The Amos Oz Reader

BOOKS BY AMOS OZ

FICTION

Where the Jackals Howl
Elsewhere, Perhaps
My Michael
Unto Death
Touch the Water, Touch the Wind
The Hill of Evil Counsel
A Perfect Peace
Black Box
To Know a Woman
Fima
Don't Call It Night
The Same Sea
Rhyming Life and Death

NONFICTION

In the Land of Israel
Israel, Palestine & Peace
Under This Blazing Light
The Slopes of Lebanon
The Story Begins
A Tale of Love and Darkness
How to Cure a Fanatic

FOR CHILDREN

Soumchi
Panther in the Basement

AMOS OZ

The Amos Oz Reader

SELECTED AND EDITED BY

Nitza Ben-Dov

HOUGHTON MIFFLIN HARCOURT
BOSTON   NEW YORK
2009

For information about permission to reproduce
selections from this book, write to Permissions,
Houghton Mifflin Harcourt Publishing Company,
6277 Sea Harbor Drive, Orlando, Florida 32887-6777.

www.hmhbooks.com

Library of Congress Cataloging-in-Publication Data
Oz, Amos.
[Selections. English. 2009]
The Amos Oz reader / Amos Oz.
p. cm.
ISBN 978-0-15-603566-8
1. Oz, Amos — Translations into English. I. Title.
PJ5054.O9A2 2009
892.4'36 — dc22   2008053532

Book design by Linda Lockowitz

Woodcuts on pages 162 and 166 by Jacob Pins

Printed in the United States of America
DOC 10 9 8 7 6 5 4 3 2 1

Credits appear on page 391.

CONTENTS

INTRODUCTION

This rich and varied selection of Amos Oz's writing from the early 1960s to the present may create the impression that there are two writers here and not one. Oz is justly known as one of Israel's leading novelists, but like several other prominent Israeli fiction writers (A. B. Yehoshua and David Grossman come to mind), he is also a public intellectual. One striking difference between the Israeli cultural situation and the American is that Israel is a place where people pay attention to what writers have to say about politics and society. The attention does not invariably imply assent, and in fact all three of the Hebrew novelists that I have just mentioned have on occasion been subjected to vilification from various quarters for their published views. Nevertheless, what a prominent writer has to say about the Occupied Territories, the invasion of Lebanon, or the nature of Zionism matters to the public. In the American setting, it is hard to imagine that, let us say, John Updike or Philip Roth would be moved to write about the American involvement in Iraq or America and globalization, and if he did, it seems likely that no one would seriously care.

Oz, then, has been a political journalist (and also a political activist) as well as a commentator for most of his career. The political journalism, as one would expect from a writer whose fiction is often cast in highly wrought lyric prose, deploys certain evocative formulations, but what chiefly distinguishes it is its predisposition to view even the most tormenting problems in the bright daylight of lucid common sense. The central issue of Zionism is particularly instructive in this regard. In a country where post-Zionism has become a fashionable rallying cry in certain intellectual circles, Oz remains a staunch Zionist. There is, however, nothing sentimental about his Zionism, and I am tempted to say that there is nothing ideological about it either. With a keen personal awareness of the difficult

European world from which both his parents came—a world, as he wryly notes in *A Tale of Love and Darkness,* in which the Jews were the only true Europeans and despised by others precisely for that reason—he looks on the existence of a Jewish state in Israel as a pragmatic solution, and one that has no viable alternatives, to the so-called Jewish question. "I am a Zionist," he writes, "because I do not want to exist as a fragment of a symbol in the consciousness of others. Neither the symbol of the shrewd, gifted, repulsive vampire, nor the symbol of the sympathetic victim who deserves compensation." He harbors none of the early Zionist illusions about coming to a land without a people, and he is keenly aware that the Zionist settlement of Palestine necessarily entailed injustice toward the natives of the country. Longings for the ancestral land may have fueled the Jewish passion to return there, but as Oz soberly observes, these longings mean nothing to the Arab inhabitants. "The Zionist enterprise," he argues, "has no other objective justification than the right of a drowning man to grasp the only plank that can save him. And that is justification enough." Elsewhere, he formulates this position in terms that have been used by other Israeli commentators—though not, as far as I know, by Arab commentators—as a clash of right against right. More recently, sobered by the bitter course of the Palestinian-Israeli conflict in recent years, he has been led to wonder whether this might also be a clash of wrong against wrong. Either way, he is clearly aware that a grim species of understanding of Zionism by the Arabs definitely exists: "We want to exist as a nation, as a State of Jews. They do not want that state."

Oz has long been a member of the peace camp in Israel, but he is too much of a political realist to contemplate either pacifism or capitulation as an alternative. Sometimes, as he somberly notes in his recent Goethe Prize speech, it is necessary to confront the forces of destruction—he does not hesitate to call them the forces of evil—with violent means. Despite his long association with Peace Now, he would surely concede that the name of that organization reflects an illusion. Given the irreconcilable differences between the two sides in the conflict over this narrow strip of land, genuine and immediate peace is simply not in the cards:

> The best we can expect, in the usual tragic way of conflicts be-
> tween individuals or between peoples, is a process of adaptation
> and psychological acceptance accompanied by a slow, painful
> awakening to reality, burdened with bitterness and reservations
> that, in the way of human wounds, heal slowly and leave per-
> manent scars.

The language here is very much the resourceful language of a novelist, spinning strands of words to evoke the emotional and psychological reality of grudgingly accepting compromise in a conflict
in which both sides have accumulated a wealth of anger, hatred,
and fear.

In his fiction, on the other hand, Oz more often uses language
not to delineate moral and emotional nuance but to conjure up dark
impulses and primal fears. There are, one must grant, elements of
change and variety in his novels and stories, as the selection in this
volume spanning more than four decades illustrates. The autobiographical *A Tale of Love and Darkness,* arguably his most brilliant
work, includes passages of sharp satire and high comedy as well as
imaginative reconstitutions of the recent European family past that
are scarcely evident in his earlier writing. But what is more central
in that book is the trauma of the mother's suicide when the future
novelist was twelve years old, a personal catastrophe that Oz could
not bring himself to write about directly or even to mention until
this late moment in his career. Much of his sensibility and much
of his fundamental conception of reality as a writer of fiction were
shaped by that terrible early loss or by the strange world to which
his poetic, deeply troubled mother introduced him. She would hold
him spellbound, he reports in *A Tale of Love and Darkness,* with
stories of mist-enshrouded castles, dark forests harboring gnomes
and ogres, magical and terrifying metamorphoses. Her suicide,
then, impressed itself on his imagination not primarily as a clinical
event but as an act of possession, the psychosis of the mother wandering in a numbed state through the rain-swept streets of Tel Aviv
on her last night on earth imagined as an irruption of the chthonic
forces she had evoked in the stories she told her son. He suggests

that his vocation as a writer was, in a way, a decision to carry on his mother's ritual of storytelling, to tell the tales she left untold.

The landscape of Oz's fiction is an Israeli landscape, and thus, inevitably, it is pregnant with the elements of political tension that he confronts so lucidly in his political journalism. But for all the accuracy of local detail, it is also a landscape drawn in the stark, even lurid, colors of the European tales of the irrational that his mother told him and is ultimately defined, however obliquely, by the shattering power of the irrational manifested in her self-chosen death.

This moment from his first novel, *Elsewhere, Perhaps,* is thoroughly characteristic of much of his fiction, especially, but not only, in its earlier phase:

> The mountains are invisible, but their presence broods over the valley. The mountains are there. Drunken gorges pouring down to attack us. Blocks of dark rock hanging high up as by a thread, threatening to sever their connection with the mountains. A hint of a movement, a patient, subdued murmur comes creeping. The mountains are there. In total silence, they are there. Standing curved columns, like giants frozen in some obscene act and turned to stone, the mountains are there.

What this amounts to is an artistically powerful expression of a paranoid vision of reality. The contours of the mountains themselves, biomorphic or anthropomorphic, appear unstable, menacing. Implicitly, and explicitly elsewhere in Oz, they hide savage creatures such as jackals and savage enemies bent on the destruction of those who live in the shadow of the mountains. The archetypal image of Oz's fiction is the small lit area of the kibbutz (itself imagined as a microcosm of the Jewish state), fenced in and defended, surrounded on all sides by an inchoate and hostile realm of darkness. This transposition of Israel's geopolitical predicament into the imagery of archaic myth is precisely the opposite of what Oz does when he comments on that predicament in his political journalism.

Paranoia is the foundation of gothic fiction, and some of Oz's strongest writing, for all his impulses to historical and social realism, is essentially gothic. In the gothic vision, the world is ultimately inscrutable, a labyrinth of shadowy turns and dark corners from which the uncanny is always ready to spring, whether driven by sexual or murderous impulse or by both. This is more or less the way reality is represented in a good deal of Oz's fiction.

The 1971 novella *Crusade,* a large portion of which is included in this volume, is probably the single most mesmerizing expression of the gothic aspect of Oz's work. The Hebrew title, *Ad Mavet,* actually means "Unto Death," and this eerie tale of a band of French crusaders making their obsession-driven way toward a Jerusalem they will never reach is a dream of transcendence in which Eros is consumed by Thanatos, eternal life proving to be the consummation of death. The crusaders brutally murder Jews who cross their path in their eastward progress, as in historical actuality the advancing crusaders murdered Jews, but they are also haunted to the point of collective madness by the idea that there is a hidden Jew lurking in their midst who must be rooted out. Thus the novella vividly concretizes the notion Oz expresses in his expository prose that a certain bent in the Christian imagination transmutes the Jew from a flesh-and-blood creature into a looming, sinister symbol. The penultimate paragraph of the story, which is at once painterly, spooky, and, as the narrator says, "abstract," is a memorable realization of the romance with madness and death characteristic of gothic fiction and may also recall Ingmar Bergman's allegorical film *The Seventh Seal:*

> Nine quivering silhouettes, Claude Crookback trudging in front, Andrés, the three brothers, four servants whose minds were long since unhinged, through meadows shining white from horizon to horizon, walking over the white earth under a white sky, on and on.

Nicholas de Lange's eloquent translation does splendid justice here to Oz's Hebrew, yet I want to note a characteristic of the prose that is most pronounced in this novella but is present in most of his fiction, in marked contrast to his journalism. The prose is patently fashioned to achieve poetic effects and is often highly stylized. The next sentence in *Crusade,* introducing the final paragraph in which the nine silhouettes, "leaving behind their loathsome flesh" will turn into "a jet of whiteness on a white canvas, an abstract purpose, a fleeting vapor, perhaps peace," begins with the phrase "Not turning homeward." This is, I think, an apt way to render the phrase in English, but the Hebrew is strange: *lo el beytam lashuv,* literally, "not to their home to return." When, after the novella's first publication, I expressed my excitement about it to the poet Yehuda Amichai, he objected vehemently to the stylization of the prose. "It is outrageous," he objected, "to say in Hebrew *lo el beytam lashuv.*" Amichai's allergy to this sort of writing is perfectly understandable because his own greatness as a Hebrew poet is intimately linked with his ability to make poetry sound naturally colloquial even in the midst of the most innovative play with allusion and metaphor. I tried to persuade him (of course, unsuccessfully) that Oz was aiming at a perfectly legitimate effect, which is the use of language as incantation, bending syntax and stretching lexical choice in strong rhythmic patterns to induce a kind of hypnotic state in the reader that enables a vision of abysmal depths beneath the surface of quotidian reality.

"I write to exorcise evil spirits," Oz says at the end of a brief autobiographical essay published in 1975. But in his 2005 Goethe Prize speech, he emphasizes instead a notion shared by many writers: that there is an ethical imperative in writing fiction, which is to imagine the other. Ultimately, there may be no contradiction between these two stated aims, or, concomitantly, between Oz's work as a novelist and as a journalist. The daylight world of the political journalism reflects the attempt of a rational person to make practical sense of a reality in which groups and individuals often act with destructive irrationality. The shadow world of his fiction is very often an attempt to enter into the tormented inwardness, the obsessions, and the perversities of characters capable of perpetrating ghastly acts, whether on a small scale or a large one. The paradigm of the kibbutz in the land where the jackal howls beyond its defended perimeters might suggest that what is at stake is a simple binary opposition between self and other, with the writer driven to imagine the dark other that threatens the self. The evidence of Oz's fiction, however, and even of some of his journalism, argues that he also sees this other as abiding within each one of us. The building blocks with which he constructs his imaginative world are taken from the Israeli reality he intimately knows: the Jerusalem of his childhood, with looming mountains and heavily armed Arab Legionnaires around it; the kibbutz where he lived for many years; the Jewish state itself, with hostile forces and hostile populations on all sides. Yet the vision of human existence articulated in his fiction, even as one sees it in this volume organized under the rubrics of kibbutz, Jerusalem, Israel, and personal history, is one that addresses readers everywhere who are constrained to live with civilization and its discontents, with the impulse to impose order on the world despite the troubling ambiguities of the disorderliness within.

—ROBERT ALTER

The Kibbutz—
"An Exemplary Nonfailure"

The Kibbutz
at the Present Time

from *Under This Blazing Light*
(Adapted from a 1974 publication)

No, I do not believe there is any such thing as a "kibbutz literature."
There are poems and books that have a kibbutz setting, and there
are poets and writers who live in a kibbutz, but the kibbutz has not
inspired any "mutation" of Hebrew literature.

For myself, I am better off, for various reasons, living in a kibbutz than I could be elsewhere, even if kibbutz life exacts its price
from me.

If I lived in Jerusalem or Tel Aviv, it is very doubtful whether
I would manage to elude the grip of the "literary world," in which
writers and academics and critics and poets sit around discussing
each other.

Not that this phenomenon is without a certain attraction, it is
just that life (as they say) is too short, and if you shut yourself away
in "literary circles" you miss something.

People sometimes ask me, both here in Israel and abroad, if
Hulda isn't too small for me, and so on. They quiz me about paro-
chial atmosphere, et cetera. They wonder how I cope with wander-
lust and the urge for adventure that they imagine writers feel more
keenly than other people. But the urge does not necessarily put on
its traveling clothes; it can be satisfied by local gossip, by peering
obliquely at the lives of different people.

Here I know a very large number of people, about three hundred.
I know them at close range, in the way that you can know someone
after twenty years in the same place. I can see genetics at work: fathers and sons, uncles and cousins, combinations of chromosomes

and the vagaries of fate. If I lived in London, Tel Aviv, Paris, I could never get to know three hundred people so intimately. Not the "literary milieu," not intellectual or academic or artistic circles, but different people: women, men, old folk, toddlers.

Of course I am not forgetting the price. The price is that a lot of different people also know me, perhaps rather better than I could wish.

However, I limit this nuisance by means of a number of stratagems (not too clever or improper) that I shall not go into here. (Or anywhere else, for that matter.)

I look around and I see a social system that, for all its disadvantages, is the least bad, the least unkind, that I have seen anywhere. And I have seen a few, because I was born and grew up in Jerusalem, in different surroundings from those of the kibbutz people, and I have spent several periods of time in other places. The kibbutz is the only attempt in modern times to separate labor from material reward, and this attempt is, in Martin Buber's phrase, "an exemplary non-failure." In my opinion this is an accurate definition. The kibbutz is the only attempt to establish a collective society, without compulsion, without repression, and without bloodshed or brainwashing. It is also, in retrospect, a unique attempt, for better or for worse, to reconstruct or revive the extended family—that clan where brothers and nephews, grandmothers and aunts, in-laws, distant relations, relations of relations, all live close together—the loss of which may turn out to be the greatest loss in modern life. It is a phenomenon that carries its own price tag: suffocation, inquisitiveness, depression, petty jealousies, the various pressures of convention, and so forth. But at times of great personal distress, at times of bereavement, illness, or old age, loneliness in the kibbutz turns out to be less harsh than the loneliness of big cities, where you are surrounded by crowds of strangers, where your actions and feelings have no worth and your joys have no meaning and sometimes even your life and death leave no trace.

In a kibbutz, when you are hurt the whole community reacts like a single organism. It is hurt with you. When you hurt someone else, the whole kibbutz can feel hurt. Of course, within this intimacy bad characteristics also thrive, whether in disguise or out in the open: self-righteousness, insensitivity, enviousness, jealousy, and narrow-mindedness. And yet, they are all part of you and you are part of the kibbutz. Flesh of its flesh. And this is all before we have even begun to talk about values, principles, beliefs, everything that I believe in and that the kibbutz offers a certain chance of achieving.

It is a good thing that the kibbutz did not have a founding father, a prophet or bearded guru who could be made into a wall poster or whose teaching could be blindly quoted. And it is a good thing that there has never been any sacred text that the kibbutz has had to live by. If the kibbutz had had a founding prophet, or a law code like the Shulhan Arukh, then it would surely not have survived beyond a single generation. Because the human condition in its continuity and its perversity is complex enough to shatter any scheme and to confound any "systematic" system.

The secret of the survival of the kibbutz into a second and third and now a fourth generation, as against the collapse of all modern communes by the end of the first generation if not sooner, lies in its secret adaptability. I say "secret adaptability," because the kibbutz likes to pretend that it is not adaptable but consistent, and that all the changes are nothing but legitimate interpretations of rigid fundamental principles. Which is true and at the same time false. It is true that there are some fundamental principles, or, it would be more accurate to say, "fundamental feelings," that are absolutely nonnegotiable. But there is a growing realistic recognition, especially in recent years, that not everything can be explained, that the world is not composed of pairs of problems and solutions that social order can join together in appropriate couples like a matchmaker. There are more problems in the world than solutions. I must stress that I do not mean that there are many unsolved problems *at the moment,* but that *in the nature of things* there are more problems in the world than solutions. Conflict, generally speaking, is not resolved, it gradually subsides, or it doesn't, and you live with it, and the flesh that has been pierced by a painful splinter grows back over it and covers it up. This truth the kibbutz has begun to learn in recent years. It is becoming less fanatical, less dogmatic, it is a society that is learning the wisdom, indulgence, and patience of age. It is not that I am untroubled or happy at the sight of such developments—I am simply pleased to see how the kibbutz has learned to react calmly, patiently, almost shrewdly, to exceptions and oddities, to changing times and tastes, as if it has whispered to itself: "So be it for the time being; now let's wait and see."

If I had to choose between kibbutz life as it was in the twenties, thirties, and forties and as it is now I would choose the present. Indeed, I would run for my life from the spirit of those days, despite all the much debated "erosion" and "decline." Not because of the material comfort (which has blessed psychological and social consequences, apart from the well-known damage that resulted from it), but particularly on account of the increased wisdom and tolerance. Some of the veterans have been sounding alarm bells for years and decades about imminent collapse, whereas I sense in fact a certain increase of self-confidence and inner strength from which come the tolerance and indulgence and also, not least, the ability to laugh at oneself.

The kibbutz is developing an organic character: it is a new kind of village, containing a few interrelated families and a few principles that do not need to be carved on the lintels and recited day and night. The kibbutz is no longer an experiment. It is growing in accordance with its own inner legitimacy, not according to a rational ideological scheme. It is ramifying, taking on different forms, striking deeper roots, producing leaves, flowers, and fruit in due season and occasionally shedding its leaves. The days when it was an "encampment" or a "nucleus" are over and gone. There is no more striking camp, no more moving from one site to another, starting afresh. The kibbutz lives in its own inner legitimacy, far from the domination of human legislators with their committees and conflicts. As with all inner legitimacy, so this, too, is mysterious, semivisible, spurning all generalizations and definitions.

Let's wait and see.

Where the Jackals Howl

from *Where the Jackals Howl* (1965)

1

At last the heat wave abated.

A blast of wind from the sea pierced the massive density of the *khamsin,* opening up cracks to let in the cold. First came light, hesitant breezes, and the tops of the cypresses shuddered lasciviously, as if a current had passed through them, rising from the roots and shaking the trunk.

Toward evening the wind freshened from the west. The *khamsin* fled eastward, from the coastal plain to the Judean hills and from the Judean hills to the rift of Jericho, from there to the deserts of the scorpion that lie to the east of Jordan. It seemed that we had seen the last *khamsin.* Autumn was drawing near.

Yelling stridently, the children of the kibbutz came streaming out onto the lawns. Their parents carried deck chairs from the verandas to the gardens. "It is the exception that proves the rule," Sashka is fond of saying. This time it was Sashka who made himself the exception, sitting alone in his room and adding a new chapter to his book about problems facing the kibbutz in times of change.

Sashka is one of the founders of our kibbutz and an active, prominent member. Squarely built, florid and bespectacled, with a handsome and sensitive face and an expression of fatherly assurance. A man of bustling energy. So fresh was the evening breeze passing through the room that he was obliged to lay a heavy ashtray on a pile of rebellious papers. A spirited straightforwardness animated him, giving a trim edge to his sentences. Changing times, said Sashka to himself, changing times require changing ideas. Above all, let us not mark time, let us not turn back upon ourselves, let us be vigorous and alert.

The walls of the houses, the tin roofs of the huts, the stack of steel pipes beside the smithy, all began to exhale the heat accumulated in them during the days of the *khamsin*.

Galila, daughter of Sashka and Tanya, stood under the cold shower, her hands clasped behind her neck, her elbows pushed back. It was dark in the shower room. Even the blond hair lying wet and heavy on her shoulders looked dark. If there were a big mirror here, I could stand in front of it and look myself over. Slowly, calmly. Like watching the sea wind that's blowing outside.

But the cubicle was small, like a square cell, and there was no big mirror, nor could there have been. So her movements were hasty and irritable. Impatiently she dried herself and put on clean clothes. What does Matityahu Damkov want of me? He asked me to go to his room after supper. When we were children we used to love watching him and his horses. But to waste the evening in some sweaty bachelor's room, that's asking too much. True, he did promise to give me some paints from abroad. On the other hand, the evening is short and we don't have any other free time. We are working girls.

How awkward and confused Matityahu Damkov looked when he stopped me on the path and told me I should come to his room after supper. And that hand in the air, waving, gesticulating, trying to pluck words out of the hot wind, gasping like a fish out of water, not finding the words he was looking for. "This evening. Worth your while to drop in for a few minutes," he said. "Just wait and see, it will be interesting. Just for a while. And quite . . . er . . . important. You won't regret it. Real canvases and the kind of paints professional artists use, as well. Actually, I got all these things from my cousin Leon who lives in South America. I don't need paints or canvases. I . . . er . . . and there's a pattern as well. It's all for you, just make sure that you come."

As she remembered these words, Galila was filled with nausea

and amusement. She thought of the fascinating ugliness of Matityahu Damkov, who had chosen to order canvases and paints for
her. Well, I suppose I should go along and see what happens and
discover why I am the one. But I won't stay in his room more than
five minutes.

2

In the mountains the sunset is sudden and decisive. Our kibbutz
lies on the plain, and the plain reduces the sunset, lessens its impact. Slowly, like a tired bird of passage, darkness descends on the
surface of the land. First to grow dark are the barns and the win-
dowless storerooms. The coming of the darkness does not hurt
them, for it has never really left them. Next it is the turn of the
houses. A timer sets the generator in motion. Its throbbing echoes
down the slope like a beating heart, a distant drum. Veins of electricity awake into life and a hidden current passes through our thin
walls. At that moment the lights spring up in all the windows of the
veterans' quarters. The metal fittings on the top of the water tower
catch the fading rays of daylight, hold them for a long moment.
Last to be hidden in the darkness is the iron rod of the lightning
conductor on the summit of the tower.

The old people of the kibbutz are still at rest in their deck chairs.
They are like lifeless objects, allowing the darkness to cover them
and offering no resistance.

Shortly before seven o'clock the kibbutz begins to stir, a slow
movement toward the dining hall. Some are discussing what has
happened today, others discuss what is to be done tomorrow, and
there are a few who are silent. It is time for Matityahu Damkov to
emerge from his lair and become a part of society. He locks the
door of his room, leaving behind him the sterile silence, and goes
to join the bustling life of the dining hall.

3

Matityahu Damkov is a small man, thin and dark, all bone and
sinew. His eyes are narrow and sunken, his cheekbones slightly

curved, an expression of "I told you so" is fixed upon his face. He joined our kibbutz immediately after World War II. Originally he was from Bulgaria. Where he has been and what he has done, Damkov does not tell. And we do not demand chapter and verse. However, we know that he has spent some time in South America. He has a mustache as well.

Matityahu Damkov's body is a cunning piece of craftsmanship. His torso is lean, boyish, strong, almost unnaturally agile. What impression does such a body make on women? In men it arouses a sense of nervous discomfort.

His left hand shows a thumb and a little finger. Between them is an empty space. "In time of war," says Matityahu Damkov, "men have suffered greater losses than three fingers."

In the daytime he works in the smithy, stripped to the waist and gleaming with sweat, muscles dancing beneath the taut skin like steel springs. He solders together metal fittings, welds pipes, hammers out bent tools, beats worn-out implements into scrap metal. His right hand or his left, each by itself is strong enough to lift the heavy sledgehammer and bring it down with controlled ferocity on the face of the unprotesting metal.

Many years ago Matityahu Damkov used to shoe the kibbutz horses, with fascinating skill. When he lived in Bulgaria it seems that his business was horse breeding. Sometimes he would speak solemnly of some hazy distinction between stud horses and workhorses, and tell the children gathered around him that he and his partner or his cousin Leon used to raise the most valuable horses between the Danube and the Aegean.

Once the kibbutz stopped using horses, Matityahu Damkov's craftsmanship was forgotten. Some of the girls collected redundant horseshoes and used them to decorate their rooms. Only the children who used to watch the shoeing, only they remember sometimes. The skill. The pain. The intoxicating smell. The agility. Galila used to chew a lock of blond hair and stare at him from a distance with gray, wide-open eyes, her mother's eyes, not her father's.

She won't come.

I don't believe her promises.

She's afraid of me. She's as wary as her father and as clever as her mother. She won't come. And if she does come, I won't tell her. If I tell her, she won't believe me. She'll go and tell Sashka everything. Words achieve nothing. But here there are people and light: supper time.

On every table gleamed cutlery, steel jugs and trays of bread.

"This knife needs sharpening," Matityahu Damkov said to his neighbors at the table. He cut his onions and tomatoes into thin slices and sprinkled them with salt, vinegar and olive oil. "In the winter, when there's not so much work to be done, I shall sharpen all the dining-room knives and repair the gutter as well. In fact, the winter isn't so far away. This *khamsin* was the last, I think. So there it is. The winter will catch us this year before we're ready for it."

At the end of the dining room, next to the boiler room and the kitchen, a group of bony veterans, some bald, some white-haired, are gathered around an evening paper. The paper is taken apart and the sections passed around in turn to the readers who have "reserved" them. Meanwhile there are some who offer interpretations of their own and there are others who stare at the pundits with the eyes of weary, good-humored old age. And there are those who listen in silence, with quiet sadness on their faces. These, according to Sashka, are the truest of the true. It is they who have endured the true suffering of the labor movement.

While the men are gathered around the paper discussing politics, the women are besieging the work organizer's table. Tanya is raising her voice in protest. Her face is wrinkled, her eyes harassed and weary. She is clutching a tin ashtray, beating it against the table to the rhythm of her complaints. She leans over the work sheets as if bending beneath the burden of injustice that has been laid or is about to be laid on her. Her hair is gray. Matityahu Damkov hears her voice but misses her words. Apparently the work organizer is trying to retreat with dignity in the face of Tanya's anger. And now she casually picks up the fruits of victory, straightens up, and makes her way to Matityahu Damkov's table.

"Now it's your turn. You know I've got a lot of patience, but there are limits to everything. And if that lock isn't welded by ten o'clock tomorrow morning, I shall raise the roof. There is a limit, Matityahu Damkov. Well?"

The man contorted the muscles of his face so that his ugliness intensified and became repulsive beyond bearing, like a clown's mask, a nightmare figure.

"Really," he said mildly, "there's no need to get so excited. Your lock has been welded for days now, and you haven't come to collect it. Come tomorrow. Come whenever you like. There's no need to hurry me along."

"Hurry you? Me? Never in my life have I dared harass a workingman. Forgive me. I'm sure you're not offended."

"I'm not offended," said Matityahu. "On the contrary. I'm an easygoing type. Good night to you."

With these words the business of the dining room is concluded. Time to go back to the room, to put on the light, to sit on the bed and wait quietly. And what else do I need? Yes. Cigarettes. Matches. Ashtray.

4

The electric current pulses in twining veins and sheds a weary light upon everything: our little red-roofed houses, our gardens, the pitted concrete paths, the fences and the scrap iron, the silence. Dim, weak puddles of light. An elderly light.

Searchlights are mounted on wooden posts set out at regular intervals along the perimeter fence. These beacons strive to light up the fields and the valleys that stretch away to the foothills of the mountains. A small circle of plowed land is swamped by the lights on the fence. Beyond this circle lies the night and the silence. Autumn nights are not black. Not here. Our nights are gray. A gray radiance rising over the fields, the plantations, and the orchards. The orchards have already begun to turn yellow. The soft gray light embraces the treetops with great tenderness, blurring their sharp edges, bridging the gap between lifeless and living. It is the way of the night light to distort the appearance of inanimate things and to infuse them with life, cold and sinister, vibrant with venom. At the same time it slows down the living things of the night, softening their movements, disguising their elusive presence. Thus it is that we cannot see the jackals as they spring out from their hiding places. Inevitably we miss the sight of their soft noses sniffing the air, their paws gliding over the turf, scarcely touching the ground.

The dogs of the kibbutz, they alone understand this enchanted motion. That is why they howl at night in jealousy, menace, and rage. That is why they paw at the ground, straining at their chains till their necks are on the point of breaking.

An adult jackal would have kept clear of the trap. This one was a cub, sleek, soft, and bristling, and he was drawn to the smell of blood and flesh. True, it was not outright folly that led him into the trap. He simply followed the scent and glided to his destruction with careful, mincing steps. At times he stopped, feeling some obscure warning signal in his veins. Beside the snare he paused, froze where he stood, silent, as gray as the earth and as patient. He pricked up his ears in vague apprehension and heard not a sound. The smells got the better of him.

Was it really a matter of chance? It is commonly said that chance is blind; we say that chance peers out at us with a thousand eyes. The jackal was young, and if he felt the thousand eyes fixed upon him, he could not understand their meaning.

A wall of old, dusty cypresses surrounds the plantation. What is it, the hidden thread that joins the lifeless to the living? In despair, rage, and contortion we search for the end of this thread, biting lips till we draw blood, eyes rolling in frenzy. The jackals know this thread. Sensuous, pulsating currents are alive in it, flowing from body to body, being to being, vibration to vibration. And rest and peace are there.

At last the creature bowed his head and brought his nose close to the flesh of the bait. There was the smell of blood and the smell of sap. The tip of his muzzle was moist and twitching, his saliva was running, his hide bristling, his delicate sinews throbbed. Soft as a vapor, his paw approached the forbidden fruit.

Then came the moment of cold steel. With a metallic click, light and precise, the trap snapped shut.

The animal froze like stone. Perhaps he thought he could outwit the trap, pretending to be lifeless. No sound, no movement. For a long moment jackal and trap lay still, testing each other's strength. Slowly, painfully, the living awoke and came back to life.

And silently the cypresses swayed, bowing and rising, bending and floating. He opened his muzzle wide, baring little teeth that dripped foam.

Suddenly despair seized him.

With a frantic leap he tried to tear himself free, to cheat the hangman.

Pain ripped through his body.

He lay flat upon the earth and panted.

Then the child opened his mouth and began to cry. The sound of his wailing rose and filled the night.

5

At this twilight hour our world is made up of circles within circles. On the outside is the circle of the autumn darkness, far from here, in the mountains and the great deserts. Sealed and enclosed within it is the circle of our night landscape, vineyards and orchards and plantations. A dim lake astir with whispering voices. Our lands betray us in the night. Now they are no longer familiar and submissive, crisscrossed with irrigation pipes and dirt tracks. Now our fields have gone over to the enemy's camp. They send out to us waves of alien scents. At night we see them bristling in a miasma of threat and hostility and returning to their former state, as they were before we came to this place.

The inner circle, the circle of lights, keeps guard over our houses and over us, against the accumulated menace outside. But it is an ineffective wall, it cannot keep out the smells of the foe and his voices. At night the voices and the smells touch our skin like tooth and claw.

And inside, in the innermost circle of all, in the heart of our illuminated world, stands Sashka's writing desk. The table lamp sheds a calm circle of brightness and banishes the shadows from the stacks of papers. The pen in his hand darts to and fro and the words take shape. "There is no stand more noble than that of the few against the many," Sashka is fond of saying. His daughter stares wide-eyed and curious at the face of Matityahu Damkov. You're ugly and you're not one of us. It's good that you have no children and one day those dull mongoloid eyes will close and you'll be dead. And you won't leave behind anyone like you. I wish I wasn't here, but before I go I want to know what it is you want of me and why you told me to come. It's so stuffy in your room and there's an old bachelor smell that's like the smell of oil used for frying too many times.

"You may sit down," said Matityahu from the shadows. The shabby stillness that filled the room deepened his voice and made it sound remote.

"I'm in a bit of a hurry."

"There'll be coffee as well. The real thing. From Brazil. My cousin Leon sends me coffee too, he seems to think a kibbutz is a kind of kolkhoz. A kolkhoz labor camp. A collective farm in Russia, that's what a kolkhoz is."

"Black without sugar for me, please," said Galila, and these words surprised even her. What is this ugly man doing to me? What does he want of me? "You said you were going to show me some canvases, and some paints, didn't you?"

"All in good time."

"I didn't expect you to go to the trouble of getting coffee and cakes, I thought I'd only be here for a moment."

"You are fair," the man said, breathing heavily, "you are fairhaired, but I'm not mistaken. There is doubt. There has to be. But it is so. What I mean is, you'll drink your coffee, nice and slow, and I'll give you a cigarette too, an American one, from Virginia. In the meantime, have a look at this box. The brushes. The special oil too. And the canvases. And all the tubes. It's all for you. First of all, drink. Take your time."

"But I still don't understand," said Galila.

A man pacing about his room in an undershirt on a summer night is not a strange sight. But the monkeylike body of Matityahu Damkov set something stirring inside her. Panic seized her. She put down the coffee cup on the brass tray, jumped up from the chair and stood behind it, clutching the chair as if it were a barricade.

The transparent, frightened gesture delighted her host. He spoke patiently, almost mockingly. "Just like your mother. I have something to tell you when the moment's right, something that I'm positive you don't know, about your mother's wickedness."

Now, at the scent of danger, Galila was filled with cold malice. "You're mad, Matityahu Damkov. Everybody says that you're mad." There was tender austerity in her face, an expression both secretive and passionate. "You're mad, and get out of my way and let me pass. I want to get out of here. Yes. Now. Out of my way."

The man retreated a little, still staring at her intently. Suddenly he sprang onto his bed and sat there, his back to the wall, and laughed a long, happy laugh. "Steady, daughter, why all the haste? Steady. We've only just begun. Patience. Don't get so excited. Don't waste your energy."

Galila hastily weighed up the two possibilities, the safe and the fascinating, and said, "Please tell me what you want of me."

"Actually," said Matityahu Damkov, "actually, the kettle's boiling again. Let's take a short break and have some more coffee. You won't deny, I'm sure, that you've never drunk coffee like this."

"Without milk or sugar for me. I told you before."

6

The smell of coffee drove away all other smells: a strong, sharp, pleasant smell, almost piercing. Galila watched Matityahu Damkov closely, observing his manners, the docile muscles beneath his string shirt, his sterile ugliness. When he spoke again, she clutched the cup tightly between her fingers and a momentary peace descended on her.

"If you like, I can tell you something in the meantime. About horses. About the farm that we used to have in Bulgaria, maybe fifty-seven kilometers from the port of Varna, a stud farm. It belonged to me and my cousin Leon. There were two branches that we specialized in: workhorses and stud horses, in other words, castration and covering. Which would you like to hear about first?"

Galila relaxed, leaning back in the chair and crossing her legs, ready to hear a story. In her childhood she had always loved the moments before the start of a bedtime story.

"I remember," she said, "how when we were children we used to come and watch you shoeing the horses. It was beautiful and strange and so . . . were you."

"Preparing for successful mating," said Matityahu, passing her a plate of crackers, "is a job for professionals. It takes expertise and intuition as well. First, the stallion must be kept in confinement for a long time. To drive him mad. It improves his seed. He's kept apart from the mares for several months, from the stallions too. In his frustration he may even attack another male. Not every stallion is suitable for stud, perhaps one in a hundred. One stud horse to a hundred workhorses. You need a lot of experience and keen observation to pick out the right horse. A stupid, unruly horse is the best. But it isn't all that easy to find the most stupid horse."

"Why must he be stupid?" asked Galila, swallowing spittle.

"It's a question of madness. It isn't always the biggest, most handsome stallion that produces the best foals. In fact a mediocre horse can be full of energy and have the right kind of nervous temperament. After the candidate had been kept in confinement for a few months, we used to put wine in his trough, half a bottle. That was my cousin Leon's idea. To get the horse a bit drunk. Then we'd fix it so he could take a look at the mares through the bars and get a whiff of their smell. Then he starts going mad. Butting like a bull. Rolling on his back and kicking his legs in the air. Scratching himself, rubbing himself, trying desperately to ejaculate. He screams and starts biting in all directions. When the stallion starts to bite, then we know that the time has come. We open the gate. The mare is waiting for him. And just for a moment, the stallion hesitates. Trembling and panting. Like a coiled spring."

Galila winced, staring entranced at Matityahu Damkov's lips.

"Yes," she said.

"And then it happens. As if the law of gravity had suddenly been revoked. The stallion doesn't run, he flies through the air. Like a cannonball. Like a spring suddenly released. The mare bows and lowers her head and he thrusts into her, blow after blow. His eyes are full of blood. There's not enough air for him to breathe and he gasps and chokes as if he's dying. His mouth hangs open and he pours saliva and foam on her head. Suddenly he starts to roar and howl. Like a dog. Like a wolf. Writhing and screaming. In that moment there is no telling pleasure from pain. And mating is very much like castration."

"Enough, Matityahu, for God's sake, enough."

"Now let's relax. Or perhaps you'd like to hear how a horse is castrated?"

"Please, enough, no more," Galila pleaded.

Slowly Matityahu raised his maimed hand. The compassion in his voice was strange, almost fatherly: "Just like your mother. About that," he said, "about the fingers and about castration as well, we'll talk some other time. Enough now. Don't be afraid now. Now we can rest and relax. I've got a drop of cognac somewhere. No? No. Vermouth then. There's vermouth too. Here's to my cousin Leon. Drink. Relax. Enough."

7

The cold light of the distant stars spreads a reddish crust upon the fields. In the last weeks of the summer the land has all been turned over. Now it stands ready for the winter sowing. Twisting dirt tracks cross the plain, here and there are the dark masses of plantations, fenced in by walls of cypress trees.

For the first time in many months our lands feel the first tentative fingers of the cold. The irrigation pipes, the taps, the metal fittings, they are the first to capitulate to any conqueror, summer's heat or autumn's chill. And now they are the first to surrender to the cool moisture.

In the past, forty years ago, the founders of the kibbutz entrenched themselves in this land, digging their pale fingernails into the earth. Some were fair-haired, like Sashka, others, like Tanya, were brazen and scowling. In the long, burning hours of the day they used to curse the earth scorched by the fires of the sun, curse it in despair, in anger, in longing for rivers and forests. But in the darkness, when night fell, they composed sweet love songs to the earth, forgetful of time and place. At night forgetfulness gave taste to life. In the angry darkness oblivion enfolded them in a mother's embrace. "There," they used to sing, not "Here."

There in the land our fathers loved,
There all our hopes shall be fulfilled.
There we shall live and there a life
Of health and freedom we shall build . . .

People like Sashka were forged in fury, in longing, and in dedication. Matityahu Damkov, and the latter-day fugitives like him, know nothing of the longing that burns and the dedication that draws blood from the lips. That is why they seek to break into the inner circle. They make advances to the women. They use words similar to ours. But theirs is a different sorrow, they do not belong to us, they are extras, on the outside, and so they shall be until the day they die.

The captive jackal cub was seized by weariness. The tip of his right paw was held fast in the teeth of the trap. He sprawled flat on the turf as if reconciled to his fate.

First he licked his fur, slowly, like a cat. Then he stretched out his neck and began licking the smooth, shining metal. As if lavishing warmth and love upon the silent foe. Love and hate, they both breed surrender. He threaded his free paw beneath the trap, groped slowly for the meat of the bait, withdrew the paw carefully and licked off the savor that had clung to it.

Finally, the others appeared.

Jackals, huge, emaciated, filthy, and swollen-bellied. Some with running sores, others stinking of putrid carrion. One by one they came together from all their distant hiding places, summoned to the gruesome ritual. They formed themselves into a circle and fixed pitying eyes upon the captive innocent. Malicious joy striving hard to disguise itself as compassion, triumphant evil breaking through the mask of mourning. The unseen signal was given, the marauders of the night began slowly moving in a circle as in a dance, with mincing, gliding steps. When the excitement exploded into mirth the rhythm was shattered, the ritual broken, and the jackals cavorted madly like rabid dogs. Then the despairing voices rose into the night, sorrow and rage and envy and triumph, bestial laughter and a choking wail of supplication, angry, threatening, rising to a scream of terror and fading again into submission, lament, and silence.

After midnight they ceased. Perhaps the jackals despaired of their helpless child. Quietly they dispersed to their own sorrows. Night, the patient gatherer, took them up in his arms and wiped away all the traces.

8

Matityahu Damkov was enjoying the interlude. Nor did Galila try to hasten the course of events. It was night. The girl unfolded the canvases that Matityahu Damkov had received from his cousin Leon and examined the tubes of paint. It was good quality material, the type used by professionals. Until now she had painted on oiled sackcloth or cheap mass-produced canvases with paints borrowed from the kindergarten. She's so young, thought Matityahu Damkov, she's a little girl, slender and spoiled. I'm going to smash her to pieces. Slowly. For a moment he was tempted to tell her the truth outright, like a bolt from the blue, but he thought better of it. The night was slow.

In oblivion and delight, compulsively, Galila fingered the fine brush, lightly touching the orange paint, lightly stroking the canvas with the hairs of the brush, an unconscious caress, like fingertips on the hairs of the neck. Innocence flowed from her body to his, his body responded with waves of desire.

Afterward Galila lay without moving, as if asleep, on the oily, paint-splashed tiles, canvases and tubes of paint scattered about her. Matityahu lay back on his single bed, closed his eyes, and summoned a dream.

At his bidding they come to him, quiet dreams and wild dreams. They come and play before him. This time he chose to summon the dream of the flood, one of the severest in his repertoire.

First to appear is a mass of ravines descending the mountain slopes, scores of teeming watercourses, crisscrossing and zigzagging.

In a flash the throngs of tiny people appear in the gullies. Like little black ants they swarm and trickle from their hiding places in the crevices of the mountain, sweeping down like a cataract. Hordes of thin dark people streaming down the slopes, rolling like an avalanche of stone and plunging in a headlong torrent to the levels of the plain. Here they split into a thousand columns, racing westward in furious spate. Now they are so close that their shapes can be seen: a dark, disgusting, emaciated mass, crawling with lice and fleas, stinking. Hunger and hatred distort their faces. Their eyes blaze with madness. In full flood they swoop upon the fertile valleys, racing over the ruins of deserted villages without a moment's pause. In their rush toward the sea they drag with them all that lies in their path, uprooting posts, ravaging fields, mowing down fences, trampling the gardens and stripping the orchards, pillaging homesteads, crawling through huts and stables, clambering over walls like demented apes, onward, westward, to the sands of the sea.

And suddenly you too are surrounded, besieged, paralyzed with fear. You see their eyes ablaze with primeval hatred, mouths hanging open, teeth yellow and rotten, curved daggers gleaming in their hands. They curse you in clipped tones, voices choking with rage or with dark desire. Now their hands are groping at your flesh. A knife and a scream. With the last spark of your life you extinguish the vision and almost breathe freely again.

"Come on," said Matityahu Damkov, shaking the girl with his right hand, while the maimed hand, his left, caressed her neck. "Come on. Let's get away from here. Tonight. In the morning. I shall save you. We'll run away together to South America, to my cousin Leon. I'll take care of you. I'll always take care of you."

"Leave me alone, don't touch me," she said.

He clasped her in a powerful and silent embrace.

"My father will kill you tomorrow. I told you to leave me alone."

"Your father will take care of you now and he'll always take care of you," Matityahu Damkov replied softly. He let her go. The girl stood up, buttoning her skirt, smoothing back her blond hair.

"That isn't what I want. I didn't want to come here at all. You're taking advantage of me and doing things to me that I don't want and saying all kinds of things because you're mad and everyone knows you're mad, ask anyone you like."

Matityahu Damkov's lips broadened into a smile.

"I won't come to you again, not ever, And I don't want your paints. You're dangerous. You're as ugly as a monkey. And you're mad."

"I can tell you about your mother, if you want to hear. And if you want to hate and curse, then it's her you should hate, not me."

The girl turned hurriedly to the window, flung it open with a desperate movement and leaned out into the empty night. Now she's going to scream, thought Matityahu Damkov in alarm, she'll scream and the opportunity won't come again. Blood filled his eyes. He swooped upon her, clapped his hand over her mouth, dragged her back inside the room, buried his lips in her hair, probed with his lips for her ear, found it, and told her.

9

Sharp waves of chill autumn air clung to the outer walls of the houses, seeking entry. From the yard on the slope of the hill came the sounds of cattle lowing and herdsmen cursing. A cow having difficulty giving birth, perhaps, the big torch throwing light on the blood and the mire. Matityahu Damkov knelt on the floor and gathered up the paints and the brushes that his guest had left scattered there. Galila still stood beside the open window, her back to the room and her face to the darkness. Then she spoke, still with her back to the man.

"It's doubtful," she said. "It's almost impossible, it isn't even logical, it can't be proved, and it's crazy. Absolutely."

Matityahu Damkov stared at her back with his mongoloid eyes. Now his ugliness was complete, a concentrated, penetrating ugliness.

"I won't force you. Please. I shall say nothing. Perhaps just laugh to myself quietly. For all I care you can be Sashka's daughter or even Ben-Gurion's daughter. I shall say nothing. Like my cousin Leon I shall say nothing. He loved his Christian son and never said I love you, only when this son of his had killed eleven policemen and himself did he remember to tell him in his grave, I love you. Please."

Suddenly, without warning, Galila burst into laughter. "You fool, you little fool, look at me, I'm blond, look!"

Matityahu said nothing.

"I'm not yours, I'm sure of it because I'm blond, I'm not yours or Leon's either, I'm blond and it's all right! Come on!"

The man leaped at her, panting, groaning, groping his way blindly. In his rush he overturned the coffee table, he shuddered violently and the girl shuddered with him.

And then she recoiled from him, fled to the far wall. He pushed aside the coffee table. He kicked it. His eyes were shot with blood, and a sound like gargling came from his lips. She suddenly remembered her mother's face and the trembling of her lips and her tears, and she pushed the man from her with a dreamy hand. As if struck, they both retreated, staring at each other, eyes wide open.

"Father," said Galila in surprise, as if waking on the first morning of winter at the end of a long summer, looking outside, and saying, Rain.

10

The sun rises without dignity in our part of the world. With a cheap sentimentality it appears over the peaks of the eastern mountains and touches our lands with tentative rays. No glory, no complicated tricks of light. A purely conventional beauty, more like a picture postcard than a real landscape.

But this will be one of the last sunrises. Autumn will soon be here. A few more days and we shall wake in the morning to the sound of rain. There may be hail too. The sun will rise behind a screen of dirty gray clouds. Early risers will wrap themselves in overcoats and emerge from their houses fortified against the daggers of the wind.

The path of the seasons is well trodden. Autumn, winter, spring, summer, autumn. Things are as they have always been. Whoever seeks a fixed point in the current of time and the seasons would do well to listen to the sounds of the night that never change. They come to us from out there.

The Way of the Wind*

from *Where the Jackals Howl* (1965)

1

Gideon Shenhav's last day began with a brilliant sunrise.

The dawn was gentle, almost autumnal. Faint flashes of light flickered through the wall of cloud that sealed off the eastern horizon. Slyly the new day concealed its purpose, betraying no hint of the heat wave that lay enfolded in its bosom.

Purple glowed on the eastern heights, fanned by the morning breeze. Then the rays pierced through the wall of cloud. It was day. Dark loopholes blinked awake at daylight's touch. Finally the incandescent sphere rose, assaulted the mountains of cloud, and broke their ranks. The eastern horizon was adazzle. And the soft purple yielded and fled before the terrible crimson blaze.

The camp was shaken by reveille a few minutes before sunrise. Gideon rose, padded barefoot out of his hut, and, still asleep, looked at the gathering light. With one thin hand he shaded his eyes, still yearning for sleep, while the other automatically buttoned up his battle dress. He could already hear voices and metallic sounds; a few eager boys were cleaning their guns for morning inspection. But Gideon was slow. The sunrise had stirred a weary restlessness inside him, perhaps a vague longing. The sunrise was over, but still he stood there drowsily, until he was pushed from behind and told to get cracking.

---

*The Hebrew word *ruah* has multiple meanings: wind, spirit, intellect, ghost, to mention only a few. In this story it also refers to the ideological convictions of the old man. The title is borrowed from Ecclesiastes 11:5. — TRANS.

He went back into the hut, straightened his camp bed, cleaned his submachine gun, and picked up his shaving kit. On his way, among whitewashed eucalyptus trees and clustering notices commending tidiness and discipline, he suddenly remembered that today was Independence Day, the Fifth of Iyar. And today the platoon was to mount a celebratory parachute display in the Valley of Jezreel. He entered the washroom and, while he waited for a free mirror, brushed his teeth and thought of pretty girls. In an hour and a half the preparations would be complete and the platoon would be airborne, on its way to its destination. Throngs of excited civilians would be waiting for them to jump, and the girls would be there, too. The drop would take place just outside Nof Harish, the kibbutz that was Gideon's home, where he had been born and brought up until the day he joined the army. The moment his feet touched the ground, the children of the kibbutz would close around him and jump all over him and shout, "Gideon, look, here's our Gideon!"

He pushed in between two much bigger soldiers and began to lather his face and try to shave.

"Hot day," he said.

One of the soldiers answered, "Not yet. But it soon will be."

And another soldier behind him grumbled, "Hurry it up. Don't spend all day jawing."

Gideon did not take offense. On the contrary, the words filled him with a surge of joy for some reason. He dried his face and went out onto the parade ground. The blue light had changed meanwhile to gray-white, the grubby glare of a *khamsin*.

2

Shimshon Sheinbaum had confidently predicted the previous night that a *khamsin* was on its way. As soon as he got up he hurried over to the window and confirmed with calm satisfaction that he had been right yet again. He closed the shutters, to protect the room from the hot wind, then washed his face and his shaggy shoulders and chest, shaved, and prepared his breakfast, coffee with a roll brought last night from the dining hall. Shimshon Sheinbaum loathed wasting time, especially in the productive morning hours: you go out, walk to the dining hall, have a chat, read the paper, discuss the news, and that's half the morning gone. So he always made do with a cup of coffee and a roll, and by ten past six, after the early news summary, Gideon Shenhav's father was sitting at his desk. Summer and winter alike, with no concessions.

He sat at his desk and stared for a few minutes at the map of the country that hung on the opposite wall. He was straining to recapture a nagging dream which had taken hold of him in the early hours, just before he had awakened. But it eluded him. Shimshon decided to get on with his work and not waste another minute. True, today was a holiday, but the best way to celebrate was to work, not to slack off. Before it was time to go out and watch the parachutists — and Gideon, who might actually be among them and not drop out at the last minute — he still had several hours of working time. A man of seventy-five cannot afford to squander his hours, especially if there are many, painfully many, things he must set down in writing. So little time.

The name of Shimshon Sheinbaum needs no introduction. The Hebrew Labor Movement knows how to honor its founding fathers, and for decades now Shimshon Sheinbaum's name has been invested with a halo of enduring fame. For decades he has fought body and soul to realize the vision of his youth. Setbacks and disappointments have not shattered or weakened his faith, but, rather, have enriched it with a vein of wise sadness. The better he has come to understand the weakness of others and their ideological deviations, the more ferociously he has fought against his own weaknesses. He has sternly eliminated them, and lived according to his principles, with a ruthless self-discipline and not without a certain secret joy.

At this moment, between six and seven o'clock on this Independence Day morning, Shimshon Sheinbaum is not yet a bereaved father. But his features are extraordinarily well suited to the role.

A solemn, sagacious expression, of one who sees all but betrays no reaction, occupies his furrowed face. And his blue eyes express an ironic melancholy.

He sits erect at his desk, his head bent over the pages. His elbows are relaxed. The desk is made of plain wood, like the rest of the furniture, which is all functional and unembellished. More like a monastic cell than a bungalow in a long-established kibbutz.

This morning will not be particularly productive. Time and again his thoughts wander to the dream that flickered and died at the end of the night. He must recapture the dream, and then he will be able to forget it and concentrate on his work. There was a hose, yes, and some sort of goldfish or something. An argument with someone. No connection. Now to work. The Poalei Zion Movement appears to have been built from the start on an ideological contradiction that could never be bridged, and which it only succeeded in disguising by means of verbal acrobatics. But the contradiction is only apparent, and anyone who hopes to exploit it to undermine or attack the movement does not know what he is talking about. And here is the simple proof.

Shimshon Sheinbaum's rich experience of life has taught him how arbitrary, how senseless is the hand that guides the vagaries of our fate, that of the individual and that of the community alike. His sobriety has not robbed him of the straightforwardness which has animated him since his youth. His most remarkable and admirable characteristic is his stubborn innocence, like that of our pure, pious forebears, whose sagacity never injured their faith. Sheinbaum has never allowed his actions to be cut loose from his words. Even though some of the leaders of our movement have drifted into political careers and cut themselves off completely from manual labor, Sheinbaum has never abandoned the kibbutz. He has turned down all outside jobs and assignments, and it was only with extreme reluctance that he accepted nomination to the General Workers' Congress. Until a few years ago his days were divided equally between physical and intellectual work: three days gardening, three days theorizing. The beautiful gardens of Nof Harish are largely his handiwork. We can remember how he used to plant and prune and lop, water and hoe, manure, transplant, weed, and dig up. He did not permit his status as the leading thinker of the movement to exempt him from the duties to which every rank-and-file member is liable: he served as night watchman, took his turn in the kitchens, helped with the harvest. No shadow of a double standard has ever clouded the path of Shimshon Sheinbaum's life; he is a single complex of vision and execution, he has known no slackness or weakness of will—so the secretary of the movement wrote about him in a magazine a few years ago, on the occasion of his seventieth birthday.

True, there have been moments of stabbing despair. There have been moments of deep disgust. But Shimshon Sheinbaum knows how to transform such moments into secret sources of furious energy. Like the words of the marching song he loves, which always inspires him to a frenzy of action: *Up into the mountains we are climbing, / Climbing up toward the dawning day; / We have left all our yesterdays behind us, / But tomorrow is a long long way away.* If only that stupid dream would emerge from the shadows and show itself clearly, he could kick it out of his mind and concentrate at last on his work. Time is slipping by. A rubber hose, a chess gambit, some goldfish, a great argument, but what is the connection?

For many years Shimshon Sheinbaum has lived alone. He has channeled all his vigor into his ideological productions. To this life's work he has sacrificed the warmth of a family home. He has managed, in exchange, to retain into old age a youthful clarity and cordiality. Only when he was fifty-six did he suddenly marry Raya Greenspan and father Gideon, and after that he left her and returned to his ideological work. It would be sanctimonious to pretend, however, that before his marriage Shimshon Sheinbaum maintained a monastic existence. His personality attracted women just as it attracted disciples. He was still young when his thick mop of hair turned white, and his sun-beaten face was etched with an appealing pattern of lines and wrinkles. His square back, his strong shoulders, the timbre of his voice — always warm, skeptical, and rather ruminative — and also his solitude, all attracted women to him like fluttering birds. Gossip attributes to his loins at least one of the urchins of the kibbutz, and elsewhere, too, stories are current. But we shall not dwell on this.

At the age of fifty-six Shimshon Sheinbaum decided that it befitted him to beget a son and heir to bear his stamp and his name into the coming generation. And so he conquered Raya Greenspan, a diminutive girl with a stammer who was thirty-three years his junior. Three months after the wedding, which was solemnized before a restricted company, Gideon was born. And before the kibbutz had recovered from its amazement, Shimshon sent Raya back to her former room and rededicated himself to his ideological work. This episode caused various ripples, and indeed, it was preceded by painful heart-searchings in Shimshon Sheinbaum himself.

Now let's concentrate and think logically. Yes, it's coming back. She came to my room and called me to go there quickly to put a stop to that scandal. I didn't ask any questions, but hurried after her. Someone had had the nerve to dig a pond in the lawn in front of the dining hall, and I was seething because no one had authorized such an innovation, an ornamental pond in front of the dining hall, like some Polish squire's château. I shouted. Who at, there is no clear picture. There were goldfish in the pond. And a boy was filling it with water from a black rubber hose. So I decided to put a stop to the whole performance there and then, but the boy wouldn't listen to me. I started walking along the hose to find the faucet and cut off the water before anybody managed to establish the pond as a fait accompli. I walked and walked until I suddenly discovered that I was walking in a circle and the hose was not connected to a faucet but simply came back to the pond and sucked up water from it. Stuff and nonsense. That's the end of it. The original platform of the Poalei Zion Movement must be understood without any recourse to dialectics, it must be taken literally, word for word.

3

After his separation from Raya Greenspan, Shimshon Sheinbaum did not neglect his duties as his son's mentor, nor did he disclaim responsibility. He lavished on him, from the time the boy was six or seven, the full warmth of his personality. Gideon, however, turned out to be something of a disappointment, not the stuff of which dynasties are founded. As a child he was always sniveling. He was a slow, bewildered child, mopping up blows and insults without retaliating, a strange child, always playing with candy wrappers, dried leaves, silkworms. And from the age of twelve he was constantly having his heart broken by girls of all ages. He was always lovesick, and he published sad poems and cruel parodies in the children's newsletter. A dark, gentle youth, with an almost feminine beauty, who walked the paths of the kibbutz in obstinate silence. He did not shine at work; he did not shine in communal life. He was slow of speech and no doubt also of thought. His poems seemed to Shimshon incorrigibly sentimental, and his parodies venomous, without a trace of inspiration. The nickname Pinocchio suited him, there is no denying it. And the infuriating smiles he was perpetually spreading across his face seemed to Shimshon a depressingly exact replica of the smiles of Raya Greenspan.

And then, eighteen months before, Gideon had amazed his father. He suddenly appeared and asked for his written permission to enlist in the paratroopers—as an only son, this required the written consent of both parents. Only when Shimshon Sheinbaum was convinced that this was not one of his son's outrageous jokes did he agree to give his consent. And then he gave it gladly: this was surely an encouraging turn in the boy's development. They'd make a man of him there. Let him go. Why not.

But Raya Greenspan's stubborn opposition raised an unexpected obstacle to Gideon's plan. No, she wouldn't sign the paper. On no account. Never.

Shimshon himself went to her room one evening, pleaded with her, reasoned with her, shouted at her. All in vain. She wouldn't sign. No reason, she just wouldn't. So Shimshon Sheinbaum had to resort to devious means to enable the boy to enlist. He wrote a private letter to Yolek himself, asking a personal favor. He wished his son to be allowed to volunteer. The mother was emotionally unstable. The boy would make a first-rate paratrooper. Shimshon himself accepted full responsibility. And incidentally, he had never before asked a personal favor. And he never would again. This was the one and only time in his whole life. He begged Yolek to see what he could do.

At the end of September, when the first signs of autumn were appearing in the orchards, Gideon Shenhav was enrolled in a parachute unit.

From that time on, Shimshon Sheinbaum immersed himself more deeply than ever in ideological work, which is the only real mark a man can leave on the world. Shimshon Sheinbaum has made a mark on the Hebrew Labor Movement that can never be erased. Old age is still far off. At seventy-five he still has hair as thick as ever, and his muscles are firm and powerful. His eyes are alert, his mind attentive. His strong, dry, slightly cracked voice still works wonders on women of all ages. His bearing is restrained, his manner modest. Needless to say, he is deeply rooted in the soil of Nof Harish. He loathes assemblies and formal ceremonies, not to mention commissions and official appointments. With his pen alone he has inscribed his name on the roll of honor of our movement and our nation.

4

Gideon Shenhav's last day began with a brilliant sunrise. He felt he could even see the beads of dew evaporating in the heat. Omens blazed on the mountain peaks far away to the east. This was a day of celebration, a celebration of independence and a celebration of parachuting over the familiar fields of home. All that night he had nestled in a half dream of dark autumnal forests under northern skies, a rich smell of autumn, huge trees he could not name. All night long, pale leaves had been dropping on the huts of the camp.

Even after he had awakened in the morning, the northern forest with its nameless trees still continued to whisper in his ears.

Gideon adored the delicious moment of free fall between the jump from the aircraft and the unfolding of the parachute. The void rushes up toward you at lightning speed, fierce drafts of air lick at your body, making you dizzy with pleasure. The speed is drunken, reckless, it whistles and roars and your whole body trembles to it, red-hot needles work at your nerve ends, and your heart pounds. Suddenly, when you are lightning in the wind, the chute opens. The straps check your fall, like a firm, masculine arm bringing you calmly under control. You can feel its supporting strength under your armpits. The reckless thrill gives way to a more sedate pleasure. Slowly your body swings through the air, floats, hesitates, drifts a little way on the slight breeze, you can never guess precisely where your feet will touch ground, on the slope of that hill or next to the orange groves over there, and like an exhausted migrating bird you slowly descend, seeing roofs, roads, cows in the meadow, slowly, as if you have a choice, as if the decision is entirely yours.

And then the ground is under your feet, and you launch into the practiced somersault which will soften the impact of landing. Within seconds you must sober up. The coursing blood slows down. Dimensions return to normal. Only a weary pride survives in your heart until you rejoin your commanding officer and your comrades and you're caught up in the rhythm of frenzied reorganization.

This time it is all going to happen over Nof Harish.

The older folk will raise their clammy hands, push back their caps, and try to spot Gideon among the gray dots dangling in the sky. The kids will rush around in the fields, also waiting excitedly for their hero to touch down. Mother will come out of the dining hall and stand peering upward, muttering to herself. Shimshon will leave his desk for a while, perhaps take a chair out onto his little porch and watch the whole performance with pensive pride.

Then the kibbutz will entertain the unit. Pitchers of lemonade glistening with chilly perspiration will be set out in the dining hall, there will be crates of apples, or perhaps cakes baked by the older women, iced with congratulatory phrases.

By six-thirty the sun had grown out of its colorful caprice and risen ruthlessly over the eastern mountain heights. A thick heat weighed heavily on the whole scene. The tin roofs of the camp huts reflected a dazzling glare. The walls began to radiate a dense, oppressive warmth into the huts. On the main road, which passed close to the perimeter fence, a lively procession of buses and trucks was already in motion: the residents of the villages and small towns were streaming to the big city to watch the military parade. Their white shirts could be discerned dimly through the clouds of dust, and snatches of exuberant song could be caught in the distance.

The paratroopers had completed their morning inspection. The orders of the day, signed by the chief of staff, had been read out and posted on the bulletin boards. A festive breakfast had been served, including a hard-boiled egg reposing on a lettuce leaf ringed with olives.

Gideon, his dark hair flopping forward onto his forehead, broke into a quiet song. The others joined him. Here and there someone altered the words, making them comical or even obscene. Soon the Hebrew songs gave way to a guttural, almost desperate Arabic wail. The platoon commander, a blond, good-looking officer whose exploits were feted around the campfires at night, stood up and said, That's enough. The paratroopers stopped singing, hastily downed the last of their greasy coffee, and moved toward the runways. Here there was another inspection; the commanding officer spoke a few words of endearment to his men, calling them "the salt of the earth," and then ordered them into the waiting aircraft.

The squadron commanders stood at the doors of the planes and checked each belt and harness. The CO himself circulated among the men, patting a shoulder, joking, predicting, enthusing, for all the world as though they were going into battle and facing real danger. Gideon responded to the pat on his shoulder with a hasty smile. He was lean, almost ascetic-looking, but very suntanned. A sharp eye, that of the legendary blond commander, could spot the blue vein throbbing in his neck.

Then the heat broke into the shady storage sheds, mercilessly flushing out the last strongholds of coolness, roasting everything with a gray glow. The sign was given. The engines gave a throaty roar. Birds fled from the runway. The planes shuddered, moved forward heavily, and began to gather the momentum without which takeoff cannot be achieved.

5

I must get out and be there to shake his hand.

Having made up his mind, Sheinbaum closed his notebook. The months of military training have certainly toughened the boy. It is hard to believe, but it certainly looks as though he is beginning to mature at last. He still has to learn how to handle women. He has to free himself once and for all from his shyness and his sentimentality: he should leave such traits to women and cultivate toughness in himself. And how he has improved at chess. Soon he'll be a serious challenge to his old father. May even beat me one of these days. Not just yet, though. As long as he doesn't up and marry the first girl who gives herself to him. He ought to break one or two of them in before he gets spliced. In a few years he'll have to give me some grandchildren. Lots of them. Gideon's children will have two fathers: my son can take care of them, and I'll take care of their ideas. The second generation grew up in the shadow of our achievements; that's why they're so confused. It's a matter of dialectics. But the third generation will be a wonderful synthesis, a successful outcome: they will inherit the spontaneity of their parents and the spirit of their grandparents. It will be a glorious heritage distilled from a twisted pedigree. I'd better jot that phrase down, it will come in handy one of these days. I feel so sad when I think of Gideon and his friends: they exude such an air of shallow despair, of nihilism, of cynical mockery. They can't love wholeheartedly, and they can't hate wholeheartedly, either. No enthusiasm, and no loathing. I'm not one to deprecate despair per se. Despair is the eternal twin of faith, but that's real despair, virile and passionate, not this sentimental, poetic melancholy. Sit still, Gideon, stop scratching yourself, stop biting your nails. I want to read you a marvelous passage from Brenner. All right, make a face. So I won't read. Go outside and grow up to be a Bedouin, if that's what you want. But if you don't get to know Brenner, you'll never understand the first thing about despair or about faith. You won't find any soppy poems here about jackals caught in traps or flowers in the autumn. In Brenner, everything is on fire. Love, and hatred as well. Maybe you yourselves won't see light and darkness face to face, but your children will. A glorious heritage will be distilled from a twisted pedigree. And we won't let the third generation be pampered and corrupted by sentimental verses by decadent poetesses. Here come the planes now. We'll put Brenner back on the shelf and get ready to be proud of you for a change, Gideon Sheinbaum.

6

Sheinbaum strode purposefully across the lawn, stepped up onto the concrete path, and turned toward the plowed field in the southwest corner of the kibbutz, which had been selected for the landing. On his way he paused now and again at a flower bed to pull up a stray weed skulking furtively beneath a flowering shrub. His small blue eyes had always been amazingly skillful at detecting weeds. Admittedly, because of his age he had retired a few years previously from his work in the gardens, but until his dying day he would not cease to scan the flower beds mercilessly in search of undesirable intruders. At such moments he thought of the boy, forty years his junior, who had succeeded him as gardener and who fancied himself as the local watercolorist: he had inherited beautifully tended gardens, and now they were all going to seed before our very eyes.

A gang of excited children ran across his path. They were fiercely absorbed in a detailed argument about the types of aircraft that were circling above the valley. Because they were running, the argument was being carried out in loud shouts and gasps. Shimshon seized one of them by the shirttail, forcibly brought him to a halt, put his face close to the child's, and said, "You are Zaki."

"Leave me alone," the child replied.

Sheinbaum said, "What's all this shouting? Airplanes, is that all you've got in your heads? And running across the flower beds like that where it says Keep Off, is that right? Do you think you can do whatever you like? Are there no rules anymore? Look at me when I'm speaking to you. And give me a proper answer, or . . ."

But Zaki had taken advantage of the flood of words to wriggle out of the man's grasp and tear himself free. He slipped in among the bushes, made a monkey face, and stuck out his tongue.

Sheinbaum pursed his lips. He thought for an instant about old age, but instantly thrust it out of his mind and said to himself, All right. We'll see about that later. Zaki, otherwise Azariah. Rapid calculation showed that he must be at least eleven, perhaps twelve already. A hooligan. A wild beast.

Meanwhile the young trainees had occupied a vantage point high up on top of the water tower, from which they could survey the length and breadth of the valley. The whole scene reminded Sheinbaum of a Russian painting. For a moment he was tempted to climb up and join the youngsters on top of the tower, to watch the display comfortably from a distance. But the thought of the manly handshake to come kept him striding steadily on, till he reached the edge of the field. Here he stood, his legs planted well apart, his arms folded on his chest, his thick white hair falling impressively over his forehead. He craned his neck and followed the two transport planes with steady gray eyes. The mosaic of wrinkles on his face enriched his expression with a rare blend of pride, thoughtfulness, and a trace of well-controlled irony. And his bushy white eyebrows suggested a saint in a Russian icon. Meanwhile the planes had completed their first circuit, and the leading one was approaching the field again.

Shimshon Sheinbaum's lips parted and made way for a low hum. An old Russian tune was throbbing in his chest. The first batch of men emerged from the opening in the plane's side. Small dark shapes were dotted in space, like seeds scattered by a farmer in an old pioneering print.

Then Raya Greenspan stuck her head out of the window of the

kitchen and gesticulated with the ladle she was holding as though admonishing the treetops. Her face was hot and flushed. Perspiration stuck her plain dress to her strong, hairy legs. She panted, scratched at her disheveled hair with the fingernails of her free hand, and suddenly turned and shouted to the other women working in the kitchens, "Quick! Come to the window! It's Gidi up there! Gidi in the sky!"

And just as suddenly she was struck dumb.

While the first soldiers were still floating gently, like a handful of feathers, between heaven and earth, the second plane came in and dropped Gideon Shenhav's group. The men stood pressed close together inside the hatch, chest against back, their bodies fused into a single tense, sweating mass. When Gideon's turn came he gritted his teeth, braced his knees, and leapt out as though from the womb into the bright hot air. A long wild scream of joy burst from his throat as he fell. He could see his childhood haunts rushing up toward him as he fell he could see the roofs and treetops and he smiled a frantic smile of greeting as he fell toward the vineyards and concrete paths and sheds and gleaming pipes with joy in his heart as he fell. Never in his whole life had he known such overwhelming, spine-tingling love. All his muscles were tensed, and gushing thrills burst in his stomach and up his spine to the roots of his hair. He screamed for love like a madman, his fingernails almost drawing blood from his clenched palms. Then the straps drew taut and caught him under the armpits. His waist was clasped in a tight embrace. For a moment he felt as though an invisible hand were pulling him back up toward the plane into the heart of the sky. The delicious falling sensation was replaced by a slow, gentle swaying, like rocking in a cradle or floating in warm water. Suddenly a wild panic hit him. How will they recognize me down there? How will they manage to identify their only son in this forest of white parachutes? How will they be able to fix me and me alone with their anxious, loving gaze? Mother and Dad and the pretty girls and the little kids and everyone. I mustn't just get lost in the crowd. After all, this is me, and I'm the one they love.

That moment an idea flashed through Gideon's mind. He put his hand up to his shoulder and pulled the cord to release the spare chute, the one intended for emergencies. As the second canopy opened overhead he slowed down as though the force of gravity had lost its hold on him. He seemed to be floating alone in the void, like a gull or a lonely cloud. The last of his comrades had landed in the soft earth and were folding up their parachutes. Gideon Shenhav alone continued to hover as though under a spell with two large canopies spread out above him. Happy, intoxicated, he drank in the hundreds of eyes fixed on him. On him alone. In his glorious isolation.

As though to lend further splendor to the spectacle, a strong, almost cool breeze burst from the west, plowing through the hot air, playing with the spectators' hair, and carrying slightly eastward the last of the parachutists.

7

Far away in the big city, the massed crowds waiting for the military parade greeted the sudden sea breeze with a sigh of relief. Perhaps it marked the end of the heat wave. A cool, salty smell caressed the baking streets. The breeze freshened. It whistled fiercely in the treetops, bent the stiff spines of the cypresses, ruffled the hair of the pines, raised eddies of dust, and blurred the scene for the spectators at the parachute display. Regally, like a huge solitary bird, Gideon Shenhav was carried eastward toward the main road.

The terrified shout that broke simultaneously from a hundred throats could not reach the boy. Singing aloud in an ecstatic trance, he continued to sway slowly toward the main electric cables, stretched between their enormous pylons. The watchers stared in horror at the suspended soldier and the power lines that crossed the valley with unfaltering straightness from west to east. The five parallel cables, sagging with their own weight between the pylons, hummed softly in the gusty breeze.

Gideon's two parachutes tangled in the upper cable. A moment later his feet landed on the lower one. His body hung backward in a slanting pose. The straps held his waist and shoulders fast, preventing him from falling into the soft plowland. Had he not been insulated by the thick soles of his boots, the boy would have been struck dead at the moment of impact. As it was, the cable was already protesting its unwonted burden by scorching his soles. Tiny sparks flashed and crackled under Gideon's feet. He held tight with both hands to the buckles on the straps. His eyes were open wide and his mouth was agape.

Immediately a short officer, perspiring heavily, leapt out of the petrified crowd and shouted, "Don't touch the cables, Gidi. Stretch your body backward and keep as clear as you can!"

The whole tightly packed, panic-stricken crowd began to edge slowly in an easterly direction. There were shouts. There was a wail. Sheinbaum silenced them with his metallic voice and ordered everyone to keep calm. He broke into a fast run, his feet pounding on the soft earth, reached the spot, pushed aside the officers and curious bystanders, and instructed his son, "Quickly, Gideon, release the straps and drop. The ground is soft here. It's perfectly safe. Jump."

"I can't."

"Don't argue. Do as I tell you. Jump."

"I can't, Dad, I can't do it."

"No such thing as can't. Release the straps and jump before you electrocute yourself."

"I can't, the straps are tangled. Tell them to switch off the current quickly, Dad, my boots are burning."

Some of the soldiers were trying to hold back the crowd, discourage well-meaning suggestions, and make more room under the power lines. They kept repeating, as if it were an incantation, "Don't panic please don't panic."

The youngsters of the kibbutz were rushing all around, adding to the confusion. Reprimands and warnings had no effect. Two angry paratroopers managed to catch Zaki, who was idiotically climbing the nearest pylon, snorting and whistling and making faces to attract the attention of the crowd.

The short officer suddenly shouted: "Your knife. You've got a knife in your belt. Get it out and cut the straps!"

But Gideon either could not or would not hear. He began to sob aloud.

"Get me down, Dad, I'll be electrocuted, tell them to get me down from here, I can't get down on my own."

"Stop sniveling," his father said curtly. "You've been told to use your knife to cut the straps. Now, do as you've been told. And stop sniveling."

The boy obeyed. He was still sobbing audibly, but he groped for the knife, located it, and cut the straps one by one. The silence was total. Only Gideon's sobbing, a strange, piercing sound, was to be heard intermittently. Finally one last strap was left holding him, which he did not dare to cut.

"Cut it," the children shrilled, "cut it and jump. Let's see you do it."

And Shimshon added in a level voice, "Now what are you waiting for?"

"I can't do it," Gideon pleaded.

"Of course you can," said his father.

"The current," the boy wept. "I can feel the current. Get me down quickly."

His father's eyes filled with blood as he roared, "You coward! You ought to be ashamed of yourself!"

"But I can't do it, I'll break my neck, it's too high."

"You can do it and you must do it. You're a fool, that's what you are, a fool and a coward."

A group of jet planes passed overhead on their way to the aerial display over the city. They were flying in precise formation, thundering westward like a pack of wild dogs. As the planes disappeared, the silence seemed twice as intense. Even the boy had stopped crying. He let the knife fall to the ground. The blade pierced the earth at Shimshon Sheinbaum's feet.

"What did you do that for?" the short officer shouted.

"I didn't mean it," Gideon whined. "It just slipped out of my hand."

Shimshon Sheinbaum bent down, picked up a small stone, straightened up, and threw it furiously at his son's back.

"Pinocchio, you're a wet rag, you're a miserable coward!"

At this point the sea breeze also dropped.

The heat wave returned with renewed vigor to oppress both men and inanimate objects. A red-haired, freckled soldier muttered to himself, "He's scared to jump, the idiot, he'll kill himself if he stays up there." And a skinny, plain-faced girl, hearing this, rushed into the middle of the circle and spread her arms wide.

"Jump into my arms, Gidi, you'll be all right."

"It would be interesting," remarked a veteran pioneer in working clothes, "to know whether anyone has had the sense to phone the electric company to ask them to switch off the current." He turned and started off toward the kibbutz buildings. He was striding quickly, angrily, up the slight slope when he was suddenly alarmed by a prolonged burst of firing close at hand. For a moment he imagined he was being shot at from behind. But at once he realized what was happening: the squadron commander, the good-looking blond hero, was trying to sever the electric cables with his machine gun.

Without success.

Meanwhile, a beaten-up truck arrived from the farmyard. Ladders were unloaded from it, followed by the elderly doctor, and finally a stretcher.

At that moment it was evident that Gideon had been struck by a sudden decision. Kicking out strongly, he pushed himself off the lower cable, which was emitting blue sparks, turned a somersault, and remained suspended by the single strap with his head pointing downward and his scorched boots beating the air a foot or so from the cable.

It was hard to be certain, but it looked as though so far he had not sustained any serious injury. He swung limply upside down in space, like a dead lamb suspended from a butcher's hook.

This spectacle provoked hysterical glee in the watching children. They barked with laughter. Zaki slapped his knees, choking and heaving convulsively. He leapt up and down screeching like a mischievous monkey.

What had Gideon Shenhav seen that made him suddenly stretch his neck and join in the children's laughter? Perhaps his peculiar posture had unbalanced his mind. His face was blood-red, his tongue protruded, his thick hair hung down, and only his feet kicked up at the sky.

8

A second group of jets plowed through the sky overhead. A dozen metallic birds, sculpted with cruel beauty, flashing dazzlingly in the bright sunlight. They flew in a narrow spearhead formation. Their fury shook the earth. On they flew to the west, and a deep silence followed.

Meanwhile, the elderly doctor sat down on the stretcher, lit a cigarette, blinked vaguely at the people, the soldiers, the scampering children, and said to himself, We'll see how things turn out. Whatever has to happen will happen. How hot it is today.

Every now and again Gideon let out another senseless laugh. His legs were flailing, describing clumsy circles in the dusty air. The blood had drained from his inverted limbs and was gathering in his head. His eyes were beginning to bulge. The world was turning dark. Instead of the crimson glow, purple spots were dancing before his eyes. He stuck his tongue out. The children interpreted this as a gesture of derision. "Upside-down Pinocchio," Zaki shrilled, "why don't you stop squinting at us and try walking on your hands instead?"

Sheinbaum moved to hit the brat, but the blow landed on thin air because the child had leapt aside. The old man beckoned to the blond commander, and they held a brief consultation. The boy was in no immediate danger, because he was not in direct contact with the cable, but he must be rescued soon. This comedy could not go on forever. A ladder would not help much: he was too high up. Perhaps the knife could be got up to him again somehow, and he could be persuaded to cut the last strap and jump into a sheet of canvas. After all, it was a perfectly routine exercise in parachute training. The main thing was to act quickly, because the situation was humiliating. Not to mention the children. So the short officer removed his shirt and wrapped a knife in it. Gideon stretched his hands downward and tried to catch the bundle. It slipped between his outstretched arms and plummeted uselessly to the ground. The children snickered. Only after two more unsuccessful attempts did Gideon manage to grasp the shirt and remove the knife. His fingers were numb and heavy with blood. Suddenly he pressed the blade to his burning cheek, enjoying the cool touch of the steel. It was a delicious moment. He opened his eyes and saw an inverted world. Everything looked comical: the truck, the field, his father, the army, the kids, and even the knife in his hand. He made a twisted face at the gang of children, gave a deep laugh, and waved at them with the knife. He tried to say something. If only they could see themselves from up here, upside down, rushing around like startled ants, they would surely laugh with him. But the laugh turned into a heavy cough; Gideon choked and his eyes filled.

9

Gideon's upside-down antics filled Zaki with demonic glee.

"He's crying," he shouted cruelly, "Gideon's crying, look, you can see the tears. Pinocchio the hero, he's sniveling with fear-o. We can see you, we can."

Once again Shimshon Sheinbaum's fist fell ineffectually on thin air.

"Zaki," Gideon managed to shout in a dull, pain-racked voice, "I'll kill you, I'll choke you, you little bastard." Suddenly he chuckled and stopped.

It was no good. He wouldn't cut the last strap by himself, and the doctor was afraid that if he stayed as he was much longer he was likely to lose consciousness. Some other solution would have to be found. This performance could not be allowed to go on all day.

And so the kibbutz truck rumbled across the plowland and

braked at the point indicated by Shimshon Sheinbaum. Two ladders were hastily lashed together to reach the required height, and then supported on the back of the truck by five strong pairs of hands. The legendary blond officer started to climb. But when he reached the place where the two ladders overlapped, there was an ominous creak, and the wood began to bend with the weight and the height. The officer, a largish man, hesitated for a moment. He decided to retreat and fasten the ladders together more securely. He climbed down to the floor of the truck, wiped the sweat from his forehead, and said, "Wait, I'm thinking." Just then, in the twinkling of an eye, before he could be stopped, before he could even be spotted, the child Zaki had climbed high up the ladder, past the join, and leapt like a frantic monkey up onto the topmost rungs; suddenly he was clutching a knife—where on earth had he got it from? He wrestled with the taut strap. The spectators held their breath: he seemed to be defying gravity, not holding on, not caring, hopping on the top rung, nimble, lithe, amazingly efficient.

10

The heat beat down violently on the hanging youth. His eyes were growing dimmer. His breathing had almost stopped. With his last glimmer of lucidity he saw his ugly brother in front of him and felt his breath on his face. He could smell him. He could see the pointed teeth protruding from Zaki's mouth. A terrible fear closed in on him, as though he were looking in a mirror and seeing a monster. The nightmare roused Gideon's last reserves of strength. He kicked into space, flailed, managed to turn over, seized the strap, and pulled himself up. With outstretched arms he threw himself onto the cable and saw the flash. The hot wind continued to tyrannize the whole valley. And a third cluster of jets drowned the scene with its roaring.

11

The status of a bereaved father invests a man with a saintly aura of suffering. But Sheinbaum gave no thought to this aura. A stunned, silent company escorted him toward the dining hall. He knew, with utter certainty, that his place now was beside Raya.

On the way he saw the child Zaki, glowing, breathless, a hero. Surrounded by other youngsters: he had almost rescued Gideon. Shimshon laid a trembling hand on his child's head, and tried to tell him. His voice abandoned him and his lips quivered. Clumsily he stroked the tousled, dusty mop of hair. It was the first time he had ever stroked the child. A few steps later, everything went dark and the old man collapsed in a flower bed.

As Independence Day drew to a close the *khamsin* abated. A fresh sea breeze soothed the steaming walls. There was a heavy fall of dew on the lawns in the night.

What does the pale ring around the moon portend? Usually it heralds a *khamsin*. Tomorrow, no doubt, the heat will return. It is May, and June will follow. A wind drifts among the cypresses in the night, trying to comfort them between one heat wave and the next. It is the way of the wind to come and to go and to come again. There is nothing new.

An Extended Family

from Elsewhere, Perhaps (1966)

14

MOUNTING EVIDENCE

During the days preceding the festival, gossip reached fever pitch. If the signs were to be believed, something very strange and disturbing had happened in our kibbutz. One night Israel Tsitron, who was on duty as night watchman, overheard a quarrel. From him we learned that all was not well between Noga and her boyfriend, the widow's son, Rami. This was confirmed by the evidence of Dafna Isarov, even if there were some who disputed the details of her disturbing story. According to Dafna, one evening, one Friday night, Rami Rimon had burst into the room that she and Noga shared and attacked Noga by main force. Later, Ezra Berger had appeared and had clashed with Rami, at first with words but later with blows. Eventually, Rami had burst out of the room, looking, Dafna said, very strange. A strange friendship had certainly come into being—so testified the widow Fruma Rominov*—between Reuven Harish's daughter and Bronka's husband.

Of course. Now that this news has come to our notice, we connect

---

*Though Fruma and Rami have different last names, they are mother and son; at the initiative of the first prime minister of Israel, David Ben-Gurion, Jews from all over the world who gathered in the young state changed their Diasporic names (German, Polish, Arabic) to Hebrew biblical names in order to signify a new generation and a new era in Jewish-Israeli life.

it with what we have seen with our own eyes but not thought much about. For some days now we have observed the man and the girl chatting together in the early afternoon by the garage. Up to now we have seen nothing wrong in these conversations. If the rumors are true, we have been very naïve. It is alleged that Ezra Berger buys his little friend embroidery thread over and above the kibbutz ration and pays for it out of his own pocket. In return, the girl has made him an embroidered bag for his sandwiches. Nina Goldring, who supplies the sandwiches, has seen the bag with her own eyes. It has a bear embroidered on it.

Is it right or proper for the two of them to meet in broad daylight in the middle of the yard, in the shadow of the huge truck, and for the older man to finger the girl's chin and mutter his pointless proverbs to her? Is it right for her to respond with musical laughter and even slap him on his hairy shoulder? No, it's not right, it's not proper, it smacks of licentiousness.

If we are to believe Dafna, things have gone even further. Noga has got into the habit of getting up in the middle of the night and stealing across to the shed behind the laundry building to meet the driver on his return. Admittedly, Dafna is suspected of exaggerating. It would be only natural. But there is no denying that the affair has gone too far. There is more to it than meets the eye. We are cautious in our judgment. We base our opinion not on Dafna's evidence, which is not universally accepted, but on that of Mundek Zohar, who is a reliable witness. His evidence is decisive, and we shall record it presently. Of Noga Harish it was said that her mother Eva's hot blood flowed in her veins. Of Ezra Berger, Herzl Goldring said, "Is it any wonder that his Oren is a delinquent? The apple never falls far from the tree." There were some (Fruma Rominov seems to have been the first to voice this alarming idea) who said that this was Ezra's way of having his revenge. And so on.

For some days we scrutinized the faces of Reuven and Bronka, looking for signs. "He who sows the wind will reap the whirlwind," said Grisha Isarov, parodying the truck driver's cryptic style of utterance.

Einav, quietly waiting for the end of her pregnancy, said to her husband Tomer one evening, "He's in the news, your father."

Tomer shrugged his shoulders and said nothing.

"I think you ought to do something about it. It's your family, after all."

But Tomer, whose young body had no rival in the arduous work of haymaking, gave his wife a sneering look, spread out his massive arms and said, "Why me? I'm not his father. If the old man wants to make a fool of himself, good luck to him. Mother's not much better than he is."

True, Bronka is no better than her husband. It was she who started it all. But this fact does nothing to relieve her present unhappiness. Often, in bed, she turns her face to the wall and cries. Reuven bites his lip and does not talk about it. What can he say? He strokes her cheek affectionately and says nothing. His heart is heavy. He has not changed his habits, though. Every evening he crosses the lawn to Bronka and stays with her until just before Ezra gets back. But for some days now he has resumed the habit of the early days of their friendship, when it was still pure and intellectual. He is content to sit with her, drink coffee, munch grapes, talk awkwardly about art, until Bronka buries her face in her hands and collapses into long fits of sobbing.

If there is a letter from Zechariah-Siegfried in Munich, Bronka gives it to Reuven so that he can read his wife's brief lines. Then they sit side by side on the divan, holding hands. Reuven is as silent as a boy who is in love for the first time. Bronka, too, is silent. She is knitting a hat for her future granddaughter. Sometimes he brings a book with him, and they read it together, as in the good old days. Once Bronka gazed at Reuven's lips and said, "What's going to happen? Tell me, tell me."

"It's going to be bad," said Reuven.

Still the worst did not happen. It is true that Noga sometimes woke up in the middle of the night and slipped through the darkness behind the shrubbery to meet the man on his return. But Ezra, with clumsy affection, rested her head on his sweaty chest, stroked it consolingly, and sent her back to bed. Once he even kissed her. Mundek Zohar, who was on duty that night, saw it with his own eyes and is ready to swear to it, and Mundek is a reliable witness. But it was so dark that the watchman could not see the girl's hot tears, and so he misjudged the nature of the kiss. It was a warm-hearted, paternal kiss, the purest thing in the world.

15

WOMAN

At the end of the week came the *khamsin*. From the mountain range in the east a murderous dryness flowed down to engulf us. The sky was gray, as if the desert had risen to float upside down over our tiny roofs. The heat tore at our vitality with its cruel claws, bringing desperate weariness, tormenting the body and oppressing the soul. Hens died by the dozen, despite the elaborate cooling system. Obstinacy took hold of the cows, and Herbert Segal was reduced to driving them into the milking shed with a whip. The trees grew gray and whispered drily. Scorched yellow patches appeared in the lawns. The men and women of the kibbutz quarreled violently over trifles. Decency restrains us from relating the words that Fruma Rominov hurled at Bronka Berger on one of these terrible days. But this much we may say, that Bronka, shaken, arrived at Reuven Harish's room during the afternoon, beckoned to him to come outside, so that the children should not hear, and announced breathlessly that she could not put up with any more of it, and that it was up to him, for God's sake, to do what any real father would have done long ago.

And so it was Fruma Rominov's judgment that brought about, even though indirectly, the conversation between father and daughter that up to now Reuven Harish had tried to avoid.

They were strolling together in front of the kibbutz office. It was eight o'clock in the evening. The air was dark and stifling. They spoke softly.

"I wanted to ask you if you think, Noga."

"What sort of question's that, Daddy? I don't understand what you mean."

"If you think. If you've thought a single thought these last weeks, or if you've given up thinking altogether."

"I'm not the tourists, Daddy, so please talk frankly to me, don't beat about the bush."

"I'll talk, Noga. I'll talk. I'll talk in a moment. I won't beat about the bush. And I want you to talk to me, too, completely openly. Sincerely."

"Don't I always?"

"Perhaps. Tell me, Noga, do you know what people here have been saying about you recently?"

"What have people here been saying about me recently, Daddy?"

"You know very well what they've been saying. Gossip. Nasty gossip."

"It's always unhappy people who say unkind things."

"I . . . I want us to understand each other, Noga. Don't force me to say unkind things, too."

"Why, are you unhappy?"

"Why are you fighting against me, Noga? It hurts me. I don't want us to fight. I want you to be happy."

"It's hot, Daddy. I'm hot. We're all hot. It's the *khamsin*. Why do you want to talk about gossip now? Why do you think that life is all about talking? There are other things. Not just words. Words aren't everything. Why must you always explain everything? Why has everything got to be explained? The sky won't fall if something isn't explained."

"There are things . . ."

"Yes. I know. There are things. Fruma said something nasty to Bronka. I know, Dafna heard it and told me. I hate words. It's because of those words that you've come to talk to me now, when we're so hot. That's enough. Let's stop."

"Never mind about Fruma and never mind about Bronka. I want to talk to you, Noga. About you."

"You want to talk and you talk all the time but you don't really talk."

"I am talking. I'm talking about your new . . . friendship, to call a spade a spade. I only want to know one thing: if you think at all."

"Friendship?"

"Yes."

"Ezra?"

"I . . . yes. Ezra."

"Tell me, do you feel . . . embarrassed? Do you find it difficult to ask me things straight out? I've got to keep away from Ezra because Bronka . . . Oh, it's simple, it's simple, Daddy, so simple, and you're walking on tiptoe as if I were made of glass. I'm not made of glass. I understand. It's simple. Either you and Bronka or me and Ezra, and you were first, so you have first claim. It's so simple, Daddy."

"Noga . . . Stella, listen . . . Why do you . . . Why do you have to put it . . . Listen to me for a moment."

"I'm listening, Daddy, I'm listening to every word, all the time. You don't have to ask me to listen. I'm all ears."

Reuven Harish is a little perplexed. In his embarrassment he tugs lightly at his upper lip, searching for the right words. The heat blurs his mind. The perspiration from his hand smudges his face, and the perspiration from his face sticks to his hand. A strange stabbing stirs in his chest but dies down before it becomes painful. Stella, meanwhile, a naughty little deer, turns her back on him and paws the earth with her foot. On her face is a grimace, which is almost a smile. Reuven tries to stroke her neck. She moves out of reach.

"Let me put it another way, Noga. Look. You're not a child, right? I'm not trying to interfere with your private life. But I don't want you to ruin your life. That's all. That's the only thing I'm talking about."

"You're sweet, Daddy," Noga says suddenly. "You're really sweet."

Her face shines in the dark. But her teeth, strangely, chatter as if she were ill. He's suffering. He's suffering, and now he's going to start talking about Mother. Oh, poor Daddy, silly Daddy, if only you realized that I'm on your side, only I can't say so because . . .

Reuven is suffering. This is not how he imagined the conversation. She's eluding me. I talk to her, and she dances circles round me. What is she thinking? You can never tell what they're thinking. They dance. You talk, and they dance. They're both the same. Outwardly they look calm, but inside, a raving demon. But not her. I won't let her. She's mine.

Affectionately, half-jokingly, Reuven asked, "To come to the point, Stella, what demon's got into you?"

Affectionately, half-jokingly, Noga answered, "A wonderful demon, Daddy. A sad, wise demon, full of love. Sometimes he's frightening, but he's a gentle demon. A tired demon."

"Now I'll tell you something," Reuven said. "Something about your mother."

"No," said Noga. "Not that. I won't listen."

"Yes. You will listen. You must listen," said Reuven Harish, pressing home to the full his unexpected advantage.

"No. I don't have to. I won't listen. I won't listen to anything."

"When that wretch Hamburger came, your mother loathed him. I'm not exaggerating: she loathed him, but she behaved politely. He was a close relative; they had grown up in the same house together, but apparently the war corrupted him. That was what your mother thought. She said that he wasn't himself. He wasn't the little boy who had been betrothed to her when she was a little girl. He was someone else. A clown imitating the speech and manners of that dead boy. Well, then. Actually he spent the war in Switzerland, making money by speculating. I'll tell you about that too, sometime. Your mother said she hoped he'd leave soon. Tomorrow. At once. I was the one who urged her to behave politely toward him. After all, he'd had a hard life. He'd suffered a lot. But your mother hated him. He was clever. He used to say things like 'tame partridge' and laugh a slimy laugh. Your mother asked him to shut up, for heaven's sake. He would wink and say, for instance, '*Gold und Silber*' or '*Raus, raus, Dichter.*' These remarks hurt your mother terribly. He talked a great deal about women, by the way."

"I'm not listening."

"I looked after him most of the time because your mother didn't like to be near him. I took the wretched creature to Jerusalem, Sodom, Elat. Every place, every sight, every name reminded him of some obscenity or dirty joke. He made a point of spending a lot of money on me. Tried to be friendly with his great toothy horse smiles. He had enormous teeth. He talked about women. And he winked."

"I'm not listening."

"Once we were coming out of the dining hall, he and your mother and I, and he asked with a wink if it was true that we practiced free love here. The smile showed all those teeth of his. Your mother was so disgusted she ran off. When she came back, he sang some German nursery rhyme about Franzi the gardener peeping into the cellar and watching the prince's children praying. Make him go away tomorrow, your mother said that night, Make him go at once. Tomorrow. He didn't stay with us long. Perhaps a fortnight. Then suddenly . . ."

"I'm not listening to a word you're saying. You're talking to thin air."

"Then one day I went to Tel Aviv, Stella dear, one awful day, and the next day I came home and there was nothing left. Some madness had taken hold of your mother. She went off with that swine. But in her heart, Noga my darling, in her heart I know she regrets it all. Her infatuation ruined her. Me. Us. She wrote me a long letter from Europe a month later, pouring her heart out. Her Isaac was a little angel once; they used to play duets together on the piano when they were little, read poetry, write, draw, but suffering had corrupted him, and she felt it was up to her, and her alone, to purify him. That was how we lost your mother. You were just a little toddler then."

"Daddy, don't say any more. Be nice. Please, please stop, Daddy."

"Her infatuation ruined everything. I'm not beating about the bush now. I'm telling you straight out, Noga."

"You did the same to someone else."

"No, I didn't. How can you compare it? Bronka and I . . ."

"You and Bronka. Me and Ezra. That's life. It's not made of words. It's ugly. I want you to stop now. Stop talking."

• • •

Then, for no reason, the girl dragged her father over to the shadow of a nearby tree and kissed his face, uttering as she did so a sob that sounded like a smothered laugh or a puppy's crying. Reuven stifled his words and gently stroked his daughter's hair and murmured, "Stella, Stella," and whispered to her to be careful, and Noga—in the soft low voice of another woman—told Reuven that she loved him now and always, while the *khamsin* raged relentlessly, unmoved even by powerful emotions.

Noga went to the abandoned stable to wait for Ezra's return. The darkness and the ancient smells of decay frightened her for once, and so she waited at the entrance to the stable. She sat down on a dark, rotting board and thought. Suffering corrupted him, and she felt it was up to her, and her alone, to purify him. This is where we found the rope. It wasn't very long ago. It's a long time since there were horses here. Horses aren't used anymore. They've had their day. A horse is a splendid animal. A horse is a powerful animal. There's a contradiction in a horse. He can be wild and rush over the plains. A horse has a wild smell when he sweats. I feel dizzy when I think of a horse's smell. He had enormous teeth, like a horse, Daddy said. A galloping horse is the most beautiful animal in the world. He spent the war in Switzerland, making money by speculating. Speculation is wrong. Franzi the gardener, what did Franzi the gardener see, what were the prince's children doing in a dark cellar? And what did he mean by "tame partridge"? How clumsy he looked when he poured the water I brought him down his throat without putting the mug to his lips, and the water splashed onto his chin and trickled down his neck and vanished into the hair on his chest. How strong. When he's driving, he thinks about the Bible, about Rachel and Leah, for instance, and their children. "Leah" can mean "tired" in Hebrew. That's pretty, but sad. He didn't even know what turquoise was, but I taught him because I'm responsible for him. What does *Raus, raus, Dichter* mean? I wish I knew. Outside it's hot in the stable it's nice and cool I'm frightened to go inside don't be frightened Franzi the gardener is a good man he won't tell on the little princess. Mummy was prettier than me. Her light blue dressing gown I wore once and he met me on the path and said *Gold und Silber* and looked at me not at my face then he turned his head and looked away. Daddy's sure she regrets it all in her heart. You don't regret in your heart. Only in literary language. He asked if we practiced free love here. Mummy wanted him to go away. But I'm Daddy's daughter, too. Green eyes. It's true. Now listen carefully, Ezra, there's one thing you've got to remember. I love a horse because he's wild and I have to purify because I'm responsible. It's almost midnight. Not long now. Soon you'll . . . Old Franzi, the gardener, shame on his peeping eyes. And, you know, there's a contradiction in the color turquoise: it's blue and it's green, like a horse, which can be mild or wild.

Ezra spent a long time tonight with his friends the fishermen in Tiberias. He got home to the kibbutz at one o'clock in the morning. Noga had leaped up onto the running board before the truck stopped. She put her head into the cab and smiled, and her teeth chattered. She must be ill, flushed with fever. Go to bed, little girl, you're trembling all over, are you crazy. Yes, Ezra, yes, yes. You're not well, little one, get moving, Turquoise, forward march—to bed, do you hear, little baby, don't argue now. No, I can't hear, Ezra, I can't hear a word. You're ill, silly, you've got a temperature. *Little bear is feeling ill, stayed up late and caught a chill.* Don't talk, Ezra, I don't want you to talk, I want you to put your arms round me and explain to me what "tame partridge" means and two more words I've forgotten. No, you're confused, Turquoise, you don't know what you're doing. I do know. I know what I want. I want you to put your arms round me and not talk and not talk in proverbs. And not talk.

Ezra took hold of her thin arm and tried to take her to her room. Noga wouldn't let him. She fought back. She stood rooted to the spot. Ezra didn't want to take her to her room by force. Perplexed, he paused and looked at her, desperately tired. The night air was still thick and oppressive. In the distance dogs howled wildly, and the jackals howled in answer. The night was full of dim anger.

Trembling all over, Noga clung to the man's powerful body. He tried to prize her loose. She gripped his clothes with her nails. Delicious kisses on his hairy, sweat-matted chest. Backward she dragged him step by tiny step into the thick darkness of the myrtle bushes. Who taught her tongue to lick his salty neck so tenderly? Or her fingers to play so cleverly on the back of his head? Overcome, he fell, his heavy hands on her shoulders. His voice betrayed him, no longer forming words, only dry groans. Noga was terrified. She regretted it now and tried to escape. His grip was heavy, frightening. Her eyes flickered and went out. Her body awoke and filled with sweet gushes. Warm shudders flowed from one sweet part of her to another. Her breath came in pants, her mouth stretched wide open, her tiny teeth dug again and again into the blind flesh. The ground beneath her stirred, sending quivering ripples through her. On spreading ripples her body floated. Torrents flooded over her, bursting out strong and cruel from forgotten lairs. Wave after wave after wave. The confusion whirled in a cycle, in a burning rhythm. Boiling water battered her body. Boiling oil. Burning poison. Sweet seething poison slicing down into the marrow of her bones. An imprisoned scream, flash after flash swept away into the water, the waves were not black, they were gleaming, dazzling flares capering in the water, a streaming jet swept her sick body toward roaring waterfalls.

Two or three hours later. Dawn light outlining the slats of the shutters. She turns between her sheets. Strange, secret sensations. Her body curls up compulsively, her knees drawn up to her chin, pressing against her breasts, her fingers caressing her skin. Drop by drop, like rain in a gutter, a song dripped inside her:

> *From the Dead Sea to Jericho*
> *The pomegranate sweetly smells,*
> *A pair of eyes, a pair of doves,*
> *And a voice like the sound of bells.*

She can hear them in her skin. She can hear the bells.

16

HATRED

For six more days the *khamsin* oppressed us relentlessly. If you reached out to touch a bench, a wall, an irrigation tap, a stair rail, the inanimate object responded with incandescent hatred. Reuven Harish found relief from the oppression — incredible though it may seem — by casting it in a poetic mold.

> *Blazing heat, down you beat*
> *On scorpion's lair and snake's retreat.*
> *Leaving your arid desert seat,*
> *The home of Genie and Afrit,*
> *You stamp the plains with scorching feet,*
> *Stifling everything you meet.*
> *Panting souls find no retreat,*
> *Strongest men admit defeat;*
> *Gasping voices beg, entreat*
> *Relief from yellow, parching heat.*

Meanwhile, the enemy's provocations intensified. Frequent shots were fired into our fields, by day as well as by night. There were no casualties, however. The enemy were careful not to overstep the mark. They were content to harass us and remind us that they were there, bent on our destruction.

At the end of the week a small army unit dug itself into the vineyards and pointed machine guns at the enemy positions installed halfway up the slope, on the territory that was the bloodstained subject of dispute between the two states. Our troops had orders not to provoke the enemy. If the enemy launched a serious action, if a stray tractor was cut off by firing, they were to cover it and extricate it. But they were forbidden to return random fire, so as not to aggravate the prevailing tension. They also had orders to dig some trenches, so that people working in outlying fields could take cover if attacked. Digging trenches during the stifling *khamsin*, even at night, is not the most pleasant of tasks. Our soldiers found assistance from an unexpected quarter: Oren Geva and his friends appeared one afternoon to offer their help. Before the commanding officer could manage to dismiss the intruders with a reprimand, they had already dug two or three magnificent trenches. The officer shrugged his shoulders and showed them where and how.

This new problem provoked conflicting opinions among the schoolteachers on the kibbutz. According to Herbert Segal, in addition to the obvious danger to which our children were exposed, it would also encourage militaristic attitudes. It was the forceful opinion of Reuven Harish, curiously, that swayed the balance. In the first place, he said, who could stop them. Second, it would provide a constructive outlet for their excess energies.

For several days the lads threw themselves into their work with a will. They worked well and they were handsomely rewarded: a pat on the back from the commanding officer for Oren Geva, the satisfaction of being in the front lines, some rich additions to their vocabulary, the privilege of secretly handling the gleaming weapons, and even—pray that no word of it reaches hostile ears—unofficial permission to clean and oil a submachine gun.

In the dining hall after supper small groups gather to discuss the situation. Some decipher and interpret the signs; others hold that the enemy is simply out to demonstrate his presence; others maintain that we are witnessing the prelude to a big show, such as we saw three months ago, when they began by ambushing a tractor and ended up battering a kibbutz with heavy gunfire.

The other topic of conversation is the question of reprisals. Most of the older members think that it would be better for us not to heap coals on the fire. So long as the enemy refrains from launching a real attack, argues Mundek Zohar, head of the regional council, we are better off showing our contempt by maintaining a dignified silence. Podolski looks up from the work rotas to agree with Mundek Zohar and adds that we mustn't allow ourselves to play into their hands by doing what they want us to do.

The youngsters think differently, as is only natural. Tomer Geva lays a large hand on Podolski's lean shoulder and says, "Podolski, Podolski, I'm very sad to have to inform you that the dear Arabs haven't read Tolstoy or Rosa Luxemburg, and I'm afraid they're not too well up in Mahatma Gandhi, either. But there's one language they're perfectly at home in. Without a crushing blow, a really juicy blow, as they say, we'll never stop the bastards and their blasted nuisance."

Grisha Isarov, though not a young man, has a youthful temperament. He endorses Tomer's sentiments and remarks, "Prevention is better than cure, Mundek, and your fine ideas can cost lives. As for you, Podolski, you've nothing to fear. They're brave when they scent weakness and cowards when you show them a fist. I've known them for thirty years now. They haven't changed and they'll never change. Once, in '46, I went out to set an ambush for a gang of them. Not an ordinary ambush, though . . ."

Meanwhile, the military authorities maintained a total silence. One Friday evening we had a visit from a group of high-ranking officers. We received them in the dining hall with cold drinks and fruit. They answered all our questions with a smile and a shake of the head. Afterward, they strolled around outside for twenty minutes, exchanging a few words in an undertone, while an undersized captain ran around energetically rolling and unrolling maps for them. At the same time, he made signs to the curious youngsters to keep their distance. Gai Harish's young gang observed the visitors from a respectful distance, their mouths agape, their heads cocked, their fair hair falling over their foreheads, and wonder blazing in their eyes.

Grisha Isarov's prestige took a mighty leap that night. Among the senior officers he discovered an old comrade from the days of the Jewish Brigade. They fell on each other and exchanged hearty bear hugs, while the youngsters looked on in amazement. Grisha was even allowed to join the officers for the last few minutes of their conference, but unfortunately he did not manage to adapt his voice to their hushed tones but expressed his opinions at the top of his voice. The seven Isarov children, including Dafna, basked in a halo of glory that night.

On Sunday another small group of officers visited us, this time a group of lower rank. They inspected the shelters and the trenches and looked rather apprehensively at the telephone wire that emerged from the kibbutz office and ran along the lawn on a series of rough wooden poles. One of them detached himself from the group to peer into the surgery and examine the nurse's supplies. Finally, they sat down at an isolated table in the dining hall to jugs of fruit juice and baskets of fruit. They invited Tsvi Ramigolski, the secretary of the kibbutz, to join them, together with Grisha Isarov, with his tousled mustache and his wading boots, and two or three younger men, such as Tomer Geva, who had served as officers in the army.

What a pity that the latter group haughtily refused to pass on to us the gist of that fascinating conversation. In reply to your questions they merely shook their heads secretively. If you persisted and pestered them and swore yourself to secrecy, they relented enough to dismiss you with a half sentence, such as, "It's going to be hot."

Oren's gang, too, in their usual sly way, were prepared to inform you, "It's going to be a big show."

The youngest group, Gai and his friends, promptly translated the hints into action. On Monday evening the kibbutz yard was full of shouting and bustle, scampering footsteps and sounds of battle, and at nightfall the little hill that faces the kibbutz gates to the west was stormed, and the Israeli flag planted on it with great pomp and circumstance.

Even to someone like ourselves, far removed from military matters, it was perfectly obvious that something was afoot in the stifling heat of the *khamsin*. Grisha Isarov, who was responsible for security, had already taken several hours off his work in the fishponds and enlisted the help of two or three other members in cleaning out and putting straight the shelters and the trenches.

Grisha Isarov, a man of forty or so, was not one of the founders of our kibbutz. He joined us two years before the Second World
War. When war broke out, he volunteered for the Jewish Brigade
and reached the rank of sergeant major in Her Majesty's Armed
Forces. After the war he returned to the kibbutz, heavier, mustached, and with an inexhaustible fund of anecdotes. No wonder
that Esther Klieger, a nursery school teacher with an amazing knack
for carving abstract sculptures out of tree stumps, succumbed to his
charms. Grisha did not rest quietly for long. Within three or four
months of returning from the war in Italy, he had succeeded in getting Esther with child, marrying her, and joining the underground
army. His exploits as a company commander in the struggle for independence he will be happy to recount to you till midnight, and
if he is busy in the fishponds, then you can hear the stories either
from his plump daughter Dafna or from any one of his six other
children, who are all as heavily built as their father and all marked,
boys and girls alike, with a fine down on their upper lip, which
Grisha jokingly refers to as the badge of his unit.

If it had not been for a certain unfortunate incident, Grisha
might have risen to high rank in the army; he might have joined the
group of senior officers that Friday night in his own right and not
as a favor. The details of the misdemeanor that put a premature end
to Grisha Isarov's promising military career are not known for certain. According to our old ally, gossip, it concerned a punishment
inflicted on one of the men under his command that exceeded the
bounds of military regulations. According to Grisha himself, the
modern Israeli army is better suited to tin soldiers than to fighting
men. A man of his caliber would not waste his life and talents in an
army of halberdiers and gay hussars commanded by chocolate-box
admirals.

Anyway, a couple of years after the end of the War of Independence Grisha returned to Metsudat Ram for good and shouldered
the arduous responsibility of the fishponds. His bluff, hearty manner endears him to all around him. His numerous progeny, too,
give rise to good-humored jests. Grisha Isarov also manages the

security of the kibbutz with wholehearted enthusiasm, though not without a hint of frivolity. Occasionally, for instance, he straightens his massive back, lays down the fishnets, and hurls vehement Arabic curses at the enemy positions. Or sometimes he sways his hips at them like an enormous belly dancer and gives a hideous laugh. But he is not the kind of man to overlook such trivial tasks as repairing a torn stretcher, taking stock of the ammunition, or his recent effort of cleaning out and putting straight the shelters and trenches.

It was a difficult period for Herzl Goldring. He hardly had time to play his accordion. Because of the heat, the plants needed to be watered at least twice as often as normally, and even that did little good. There were not enough rubber hoses for the job. Time and again he had pestered Yitzhak Friedrich, the treasurer, for a small sum to buy plastic hose pipes, but each time Frederick the Great had fobbed him off with excuses: either It's the beginning of the month, and how can we tell whether we'll have enough cash to see it out, or else It's the end of the month, and who has cash to lay out at the end of the month. If he'd asked for a large amount, he'd have got it by now. But if you need a small sum for a vital purpose, they fob you off with one excuse after another. It's symptomatic of the whole place. So Herzl Goldring grumbles to his wife, Nina, as they sit on their little veranda in the evening with the light out.

All round the kibbutz grounds you see plants drooping, withering, fainting with the heat. Before you've fixed up the hose to water the flowers on one side of the kibbutz, those on the other side have started to wilt. And Herzl Goldring is a man who feels physical pain at the sight of a dying plant, because he loves his work.

Herzl Goldring's dedication to his flower beds is a byword in the kibbutz. He belongs to the German faction, and in his heart of hearts he has never managed to reconcile himself to the ways of the Russians. They're so inconsistent. One day they're all sympathy and plead to be allowed to help you after their work, laying and weeding the lawns; another day they turn a deaf ear to all your requests and entreaties and empty a barrowload of building rubble on the same lawn that they so eagerly volunteered to help make. True, Herzl's wife is also a Russian. But Nina is unique among her countrywomen for her reserved manner. For many years she has borne the burden of managing the kitchen stores, generating a spirit of economy, cleanliness, and open-mindedness. Like her husband, she is gifted with a fine aesthetic sense. Their room, tastefully furnished in a European style, is gleaming and spotless. True, the pretty rugs, bookcases, and chest of drawers were acquired with money that Herzl received from the German government in reparation for his family's lost fortune, but he should not be judged harshly on this account. The money he received was paid over almost in its entirety to Yitzhak Friedrich. We must not criticize him for keeping a small sum to furnish his home and buy himself an accordion. What else was there left in his life? Their only daughter had died in her infancy of diphtheria. Being childless, they naturally wanted to make the most of their modest home. It was a venial human weakness.

As rumor has it, the Goldrings are not a happy couple. Every evening they sit in easy chairs on the darkened veranda, saying nothing, doing nothing. Sometimes Herzl has to go and turn off a sprinkler; he promises Nina not to be long, and he keeps his word. Their house is quiet. The only sounds in the evening come from the radio and from Herzl's accordion. He plays march tunes, to our perpetual surprise. The Goldrings have their supper early, before the dining room gets too full. They greet everyone, strangers included, but it is impossible to engage them in friendly conversation. Herzl agrees blankly with everything you say to him, as if he only wants to be left in peace. Nina reacts with exaggerated concern, as if she is trying hard to make you think that she is interested in you, whereas in fact she is only interested in making you believe that she is interested in you.

Herzl takes no part in kibbutz meetings, except to complain from time to time about the destruction of his plants. On such occasions he reddens, wrinkles his nose, and announces indifferently that if they want his resignation, he is prepared to tender it on a moment's notice. If his arguments are accepted, he goes on to say that actions speak louder than words, and leaves the meeting immediately, since the other items on the agenda are no concern of his. If they are not accepted, he states that his resignation takes effect forthwith, and leaves the meeting immediately, for the same reason. But at six o'clock the next morning he shatters the silence of the yard with his lawn mower, as usual, and makes no reference to his threat. Every few days he loses his temper for some trivial reason and snarls an acid "I wish you were dead" at someone, then returns to his customary politeness. Some of our young people, either because of the irritating noise of his lawn mower or for some other reason, have nicknamed Herzl Goldring the Dentist. The title is not witty, and it does not meet with our approval.

Despite everything, he is a wonderful gardener, and his devotion, imagination, and taste have turned our kibbutz into a garden of delights. Thanks to him, we have none of the unsightly plots, beds of weeds, and piles of rubble that you find in the grounds of some kibbutzim. It would be even lovelier if it were not for the mischievous Russians. That has been Herzl Goldring's opinion for many years. They lack the most basic cultured instincts. Is culture a matter of book learning and long words? No. Far from it. No, Reuven Harish, culture is a matter of everyday life, of taking trouble over details, of cultivating a general aesthetic sense. These people walk across the lawns, making ugly bare strips, dump rubbish among the bushes, trample down the young seedlings, and why? Just to take a shortcut or out of pure thoughtlessness. How sad that our children, including those of the Germans, pick up this corrupt culture, this false culture. It gets worse every day. Corruption is like bindweed: if you don't eradicate it ruthlessly, it kills everything.

Herzl Goldring looks at you through his sunglasses. His look is embarrassed, not embarrassing, but nevertheless you feel ashamed, you lower your eyes, you stammer an excuse and promise Herzl Goldring never to cut his foliage to decorate your room. However, you are bound to break your promise. But why the hell should a man feel ashamed of any step he takes in his own home? Is it any wonder that Herzl Goldring hates you bitterly in the hidden depths of his heart?

Every day at half past four in the afternoon the mail arrives in a red van that announces its presence with a hollow, cowlike blast on its horn. Tsvi Ramigolski gets up from his desk, over which hangs a photograph of his dead brother, Aaron. "All right, I'm coming," he murmurs abstractedly, as if someone will hear him and stop hooting. He hurries out into the dusty square in front of the hut. Halfway there he claps his hand to his forehead and goes back to pick up the outward-bound mail that in his haste he has forgotten. Then he presses through the impatient crowd thronging round the van, exchanges bundles, and shouts out the names of those who have letters. Gai Harish clutches the lucky ones and begs for the stamps. Oren Geva eyes the silver emblem on the hood of the van and thinks inscrutable thoughts. Herbert Segal, meanwhile, receives a new record with religious awe and scrutinizes the writing on the wrapper. Mendel Morag is here, too, to send a parcel of cakes to his relatives.

We live in a small, far-off land, in its northeastern extremity, in a small village a long way from the nearest town. Like all isolated communities, always and everywhere, we love getting letters. Let us imagine that we have the right to peep at letters that are not addressed to us and see what excitements we can espy.

Here, for instance, is a letter from Rami Rimon to his onetime girlfriend. It contains no reproach and no words of conciliation. It is a very short letter: the obligatory words of greeting, then a brief description of his preliminary training. What news at home? I'm holding my own, and I've had some pieces of good luck I'll tell you about some other time. Food's not bad. Not enough sleep. One can get used to anything, though. You forget some things and learn others. I hope things on our border don't get too hot before I get there, because I want to be in on the action. Nothing else to report. If you can, say a few nice words to my mother now and then. It must be hard on her. Write to me if you feel like it.

Fruma, too, has had a letter from her son. Rami's letter to his mother is even shorter than the one to Noga. No description of his training, not even a brief one. No mention of the shortage of sleep. All he says is that he is well, that the others in his tent are all pleasant boys, though a mixed bunch, that he's in excellent health. He hopes she isn't mourning for him day and night. He'll come home on leave soon. Finally, as if after reconsideration, he remarks that the cookies were lovely, Mom, and it would be nice if you sent me some more.

Fruma, of course, will bake some and send them off very soon. What a pity her relations with other people nowadays are so bitterly quarrelsome.

Dr. Nehemiah Berger writes from Jerusalem to his brother and sister-in-law. He thanks them for being kind enough to invite him to stay. He is almost on his way. No, he is not afraid of the situation on the border. On the contrary, he sometimes finds Jerusalem terribly dreary. He is so bored that he is unable to concentrate on his research, so he is wasting his time on ridiculous translations that earn him his living. What a tragicomic paradox: one earns five times as much for a mechanical translation as for original research. He's not afraid of the heat in the valley, either. Jerusalem may be cooler but it is the dryness that makes him ill and drains the intellectual juices that are vital for creative work. Above all, he confesses to an overpowering longing to see his relatives again. What sort of life do I lead here? No wife, no children, only painful research work, and who can say whether I shall live to complete it? Sometimes I say to myself, Nehemiah, the history of Jewish socialism is a complex structure of wonders and miracles. Who are you to try to plumb its depths? There's one thing I know, and I'll maintain it till my dying day: anyone who says that socialism is an imported plant in our garden doesn't know what he's talking about. We never dissociated our national messianic aspirations from the goal of social salvation. But to prove it one has to explore paths thousands of years old, picking up a fragment here and there, without getting lost in the details and losing sight of the fundamental thesis. It's wearisome work. And who can I talk to about it except to you, my dear Ezra and Bronka, my nearest and dearest, and your dear children? Which reminds me, how is Einav? It can't be long now till the birth. I hope and pray it goes well. Our brother Zechariah sent me a picture postcard. He may be coming over, but he doesn't give any details. Does he write to you regularly? Give my love to Oren and little Tomer — he's probably not so little anymore — and to Einav. I'll be on my way to see you soon. All the best. Your loving brother, Nehemiah.

And what about Siegfried? Siegfried's letter is rather strange, brimming with an odd joy. Has peace finally come to your land? A curse on the enemies of Israel who do not let us find our redemption quietly. Look after yourselves. Wouldn't it be better for our dear Einav to move away from the border till she's had her child? We have a brother in the capital who would be happy to look after her. Think over my advice. Everything is flowing smoothly here. I'm doing good business and "pouring out my wrath on the Gentiles." I've taken on an ex-Gestapo officer as a doorman. You would be as happy as I am if you could only see him bowing and scraping. I'm so happy to have my enemies in my power. Revenge is certainly sweet. Sweeter than honey. I've got the gold and silver now and they all dance attendance on me, with *"Jawohl, Herr Berger,"* *"Bitte, Herr Berger,"* *"Danke, Herr Berger,"* *"Wunderbar, Herr Berger."* When I see you in a few weeks' time I'll tell you all about it, and we can enjoy the enemy's humiliation together. There is justice in this world, that's what I say, even if our national poet Bialik isn't right when he says "justice will be done when I depart this world." Here am I, the son of a Polish-Jewish cantor who was burned in the furnaces of Sobibor, lording it over the son of a Prussian Junker, the grandson of a Prussian Junker, the great-grandson of the Devil himself, and he is grateful to me for paying him a couple of pence more than doormen get paid in other clubs. It's a miracle, that's what I say. Signs and wonders, mighty hand and outstretched arm! Incidentally, Hamburger has just bought another car. He's got two now, one for himself and one for his wife. What a pity that he's so blinded by wealth he can't see the wonder of it. He's also taken on a liveried chauffeur. Eva will tell you her news herself. I'll leave her some room.

Eva says, Thank you for the pretty picture. Here in Munich the weather is cold and rainy. The rain never stops. It has a certain beauty, but I feel sad when I remember the weather in the valley. Life is quiet and pleasant here. But no life is entirely free from sadness. And all sorts of strange thoughts. Be well. Tell me how Stella is getting on at school. Do you think Reuven would be good enough to cut off a lock of her hair and send it to me via you? Would you ask him? Please. I pray that my daughter won't hate me. Yours, Eva.

Ezra Berger reads the letter from his two brothers, the one in Germany and the other in Jerusalem, and thinks them over during one of the long silences between himself and his little friend. Amazing things happen. Wonders and miracles, as Zechariah says. Father used to say to us, Love work and hate power and put your heart into everything you do. But nobody could say that Father put his heart into being a cantor. May he rest in perfect peace. When Nehemiah ran away to Lvov, to the university, Father went into mourning for him. When Ezra joined the movement and came to Palestine, Father said we all have our trials to bear. When Siegfried went off and became Siegfried, Father said it's a very sore trial. Two's company, three's a crowd, little Noga. There's a great truth in that. Pour out your wrath on the Gentiles, Zechariah said when he came here in 1948. That was his be-all and end-all. I remember a terrible argument he had with Nehemiah. I'm going to go back there, he said, and be a dirty Jew. A filthy Yid. That's what he said. Yes, I said, you're right, men aren't made of myrrh and frankincense, but you're my brother and you weren't born to be a scoundrel. Nehemiah's argument was different. Stay here, have lots of children. That's our revenge. Zechariah laughed and paraphrased an old saying. Their world stands on three things, he said, murder, fornication, and greed. Those are its three legs. I'm going to smash one or two of those legs, just as they smashed me. As our dear father used to say: Hate power, hate work, hate your enemies, and you'll float like pure oil on sewage. Our brother Zechariah said this, too, that day: A true Jew, gentlemen, must pierce the darkness and eat away the rotten foundations of the earth, as our national poet Bialik puts it. If they bruise our head, we must bruise their heel, and their heels are murder, profit, and debauchery. Murder is forbidden in the Torah, but even the Devil wouldn't stop me debauching them and bleeding their money out of them. So Zechariah went to Munich, and Nehemiah lives in Jerusalem. "It is better for me to die than to live." "Would God I had died for you." Those verses may be allegorical, or something, but they're not true. That's what I think, little Turquoise. Here am I sitting under my vine and under my fig tree, as the Bible says, and my wife as a fruitful vine by the side of my house, and where's Ramigolski now? Ramigolski is a white skeleton without a wrapping. My fate has been better than Zechariah's, better than Nehemiah's, better than my friend Ramigolski's. My lot has been a happy one. But it doesn't matter. It doesn't mean a thing. I was thinking and I happened to talk aloud, like a man crying out when he dreams. Listen, Turquoise, my brother who lives in Germany can interpret dreams. Really. We didn't throw him in a pit and show his striped robe to our father. You don't understand? I'll explain. A: Who wears striped robes nowadays? Only the Arabs. B: Our father was burned. C: Our brother, who interprets dreams, doesn't feed the Gentiles; he pours out his wrath on them. D: Conclusion. There is no conclusion. The conclusion is that the analogy doesn't work, and it's best to forget about it, because I'm tired and it's half past midnight.

Between Ezra and Bronka there is silence.

Since they live in a small apartment, they sometimes accidentally touch or bump into one another. Then they look at each other. Bronka pales. Ezra mutters, "Sorry."

Bronka does not ask. Ezra doesn't expect her to ask. All she ever asks is, for instance, "Have you written to your brothers yet?"

And Ezra, as if weighing her words before he answers, says, "Not yet. Maybe I'll have time on Saturday. We'll see."

Ezra spends most of his time in his truck. What little free time he has is divided between his friends the fishermen of Tiberias and his little friend in the grove beside the swimming pool. It is surprising, in view of this, that he did not forget Bronka's birthday. On one of his journeys he bought her a pretty vase, and set it silently on her bedside table. As for Bronka, she did not refuse her present. As she buttoned up her housecoat, early in the morning, with her back to him, she said, "Thank you. It was kind of you."

Ezra replied tersely, "Yes."

Bronka said, "Perhaps you could take the curtains down for me, too. They've got to be washed; they're all dusty."

And Ezra, "Why not? May I stand on this chair, or must I go and borrow a stepladder from the stores?"

Every Sunday, the beginning of the week, Bronka lays at the foot of her husband's bed a clean, neatly folded shirt and pair of trousers. Every Friday she takes his dirty working clothes, turns the pockets inside out, and puts them in the laundry bag. And every night, when Ezra gets back from his journey, he finds a cup of tea waiting for him as usual on the table, covered with a saucer to keep it warm. Every three or four days Tomer visits his parents' house to see to the little garden. Oren empties the garbage bins every three days, provided his mother reminds him and provided he is not suffering from one of the dark moods that take hold of him from time to time for no apparent reason. And Einav, on those evenings when Bronka does not feel well, brings her her supper on a tray, covered with a white napkin. Recently, Bronka has been unwell for three days running. Ezra did not give up his second daily trip, but he bought his wife a book about symphonic music in Tel Aviv to take her mind off her illness and her thoughts.

Now for an act of heroism.

On Saturday evening, when the other members were all gathered for their weekly meeting, Tomer Geva started up a gray tractor, switched on the headlights, and set out to turn off the irrigation taps in the outlying fields. On the way he thought about various things, about his father, for instance, who had still not lost his youthful vigor. A great mystery this, which impresses Arabs and women; it is the only thing that lets you live your life, and without it you're nothing. On the way he almost ran over a jackal that was caught in the headlights and was saved only by its instincts. The creature escaped and was swallowed up in the great darkness, running in terrified zigzags across the fields to the end of the dark, where it rested and wept and laughed with madness in its voice.

The oppressive heat was still making itself felt. And the dogs howled, as dogs do on hot nights. The swish of the sprinklers clashed with the crickets' chirping. Amid these sounds, hideous and deafening, came the vicious howl of bullets close to Tomer's ear. Tomer hesitated for only a fraction of a second. He determined the direction of the shots. With a flick of his hand he put out the lights. He leaped out and landed on the rough earth. The tractor continued at its former pace but headed to the left, down the slope. The bullets pursued the tractor, and the youth was saved, though wounded, apparently, in the arm. The tractor, driverless, rushed down the slope. The bullets pierced it with fierce savagery. There was a roar, flashes rent the darkness, a dull shock, a guttural shriek, then silence.

Who else except these wretches would have laid an ambush in a wadi and opened fire at night at a range of a hundred yards? The tractor had rolled straight into the thick of them. Terrified as if it had been an armored car, they had thrown a hand grenade at it and run.

The next afternoon, after Tomer had been operated on and two bullets removed from his arm, his family and friends gathered round his hospital bed. Congratulations, explanations, and jokes assailed the patient. Even Einav's tears could not detract from the warmhearted atmosphere. We may quote Oren's words. First, the tractor is finished. Done for. The grenade smashed it to smithereens. Perhaps one or two pieces of the engine could still be used. Secondly, there was an investigation. With a tracker and dogs. You should have seen the dogs, Tomer. They ran through the vineyard. You're the talk of the whole valley. A single boy defeated a whole ambush unarmed. They found traces of blood on the way out of the wadi. They blew themselves up with their own grenade. The boy took the tractor and turned it on them. Third, Tomer, reinforcements have been brought up. On both sides. We're flexing our muscles. If we have another squeak out of them — that's what they said to the wogs — we'll smash their whole army. Now we're waiting for them to squeak. So we can smash them. If you'd been better, they'd have done it tonight. Crushed them bone by bone. Squashed them. Till there was nothing left.

Oren's dark eyes flashed with excitement. Hatred hardened the set of his jaws and his mouth. There was no smile on his face, only icy rage. Tomer lifted himself up in bed and gave his brother's chin a friendly punch with his good hand. He smiled a forced, fleeting smile, but it met with no response. Oren was not disposed to let affection interfere with serious business. Let us take a look at his face. If we interpret the signs rightly, an enthralling idea is going through the boy's mind. Despite his self-control, he is biting his lower lip. He looks excited.

Secret Adaptability

from *A Perfect Peace* (1982)

4

That night, in the darkness of the barber's half of the shack near the farm sheds, Azariah Gitlin lay with open eyes, listening to the groans of the old, wind-tossed eucalyptus trees and to the tiny fists of rain on the tin roof while his mind whirred with musings about himself, his secret mission, and the love of the members of Kibbutz Granot that should and would be his as soon as they realized who he really was.

He thought of the kibbutzniks' eyes following his entrance into the dining room, of the old pioneers, their faces brown as mahogany even in the dead of winter, of the young men, so bulky and slow-moving that some of them seemed like drowsy wrestlers, and of the young women, whispering to each other, no doubt about him, as they watched him come in — buxom, golden girls who, for all their simple dress, brimmed with a saucy femininity that suggested a knowledge of things you never dream of.

Azariah longed to get to know all these people right away, to talk to them, to win their hearts, to arouse their strongest emotions, to slip past their defenses and touch their private lives as profoundly as he could. If only he could skip over the awkwardness of the first few days and step right into the middle of things. He wanted to let them all know that now that he had arrived their life would never be the same. Perhaps he would give guitar recitals in the dining room that would stir the weariest heart among them. Then he would share the ideas he had suffered so hard to arrive at during his long years of solitude, his very own thoughts about justice, politics, love, art, and the meaning of life. He would make these people admire him, love him, for his passionate inner strength. Around him would gather the young ones whose spirits had been dulled by their humdrum lives and the toll of hard physical work. He would give lectures that would rekindle their enthusiasm. He would found a discussion club. He would write articles for their newsletter. He would astonish even Yolek with his historical insights into the Ben-Gurion era. His arguments would carry the day in every debate.

Before long, all would know that a rare soul had come to live among them. They would begin coming to him with their problems and with requests for his opinions. In their dimly lit bedrooms, they would talk about him in hushed tones. An uncanny fellow, they would say. And the loneliness in his eyes! the young women would add. They would choose him to represent their kibbutz. He would appear at movement conferences where he would blaze new trails and demolish old shibboleths. Oh, how he would astound them with the revolutionary power of his thought! His words would batter down the breastworks, as strangers he had never met would be discussing him in a hundred different places. At first they would say: You know who we mean, that new fellow who got up at the last conference and gave it to them but good in four brilliant minutes that they'll never forget. After a while it would be: Azariah? He's the latest discovery, a rising new star; we're sure to hear more of him.

Eventually people would ask, Can you believe that there are still some fossils who refuse to accept the Gitlin approach? The leaders of the movement, still reluctant to commit themselves, yet consumed by curiosity and doubt, would declare, That's all very well, but why doesn't he come around for a serious talk? Let's have a good look at him and hear what he has to say. And when he had left their offices, they would confess, No question about it, he swept us off our feet. The boy's a real find. In time the press would sniff him out, too. And the radio. Inquiries would be made and background information sought from the kibbutz. The mystery of his origins and life story would amaze them. How little is actually known about him, they would report. One winter night he simply walked in from the dark.

Crotchety reactionaries would argue with him in the weekend magazine sections. At great length they would attempt to squelch his explosive ideas, but in vain. Four or five lines of rebuttal would suffice to crush them, such was the elegant but merciless juggernaut of his wit. Yet in closing, he would always pat their elderly shoulders: Nonetheless, I must credit my opponents for their contributions to the intellectual outlook of their own generation.

A nationwide debate would arise over the new concept, whose founder and leading spokesman was Azariah Gitlin. Fresh forces would rally around him. Young women would write letters to the editor in his defense. Budding poetesses would seek his company. One would even dedicate a poem to him entitled "The Eagle's Lonely Sorrow." Celebrities, famous pundits, representatives of the foreign press would come to exchange views. He would be referred to as a visionary for the times. And all the while he would stubbornly refuse to leave the barber's room or the shack. Repeatedly, to everyone's amazement, he would turn down the kibbutz's offer of a better room. In this ramshackle cabin, small groups of young activists would assemble from all over the country. How startled they would be to discover that Azariah Gitlin's sole earthly possessions were a metal bed, a wobbly table, a decrepit old chest, one chair, and a guitar. These and the numerous bookshelves lining the walls would bear silent witness to the ascetic severity of his life and to long nights of arduous thought. Why, the carpenter who volunteered one morning to make those shelves was the very same brusque young man who had been the first to encounter him upon his arrival in the kibbutz.

His guests would sit on the floor, hanging on his every word, only rarely interrupting to ask for a clarification. There was no way, the pretty girls would whisper to one another, absolutely no way to persuade him to move to better quarters. Here is where he was put that first night, and here is where he is going to stay. The man has absolutely no material wants. Sometimes, late at night, we wake and hear as in a dream the chords of his guitar. Between sessions, one of these barefoot girls would volunteer to make coffee for all of those assembled. With a generous smile he would thank her. Later, the visitors would take their leave, and a new group would arrive, some from afar, for inspiration, guidance, or simply to bask in his presence. He would exhort them all to prepare for a protracted struggle. He would preach the need for perseverance. He would reject out of hand all political gimmicks and tactical adventures.

Of course, he would make deadly enemies. He would take them on in the newspapers, compassionately yet ironically citing Spinoza or some other celebrated thinker, as required. His tone would be forgiving, as if the old guard consisted not of angry ancients but of hotheaded young Turks, whose attacks on him he so pitied that he would not stoop to rub salt into their bruised and battered pride.

One day, perhaps even by next summer, Prime Minister Eshkol would inquire of his inner circle about this eighth wonder of the world. Why not bring the lad to see me so that I can size him up myself? When Azariah was invited to Eshkol's office, the secretary would allot him ten minutes. Half an hour later, Eshkol would order her to hold the calls. He would be sitting in his chair not uttering a word, overwhelmed by Azariah's analysis of the nation's affairs. From time to time he would dare to pose a question, jotting down the answers in pencil on little scraps of paper. The hours would go by. Evening would descend outside the windows, yet Eshkol would refrain from turning on the lights, so rapt would he be in the revelations of Azariah's monastic years. Finally, he would rise from his seat, lay his hands on Azariah's shoulders, and say, "*Yingele,* from now on you're staying with me. Consider yourself nationalized. As of seven o'clock tomorrow morning, your place will be here at my side, in that room over there that can be reached only through my private office so you'll be on tap whenever I need you. But for now, what I'd like to ask is your opinion of Nasser's true intentions and how we can rally our nation's youth around the flag."

It would be late at night before he finally emerged from the prime minister's office. Shapely secretaries would exchange whispers as he passed, his shoulders slightly stooped, his face exhibiting neither pride nor triumph, but responsibility tempered by sadness.

And one day Yolek Lifshitz, the secretary of Kibbutz Granot, would say to his friend Hava, "Well? Who was it who discovered our Azariah, eh? It was me, that's who, although I was nearly dumb enough to chuck him down the stairs. I'll never forget how he turned up here that winter night, a shady-looking character if ever there was one, and wetter than a drowned cat. Just look what's become of him now!"

The one thing Azariah did not think about was the work awaiting him in the tractor shed the next day. Since he had failed, after a desultory search, to find the light switch, the dusty, naked bulb still shone feebly from the ceiling. A haze settled over his mind. Unable to get warm beneath the thin woolen blanket, he lay shivering from the cold. Sometime after midnight he heard a monotonous chant from the other side of the plywood partition, a kind of shrill prayer or incantation in a language that was neither Hebrew nor anything else, its accents guttural like the desert's and as though risen from the depths of some evil slumber:

"Why do the heath'm rage 'n' people imag'm vain things 'bout God 'n' 'bout His Messiah . . . He was lowly 'n' we 'steemed 'm not . . . He was more hon'lable than thirty but he 'tained not to Thee . . . And King David 'pointed 'm over his guard . . . Asael brother of Yo-o-av . . . 'n' his cousin Elha-a-nan . . . 'n' Helez the Paltite . . . 'n' Ira son of Ikesh Tekoo-o-ite . . . 'n' Zalmon A-hoooo-hite . . . He was loath'en'd, he had'a no form nor come-leeee-ness . . ."

Azariah Gitlin got out of bed and tiptoed barefoot to the partition. Through a crack in the plywood he glimpsed a tall, thin man sitting on a low stool, wrapped in a blanket reaching over his head, a needle in each hand and on his knees a ball of red yarn. He was knitting.

Azariah returned to bed and tried cuddling up beneath the blanket. The wind howling outside knifed into the shack through the chinks between the planks, and the rough woolen blanket scratched his skin. Desperately trying to reanimate the magical power of his thoughts, he lay there half awake and half asleep until nearly morning, longing for the women who would come to love him, comfort him, and wait on him body and soul. Two of them, young and full-bodied, who would be utterly shameless about having him in their power, lying as he was on his back with his eyes shut tight and his heart pounding madly away.

The morning was vile. Misty vapors swirled among the houses. It was biting cold.

At half past six, as requested by a note slipped under his door, Yonatan Lifshitz arrived to take the new mechanic to work. He found him fully awake and engaged in light calisthenics. Over greasy coffee in a corner of the dining hall, whose fluorescent lights were already on because of the dimness of the morning, the newcomer talked a blue streak and Yonatan understood hardly a word. It struck him as comical that his charge had dressed for work in clean clothes and a pair of ordinary walking shoes. The questions he put to Yonatan were queer, too. When and how had Kibbutz Granot been founded? Why had it been built on the slope of the hill instead of on the hilltop or in the valley below? Was there archival material available from its pioneering days? Was there any point in trying to get the founders of the kibbutz to talk about those times for the record? Would they tell the truth, or would they simply glorify their own works? And the price they paid: Had many of them really lost their lives to Arab marauders, malaria, heat stroke, killing work?

Most of these queries the young man answered himself, and with considerable astuteness, perhaps even some knowledge. Now and then he let drop some bon mot about the eternal, tragic conflict between high ideals and gray realities, or between the social vision of the revolutionary and the passions of the human heart. At one point Yonatan thought he caught the phrase "the clear, certain premises of our mental life," and he began to feel a weary longing for some clear, bright faraway meadow bathed in sunlight by the banks of a broad river, perhaps in Africa. Once that image faded, he had a faint desire to know what might be eating this young man so early in the morning. Yet this desire, too, faded rapidly. The rawness of the weather and his own fatigue made Yonatan bunch up inside his clothes. Water leaking through his torn boot was freezing the tips of his toes. What was there to keep him from proclaiming himself sick, like his father and half the kibbutz, and going back to his room this very minute? No. On a day that should have been declared an official bed day, he had to show this yackety mechanic the rounds.

"Let's go," he said, disgruntled, pushing away his mug. "Come on, let's head for the tractor shed. Have you finished your coffee?"

Azariah jumped up from his seat. "A long while ago. I'm one hundred percent at your service."

To this remark he added his full name, volunteered the information that the secretary of the kibbutz had told him that Yonatan's name was Yonatan and that he and Hava were his parents. He concluded by quoting some little proverb.

"This way," said Yonatan. "Watch out. These steps are slippery."

"The laws of nature are such," said Azariah, "that there are no accidents. Whatever happens is necessary and predestined, even slipping on these steps."

Yonatan did not reply. He neither liked nor trusted words. Yet he was well aware that most people were in need of more love than they ever received and that this sometimes made them try to make friends with total strangers in the most ludicrous ways, including talking too much. He's like a lost wet puppy, thought Yonatan, wagging not only his tail but his whole rear end to get me to like him and pet him. Fat chance! You're barking up the wrong tree, pal.

While the two of them passed farm sheds, navigated puddles, and sloshed through mud, the young man kept up his steady stream of talk. Yonatan withdrew from his silence only twice — once to ask the newcomer if he had been born in Israel, and again to inquire if he had ever worked on, or at least had a good look at, a D-6 Caterpillar engine.

Azariah answered no to both questions. He had been born in the Diaspora (it struck Yonatan as odd that he didn't say "abroad" or simply name the country he had come from) and knew nothing about Caterpillar tractors. Not that it mattered. In his opinion, backed by experience, engines everywhere, whatever their differences, were close relatives. Once you had doped out one, you understood them all. Anyway, he would do his best. The worm and the man both do what they can. Yonatan wondered where his father had ever managed to dig up such a creep.

The corrugated tin walls of the tractor shed only made the cold day worse. The slightest contact with anything metal froze one's fingers at once. Congealed oil, dust, mildew, and filth were everywhere. In the joints of the rafters, among the tool chests and crates of spare parts, even on the tractors, tribes of spiders had spun upside-down cathedrals. Tools were scattered, as if in anger, about an abandoned-looking yellow machine smeared with mud and black oil, its innards exposed. On the treads, on the tattered driver's seat, in the folds of the hood that had been thrown to the floor were wrenches, pliers, screwdrivers, bolts, and iron rods. A beer bottle half filled with some slimy liquid, rubber belts, torn sacks, and rusted gears lay all over. And the whole derelict place was pervaded by the acrid chemical smell of lubricants, burned rubber, and kerosene and diesel fumes.

Yonatan, whose mood blackened every time he entered the shed, glanced about with a sullen, defiant look. The new mechanic began hopping around the tractor engine in his spotless clothes like some sort of vainglorious grasshopper. Finally he came to a halt at the front of the engine, struck a pose as if for an official photograph, and joyously launched into a manifesto.

"A brand-new time, a brand-new place, and I'm brand-new, too. Every beginning is a birth, and every ending, no matter what is ended, brings with it the taint of death. All things should be accepted calmly and with a light heart, because fate in its many disguises always stems from the same eternal decree, just as it must forever be the essence of a triangle that the sum of its three angles always equals one hundred and eighty degrees. If you were to think

about this fact for a minute, Yonatan, you would be surprised to realize that not only is it true, it can also give us the most wonderful
peace of mind. To accept all things, to understand all things, and
to respond to all things with perfect inner tranquillity! Mind you,
I don't deny that a part of what I say comes from the philosopher
Spinoza, who, by the way, was a diamond polisher by profession.
Well, I've told you in a nutshell what I believe in. And you, Yonatan,
what do you believe in?"

"I," said Yonatan distractedly, unintentionally kicking over an
empty can of engine oil, "am freezing my ass off and getting sick.
If you ask me, we should pour a little gasoline beneath that barrel
of diesel oil over there, put a match to it, make a great big bonfire,
and burn down this whole fucking tractor shed with all its fucking
tractors once and for all. Just to get warm. Look, this is the patient.
With a little goodwill you can get it to turn over, but after two or
three minutes it conks out. Don't ask me why. I don't know why.
All I know is that a note slipped under my door last night told me
to take the new mechanic living next to Bolognesi to the tractor
shed in the morning. If you really are one, why don't you see what's
wrong with this damn thing while I sit down and rest my legs."

Azariah Gitlin complied with enthusiasm. Having rolled up his
pants cuffs with his fingertips in a way that reminded Yonatan of
a fashion model fingering the hem of her dress in a newsreel, the
young man climbed gingerly onto one of the tractor treads to study
the engine. From this vantage point, without turning around to face
Yonatan, he posed two or three simple questions that the latter was
able to answer. When he asked yet another, Yonatan replied from
his seat on an overturned crate, "If I knew the answer to that, I
wouldn't need you here in the first place."

Azariah Gitlin did not take offense. He nodded several times,
as if understanding Yonatan's dilemma only too well, made some
vague remark about the importance of creative intuition even in
purely technical matters, and patiently blew a puff of warm breath
across his musicianly fingers.

"Well, what do you say?" asked Yonatan indifferently, noting at the same time, much to his surprise, a glow of affection on the new-comer's face. For whom or what that affection was meant, however, he had not the slightest inkling.

"I have a big favor to ask of you," Azariah sang out.

"Yes?"

"If it's not too much trouble, could you please try starting it up? I want to listen to it. And, of course, to look too. Then we'll see what conclusions we can come to."

Yonatan's reservations, which had been growing steadily, now turned to outright distrust. Nevertheless, he climbed into the driver's seat and switched on the ignition. It took four or five tries before the staccato retching of the starter yielded to the hoarse, steady, earsplitting roar of the engine. As though repressing some unconscionable desire, the ponderous engine began to shake and shudder.

Meticulously, taking care not to dirty his clean clothes, Azariah stepped down from the tread and backed away from the engine. Like an artist who retreats to the opposite end of his studio to get a better view of his canvas, he chose to stand at the maximum distance, in the far corner of the shed, beside the oil and fuel drums, flanked by some filthy straw brooms and a pile of old, used springs. Shutting his eyes in a gesture of supreme concentration, he listened to the raucous growl of the engine as if it were a madrigal sung by a distant choir, among whose myriad voices it was his job to pick out the only one that was flat.

As absurd as this performance seemed to Yonatan, watching from his seat on the crate, it was also somehow touching. Was it because the young stranger was so very strange?

A sharp, high whistle rose above the din. Like a public speaker suffering from throat strain, the tractor broke into a series of hoarse coughs. These were progressively stifled until brief stretches of silence could be heard. Finally, after five or six sharp backfires, the engine fell silent. From outside the shed, shrill, bitter, and piercing, came the caws of birds screaming in the wind. Azariah Gitlin opened his eyes.

"That's it?" he asked with a smile.

"That's it," said Yonatan. "It's the same every time."

"Did you ever try putting it into gear as soon as it starts?"

"What do you think?" said Yonatan.

"And what happened?"

"What do you think?"

"Listen," concluded Azariah, "it's all very strange."

"You're telling me." Yonatan said dryly. He no longer had the slightest doubt that the newcomer was not just another queer fish but an out-and-out impostor.

"What I'm telling you," said Azariah Gitlin gently, "is that curiosity may have killed the cat, but it's haste that killed the bear."

Yonatan did not reply.

"And now," said Azariah Gitlin, "I need some time to think. If you don't mind, I'll take a few minutes to do it."

"To think?" snickered Yonatan. "Why not? Be my guest." He rose, picked up a ripped, greasy sack, sat down again on the crate, wrapped the tattered burlap around his torn boot, and lit himself a cigarette. "Fine. You go ahead and think. When you're done, raise your right hand."

He had not yet finished the cigarette when, to his utter amazement, the young man declared, "I'm done."

"You're done what?"

"I'm done thinking."

"And what, may I ask, did you think of?"

"I thought," said Azariah hesitantly, "that maybe, when you finish your cigarette, we might start working on this tractor."

The entire repair job was performed by Yonatan himself and took no more than twenty minutes. Clean, pale, and alert, Azariah Gitlin stood looking on, telling him exactly what to do as if reading instructions from a manual, presiding over the operation from afar like one of those grand masters Yonatan had read about who play blind chess without pieces or a board. Only once in the course of the proceedings did the young man bother to step onto a tread and peer into the bowels of the engine. Using the tip of a screwdriver, he adjusted a contact with a watchmaker's precision and then climbed down again, taking great pains to avoid the grime.

As soon as the tractor was started up, it began to gurgle steadily and softly like a purring animal. The gears were successfully tested. The engine ran for ten minutes without a hitch. At last Yonatan switched it off and said in a voice that sounded too loud in the sudden silence, "Yup. That's it."

He couldn't decide whether the newcomer was a magician or a mechanical genius, or whether the whole problem had been so simple to begin with that he could have easily solved it himself had he not been so tired, cold, and preoccupied during the last few days.

Azariah Gitlin, on the other hand, celebrated his little triumph with a delirious outbreak, slapping his companion repeatedly on the back and singing his own praises until Yonatan was thoroughly revolted. He reveled in recounting the times he had miraculously confounded his enemies, among whom were an evil major called Zlotshin, or Zlotshnikov, a beautiful female officer in an army garage with deeply ambivalent feelings about him, and that Ph.D. idiot in engineering from the Haifa Technion who had failed to come up with some mechanical solution that he, Azariah, had hit upon at once. He talked about his brainstorms, about the human brain in general, about Major Zlotkin or Zlotnik, who had been driven mad by envy, about her seductive advances, about some revolutionary technical device developed by him but cunningly pirated away by Major Zlotshkin's brother-in-law, who made a mint with it and bought some nice little island in the eastern Aegean, from which he bombarded Azariah with letters full of threats, expressions of admiration, and offers of joint ventures.

Yonatan half listened to all this in ponderous silence. At last Azariah fell silent too, only to wipe off a bluish oil stain that had spattered on the tip of his shoe.

"All right," said Yonatan. "It's a quarter past eight. Let's go have breakfast in the dining hall. Then we'll come back and see what else needs to be done around here."

On their way to the dining hall, still compulsively talking, Azariah told two different jokes about passengers on Polish trains, one involving an anti-Semitic priest and the other a big fat general, both of whom, the first despite his great malice and the second despite his great strength, were outwitted by the Jews. He alone laughed at the punch lines, which caused him nervously to joke some more about all the old canards that no one laughed at but their tellers.

Yonatan noticed for the first time that the newcomer had a faint accent. It was so well concealed as to be barely identifiable. The *l*s were a bit too soft, the *r*s slightly prolonged, and the *k*s sometimes expelled from the palate as if he had swallowed something distasteful. Obvious effort had gone into overcoming this accent. Perhaps this effort, or the speed with which he spoke, was why Azariah so often tripped over his own words, nearly choking on some of them. At such times he would break off in mid-sentence, only to fling himself back into the breach at once.

No two lonelinesses are ever alike, thought Yonatan. If two people could really have anything in common, it might be possible for them to become truly close. Just look at this poor bastard trying so hard to cheer me up and make me laugh when he's so unhappy himself. You can see he's all twisted inside — too sensitive, too cocksure, too obsequious, and all at the same time. We get all kinds of strange types here, and they go on being strange to the end. Some of them go all out to make friends with us and fit in, but after a couple of weeks or months, they can't take it anymore and they split. Either we forget all about them or remember them only because of something funny, like that middle-aged divorcée two years ago who decided to make a play for old Stutchnik, of all people. Rachel Stutchnik caught them one night listening to Brahms in the music room, him in her lap. Easy come, easy go. Maybe he thinks that being the secretary's son, I've been appointed to look him over and report back. Why else would he be freaking out like this to make me love him at first sight? But who could love a weirdo like him? I'd be the last one to. Especially now, when I can't even stand my own self. Maybe some other time I might have tried to like him or get him to calm down. He'll climb the walls here, and when he's had it, he'll clear out. Relax, pal. Take it easy.

A light, pinpointy rain was falling. The wind sharpened the pins and sent them flying in every direction. The electric wires were pricked by them too and hummed an odd tune.

"After breakfast," said Yonatan, "you should go to the storeroom and ask for a pair of work clothes. You'll find Peiko's old boots in that crate behind the diesel oil. Peiko's the man who ran this place for years."

When the two of them stopped to wash up at the stand outside the dining hall, Azariah's long, wistful, delicate fingers caught Yonatan's eye. The sight of them made him think of Rimona. And at that very moment he saw her sitting with some friends at the far end of the hall, grasping a mug of tea with both hands. He knew that it was still full and that she was holding it, as usual, to warm her fingers. For a second he wondered what she might be thinking about this morning, but he scolded himself at once. What do I care what she's thinking? All I want is to be far away from them all.

Through breakfast Azariah Gitlin kept coming on strong, both to Yonatan and to the two other people who joined their table, Yashek and little Shimon from the sheep pen. Having introduced himself, he asked if he might have their names as well. Then, with a peculiar sort of merriment, he told them about his sleepless night in the barber's room, where, as if in some horror movie, a cracked voice on the other side of the wall began speaking at the stroke of midnight. He saw—waking or dreaming, he still couldn't say—a ghost mumbling all sorts of Biblical abracadabra in a dead tongue, Chaldean perhaps or Hittite.

He then related the tale of the tractor, fishing for compliments from Yonatan so that the other two men might be suitably impressed. Indeed, though less than a day had passed since his arrival in the kibbutz, and he had been urged to rest up for a few days before beginning work, a sixth sense had told him that there was no time to waste, which was why he rose early this morning and ran to the tractor shed, thus proving—or rather, demonstrating—no, the right word was justifying—yes, justifying the faith placed in him and the high hopes pinned on him. Of course, whatever praise he deserved was due to his intuition more than his knowledge or skill, since the minute he heard the sound of the engine he had had a brainstorm. As the saying went, "If his wagon is stuck in the mud, tell Ivan not to push but to put on his thinking cap."

Whenever one of his tablemates reacted to all this exuberance with a vague smile, Azariah guffawed loudly and redoubled his efforts. And when Yonatan poured two mugs of coffee and handed him one, he couldn't find enough words to thank him.

"A guiding hand brought Comrade Yonatan and me together from the start. You should have seen his warmth, his patience, his . . . when he broke me in on my new job. Such refinement, such tact! Why, he never says a word about himself."

"Knock it off," said Yonatan.

"What's the matter?" asked Yashek. "Why don't you let someone say a good word about you for a change?"

Little Shimon took a crumpled newspaper out of his pocket and turned to the sports section. The front-page headlines told of a brief, bitter battle between Israeli and Syrian armored forces along the northern border. At least three enemy tanks had been hit and gone up in flames. Syrian earthmoving equipment engaged in the Jordan diversion project had also been destroyed. A photograph showed the grinning general of the northern command surrounded by grinning soldiers in full battle gear.

Seeing this, Yashek remarked that he saw no end in sight.

Little Shimon, hiding behind the sports section, declared gruffly that if it weren't for the Russians he would take care of the Arabs quickly enough with one or two healthy kicks in the rear.

"We like to think everything depends on us. But it doesn't. Eshkol isn't exactly Napoleon. Some things don't depend on anyone," Yonatan said, more to himself than to the others.

At this point Azariah burst back into the conversation. He warned of the dangers of shortsightedness, explained where Ben-

Gurion had been mistaken on the one hand and Eshkol wrong on the other, quickly sketched the sinister mentality of the Russians while appealing to Svidrigailov and Ivan Karamazov, argued that Slavs were constitutionally incapable of moral inhibitions, and sought to cast a new light on the subject of Jewish destiny. Raising his voice insistently to court Yashek's attention and paying no heed to the glances being cast at him from neighboring tables, he undertook to expound the dialectic distinction between strategic ends and political means, and between both of these and the "national idea" that every civilization was based on. He predicted an imminent war, deplored the blindness prevailing everywhere, sketched possible international complications, suggested ways out of them, and, in light of all these factors, posed two basic questions for which he immediately volunteered the answers.

There was in all this an irresistible passion and a nervous power of imagination that, despite its bizarreness, caused even Yashek to nod twice and say, "That's so, that really is so." Thus egged on, Azariah launched into a fresh harangue on the wisdom of looking for what Spinoza called the Ratio, that is, for the permanent laws underlying the multifarious phenomena wrongly labeled coincidence. But he soon noticed that the others had finished their breakfast and were waiting for him to pause for breath so they could get up and go. This realization, at the very time he was desperately trying to extricate himself from a lengthy sentence, led him to break off completely and turn back to his food. He began gulping it down so as not to keep anyone waiting, only to have it go down the wrong pipe and trigger an outburst of coughing.

"Take your time," Yonatan said calmly. "These two goof-offs are in a hurry because they haven't earned the salt in their salad yet, but we've already done a damn good job on that Caterpillar. Now we have all day." Outside, the gray rain continued to fall, stubbornly and insensibly, like a frozen madness.

That evening Azariah Gitlin, carrying his guitar, knocked on the Lifshitzes' door. Freshly shaved and washed, his curly locks dripping wet from the rain, he begged pardon for having come uninvited. Nevertheless, he had read somewhere that the kibbutzim had—and rightly so—done away with the rules of formal etiquette. Moreover, Yolek had suggested last night that he drop in on Yonatan and Rimona to get acquainted. Besides which, the room to which he had been assigned—the electric bulb was so weak he couldn't read a paper or book, much less write. And so he had decided to try his luck and drop by for a visit.

Yes, thank you, he would love a cup of coffee. There was an old Russian proverb that went, "The man who has no other friend will be the Devil's in the end." Not an exact translation, but at least he had preserved the rhyme. Were they sure he wasn't intruding? With their kind permission, he promised not to overstay his welcome. He had brought his guitar because it had occurred to him that Yonatan and his friend might like music, in which case he would gladly play a few simple tunes. Indeed, the three of them might even sing a bit. He had said "friend" rather than "wife" because that was the word, so right-sounding for a kibbutz, that he had heard Comrade Yolek use last night. How nice it was here.

Yes, their furniture was simple and comfortable, nothing fancy about it, and everything in the best of taste. Such coziness was just what his weary soul needed. He had no friends. Not one. For which he blamed only himself. Until now he hadn't known how to make friends and hadn't tried to find out. But from now on he would, so to speak, put his cards on the table and turn over a new leaf. And please excuse him for talking so much. Though the two of them might think him garrulous, they couldn't be more wrong. Yet the moment he set foot in the kibbutz he had felt himself among kindred souls, and this had made him open up. Everywhere in the world people were light-years away from one another, whereas here he felt such warmth, such togetherness . . . Look, he wanted to show them his identity pass, not to prove who he was, but because of a pressed cyclamen between its pages that he had picked a year ago. He wanted to give this cyclamen to his friend Yonatan's friend. Please. It was, after all, only a token.

Rimona put the kettle on to boil. Yonatan set out a plate of small cakes and the Bokhara creamer. Tia shuffled over to the guest, pressed her nose against his knees, sniffed, sighed, and crawled off to lie beneath the couch, from where only her tail protruded; it thumped several times on the rectangular gray rug spread on the floor by the coffee table. Four carefully arranged rows of books stood on the shelves. Heavy brown curtains covered the window and the door leading out to the porch.

The whole room seemed to be at peace, even the picture on the wall, in which a dark bird perched on a red brick fence. Shamelessly piercing the surrounding murk like a golden spear was a diagonal shaft of sunlight. Lancing a brick at the bottom of the picture, it caused it to blossom into a nimbus of blinding light. The bird looked weary; its bill was slightly, thirstily agape, its eyes closed.

The electric kettle whistled. Rimona brought the coffee to the table. "You must like your new job," she said. "Yonatan tells me you're very good at it."

Careful to avoid her eyes, Azariah told her how happy it made him to have Yonatan as his first friend on the kibbutz. And of course, though two men stood no more chance of meeting than two mountain peaks if it wasn't predestined, he hardly need say that one's first encounters in a new place could be fateful. Incidentally, he had once read a fascinating article about the place of women in a kibbutz, but he did not agree with it. That is, he reserved his views on the subject. What did Rimona think? He himself suspected that the problem had yet to be solved.

"It's too bad," said Rimona, "that you came in the middle of winter instead of the beginning of summer. In winter everything is so sad and closed in. In summer the flowers are all in bloom, the lawns are green, the nights are much shorter and not so dark, and the days are very, very long. They're so long that sometimes a single one can seem like a week. And from our porch you can see the sunset."

"Except that by summer," said Yonatan, "we would have found someone else to work with the tractors and we might not have had room for you. The fact is that you came in the nick of time. To think that for three days I stood there like an idiot, staring at a simple gas block without realizing what the trouble was!"

"If you'll permit me to express a very different opinion," said Azariah, "I personally do not believe in chance. Everything that happens does so for a precise if unknowable reason. 'If the carriage is meant to break down, all the czar's coachmen can't get it to town.' Think, for instance, of an ordinary citizen named Yehoshafat Cantor, an arithmetic teacher, bachelor, stamp collector, and member of his building's tenants' committee. He steps out one evening for ten minutes of fresh air and gets in the way of a bullet fired accidentally, let us say, by a private detective cleaning his handgun on his back porch. The blast blows Cantor's head off. I say to you without the slightest hesitation that all the natural, social, and psychological sciences cannot begin to reconstruct the myriad events that conspired with uncanny precision to bring about this tragic death. Why, we're talking about the most incredible chain of circumstances, one involving infinitesimal fractions of seconds and millimeters, one composed of countless variables of time and space and weather, of optics and ballistics, of human wills and obstructions to those wills, of genetics, personal habits, education, of major and minor decisions, mishaps, errors, customs, the length of a news broadcast, the leap of a cat from a garbage pail, a child annoying its mother in a nearby alleyway, et cetera ad infinitum. And each single one of these circumstances has its own chain of causes going back to still other causes. All it takes is for one of these countless variables to be off, so to speak, by a hair's breadth to change the whole outcome. The bullet now flies in front of Cantor's nose, or passes through his sleeve, or parts the hair on his head. It may even blow out the brains of someone else—me, for example, or, perish the thought, one of you. Any one of these or other possibilities would in turn take its place in a new chain of circumstances leading to still other events beyond human ken, and so on and so forth.

"And what do we so cleverly do about it? In our ignorance, bewilderment, and fear—and perhaps, I should add, in our laziness and arrogance—we say that an unfortunate accident took place. And with this lie, this vulgar, ignorant falsehood we write the matter off.

"I can't remember when I last had such strong, good coffee. That may be one reason I'm talking too much. I've hardly said a word to a living soul for ages because I haven't had a soul to say one to. Even though the Bible teacher around whom I just constructed my little hypothesis may never actually exist, one grieves all the same for the death of a decent, dedicated man who may not have set the world on fire in the classroom, so to speak, but who never did the slightest harm to his country or his fellow man. These are delicious. Did you bake them yourself, Rimona?"

"They come from a box," said Rimona.

"I noticed this morning," said Yonatan, "that every little thing excites him."

"I'm sorry about that teacher," said Rimona.

"Yonatan," said Azariah, "has a sharp eye, so to speak. There's no point in pretending that I'm not excitable. Still, I'll say it again, my own governess never made pastry as good as this when I was a boy. I won't tire you now with stories about my governess, but sometime when your children are here I'll tell them all about her. Children love listening to me, especially the little ones. Maybe you know the legend of the Jewish peddler who came to a village of terrible Jew-killers and lured all their children after him with his flute until they drowned in a river. Little children would follow me through hell and high water, because I tell them the loveliest stories that are frightening but not too frightening."

"We happen," said Yonatan in a slow, sleepy voice, "not to have any children."

Azariah glanced up just as a profoundly bitter smile began to form around Rimona's lips without ever touching them. Before dying away, it momentarily reached her shaded eyes. Looking at neither of them, she said, "We had a little girl but lost her," adding, after a pause, "Whether or not it just happened, as you say, I don't know. But I'd like to know why it *had* to happen."

There was a silence. Yonatan rose, tall and very lean. He collected the empty coffee mugs and took them to the sink. While
he was out of the room, Azariah noticed that Rimona's blond hair
fell over her back and shoulders, more to the left than the right.
He noticed the slender stem of her neck and the fine lines of her
forehead and cheeks. She was, he thought, beautiful, and Yonatan
was handsome, and he loved them both, even as he envied them.
He winced to think of having pained them by mentioning children, and he felt shame and self-loathing to be almost glad to hear
that they had none. I must make them happy now and always, he
thought. I must get so close they'll never be able to do without me.
Her pale, Christian beauty is so painful. I'll never let her know
how vile I really am.

Azariah Gitlin vaguely began to hope that this girl might hurt
him, do him some wrong, which she would have to make amends
for. And yet he couldn't imagine how this might come about.

When Yonatan returned to the room, Azariah looked down at
the floor and did not see him shut the copy of *Witches and Witch
Medicine* that was lying open at the end of the couch. As he put it
back in its place on the middle shelf, Azariah politely asked if he
might smoke.

Yonatan took from his shirt pocket the pack of expensive American cigarettes that Azariah had given him that afternoon as a present and handed it to him.

"Long ago," said Azariah, "in ancient Greece, there was a philosopher who believed that the soul resides in the body like a sailor in
a ship. As lovely as that image is, it must be rejected. Another Greek
philosopher wrote that the soul dwells in the body like a spider in its
web, which in my own humble opinion is much closer to the truth.
Using the powers of observation that I developed during my long,
unhappy years of wandering, I noticed a good quarter of an hour
ago that someone here must like to play chess. If I may be permitted
to hazard a guess, that someone is you, Yonatan, not your friend."

As Yonatan opened the board and set up the pieces, Azariah
delivered himself of a few boastful remarks, only to retract them

at once and apologetically point out, "A great philosopher once observed that the winner of the Olympic medal was not necessarily the fastest man in Greece but simply the fastest man in the race."

Yonatan Lifshitz and Azariah Gitlin smoked and played in silence while Rimona sat by the radio with her bag of embroidery unopened in her lap, so intensely absorbed was she in a dream of her own. Yonatan's eyes kept filling with tears that he neither wiped away nor bothered to explain to his guest. Rimona had still not removed the pine branches from the vase, since she had found no flowers to replace them.

After six or seven moves, Azariah blundered. He did his best to come up with a smile, remarking that, even though the game was as good as over almost before it had begun, for him it was no more than a first probe. Yonatan suggested that they begin again.

But Azariah refused. He blamed the rolls of thunder outside for his inability to concentrate and, with a kind of irritable sportsmanship, insisted on playing to the bitter end. "He who has never tasted defeat will never know that triumph is sweet."

At this Rimona pressed her embroidery to her lap and looked up at him only to notice the many tiny, agitated wrinkles that came and went around his eyes. He had already single-handedly eaten every pastry on the large plate except for a sole survivor, a last concession to good manners that he kept absentmindedly picking up and putting down again. Once he even raised it all the way to his lips before giving a last-minute start and gently replacing it. Rimona opened her bag and began to embroider.

"That man you said was killed by the bullet. If he died instantly, that means he didn't suffer. Did you say his name was Yehoshafat?"

"That's right," said Azariah. "But I'm afraid I've only made you laugh at me. I always say the opposite of what I should."

"Your move," said Yonatan.

With a sudden burst of fervor, Azariah slid his remaining bishop along a diagonal that reached nearly from one end of the board to the other.

"Not bad," said Yonatan.

"Watch out!" crowed Azariah. "I'm just warming up!"

Indeed, within the space of a few moves, after recklessly sacrificing a knight and two pawns, the young man had reversed an apparently hopeless situation and was even threatening Yonatan's king.

"Do you see that?" he asked, flushed with success. At that exact moment, however, he seemed to run out of inspiration, unnecessarily losing another pawn and the initiative. Yonatan continued to play patiently, cagily, with calculated precision. Azariah, on the other hand, kept throwing away ingeniously gained advantages and committing mistakes that would have made a beginner blush.

Rimona put down her embroidery and went to open the window to air out the smoke-filled room. Tia rose too, arched her back, and moved closer to the table, panting in short, rapid breaths, her pink tongue hanging out, her eyes glued on her master and her ears cocked forward, as if straining not to miss a word or a move. Azariah Gitlin burst out laughing. "Give me time," he said, "and I'll teach your dog to play chess. You'd be surprised at what a dog can learn. Once, when I lived in a camp for new immigrants, I taught a Yemenite's goat to dance the hora."

Rimona shut the window, returned to the couch, and said, as if continuing her thoughts out loud, that it must be sad to have to spend so many hours alone in the barber's shack. In the bottom closet, she believed, was a small, unused electric kettle that they could lend to Azariah. Before he left she would also give him some coffee and sugar and a few pieces of the pastry that he liked so much.

"Check," said Azariah. His voice was cold.

"But what good does that do?" marveled Yonatan. "I can go here or here. Or here."

"I'm just pressing home the attack," said Azariah with a nervous giggle. "Thank you, Rimona," he added. "When you're being so nice to me, how could I possibly go and hurt Yonatan's feelings by inflicting, so to speak, a defeat on him."

"Your move," said Yonatan.

"As a gesture of friendship I offer you a draw."

"Hold on there," said Yonatan. "Why don't you first take a good look at what's happening to your rook. You're in bad trouble."

"If so, it's because I lost all interest in this banal, repetitious, and, if you don't mind my saying so, boring game at least ten minutes ago." Azariah's reply was almost a singsong.

"You," said Yonatan, "have lost."

"So I have," said Azariah, trying to force a comically gay expression.

"And I," said Yonatan, "have won."

"There now," said Rimona. "The kettle's boiling again."

They drank more coffee and Azariah demolished another plate of pastry. When it was all gone, he took his guitar out of its battered case, moved away from his hosts, and sat down on a footstool near the kitchen door. Tia went with him, sniffing at his shoes. At first he picked out two or three simple popular tunes, sometimes humming softly along, but then he started playing a melancholy melody that neither of them knew.

"That was sad," said Rimona.

Azariah flinched. "You didn't like it? I can play all kinds of things. Just tell me what."

"It was beautiful," said Rimona.

Thoughtfully, Yonatan gathered the survivors from the board and arranged them in two rows, black and white, on the table.

"That was just fine," he said. "I don't know much about music, but I could see that you played that piece very carefully, as if you were worried you might get carried away and snap the strings. It made me think of how quickly you figured out what was wrong with the Caterpillar. If you'd like, I'll say a word about you to Srulik. He's in charge of music around here. For now, though, we'd better think of going to the dining hall for supper."

"Comrade Yolek," said Azariah, "mistook me for that Srulik yesterday. I myself, of course, do not believe in pure coincidence. Everything happens for a reason."

• • •

Before he left, Rimona gave Azariah Gitlin the electric kettle, a bag of sugar, a can of coffee, and yet more pastry. Yonatan rummaged through drawers and found a new light bulb for Azariah's room. One look at it, though, was enough to establish that it wouldn't be any brighter than the old one.

Over supper Azariah once again began to lecture his hosts, which struck Yonatan as tiresome. He went on chewing in silence on a piece of bread while helping himself generously to the salad and a double portion of omelette. Rimona, however, listened attentively to every word. At one point, when she asked Azariah what he would do to stave off political disaster, it so went to his head that he forgot all about the vegetables she had just put on his plate. He began rehearsing an ingenious plan for engineering a big-power confrontation that would enable little Israel to slip safely away and even come out ahead.

During this recital, Etan R. stopped by their table and interrupted Azariah with a grin: "Well, well, I see you didn't get lost after all. I live in the last room by the swimming pool. If by any chance you find any justice around here, come tell me about it right away so we can nip it in the bud."

From across the hall, Yonatan's mother, Hava, waved hello. Little Shimon, mug in hand, came over to ask Yonatan to lend him the newcomer for a few days in the hope he might work some miracles in the sheep pen as well.

Before they parted and went their separate ways, Rimona invited Azariah, touching his elbow, to come again some evening to chat and play chess and to bring his guitar if he felt like it.

Once back in the barber's shack, Azariah thought of the picture that hung in Yonatan and Rimona's room, the dark, thirsty bird atop the brick wall, the surrounding murk, the diagonal shaft of sunlight, and the flaming wound that shaft inflicted on a single brick in a lower corner. So I'm invited back to chat and play music and chess. She'll have to make up to me a lot more than that if she expects to be forgiven. Her baby girl died and now she doesn't even have that.

"He's a loudmouth, a cheat, a brownnose, and a bullshitter," said Yonatan to Rimona, "and yet you can't help kind of liking him. I'm going over to talk to Udi about the fruit shipments. I won't be late."

A thick night hung over the kibbutz. The air was cold and raw, and the biting wind did not flag. It's a funny thing, thought Rimona, smiling in the darkness.

In the days that followed, Azariah Gitlin made still more repairs. His energy knew no bounds. He greased, tuned, and tightened; took apart and reassembled; changed dying batteries and readjusted fan belts; washed, waxed, and polished. He undertook to reorganize the shed by arranging the work tools in a logical order, putting up a broad wooden board on which to hang screwdrivers, wrenches, and pliers according to size, labeling all the drawers and shelves, and scrubbing the filthy concrete floor with detergents. He persuaded Yonatan to climb up to the rafters to get rid of the spiderwebs and birds' nests underneath the tin roof. He cataloged the spare parts and took a full inventory. As a crowning touch, he clipped a large colored photograph of the rotund Minister of Welfare from an illustrated weekly magazine and taped it to the wall. Every day from now on, plump-cheeked and jovial, Dr. Yosef Burg would look down on the men at work, imparting a self-satisfied bliss.

Azariah arrived early each morning in dark blue work clothes that were slightly too big on him and stood waiting for Yonatan to appear with the keys to the shed. Invariably, Yonatan would be sleepy, grouchy, and often teary-eyed, and Azariah would try to cheer him up with a story about one of the old grand masters, giants like Alekhine, Capablanca, and Lasker, compared to whom such current aces as Botvinnik and Petrosian were, so to speak, abject nonentities. To be sure, his entire fund of knowledge on the subject came from the chess journals that Yonatan had lent him and that he studied exhaustively while lying in bed.

One evening Azariah made his way to Yolek and Hava's and harangued them from eight o'clock until nearly midnight on the cyclic nature of Jewish destiny, its recurrent pattern of destruction and redemption, repeatedly referring not only to his own ideas but to a number of articles by Yolek Lifshitz in issues of the Labor Party monthly that he had come across in the recreation hall. He also expounded on the place of the creative individual in kibbutz society. Though his knowledge was as limited as his fervor was unbounded, he did manage now and then to come up with an original enough thought to make Yolek remark after he was gone, "Take it from me, Hava. I'm rarely wrong about these things. That boy has a real spark in him. If he's lucky enough to find a good girl, something may come of him yet."

"He's very strange and very sad," replied Hava. "If you ask me, this will come to no good end. You and your big discoveries!"

Azariah managed to gamble away his last two packs of American cigarettes before he had a chance to give them as gifts to new-found friends. One night he landed in the last room adjoining the swimming pool, reintroduced himself to Etan R., met the two girls who had been living with Etan since the onset of winter, and began to talk about citrus fruit. When he claimed that a grapefruit was simply a cross between an orange and a lemon, Etan not only objected but challenged him to a bet. Azariah immediately appointed the two girls as judges, asked for their verdict, and deferred without protest to their lack of support, laying his two packs of cigarettes on the table. Before leaving, he promised to bring the relevant volume of the *Encyclopaedia Britannica,* for he intended to prove that there was a fruit, perhaps the tangerine, that was half a lemon and half an orange after all.

From Etan R.'s he went to pay a call on Srulik, the music man, for whom he played his guitar for a good ten minutes, smiling all the while but blinking frantically like a cat that wants to have its ears scratched. Indeed, the cat succeeded, for Srulik decided to let him try out for the kibbutz chamber quintet.

On Thursday he visited Yonatan and Rimona again to return part of the coffee and sugar they had given him. After all, he was now getting supplies from the kibbutz commissary in accordance with Secretary Yolek's instructions. He presented Rimona with a wicker shade he had made for the lamp, pointing out that it was only a token gift.

The next night a guest lecturer from the executive committee of the national trade union spoke in the dining hall on the plight of Soviet Jewry, reading from a large number of crumbling old letters that had reached him in devious ways from behind the Iron Curtain. His audience was composed almost exclusively of the older members of the kibbutz, the younger ones, with a single exception, having found other entertainment. Srulik the music man, who was sitting next to him, later swore to all his acquaintances that several especially heartrending passages had made the newcomer shed a tear. By the time the question period arrived, however, Azariah had either got a grip on himself or had had a change of heart, for he not only asked a question but refused to accept the answer given and continued to query the lecturer until a full-fledged argument broke out.

In one way or another, Azariah Gitlin was considered odd by most people who met him or who had heard about him from others. "Yolek's Spinoza," he was frequently called behind his back. High school wits amended this to "Chimpanoza." Etan R. mimicked Azariah's manner and speech standing knee-deep in mud, dripping wet and orating about the nature of justice, which, after all, could be found only on a kibbutz, and at the same time demanding an urgent meeting with its "head." Yet not even Etan could help acquiescing, albeit with a shrug, when little Shimon claimed that the new mechanic could talk politics for hours and make them sound as thrilling as a detective or science-fiction story. There was nothing dull about him, provided, of course, that one had the time to listen.

Apart from an occasional smirk or snide remark, no one would have dreamed of hurting Azariah Gitlin. It took all kinds. If a bizarrely philosophical, overtalkative, and somewhat pathetic young man just happened to land among them, what harm was he doing?

He worked hard, he did what he was told, and some said that he wasn't even half bad at it. Besides, you could see that he had had a hard life. Sometimes, during an argument in a committee, someone would cautiously poke fun at Yolek by saying, "Come on, Yolek, you're beginning to sound like that Spinoza of yours."

What was on our minds was neither Azariah Gitlin nor the headlines in the newspapers but the flooding taking place in the low-lying fields. The winter crops were in danger of rotting in the ground.

As for Yonatan, he returned to his silence. Rimona, too, never brought up the conversation they had had. She took to poring over a little English book from India about the depths of karmic suffering and the heights of astral purity. She had borrowed it from Azariah, and its margins bore his penciled comments in an agitated hand. Every evening, without fail, she sat down with it. The stove burned with a blue flame as always, and soft music continued to come over the radio.

All was calm between Rimona and Yonatan.

Jerusalem—
An Alien City

An Alien City

from *Under This Blazing Light*
(First published in 1968)

I was born in Jerusalem; I lived there as a child; when I was nine I went through the siege and the shelling of Jerusalem. That was the first time I saw a corpse. A shell fired from the Arab Legion's gun battery on Nebi Samwil hit a pious Jew and ripped his stomach open. I saw him lying there in the street. He was a short man with a straggly beard. His face as he lay there dying looked pale and surprised. It happened in July 1948. I hated that man for a long time because he used to come back and scare me in my dreams. I knew that Jerusalem was surrounded by forces that wanted me dead.

Later I moved away from Jerusalem. I still love the city as one loves a disdainful woman. Sometimes, when I had nothing better to do, I used to go to Jerusalem to woo her. There are some lanes and alleys there that know me well, even if they pretend not to.

I liked Jerusalem because it was a city at the end of the road, a city you could get to but never go through, and also because Jerusalem was never really part of the State of Israel: with the exception of a few streets, it always maintained a separate identity, as though it was deliberately turning its back on all those flat white commercial towns: Tel Aviv, Holon, Herzlia, Netanya.

Jerusalem was different. It was the negation of the regular whitewashed blocks of flats, far from the plains of citrus groves, the gardens with their hedges, the red roofs and irrigation pipes sparkling in the sun. Even the summer blue of Jerusalem was different: the city repudiated the dusty off-white sky of the coastal plain and the Sharon valley.

A shuttered, wintry city. Even in the summer it was a wintry city. Rusty iron railings; gray stone, shading into pale blue or pink; dilapidated walls; boulders; morose, inward-looking courtyards.

And the inhabitants: a taciturn, sullen race, always seemingly quelling an inner dread. Devout Jews, Ashkenazim in fur hats, and elderly Sephardim in striped robes. Mild-mannered scholars straying as though lost among the stone walls. Dreamy maidens. Blind beggars mouthing prayers or curses. Street idiots with a certain spark.

For twenty years Jerusalem stubbornly turned its back on the rhythm of free life: a very slow city in a frantic country; a remote, hilly old suburb of a flat land full of new building and threatening to explode from the pressure of seething energy.

The gloomy capital of an exuberant state.

And the suffocation: there were ruined streets, blocked alleys, barricades of concrete and rusty barbed wire. A city which was nothing but outskirts. Not a city of gold but of corrugated iron sheets, bowed and perforated. A city surrounded by the sound of alien bells at night, alien smells, alien vistas. A ring of hostile villages enclosed the city on three sides: Shu'afat, Wadi Joz, Issawiya, Silwan, Bethany, Tsur Bahr, Beit Safafa. It seemed as though they had only to clench their fist to crush the city. In the winter night you could sense a malicious purpose coursing from over there.

And there was fear in Jerusalem: an inner fear that must never be named or expressed in words, but that gathered, accumulated, solidified in winding alleys and isolated lanes.

The city fathers, the authorities, the council-housing estates, the newly planted trees, the traffic lights, all tried to tempt Jerusalem to be absorbed into the State of Israel, but Jerusalem, apart from one or two streets, refused to be absorbed. For twenty years Jerusalem stubbornly maintained a faded Mandatory character. It remained gloomy Jerusalem: not part of Israel, but somehow over against it.

I also loved Jerusalem because I was born there.

It was a love without compassion: my nightmares were often set in Jerusalem. I no longer live there, but in my dreams I belong to Jerusalem and it will not let me go. I saw both of us entirely surrounded by foes, not just threatened on three sides. I saw the city falling to the enemy, spoiled and looted and burned as in the Bible, as in the legends of the Roman Wars, as in the folklore of my childhood. And I, too, in these dreams was trapped inside Jerusalem.

I was told many stories as a child about the olden days and about the siege. In all of them Jewish children were slaughtered in Jerusalem. Jerusalem always fell, either heroically or helplessly, but there was always a slaughter and the stories ended with the city going up in flames and with Jewish children being "stabbed." Sennacherib, the evil Titus, the crusaders, marauders, attackers, military rule, the High Commissioner, searches, curfews, Abdullah the desert king, the guns of the Arab Legion, the convoy to Mount Scopus, the convoy to the Etsion Bloc, an inflamed mob, excited crowds, bloodthirsty ruffians, irregular forces, everything was directed against me. And I always belonged to the minority, the besieged, those whose fate was sealed, who were living under a temporary stay of execution. This time, too, as always, the city would fall, and all of us inside would die like that pious Jew lying in the street with his pale, surprised face.

And also this:

After the War of Independence was over, the city was left with a frontier through its heart. All my childhood years were spent in the proximity of streets that must not be approached, dangerous alleyways, scars of war damage, no-man's-land, gun slits in the Arab Legion's fortifications, where occasionally a red Arab headdress could be glimpsed, minefields, thistles, blackened ruins. Twisted rusty arms reaching up among the waves of rubble. There were frequent sounds of shooting from over there, stray shots or machine-gun salvos. Passers-by caught in the Legionnaires' firing line would be suddenly killed.

And on the other side, opposite, throughout those years there was the other Jerusalem, the one that was surrounding my city, which sent alien, guttural sounds rippling toward us, and smells, and flickering pale lights at night, and the frightening wail of the muezzin toward dawn. It was a kind of Atlantis, a lost continent: I only have a few faint memories of it from my early childhood. The colorful bustle of the narrow streets of the Old City, the arched alleyway leading to the Wailing Wall, a Mandatory Arab policeman with a bushy mustache, market stalls, *buza,* tamarind, a riot of dizzying color, the tension of lurking danger.

From over there, on the other side of the cease-fire line, a seething menace has been eyeing me through most of my life. "Just you wait. We haven't finished yet. We'll get you too someday."

I can remember strolling along the streets of Mousrara at dusk, to the edge of no-man's-land. Or distant views from the woods at Tel Arza. Looking across from the observation post at Abu Tor. The shell-scarred square in front of Notre Dame. The spires of Bethlehem facing the woods at Ramat Rahel. The minarets of the villages round about. Barren hillsides falling away from the new housing in Talpiyot. The Dead Sea glimmering far away and deep down like a mirage. The scent of rocky valleys at dawn.

On Sunday, June 11, 1967, I went to see the Jerusalem on the other side of the lines. I visited places that years of dreaming had crystalized as symbols in my mind, and found that they were simply places where people lived. Houses, shops, stalls, street signs.

I was thunderstruck. My dreams had deceived me, the nightmares were unfounded, the perpetual dread had suddenly been transformed into a cruel arabesque joke. Everything was shattered, exposed: my adored, terrifying Jerusalem was dead.

The city was different now. Out-of-the-way corners became bustling hubs. Bulldozers cleared new paths through rubble I had imagined would be there forever. Forgotten areas filled with frantic activity. Throngs of devout Jews, soldiers in battle dress, excited tourists, and scantily clad women from the coastal towns all streamed eastward. There was a rising tide in Jerusalem, as though the plain were swelling upward and rushing into the breached city. Everybody was feeling festive, myself included.

What comes next is painful to write about. If I say again, "I love reunited Jerusalem," what have I said? Jerusalem is mine, yet a stranger to me; captured and yet resentful; yielding, yet withdrawn. I could take no notice: the sky is the same sky, the Jerusalem stone is the same Jerusalem stone, Sheikh Jarrah and the streets of the American colony are just like Katamon and the streets of the German colony.

But the city is inhabited. People live there, strangers: I do not understand their language; they are living where they have always lived and I am the stranger who has come in from outside. True, the inhabitants are polite. They are almost offensively polite, as if they have achieved the highest rung of happiness through being granted the honor of selling me a few colored postcards and some Jordanian stamps. Welcome. We are all brothers. It's you we have been waiting for these last twenty years, to smile and say *ahlan* and *salaam alaikum* and sell you souvenirs.

Their eyes hate me. They wish me dead. Accursed stranger.

I was in East Jerusalem three days after it was conquered. I arrived straight from El Arish in Sinai, in uniform, carrying a submachine gun. I was not born to blow rams' horns and liberate lands from the "foreign yoke." I can hear the groaning of oppressed people; I cannot hear the "groaning of oppressed lands."

In my childhood dreams Arabs in uniform carrying submachine guns came to the street where I lived in Jerusalem to kill us all. Twenty-two years ago the following slogan appeared in red letters on a courtyard wall: IN BLOOD AND FIRE JUDAEA FELL, IN BLOOD AND FIRE JUDAEA WILL RISE AGAIN. The words had been written during the night by someone from the anti-British underground. I don't know how to write about blood and fire. If I ever write anything about this war, I will not write about blood and fire, I shall write about sweat and vomit, pus and piss.

I tried my hardest to feel in East Jerusalem like a man who has driven out his enemies and recovered his ancestral inheritance. The Bible came back to life for me: kings, prophets, the Temple Mount, Absalom's Pillar, the Mount of Olives. And also the Jerusalem of Abraham Mapu and Agnon's *Tmol Shilshom*. I wanted to belong, I wanted to share in the general celebrations.

But I couldn't.

I saw resentment and hostility, hypocrisy, bewilderment, obsequiousness, fear, humiliation, and new plots being hatched. I walked the streets of East Jerusalem like a man who has broken into a forbidden place.

City of my birth. City of my dreams. City of aspirations of my ancestors and my people. And here I was, stalking its streets clutching a submachine gun, like a figure in one of my childhood nightmares: an alien man in an alien city.

It's Cold in This Jerusalem of Yours

from *My Michael* (1968)

1

I am writing this because people I loved have died. I am writing this because when I was young I was full of the power of loving, and now that power of loving is dying. I do not want to die.

I am thirty years of age and a married woman. My husband is Dr. Michael Gonen, a geologist, a good-natured man. I loved him. We met in Terra Sancta College ten years ago. I was a first-year student at the Hebrew University, in the days when lectures were still given in Terra Sancta College.

This is how we met:

One winter's day at nine o'clock in the morning I slipped coming downstairs. A young stranger caught me by the elbow. His hand was strong and full of restraint. I saw short fingers with flat nails. Pale fingers with soft black down on the knuckles. He hurried to stop me falling, and I leaned on his arm until the pain passed. I felt at a loss, because it is disconcerting to slip suddenly in front of strangers: searching, inquisitive eyes and malicious smiles. And I was embarrassed because the young stranger's hand was broad and warm. As he held me I could feel the warmth of his fingers through the sleeve of the blue woolen dress my mother had knitted me. It was winter in Jerusalem.

He asked me whether I had hurt myself.

I said I thought I had twisted my ankle.

He said he had always liked the word *ankle*. He smiled. His smile was embarrassed and embarrassing. I blushed. Nor did I refuse when he asked if he could take me to the cafeteria on the ground floor. My leg hurt. Terra Sancta College is a Christian convent that was loaned to the Hebrew University after the 1948 war. It is a cold building; the corridors are tall and wide. I felt distracted as I followed this young stranger who was holding on to me. I was happy to respond to his voice. I was unable to look straight at him and examine his face. I sensed, rather than saw, that his face was long and lean and dark.

"Now let's sit down," he said.

We sat down, neither of us looking at the other. Without asking what I wanted he ordered two cups of coffee. I loved my late father more than any other man in the world. When my new acquaintance turned his head I saw that his hair was cropped short and that he was unevenly shaven. Dark bristles showed, especially under his chin. I do not know why this detail struck me as important, in fact as a point in his favor. I liked his smile and his fingers, which were playing with a teaspoon as if they had an independent life of their own. And the spoon enjoyed being held by them. My own finger felt a faint urge to touch his chin, on the spot where he had not shaved properly and where the bristles sprouted.

Michael Gonen was his name.

He was a third-year geology student. He had been born and brought up in Holon. "It's cold in this Jerusalem of yours."

"My Jerusalem? How do you know I'm from Jerusalem?"

He was sorry, he said, if he was wrong for once, but he did not think he was wrong. He had learned by now to spot a Jerusalemite at first sight. As he spoke he looked into my eyes for the first time. His eyes were gray. I noticed a flicker of amusement in them, but not a cheerful flicker. I told him that his guess was right. I was indeed a Jerusalemite.

"Guess? Oh, no."

He pretended to look offended, the corners of his mouth smiling: No, it was not a guess. He could see that I was a Jerusalemite. "See?" Was this part of his geology course? No, of course not. As a matter of fact, it was something he had learned from cats. From cats? Yes, he loved watching cats. A cat would never make friends with anyone who was not disposed to like him. Cats are never wrong about people.

"You seem to be a happy sort of person," I said happily. I laughed, and my laugh betrayed me.

Afterward Michael Gonen invited me to accompany him to the third floor of Terra Sancta College, where some instructional films about the Dead Sea and the Arava were about to be shown.

On the way up, as we passed the place on the staircase where I had slipped earlier, Michael took hold of my sleeve once again. As if there was a danger of slipping again on that particular step. Through the blue wool I could feel every one of his five fingers. He coughed drily and I looked at him. He caught me looking at him, and his face reddened. Even his ears turned red. The rain beat at the windows.

"What a downpour," Michael said.

"Yes, a downpour," I agreed enthusiastically, as if I had suddenly discovered that we were related.

Michael hesitated. Then he added:

"I saw the mist early this morning, and there was a strong wind blowing."

"In my Jerusalem, winter is winter," I replied gaily, stressing "my Jerusalem" because I wanted to remind him of his opening words. I wanted him to go on talking, but he could not think of a reply; he is not a witty man. So he smiled again. On a rainy day in Jerusalem in Terra Sancta College on the stairs between the first floor and the second floor. I have not forgotten.

In the film we saw how the water is evaporated until the pure salt appears: white crystals gleaming on gray mud. And the minerals in the crystals like delicate veins, very fine and brittle. The gray mud split open gradually before our very eyes, because in this instructional film the natural processes were shown speeded up. It was a silent film. Black blinds were drawn over the windows to shut out the light of day. The light outside, in any case, was faint and murky. There was an old lecturer who occasionally uttered comments and explanations which I could not understand. The scholar's voice was slow and resonant. I remembered the agreeable voice of Dr. Rosenthal, who had cured me of diphtheria when I was a child of nine. Now and then the lecturer indicated with the help of a pointer the significant features of the pictures, to prevent his students' minds from wandering from the point. I alone was free to notice details which had no instructional value, such as the miserable but determined desert plants that appeared on the screen again and again around the machinery that extracted the potash. By the dim light of the magic lantern I was free, too, to contemplate the features, the arm, and the pointer of the ancient lecturer, looking like an illustration in one of the old books I loved. I remembered the dark woodcuts in *Moby Dick*.

Outside, several heavy, hoarse rolls of thunder sounded. The rain beat furiously against the darkened windows, as if it were demanding that we listen with rapt attention to some urgent message it had to deliver.

2

My late father often used to say, Strong people can do almost anything they want to do, but even the strongest cannot choose what they want to do. I am not particularly strong.

Michael and I arranged to meet that same evening in Café Atara in Ben Yehuda Street. Outside, an absolute storm was raging, beating down furiously on the stone walls of Jerusalem.

Austerity regulations were still in force. We were given ersatz coffee and tiny paper bags of sugar. Michael made a joke about this, but his joke was not funny. He is not a witty man—and perhaps he could not tell it in an amusing way. I enjoyed his efforts; I was glad that I was causing him some exertion. It was because of me that he was coming out of his cocoon and trying to be amused and amusing. When I was nine I still used to wish I could grow up as a man instead of a woman. As a child I always played with boys and I always read boys' books. I used to wrestle, kick, and climb. We lived in Kiryat Shmuel, on the edge of the suburb called Katamon. There was a derelict plot of land on a slope, covered with rocks and thistles and pieces of scrap iron, and at the foot of the slope stood the house of the twins. The twins were Arabs, Halil and Aziz, the sons of Rashid Shahada. I was a princess and they were my bodyguard, I was a conqueror and they my officers, I was an explorer and they my native bearers, a captain and they my crew, a master spy and they my henchmen. Together we would explore distant streets, prowl through the woods, hungry, panting, teasing Orthodox children, stealing into the woods round St. Symeon's convent, calling the British policemen names. Giving chase and running away, hiding and suddenly dashing out. I ruled over the twins. It was a cold pleasure, so remote.

Michael said, "You're a coy girl, aren't you?"

When we had finished drinking our coffee, Michael took a pipe out of his overcoat pocket and put it on the table between us. I was wearing brown corduroy trousers and a chunky red sweater, such as girls at the university used to wear at that time to produce a casual effect. Michael remarked shyly that I had seemed more feminine that morning, in the blue woolen dress. To him, at least.

"You seemed different this morning, too," I said.

Michael was wearing a gray overcoat. He did not take it off the whole time we sat in Café Atara. His cheeks were glowing from the bitter cold outside. His body was lean and angular. He picked up his unlit pipe and traced shapes with it on the tablecloth. His fingers, playing with the pipe, gave me a feeling of peace. Perhaps he had suddenly regretted his remark about my clothes; as if correcting a mistake, Michael said he thought I was a pretty girl. As he said it he stared fixedly at the pipe. I am not particularly strong, but I am stronger than this young man.

"Tell me about yourself," I said.

Michael said, "I didn't fight in the Palmach. I was in the signal corps. I was a wireless operator in the Carmeli Brigade."

Then he started talking about his father. Michael's father was a widower. He worked in the waterworks department of the Holon municipality.

Rashid Shahada, the twins' father, was a clerk in the technical department of the Jerusalem municipality under the British. He was a cultivated Arab, who behaved toward strangers like a waiter.

Michael told me that his father spent most of his salary on his education. Michael was an only child, and his father cherished high hopes for him. He refused to recognize that his son was an ordinary young man. For instance, he used to read the exercises that Michael wrote for his geology course with awe, commending them with such set phrases as "This is very scientific work. Very thorough." His father's greatest wish was for Michael to become a professor in Jerusalem, because his paternal grandfather had taught natural sciences in the Hebrew teachers' seminary in Grodno. He had been very well thought of. It would be nice, Michael's father thought, if the torch could be passed from one generation to another.

"A family isn't a relay race, with a profession as the torch," I said.

"But I can't tell my father that," Michael said. "He's a sentimental man, and he uses Hebrew expressions in the way that people used to handle fragile pieces of precious china. Tell me something about your family now."

I told him that my father had died in 1943. He was a quiet man. He used to talk to people as if he had to appease them and purchase a sympathy he did not deserve. He had a radio and electrical business—sales and simple repairs. Since his death, my mother had lived at Kibbutz Nof Harim with my older brother, Emanuel. "In the evenings she sits with Emanuel and his wife, Rina, drinking tea and trying to teach their son manners, because his parents belong to a generation that despises good manners. All day she shuts herself up in a small room on the edge of the kibbutz reading Turgenev and Gorki in Russian, writing me letters in broken Hebrew, knitting and listening to the wireless. That blue dress you liked on me this morning—my mother knitted it."

Michael smiled.

"It might be nice for your mother and my father to meet. I'm sure they would find a lot to talk about. Not like us, Hannah—sitting here talking about our parents. Are you bored?" he asked anxiously, and as he asked he flinched, as if he had hurt himself in asking.

"No," I said. "No, I'm not bored. I like it here."

Michael asked whether I hadn't said that merely out of politeness. I insisted. I begged him to tell me more about his father. I said that I liked the way he talked.

Michael's father was an austere, unassuming man. He voluntarily gave over his evenings to running the Holon workingmen's club. Running? Arranging benches, filing chits, duplicating notices, picking up cigarette-ends after meetings. It might be nice if our parents could meet . . . Oh, he had already said that once. He apologized for repeating himself and boring me. What was I reading at the university? Archaeology?

I told him I lived in digs with an Orthodox family in Achvah. In the mornings I worked as a teacher in Sarah Zeldin's kindergarten in Kerem Avraham. In the afternoons I attended lectures on Hebrew literature. But I was only a first-year student.

"*Student* rhymes with *prudent*." Straining to be witty, in his anxiety to avoid pauses in the conversation, Michael resorted to a play on words. But the point was not clear, and he tried to rephrase it. Suddenly he stopped talking and made a fresh, furious attempt at lighting his obstinate pipe. I enjoyed his discomfiture. At that time I was still repelled by the sight of the rough men my friends used to worship in those days: great bears of Palmach men who used to tackle you with a gushing torrent of deceptive kindness; thick-limbed tractor drivers coming all dusty from the Negev like marauders, carrying off the women of some captured city. I loved the embarrassment of the student Michael Gonen in Café Atara on a winter's night.

A famous scholar came into the café in the company of two women. Michael leaned toward me to whisper his name in my ear.

His lips may have brushed my hair. I said, "I can see right through you. I can read your mind. You're saying to yourself, 'What's going to happen next? Where do we go from here?' Am I right?"

Michael reddened suddenly like a child caught stealing sweets.

"I've never had a regular girlfriend before."

"Before?"

Thoughtfully Michael moved his empty cup. He looked at me. Deep down, underneath his meekness, a suppressed sneer lurked in his eyes.

"Till now."

A quarter of an hour later the famous scholar left with one of the women. Her friend moved over to a table in a corner and lit a cigarette. Her expression was bitter.

Michael remarked, "That woman is jealous."

"Of us?"

"Of you, perhaps." He tried to cover up. He was ill at ease, because he was trying too hard. If only I could tell him that his efforts did him credit. That I found his fingers fascinating. I could not speak, but I was afraid to keep silent. I told Michael that I loved to meet the celebrities of Jerusalem, the writers and scholars. It was an interest I had inherited from my father. When I was small, my father used to point them out to me in the street. My father was extremely fond of the phrase *world famous.* He would whisper excitedly that some professor who had just vanished into a florist's shop was world famous, or that some man out shopping was of international fame. And I would see a diminutive old man cautiously feeling his way like a wanderer in a strange city. When we read the books of the prophets at school I imagined the prophets as being like the writers and scholars my father had pointed out to me: men of refined features, bespectacled, with neatly trimmed white beards, their pace troubled and hesitant, as if they were walking down the steep slope of a glacier. And when I tried to imagine these frail old men thundering against the sins of the people I smiled; I thought that at the height of their fury their voices would dry up and they would merely emit a high-pitched shriek. If a writer or university professor came into his shop in Jaffa Road, my father would come home looking as if he had seen a vision. He would repeat solemnly casual words they had spoken, and study their utterances as if they were rare coins. He was always looking for hidden meanings in their words, because he saw life as a lesson from which one had to learn a moral. He was an attentive man. Once my father took me and my brother Emanuel to the Tel Or Cinema on a Saturday morning to hear Martin Buber and Hugo Bergmann speak at a meeting sponsored by a pacifist organization. I still remember a curious episode. When we came out of the auditorium Professor Bergmann stopped in front of my father and said, "I really did not expect to see you in our midst today, my dear Dr. Liebermann. I beg your pardon—you are not Professor Liebermann? Yet I feel certain we have met. Your face, sir, seems very familiar." Father stuttered. He blanched as if he had been accused of some foul deed. The professor, too, was confused and apologized for his mistake. Perhaps on account of his embarrassment, the scholar touched my shoulder and said, "In any case, my dear sir, your daughter—your daughter?—is a very pretty girl." And beneath his mustache a gentle smile spread. My father never forgot this incident as long as he lived. He used to recount it again and again, with excitement and delight. Even when he sat in his armchair, clad in a dressing gown, his glasses perched high on his forehead and his mouth drooping wearily, my father looked as if he was silently listening to the voice of some secret power. "And you know, Michael, still, to this day, I sometimes think that I shall marry a young scholar who is destined to become world famous. By the light of his reading lamp my husband's face will hover among piles of old German tomes; I shall creep in on tiptoe to put a cup of tea down on the desk, empty the ashtray, and quietly close the shutters, then leave without his noticing me. Now you'll laugh at me."

3

Ten o'clock.

Michael and I paid our own bills, as students do, and went out into the night. The sharp frost seared our faces. I breathed out, and watched my breath mingle with his. The cloth of his overcoat was coarse, heavy, and pleasant to touch. I had no gloves, and Michael insisted I wear his. They were rough, worn leather gloves. Streams of water ran down the gutter toward Zion Square, as if something sensational were happening in the center of town. A tightly wrapped couple walked past, their arms round each other. The girl said, "That's impossible. I can't believe it."

And her partner laughed. "You're very naive."

We stood for a moment or two, not knowing what to do. We only knew that we did not want to part. The rain stopped and the air grew colder. I found the cold unbearable. I shivered. We watched the water running down the gutter. The road was shiny. The asphalt reflected the broken yellow light of car headlamps. Disjointed thoughts flashed through my mind—how to keep hold of Michael for a little longer.

Michael said, "I'm plotting against you, Hannah."

I said, "Be careful. You might find yourself hoist on your own petard."

"I'm plotting dark deeds, Hannah."

His trembling lips betrayed him. For an instant he looked like a big, sad child, a child with most of its hair shorn off. I wanted to buy him a hat. I wanted to touch him.

Suddenly Michael raised his arm. A taxi screeched to a sodden halt. Then we were together inside its warm belly. Michael told the driver to drive wherever he felt like taking us—he didn't mind. The driver shot me a sly glance, full of filthy pleasure. The panel lights cast a dim red glow on his face, as if the skin had been peeled off and his red flesh laid bare. That taxi driver had the face of a mocking satyr. I have not forgotten.

We drove for about twenty minutes, with no idea where we were going. Our warm breath misted up the windows. Michael talked about geology. In Texas people dig for water and suddenly an oil well gushes up instead. Perhaps there are untapped supplies of oil in Israel too. Michael said "lithosphere." He said "sandstone," "chalk bed." He said "Precambrian," "Cambrian," "metamorphic rocks," "igneous rocks," "tectonics." For the first time then I felt that inner tension that I still feel whenever I hear my husband talking his strange language. These words relate to facts which have meaning for me, for me alone, like a message transmitted in code. Beneath the surface of the earth, opposed endogenic and exogenic forces are perpetually at work. The thin sedimentary rocks are in a continuous process of disintegration under the force of pressure. The lithosphere is a crust of hard rocks. Beneath the crust of hard rocks rages the blazing nucleus, the siderosphere.

I am not absolutely certain that Michael used these exact words during that taxi ride, in Jerusalem, at night, in the winter of 1950. But some of them I heard from him for the first time that night, and I was gripped. It was like a strange, sinister message, which I could not decipher. Like an unsuccessful attempt to reconstruct a nightmare that has faded from memory. Elusive as a dream.

Michael's voice as he spoke these words was deep and restrained. The panel lights glared red in the darkness. Michael spoke like a man weighed down with a grave responsibility, as if accuracy was at that moment of supreme importance. If he had taken my hand and pressed it in his I should not have withdrawn it. But the man I loved was carried away on a subdued tide of enthusiasm. I had been wrong. He could be very strong when he wanted to be. Much stronger than me. I accepted him. His words lulled me into that mood of tranquillity that I experience after a siesta: the tranquillity of waking to twilight, when time seems soft and I am tender and things around are tender.

The taxi passed through drenched streets that we could not identify because the windows were misted up. The windshield-wipers caressed the windshield. They beat in twin, steady rhythm, as if in obedience to some inviolable law. After twenty minutes' drive, Michael told the driver to stop, because he was not rich and our trip had already cost him the price of five lunches in the student restaurant at the end of Mamillah Road.

We got out of the taxi in a place that was unfamiliar, a steep alleyway paved with dressed stones. The paving stones were rain-lashed, for in the meantime the rain had started again. A fierce wind beat at us. We walked slowly. We were soaked to the skin. Michael's hair was drenched. His face was amusing; he had the look of a crying child. Once he stretched out a single finger and wiped away a drop of rain that was clinging to the tip of my chin. Suddenly we were in the square in front of the Generali Building. A winged lion, a rain-soaked, frozen lion, gazed down on us from above. Michael was ready to swear that the lion was laughing under his breath.

"Can't you hear him, Hannah? Laughing! He's looking at us and laughing. And I for one am inclined to agree with him."

I said, "Maybe it's a pity that Jerusalem is such a small city that you can't get lost in it."

Michael accompanied me along Melisanda Street, the Street of the Prophets, and then along Strauss Street, where the medical center is. We did not meet a living soul. It was as if the inhabitants had abandoned the city and left it to the two of us. We were lords of the city. When I was a child I used to play a game I called the Princess of the City. The twins acted the part of submissive subjects. Sometimes I made them act as rebellious subjects, and then I would humble them relentlessly. It was an exquisite thrill.

In winter, at night, the buildings of Jerusalem look like gray shapes frozen against a black backdrop. A landscape pregnant with suppressed violence. Jerusalem can sometimes be an abstract city: stones, pine trees, and rusting iron.

Stiff-tailed cats crossed the deserted streets. The alley walls reflected a counterfeit echo of our footsteps, making them dull and long. We stood outside the door of my house for about five minutes. I said, "Michael, I can't invite you up to my room for a hot glass of tea, because my landlord and his wife are religious people. When I took the room I promised them not to entertain men there. And it's half past eleven now."

When I said "men," we both smiled.

"I didn't expect you to invite me up to your room now," Michael said.

I said, "Michael Gonen, you're a perfect gentleman, and I'm grateful to you for this evening. All of it. If you were to invite me to share another evening like it with you, I don't suppose I should refuse."

He bent over me. Forcefully he gripped my left hand in his right. Then he kissed my hand. The movement was abrupt and violent, as if he had been rehearsing it all along the way, as if he had mentally counted to three before he bent over to kiss me. Through the leather of the glove he had lent me when we left the café, a strong, warm wave entered me. A moist breeze stirred the treetops and fell quiet. Like a duke in an English film, Michael kissed my hand through his glove, only Michael was drenched and he forgot to smile and the glove was not white.

I took off both gloves and handed them to him. He hurriedly put them on while they were still warm from the heat of my body. An invalid coughed wretchedly behind the closed shutters on the first floor.

"How strange you are today," I smiled.

As if I had known him on other days, too.

4

I have fond memories of an attack of diphtheria I suffered as a child of nine. It was winter. For several weeks I lay in my bed opposite the south-facing window. Through the window I could see a gloomy expanse of fog and rain: south Jerusalem, the shadow of the Bethlehem hills, Emek Refaim, the rich Arab suburbs in the valley. It was a winter world without details, a world of shapes in an expanse ranging in color from light to dark gray. I could see the trains too, and I could follow them with my eyes a long way along Emek Refaim from the soot-blackened station as far as the curves at the foot of the Arab village of Beit Safafa. I was a general on the train. Troops loyal to me commanded the high ground. I was an emperor in hiding. An emperor whose authority was undiminished by distance and isolation. In my dreams the southern suburbs were transformed into the St. Pierre and Miquelon Islands, which

I had come across in my brother's stamp album. Their names had caught my fancy. I used to carry my dreams over into the world of waking. Night and day were one continuous world. My high fever contributed to this effect. Those were dizzy, multicolored weeks. I was a queen. My cool mastery was challenged by open rebellion. I was captured by the mob, imprisoned, humiliated, tortured. But a handful of loyal supporters were plotting in dark corners to rescue me. I had confidence in them. I relished my cruel sufferings because out of them rose pride. My returning authority. I was reluctant to recover. According to the doctor, Dr. Rosenthal, there are some children who prefer to be ill, who refuse to be cured, because illness offers, in a sense, a state of freedom. When I recovered, at the end of the winter, I experienced a feeling of exile. I had lost my powers of alchemy, the ability to make my dreams carry me over the line that divides sleeping from waking. To this day I feel a sense of disappointment on waking. I mock at my vague longing to fall seriously ill.

After saying good night to Michael I went up to my room. I made some tea. For a quarter of an hour I stood in front of the paraffin heater warming myself and thinking of nothing in particular. I peeled an apple, sent to me by my brother Emanuel from his kibbutz, Nof Harim. I recalled how Michael had tried three or four times to light his pipe without success. Texas is a fascinating place: a man digs a hole in his garden to plant a fruit tree, and suddenly a jet of oil gushes out. This was a whole dimension I had never considered before, the hidden worlds that lay beneath every spot I tread. Minerals and quartzes and dolomites and all that kind of thing.

Then I wrote a short letter to my mother and my brother and his family. I told them all that I was well. In the morning I must remember to buy a stamp.

In the literature of the Hebrew enlightenment there are frequent references to the conflict between light and darkness. The writer is committed to the eventual triumph of light. I must say that I prefer the darkness. Especially in summer. The white light terrorizes Jerusalem. It puts the city to shame. But in my heart there is no conflict between darkness and light. I was reminded of how I had slipped on the stairs that morning in Terra Sancta College. It was a humiliating moment. One of the reasons why I enjoy being asleep is that I hate making decisions. Awkward things sometimes happen in dreams, but some force always operates that makes decisions for you, and you are free to be like the boat in the song, with all the crew asleep, drifting wherever the dream carries you. The soft hammock, the seagulls, and the expanse of water, which is both a gently heaving surface and also a maelstrom of unplumbed depths. I know that the deep is thought of as a cold place. But it is not always so, and not entirely. I read in a book once about warm streams and underwater volcanoes. At a point deep below the freezing ocean depths there is sometimes a warm cave hidden. When I was small I read and re-read my brother's copy of Jules Verne's *Twenty Thousand Leagues Under the Sea*. There are some rich nights when I discover a secret way through the watery depths and the darkness among green and clammy sea-creatures until I beat at the door of the warm cavern. That is my home. There a shadowy captain waits for me, surrounded by books and pipes and charts. His beard is black, his eyes hold a hungry gleam. Like a savage he seizes me, and I soothe his raging hatred. Tiny fish swim through us, as if we were both made of water. As they pass through they impart minute flickers of searing pleasure.

I read two chapters of Mapu's *Love of Zion* for the next day's seminar. If I were Tamar I would make Amnon crawl to me on his knees for seven nights. When he finally confessed the torments of his love in scriptural language I would order him to transport me in a sailing ship to the isles of the archipelago, to that faraway place where Red Indians turn into delectable sea creatures with silver spots and electric sparks, and seagulls float in blue space.

Sometimes at night I see a bleak Russian steppe. Frozen plains coated with a crust of bluish frost that reflects the flickering light of a wild moon. There is a sledge and a bearskin rug and the black back of a shrouded driver and furiously galloping horses and wolves' eyes glowing in the darkness round about and a solitary dead tree stands on the white slope and it is night within night on the steppe and the stars keep sinister watch. Suddenly the driver turns toward me a heavy face carved by some drunken sculptor. Icicles hang from the ends of his tangled mustache. His mouth is slightly open, as if it is he who is producing the howl of the biting wind. The dead tree that stands all alone on the slope on the steppe is not there by chance, it has a function that on waking I cannot name. But even when I wake I remember that it has a function. And so I return not entirely empty-handed.

In the morning I went out to buy a stamp. I posted the letter to Nof Harim. I ate a roll and yogurt and drank a glass of tea. Mrs. Tarnopoler, my landlady, came into my room to ask me to buy a can of paraffin on my way home. While I drank my tea I managed to read another chapter of Mapu. At Sarah Zeldin's kindergarten one of the girls said, "Hannah, you're as happy as a little girl today!"

I put on the blue woolen dress and tied a red silk kerchief round my neck. When I looked in the mirror I was delighted to see that with the neckerchief I looked like a daring girl who is suddenly likely to lose her head.

Michael was waiting for me at midday at the entrance to Terra Sancta, by the heavy iron gates with their dark metal ornaments. He was carrying a box full of geological specimens in his arms. Even if it had occurred to me, say, to shake hands with him, I could not have.

"Oh, it's you, is it?" I said. "Who do you think you're waiting for? Did anyone tell you to wait here?"

"It's not raining now and you're not soaking wet," Michael said. "When you're wet, you're much less bold."

Then Michael drew my attention to the sly, leering smile of the bronze statue of the Virgin on top of the building. Her arms were outstretched as if she were trying to embrace the whole city.

I went downstairs to the library basement. In a narrow, gloomy passage, lined with dark, sealed boxes, I met the kindly librarian, a short man who wore a skullcap. I was in the habit of exchanging greetings and witticisms with him. He, too, as if making a discovery, asked me, "What has come over you today, young lady? Good news? If you will permit me to say so, 'Bright joy illumines Hannah in a most amazing manner.'"

In the Mapu seminar, the lecturer related a typical anecdote, a story about a fanatically orthodox Jewish sect who claimed that ever since Abraham Mapu had published *The Love of Zion* there had been more benches in the houses of ill fame, heaven forbid.

What has got into everyone today? Have they been talking to each other?

Mrs. Tarnopoler, my landlady, had bought a new stove. She beamed benignly at me.

5

That evening the sky brightened a little. Blue patches drifted eastward. The air was damp.

Michael and I arranged to meet outside the Edison Cinema. Whichever of us arrived first would buy two tickets for the film, which starred Greta Garbo. The heroine of the film dies of unrequited love after sacrificing her body and her soul for a worthless man. Throughout the film I suppressed an overpowering desire to laugh. Her suffering and his worthlessness seemed like two terms in a simple mathematical equation, which I was not tempted to try to solve. I felt full to overflowing. I laid my head on Michael's shoulder and watched the screen sideways, until the pictures turned into a capering succession of different tones graded between black and white, but mainly various shades of light gray.

As we came out Michael said, "When people are contented and have nothing to do, emotion spreads like a malignant tumor."

"What a trite remark," I said.

Michael said, "Look here, Hannah, art isn't my subject. I'm just a humble scientist, as they say."

I refused to relent. "That's also trite."

Michael smiled. "Well?"

Whenever he cannot answer he smiles, just like a child who notices grown-ups doing something ridiculous — an embarrassed, embarrassing smile.

We strolled down Isaiah Street toward Geula Street. Sharp stars glittered in the Jerusalem sky. Many of the streetlamps of the British Mandate period had been destroyed by shellfire during the War of Independence. In 1950 most of them were still shattered. Shadowy hills showed in the distance at the ends of the streets.

"This isn't a city," I said, "it's an illusion. We're crowded in on all sides by the hills — Castel, Mount Scopus, Augusta Victoria, Nebi Samwil, Miss Carey. All of a sudden the city seems very insubstantial."

Michael said, "When it's been raining, Jerusalem makes one feel sad. Actually, Jerusalem always makes one feel sad, but it's a different sadness at every moment of the day and at every time of the year."

I felt Michael's arm round my shoulder. I buried my hands in the pockets of my warm corduroy trousers. Once I took one hand out and touched him under the chin. He was clean-shaven today, not like the first time we met, in Terra Sancta. I said he must have shaved especially to please me.

Michael was embarrassed. He just happened, he lied, to have bought a new razor that day. I laughed. He hesitated a moment, then decided to join in.

In Geula Street we saw a religious woman, wearing a white head scarf, open a second-floor window and squeeze half her body out as if she were about to throw herself down into the street. But she merely closed the heavy iron shutters. The hinges groaned as if with despair.

When we passed the playground of Sarah Zeldin's kindergarten I told Michael that I worked there. Was I a strict teacher? He imagined I was. What made him think that? He didn't know what to answer. Just like a child, I said, starting to say something and not knowing how to finish. Expressing an opinion and not daring to defend it. A child.

Michael smiled.

From one of the yards, on the corner of Malachi Street, came the sound of cats screeching. It was a loud, hysterical shriek, followed by two strangled wails, and finally a low sob, faint and submissive, as if there were no sense, no hope.

Michael said, "They're crying out in love. Did you know, Hannah, that cats are most in heat in winter, in the coldest days? When I'm married I shall keep a cat. I always wanted to have one, but my father wouldn't let me. I'm an only child. Cats cry out in love because they're not bound by any constraint or convention. I imagine that a cat in heat feels as if it's been grabbed hold of by a stranger and is being squeezed to death. The pain is physical. Burning. No, I didn't learn that in geology. I was afraid you'd make fun of me talking like this. Let's go."

I said, "You must have been a very spoiled child."

"I was the hope of the family," Michael said. "I still am. My father and his four sisters, they all bet on me as if I were their racehorse and as if my university education were a steeplechase. What do you do in the morning in your kindergarten, Hannah?"

"What a funny question. I do exactly what any other kindergarten teacher does. Last month, at Hanukkah, I glued paper tops and cut out cardboard Maccabees. Sometimes I sweep the dead leaves from the paths in the yard. Sometimes I tinkle on the piano. And I often tell the children stories, from memory, about Indians, islands, travels, submarines. When I was a child I adored the books my brother had by Jules Verne and Fenimore Cooper. I thought that if I wrestled and climbed trees and read boys' books I'd grow up to be a boy. I hated being a girl. I regarded grown-up women with loathing and disgust. Even now I sometimes long to meet a man like Michael Strogoff. Big and strong, but at the same time quiet and reserved. He must be silent, loyal, subdued, but only controlling the spate of his inner energies with an effort. What do you mean — of course I'm not comparing you to Michael Strogoff. Why on earth should I? Of course not."

Michael said, "If we had met as children you would have sent me sprawling. I used to get knocked down by the stronger girls when I was in the lower forms. I was what you'd call a good boy: a bit dozy, but hardworking, responsible, clean, and very honest. Nowadays I'm not at all dozy, though."

I told Michael about the twins. I used to wrestle with them furiously. Later on, when I was twelve, I was in love with both of them. I called them Halziz—Halil and Aziz. They were beautiful boys. A pair of strong, obedient seamen from Captain Nemo's crew. They hardly ever spoke. They either kept quiet, or else emitted guttural sounds. They didn't like words. A pair of gray-brown wolves. Alert and white-fanged. Wild and dark. Pirates. What can you know about it, little Michael?

Then Michael told me about his mother:

"My mother died when I was three. I remember her white hands, but I can't remember her face. There are a few photographs, but it's hard to make them out. I was brought up by my father. My father brought me up as a little Jewish socialist, with stories about Hasmonean children, shtetl children, children of illegal immigrants, children on kibbutzim. Stories about starving children in India, in the October Revolution in Russia. De Amicis's *The Heart*. Wounded children saving their towns. Children sharing their last crust. Exploited children, fighting children. My four aunts, my father's sisters, were quite different. A little boy should be clean, work hard, study hard, and get on in the world. A young doctor, helping his country and making a name for himself. A young lawyer, valiantly pleading before British judges, being reported in all the newspapers. On the day that independence was declared, my father changed his name from Ganz to Gonen. I am Michael Ganz. My friends in Holon still call me Ganz. But don't you call me Ganz, Hannah. You must go on calling me Michael."

We passed the wall of the Schneller army camp. Many years ago there was a Syrian orphanage here. The name reminded me of some ancient sadness, the reason for which I could not recall. A distant bell kept ringing from the east. I tried not to count its strokes. Michael and I had our arms round each other. My hand was frozen, Michael's was warm. Michael said jokingly, "Cold hands, warm heart."

I said, "My father had warm hands and a warm heart. He had a radio and electrical business, but he was a bad businessman. I remember him standing doing the washing-up with my mother's apron round him. Dusting. Beating bedspreads. Expertly making omelettes. Absently blessing the Hanukkah lights. Treasuring the remarks of every good-for-nothing. Always trying to please. As if everyone were judging him, and he, exhausted, were forever being forced to do well in some endless examination, to atone for some forgotten shortcoming."

Michael said, "The man you marry will have to be a very strong man."

A light drizzle began to fall, and there was a thick gray fog. The buildings looked weightless. In the district of Mekor Baruch a motorcycle went past us, scattering showers of droplets. Michael was sunk in thought. Outside the gate of my house I stood on tiptoe to kiss his cheek. He smoothed and dried my forehead. Timidly his lips touched my skin. He called me a cold beautiful Jerusalemite. I told him I liked him. If I were his wife I would not let him be so thin. In the darkness he seemed frail. Michael smiled. If I were his wife, I said, I would teach him to answer when he was spoken to, instead of just smiling and smiling as if words didn't exist. Michael choked back his resentment, stared at the handrail of the crumbling steps, and said, "I want to marry you. Please don't answer immediately."

Drops of freezing rain began to fall again. I shivered. For an instant I was glad I did not know how old Michael was. Still, it was his fault I was shivering now. I could not invite him up to my room, of course, but why couldn't he suggest we go to his place? Twice after we had come out of the cinema Michael had tried to say something, and I had cut him short, saying, "That's trite." What it was that Michael had been trying to say I could not remember. Of course I would let him keep a cat. How peaceful he makes me feel. Why will the man I marry have to be very strong?

6

A week later we went on a visit together to Kibbutz Tirat Yaar in the Jerusalem Hills.

Michael had a school friend in Tirat Yaar, a girl from his class who had married a boy from the kibbutz. He begged me to go with him. It meant a lot to him, he said, to introduce me to his old friend.

Michael's friend was tall and lean and acid. With her gray hair and her pursed lips she looked like a wise old man. Two children of uncertain ages huddled in a corner of the room. Something in my face or in my dress made them collapse periodically into bursts of muffled laughter. I felt confused. For two hours Michael engaged in animated conversation with his friend and her husband. I was forgotten after the first three or four polite phrases. I was entertained with lukewarm tea and dry biscuits. For two hours I sat and glowered, fastening and unfastening the catch of Michael's briefcase. What had he brought me here for? Why had I allowed myself to be talked into coming? What sort of a man had I landed myself with? Hardworking, responsible, honest, neat—and utterly boring. And his pathetic jokes. Such a dull man shouldn't be forever trying to be amusing. But Michael did everything he could to be witty and gay. They exchanged boring stories about boring teachers. The private life of a gym teacher called Yehiam Peled reduced Michael and his friend to howls of vicious schoolboy laughter. Then there followed an angry argument about a meeting between King Abdullah of Transjordan and Golda Meir on the eve of the War of Independence. Michael's friend's husband thumped on the table, and even Michael raised his voice. When he shouted his voice was frail and tremulous. It was the first time I had seen him in the company of other people. I had been wrong about him.

Afterward we walked in the dark to the main road. Tirat Yaar was connected to the main Jerusalem road by a lane lined with cypresses. A cruel wind nipped me all over. In the afterglow of sunset the Jerusalem Hills seemed to be plotting some mischief. Michael walked beside me, silent. He could not think of a single thing to say to me. We were strangers to each other, he and I. For one strange moment, I remember, I was overcome by a sharp feeling that I was not awake, or that the time was not the present. I'd been through all this before. Or else someone, years before, had warned me against walking in the dark along this black lane next to an evil man. Time was no longer a smooth, even flow. It had become a series of abrupt rushes. It may have been when I was a child. Or in a dream, or a frightening story. All of a sudden I was terrified of the dim figure walking silently beside me. His coat collar was turned up to hide the lower part of his face. His body was thin as a shadow. The rest of his features were hidden by a black leather student's hat pulled down over his eyes. Who is he? What do you know about him? He's not your brother, no relation at all, not even an old friend, but a strange shadow, far from human habitation, in the dark, late at night. Maybe he's planning to assault you. Maybe he's ill. You have heard nothing about him from anyone responsible. Why doesn't he talk to me? Why is he all wrapped up in his own thoughts? Why has he brought me here? What is he up to? It's night. In the country. I'm alone. He's alone. What if everything he has told me was a deliberate lie? He isn't a student. His name isn't Michael Gonen. He has escaped from an institution. He's dangerous. When did all this happen to me before? Somebody warned me, a long time ago, that this was how it would happen. What are those long-drawn-out sounds in the dark fields? You can't even see the light of the stars through the curtain of cypresses. There is a presence in the orchard. If I scream and scream, who will hear me? A stranger, walking with fast, clumsy steps, heedless of my pace. I fall back a little, deliberately. He doesn't notice. My teeth are chattering with cold and fear; the winter wind howls and bites. That silhouette doesn't belong to me; it's distant, wrapped up in itself, as if I were just a figment of its thoughts, with no reality of my own. I'm real, Michael. I'm cold. He didn't hear me. Maybe I wasn't speaking aloud.

"I'm cold, and I can't run this fast," I shouted as loud as I could.

Like a man distracted from his thoughts, Michael hurled back his reply:

"Not long to go now. We're almost at the bus stop. Be patient."

As soon as he had spoken, he vanished once more into the depths of his great overcoat. A lump rose in my throat, and my eyes filled. I felt insulted. Humiliated. Frightened. I wanted to hold his hand. I only knew his hand. I didn't know him. At all.

The cold wind spoke to the cypresses in a hushed, hostile tongue. There was no happiness in the world. Not in the cypresses, not in the crumbling track, not in the darkling hills around.

"Michael," I said, despairing. "Michael, last week you said you liked the word *ankle*. Tell me this, for heaven's sake: Do you realize that my shoes are full of water and my ankles hurt as if I were walking barefoot through a field of thorns? Tell me, who's to blame?"

Michael turned round sharply, frighteningly. He glared at me in confusion. Then he put his wet cheek against my face, and pressed his warm lips to my neck like a suckling child. I could feel every bristle on his cheek against the skin of my neck. I enjoyed the feel of the rough cloth of his coat. The cloth was a warm, quiet sigh. He unbuttoned his coat and drew me inside. We were together. I breathed in his smell. He felt very real. So did I. I was not a figment of his thoughts, he was not a fear inside me. We were real. I took in his pent-up panic. I reveled in it. You're mine, I whispered. Don't ever be distant, I whispered. My lips touched his forehead and his fingers found the nape of my neck. His touch was cautious and sensitive. Suddenly I was reminded of the spoon in the cafeteria in Terra Sancta, and how it had enjoyed being held in his fingers. If Michael had been an evil man then surely his fingers, too, would have been evil.

7

A fortnight or so before the wedding, Michael and I went to see his father and his aunts in Holon and my mother and my brother's family at Kibbutz Nof Harim.

Michael's father lived in a cramped and gloomy two-roomed flat in an estate of "workers' dwellings." Our visit coincided with a power failure. Yehezkel Gonen introduced himself to me by the light of a sooty paraffin lamp. He had a cold, and refused to kiss me in case I caught it from him just before my wedding. He was clad in a warm dressing gown, and his face was sallow. He told me he was entrusting a precious burden to my care—his Michael. Then he was embarrassed and regretted what he had said. He tried to pass it off as a joke. Anxiously, shyly, the old man enumerated all the illnesses Michael had had as a child. He lingered only on a very bad fever which had nearly proved fatal to Michael when he was ten. He stressed, finally, that Michael had not been ill since he was fourteen. Despite everything, our Michael, though not one of the strongest, was a decidedly healthy young man.

I recalled that when my father was selling a secondhand radio he used to talk to the customer in the same tones: frankness, fairness, a reserved familiarity, a quiet eagerness to please.

While Yehezkel Gonen addressed me in this tone of courteous assistance, with his son he barely exchanged two words. He merely said that he had been amazed to receive his letter, with the news it contained. He regretted that he could not make us some tea or coffee, as the electricity was cut off and he did not have a paraffin stove or even a gas ring. When Tova, God rest her, was alive—Tova was Michael's mother . . . if only she could have been with us on this occasion, everything would have been more festive. Tova had been a remarkable woman. He wouldn't talk about her now because he didn't want to mingle sorrow with gladness. One day he would tell me a very sad story.

"What can I offer you instead? Ah, a chocolate."

So, feverishly, as if he had been accused of neglecting his duty, he rummaged in his chest of drawers and produced an ancient box of chocolates, still in its original gift wrapping. "Here you are, my dears, help yourselves. Please."

"I am sorry, I didn't quite catch what it is you are studying at the university. Ah yes, of course, Hebrew literature. I shall remember in future. Under Professor Klausner? Yes, Klausner is a great man, even though he doesn't approve of the Labor Movement. I have a copy somewhere of one of the volumes of his *History of the Second Temple.* I'll find it to show you. In fact, I'd like to give you the book as a gift. It will be more useful to you than to me: your life is still ahead of you, mine is behind me now. It won't be easy to find it with the electricity not working, but for my daughter-in-law nothing is too much trouble."

While Yehezkel Gonen was bending down, wheezing, to look for the book on the bottom shelf of the bookcase, three of the four aunts arrived. They, too, had been invited to meet me. In the confusion caused by the power failure the aunts had been late, and had not managed to find Aunt Gitta and bring her with them. That was why only the three of them had come. In my honor, and in honor of the occasion, they had taken a taxi all the way from Tel Aviv to Holon so as to be on time. It had been pitch dark all the way.

The aunts turned to me with a slightly exaggerated sympathy, as if they saw through all my schemes but had decided to forgive me. They were delighted to make my acquaintance. Michael had written such nice things about me in his letter. How glad they were to discover for themselves that he had not been exaggerating. Aunt Leah had a friend in Jerusalem, a Mr. Kadishman, who was a cultured and influential man, and at Aunt Leah's request he had already made inquiries about my family. So the aunts, all four of them, knew that I came from a good home.

Aunt Jenia asked if she could have a few words with me in private. "I'm sorry, I know it's not very nice to whisper in company, but there's no need to insist on strict politeness in the family circle, and I suppose from now on you're one of the family."

We went into the other room, and sat down on Yehezkel Gonen's hard bed in the dark. Aunt Jenia switched on an electric torch, as if the two of us were alone together in the open at night. With every movement our shadows executed a wild dance on the wall, and the torch shook in her hand. I was struck by the grotesque idea that Aunt Jenia was about to ask me to get undressed. Perhaps because Michael had told me that she was a pediatric specialist.

She started in a tone of resolute affection: "Yehezkele's—I mean, Michael's father's financial position is not particularly good. Not at all good, in fact. Yehezkele is a petty clerk. There's no need to explain to a bright girl like you what a petty clerk is. Most of his salary goes toward Michael's education. What a burden that is there's no need for me to tell you. And Michael won't give up studying. I must tell you quite clearly and definitely that the family will on no account consent to his giving up his studies. There's no question of it.

"We discussed the matter on the way here, my sisters and I, in the taxi. We propose making a great effort and giving you, say, five hundred pounds each. Perhaps a bit more or a bit less. Aunt Gitta will certainly contribute, too, even though she couldn't manage to be here this evening. No, there's no need to thank us. We are a very familial family, if you can say that. Very much so. When Michael is a professor you can repay us the money, ha ha.

"It doesn't matter. The point is that even with that you won't have enough to set up a home just yet. I find the monstrous rise in prices these days absolutely appalling. Money itself drops in value every day. What I mean to say is, is your decision to get married in March final? Couldn't you put it off for a while? Let me ask another question, perfectly frankly, as one member of the family to another: Has anything happened which would prevent you putting off the date of the wedding? No? Then what's the hurry? I'll have you know that I was engaged for six years, in Kovno, before I married my first husband. Six years! I realize, of course, that in our modern age there's no question of a long engagement, no six years. But what about, say, a year? No? Oh, well. But I don't suppose you manage to save very much from your work in the kindergarten? There will be expenses for housekeeping and expenses for studying. You must realize one thing, that financial difficulties at the outset can well ruin a couple's married life. And I'm speaking from experience. Someday I'll tell you a shocking story. Allow me to speak frankly, as a doctor. I admit that for a month, two months, half a year, your sexual life will overcome all other problems. But what will happen after that? You're a bright girl, and I beg you to consider the question rationally. I have heard that your family is living in some kibbutz.

What's that? You inherit three thousand pounds under your father's will on your wedding day? That's good news. Very good news. You see, Hannele, Michael forgot to tell us that in his letter. By and large, our Michael still has his head in the clouds. He may be a scientific genius, but when it comes to real life he's nothing more than a child. Well then, so you've decided on March? March let it be. It's wrong for the older generation to force its ideas on the young. Your lives are still ahead of you, ours are behind us. Each generation must learn from its own mistakes. Good luck to you. One last thing: if ever you want any help or advice, you must be sure to come to me. I've had more experience than ten ordinary women. Now let's go back and join the others. Mazeltov, Yehezkele. Mazeltov, Micha. I wish you health and happiness."

At Kibbutz Nof Harim, in Galilee, my brother Emanuel welcomed Michael with a bear hug and hearty slaps on the shoulder, as if he had found a long-lost brother. In an energetic twenty-minute tour he showed him the whole of the kibbutz.

"Were you in the Palmach? No? So what? Never mind. The others did plenty of important work, too."

Half seriously, Emanuel urged us to come and live at Nof Harim. What's wrong? An intelligent lad can make himself useful and lead a satisfying life just as well here as at Jerusalem. "I can see at a glance that you're no ravening lion. From the physical point of view, that is. But so what? We're not a football team, you know. You could work in the henhouse, or even in the office. Rinele, Rinele, run and get that bottle of brandy we won in the Purim party raffle. Hurry up, our fine new brother-in-law is waiting. And what about you, Hannutchka — why so silent? The girl's going to get married and you'd think from her face she'd just been widowed. Michael, old chap, have you heard why they disbanded the Palmach? No, don't rack your brains — all I meant was do you know the joke? No? You're all behind the times in Jerusalem. Listen then, I'll tell you."

And finally, Mother.

My mother cried when she spoke to Michael. She told him in

broken Hebrew about my father's death, and her words were lost in her tears. She asked if she could measure Michael. Measure? Yes, measure. She wanted to knit him a white sweater. She would do everything she could to have it ready in time for the wedding. Had he got a dark suit? Would he like to wear poor, dear Yosef's suit for the ceremony? She could easily alter it to fit him. There wouldn't be much to do. It wasn't much too big and it wasn't much too small. She begged him. For sentimental reasons. It was the only present she could give him.

And in a heavy Russian accent my mother repeated over and over again, as if desperately seeking his confirmation, "Hannele is a fine girl. A very fine girl. She's got a lot of pain. You should know that too. And also — I don't know how you say . . . She's a very fine girl. You should know that too."

8

My late father occasionally used to say, It is impossible for ordinary people to tell a thoroughgoing lie. Deception always gives itself away. It is like a blanket which is too short: when you try to cover your feet your head is left uncovered, and when you cover your head your feet stick out. A man produces an elaborate excuse so as to conceal something, not realizing that the excuse itself reveals some unpleasant truth. Pure truth, on the other hand, is thoroughly destructive and leads nowhere. What can ordinary people do? All we can do is silently stand and stare. Here that is all we can do. Silently stand and stare.

Ten days before our wedding we took an old two-roomed apartment in the district called Mekor Baruch, in northwest Jerusalem. The people who lived in this neighborhood in 1950 were, besides the religious families, mostly petty clerks in the government service or in the Jewish Agency, textile retailers, cashiers in the cinemas or in the Anglo-Palestine Bank. It was already a dying suburb. Modern Jerusalem was reaching out toward the south and southwest. Our apartment was rather gloomy, and the plumbing was antiquated, but the rooms were very tall, which I liked. We discussed plans for painting the walls in bright colors and growing plants in pots. We did not know then that in Jerusalem pot plants never flourish, perhaps because of the large amounts of rust and chemical purifiers in the tap water.

We spent our spare time wandering around Jerusalem buying essentials: basic items of furniture, a few brushes and brooms and kitchen utensils, some clothes. I was surprised to discover that Michael knew how to haggle without being undignified. I never saw him lose his temper. I was proud of him. My best friend, Hadassah, who had recently married a promising young economist, expressed her opinion of Michael in these words:

"A modest and intelligent boy. Not too brilliant, perhaps, but steady."

Old family friends, long-established Jerusalemites, said, "He makes a good impression."

We walked around arm in arm. I strained to catch in the face of every acquaintance we met his inner judgment of Michael. Michael spoke little. His eyes were alert. He was pleasant and self-restrained in company. People said, "Geology? That's surprising. You'd think he was on the arts side."

In the evening I would go to Michael's room in Mousrara, where we were storing our purchases for the time being. I would sit most of the evening embroidering flowers on pillowcases. And on the clothes I embroidered our name, Gonen. I was good at embroidery.

I would sit back in the armchair we had bought to stand on the balcony of our flat. Michael sat at his desk, working on a paper on geomorphology. He was trying hard to have the work finished and present it before the wedding. He had promised himself that he would. By the light of his reading lamp I saw his long, lean, dark face, his close-cropped hair. Sometimes I thought he looked like a pupil in a religious boarding school, or like one of the boys from the Diskin orphanage whom I used to watch crossing our street on their way to the railway station when I was a child. Their heads were shaven and they walked along in pairs, holding hands. They were sad and resigned. But behind their air of resignation I could sense a suppressed violence.

Michael started shaving casually again. Dark bristles sprouted under his chin. Had he lost his new razor? No, he admitted that he had lied to me on our second evening together. He hadn't bought a new razor. He had shaved specially thoroughly to please me. Why had he lied? Because I had made him feel embarrassed. Why had he gone back now to shaving only every other day? Because now he didn't feel ill at ease in my presence. "I hate shaving. If only I were an artist, instead of a geologist, I might consider growing a beard."

I tried to visualize the picture, and burst out laughing.

Michael looked up at me in amazement. "What's so funny?"

"Are you offended?"

"No, I'm not offended. Not in the slightest."

"Then why are you looking at me like that?"

"Because at last I've managed to make you laugh. Time and time again I've tried to make you laugh, and I've never seen you laughing. Now, without trying, I've succeeded. It makes me happy."

Michael's eyes were gray. When he smiled the corners of his mouth quivered. He was gray and self-restrained, my Michael.

Every two hours I would make him a glass of lemon tea, which he liked. We rarely spoke, because I did not want to interrupt his work. I liked the word *geomorphology*. Once I got up quietly and tiptoed over barefoot to stand behind him as he bent over his work. Michael didn't know I was there. I could read a few sentences over his shoulder. His handwriting was neat and well-rounded, like a tidy schoolgirl's. But the words made me shudder: Extraction of mineral deposits. Volcanic forces pressing outward. Solidified lava. Basalt. Consequent and subsequent streams. A morphotectonic process which began thousands of years ago and is still continuing. Gradual disintegration, sudden disintegration. Seismic disturbances so slight that they can be detected only by the most sensitive instruments.

Once again I was startled by these words. I was being sent a message in code. My life depended on it. But I didn't have the key.

Then I went back to the armchair and carried on with my embroidery.

Michael raised his head and said, "I've never known a woman like you."

And then immediately, hastening to forestall me, he added, "How very trite."

I should like to record that until our wedding night I kept my body from Michael.

A few months before his death, my father called me into his room and locked the door behind us. His face was already ravaged by his illness. His cheeks were sunken and his skin was dry and sallow. He looked not at me but at the rug on the floor in front of him, as if he were reading off the rug the words he was to deliver. Father told me about wicked men who seduce women with sweet words and then abandon them to their fate. I was about thirteen at the time. Everything he told me I had already heard from giggling girls and spotty-faced boys. But my father uttered the words not as a joke but on a note of quiet sadness. He formulated his remarks as if the very existence of two distinct sexes was a disorder which multiplied agony in the world, a disorder whose results people must do everything in their power to mitigate. He concluded by saying that if I thought of him in moments of difficulty I might prevent myself from making a wrong decision.

I do not think that this was the real reason why I kept my body from Michael until our wedding night. What the real reason was I do not want to record here. People ought to be very careful when they use the word *reason*. Who told me that? Why, Michael himself. When he put his arms round my shoulders Michael was strong and self-restrained. Perhaps he was shy, like me. He didn't plead with words. His fingers entreated, but they never insisted. He would run his fingers slowly down my back. Then he would remove his hand and look first at his fingers, then at me, at me and at his fingers, as if cautiously comparing one thing with another. My Michael.

· · ·

One evening before I took my leave of Michael to go back to my room (I had less than a week left to live with the Tarnopoler family in Achvah), I said, "Michael, you'll be surprised to learn that I know something about consequent and subsequent streams which perhaps even you don't know. If you're a good boy, one day I'll tell you what I know."

Then I ruffled his hair with my hand: what a hedgehog! What it was I had had in mind I don't know.

One of the last nights, two days before the wedding, I had a frightening dream. Michael and I were in Jericho. We were shopping in the market, between rows of low mud huts. (My father, my brother, and I had been on an outing together to Jericho in 1938. It was during the Feast of Sukkoth. We went on an Arab bus. I was eight. I have not forgotten. My birthday is during Sukkoth.)

Michael and I bought a rug, some ottomans, an ornate sofa. Michael didn't want to buy these things. I chose them and he paid up quietly. The souk in Jericho was noisy and colorful. People were shouting wildly. I walked through the crowd calmly, wearing a casual skirt. There was a terrible, savage sun in the sky, such as I have seen in paintings by van Gogh. Then an army jeep pulled up near us. A short, smart British officer leaped out and tapped Michael on the shoulder. Michael suddenly turned and dashed off like a man possessed, upsetting stalls as he ran till he was swallowed up in the crowd. I was alone. Women screamed. Two men appeared and carried me off in their arms. They were hidden in their flowing robes. Only their eyes showed, glinting. Their grasp was rough and painful. They dragged me down winding roads to the outskirts of the town. The place looked like the steep alleys behind the Street of the Abyssinians in the east of new Jerusalem. I was pushed down a long flight of stairs into a cellar lit by a dirty paraffin lamp. The cellar was black. I was thrown to the ground. I could feel the damp. The air was fetid. Outside I could hear muffled, crazed barking. Suddenly the twins threw off their robes. We were all three the same age. Their house stood opposite ours, across a patch of wasteland, between Katamon and Kiryat Shmuel. They had a courtyard surrounded on all sides. The house was built round the yard. Vines grew up the walls of the villa. The walls were built of the reddish stone that was popular among the richer Arabs in the southern suburbs of Jerusalem.

I was afraid of the twins. They made fun of me. Their teeth were very white. They were dark and lithe. A pair of strong gray wolves. "Michael, Michael," I screamed, but my voice was taken from me. I was dumb. A darkness washed over me. The darkness wanted Michael to come and rescue me only at the end of the pain and the pleasure. If the twins remembered our childhood days, they gave no sign of it. Except their laughter. They leaped up and down on the floor of the cellar as if they were freezing cold. But the air was not cold. They leaped and bounced with seething energy. They effervesced. I couldn't contain my nervous, ugly laughter. Aziz was a little taller than his brother and slightly darker. He ran past me and opened a door I had not noticed. He pointed to the door and bowed a waiter's bow. I was free. I could leave. It was an awful moment. I could have left but I didn't. Then Halil uttered a low, trembling groan and closed and bolted the door. Aziz drew out of the folds of his robe a long, glinting knife. There was a gleam in his eyes. He sank down on all fours. His eyes were blazing. The whites of his eyes were dirty and bloodshot. I retreated and pressed my back against the cellar wall. The wall was filthy. A sticky, putrid moisture soaked through my clothes and touched my skin. With my last strength I screamed.

In the morning my landlady, Mrs. Tarnopoler, came into my room to tell me that I had cried out in my sleep. If Miss Greenbaum cries out in her sleep two nights before her marriage, that is surely a sign of some great trouble. In our dreams we are shown what we must do and what we are forbidden to do. In our dreams we are made to pay the price of all our misdeeds, Mrs. Tarnopoler said. Had she been my mother—she had to say it even if it made me angry with her—she would not have permitted me suddenly to marry some man I happened to have met in the street. I might have chanced to meet someone entirely different, or no one at all! Where would it all lead? To disaster. "You people get married at the spin of a bottle, like in the Purim game. I was married by a shadchan who knew how to bring about what is written in heaven because he knew both the families well and he had examined carefully what the bridegroom was made of and what the bride was made of. After all, your family is what you are. Parents, grandparents, aunts and uncles, brothers and sisters. Just as the well is the water. Tonight, before you go to bed, I'll make you a glass of mint tea. It's a good remedy for a troubled soul. Your worst enemies should have such dreams before their wedding night. All this has come upon you, Miss Greenbaum, because you people get married just like the idolaters in the Bible: a maiden meets a strange man without knowing what he is made of and arranges the terms with him and sets the date for her own wedding as if people were alone in the world."

When Mrs. Tarnopoler said the word *maiden* she smiled a worn-out smile. I did not speak.

9

Michael and I were married in the middle of March. The ceremony took place on the roof terrace of the old Rabbinate building in Jaffa Road, opposite Steimatsky's foreign bookshop, under a cloudy sky of dark gray shapes massed against a bright gray background.

Michael and his father both wore dark gray suits, and each had a white handkerchief in his top pocket. They looked so alike that twice I mistook one for the other. I addressed my husband Michael as Yehezkel.

Michael crushed the traditional glass with a hard stamp. As it broke the glass gave out a dry sound. A low rustle went through the congregation. Aunt Leah wept. My mother also wept.

My brother Emanuel had forgotten to bring a head covering. He spread a checkered handkerchief over his unruly hair. My sister-in-law Rina held me firmly, as though I were likely to faint suddenly. I have not forgotten a thing.

In the evening there was a party in one of the lecture rooms in the Ratisbone Building. Ten years ago, at the time of our wedding, most of the university departments were housed in wings of

Christian convents. The university buildings on Mount Scopus had been cut off from the city as a result of the War of Independence. Long-established Jerusalemites still believed that this was a temporary measure. Political speculation was rife. There was still a great deal of uncertainty.

The room in the Ratisbone Convent in which the party was held was tall and old, and the ceiling was sooty and covered with faded designs in peeling paint. With difficulty I could make out various scenes in the life of Christ, from the Nativity to the Crucifixion. I turned my gaze away from the ceiling.

My mother wore a black dress. It was the dress she had made herself after my father's death in 1943. On this occasion she had pinned a copper brooch on the dress, to mark the distinction between grief and joy. The heavy necklace she was wearing glittered in the light of the ancient lamps.

There were some thirty or forty students at the party. Most of them were geologists, but a few were first-year literature students. My best friend, Hadassah, came with her young husband and gave me a reproduction of a popular painting of an old Yemenite woman as a present. Some of my father's old friends had chipped in to give us a check. My brother Emanuel brought seven young friends from his kibbutz. Their gift was a gilt vase. Emanuel and his friends tried hard to be the life and soul of the party, but the presence of the students disconcerted them.

Two of the young geologists stood up and read out a very long and tiresome duologue based on the sexual connotations of geological strata. The piece was full of bawdy insinuations and double entendres. They were trying to amuse us.

Sarah Zeldin from the kindergarten, looking ancient and wrinkled, brought us a tea set. Every piece had a picture of a pair of lovers dressed in blue, and a gold line around the rim. She embraced my mother and they kissed each other. They conversed in Yiddish and their heads nodded up and down continuously.

Michael's four aunts, his father's sisters, stood round a table laden with sandwiches and chatted busily about me. They did not trouble to lower their voices. They did not like me. All these years Michael had been a responsible and well-organized boy, and now he was getting married with a haste that was bound to cause vulgar gossip. Six years Aunt Jenia had been engaged in Kovno, six years before she had finally married her first husband. The details of the vulgar gossip that our haste would cause the four aunts discussed in Polish.

My brother and his friends from the kibbutz drank too much. They were noisy. They sang rowdy variations on a well-known drinking song. They amused the girls until their laughter lapsed into shrieks and giggles. A girl from the geology department, Yardena by name, with bright blond hair and sequins all over her dress, kicked off her shoes and started dancing a furious Spanish dance on her own. The other guests accompanied her with a rhythmic clapping. My brother Emanuel smashed a bottle of orange juice in her honor. Then Yardena got up on a chair and, holding a full liqueur glass, sang a popular American song about disappointed love.

There is another incident I must record: At the end of the party my husband tried to deliver a surprise kiss on the back of my neck. He crept up on me from behind. Perhaps his fellow students had put the idea into his head. At that moment I happened to be holding a glass of wine that my brother had thrust into my hand. When Michael's lips touched my neck I jumped, and the wine was spilt on my white wedding dress. Some also fell on Aunt Jenia's brown suit. What is so important about this detail? Ever since the morning when my landlady, Mrs. Tarnopoler, had spoken to me after I cried out in my sleep I had been beset by hints and signs. Just like my father. My father was an attentive man. He went through life as if it were a preliminary course in which one learns a lesson and stores up experience.

Whoever Moves Toward the Light Moves Toward the Holy City

from "Crusade," in *Unto Death* (1971)

5

A few times it happened that darkness fell while they were still in the depths of the forest. Then they would light a great fire in the middle and surround the camp with a close circle of small bonfires for fear of vampires, wolves, and demons.

If one looked upward one could see how the light of the fire was broken by the thick ceiling of leaves. Round about, wolves howled, foxes' eyes glinted, an evil bird screeched. Or was it the wind. Or sinister imitations of the sound of fox, bird, and wind. Even the rustling of fallen leaves hinted at the certainty of another, a hostile camp whispering round about us and hedging us in. The forces of grace were being besieged.

The first signs of an approaching conflict were concrete enough. Dogs would go mad now and again and have to be put down with an arrow or a spear-thrust. A horse suddenly broke its halter in the night and galloped off into the wild darkness as if it had chosen to turn wolf. One of the whores who had attached herself to the army burst into shrieks and did not stop screaming for two days and three nights, under the influence of some spell or incubus. In the end they were compelled to abandon her to the devil who had seized hold of her. One day the Christians came to a spring, and, being parched, they drank and let their horses and servants drink, not realizing that the water was polluted. It inflicted humiliating agonies on man and beast alike. Surely a Jew had mingled with the Christians in disguise, was walking along the way with us, and cursing us.

Even the villagers received us grimly. The travelers were compelled to extract provisions, women, and drink from the stubborn peasants by force of arms. Once or twice stiff skirmishes broke out in the villages and Christian blood was spilt in vain. The parsimony of these districts was coarse and sullen. Even for an expedition of knights traveling in the name of Jesus Christ to deliver the Holy Land the villagers would not open their fists, without a stroke of the sword to extract charity by force from their clenched grasp.

And yet in several villages there were women who came of their own volition after dark and silently offered their bodies. These village women were huge and strong as horses. Their silence during the act, their stiff, stolid submission, was open to several interpretations—pride or modesty, dullness or rebellion. Claude, assailed by glimmerings of fevered fanaticism, would try his strength by admonishing these peasant women. He would rise and stand before them and speak with ecstatic piety of the Kingdom of Heaven, the corrupt nature of the flesh, of the happiness in store for those who give all with a cheerful spirit, for to him that giveth shall be given, and compassion shall be shown to him that hath compassion.

Who can tell the number of those scattered villages on the fringes of the forest, in valleys without so much as a name, in great gorges swathed in mist, in the winding courses of forgotten brooks and streams? "It is God's will," writes Claude in his chronicle of the journey, "to scatter His flock to the ends of the earth so as to gather to His bosom once more on the Day of Judgment the few, the elect, the truly deserving."

As for the Count, he drove his men just as he drove his mare Mistral. He did not give them his attention, yet his presence could not be forgotten for a moment. In his heart he was lonely. Remote from his fellow men. Remote from his surroundings, a stranger to the forest, ice cold. And now, in its remoteness, this soul would converse with itself on the necessity of love. To love, to be loved, to belong, to be—Guillaume de Touron felt a wild desire to overpower or crush some obstacle whose nature was hidden from him until the day when he would be permitted to be born anew. His shattered thoughts played with various images of death, of alienation, of breaking through. Like a drowning man struggling with his last reserves of strength to free himself from the grip of the water. But he did not know what the water was or how far it stretched.

Outwardly he merely seemed silent and watchful. Straining his senses to the utmost, in the hope of hearing a voice. Afraid to open his mouth and speak, lest he should miss the voice: he who speaks cannot listen. And yet Guillaume de Touron was endowed with a strange power over others. Despite his silence, he overran and choked everyone around him like a great creeper. Without intending to, he grasped and clung to everything, leaned on it with all his weight. It was a false impression that Count Guillaume de Touron, as often befalls men of his class, was a withdrawn and hesitant master, showing no reaction when his servants ran wild. A second glance would show that the reeds on which he leaned bent beneath him, while he, by the mere force of his nature, twisted and crushed them unawares.

From time to time he would conjure up an image of Jerusalem, drawing ever closer, but he would dismiss these inner visions, for they brought him no satisfaction.

In camp, at prayer, as they drank from the cask or from mountain streams, Guillaume de Touron would cast a gloomy eye over each man in turn, trying again and again to detect the hidden Jew.

By now his first suspicions had turned to utter certainty, as happens sometimes to a man who seems to hear in the distance a vague, menacing tune which causes him to wonder whether or not it is really there. After a while, from the effort of listening, the tune begins to lead the listener astray, to come suddenly from inside him, from his very innards.

He surveyed his men, every single one of them, their expressions and gestures, eating, at play, in sleep, and on horseback. Is there any reason in looking for signs in the sensible sphere? And what is Jewish in a Jew—surely not any outward shape or form but some abstract quality. The contrast does not lie even in the affections of the soul. Simply this: a terrible, a malignant presence. Is not this the essence of treachery: to penetrate, to be within, to interfuse, to put out roots, and to flourish in what is most delicate. Like love, like carnal union. There is a Jew in our midst. Perhaps he has divided himself up and insinuated himself partly here, partly there, so that not a man among us has escaped contagion.

Once, when the army had halted toward evening beside a Roman ruin whose remains were being eaten away by decay and strong roots, the Count turned to Claude Crookback with a question: Is it not written in one of those books that a wolf can insinuate himself so successfully into a flock of sheep that even a hunter cannot recognize him?

Claude's reply, perhaps in a slightly improved version, appears in his chronicle:

"I replied to this question from my lord the Count by means of a simple parable or allegory, in the spirit of the wisdom of the ancients. The sweetest apple is always the first to turn rotten. A wolf in sheep's clothing would naturally exaggerate his disguise. This is a sign for us: Who was it who embraced our Savior and kissed His cheek and reveled in honeyed words and signs of love, if not he who had sold him for thirty pieces of silver, the traitor Judas Iscariot. The Devil is cunning, my lord, cunning and insidious, and we Christians are men of innocence. Without the grace of Heaven we are trapped, every one of us, in the snare set at our feet."

6

Among them there was a piper, Andrés Alvárez by name. He was devoted to the slaves and outcasts and harlots and believed in the power of his music to soften even the most unruly spirit. He even experimented with the horses and dogs. He had forsworn meat and wine, and wore a heavy stone on a chain round his neck to humble himself to the dust, for he thought of himself as "meek and lowly." Perhaps he was trying to purge his body of some sin he had committed or had intended to commit a long time before. He nicknamed himself "Worthy of Death," and wanted to be killed on the road to Jerusalem. Suspicion fell on this man. He was ordered to pass his hand through the fire so that it could be ascertained what he was. Because of his terror, and perhaps indeed out of joy at the purifying ordeal which lay ahead, he was seized with great excitement and was bathed in sweat. When he passed his hand through the fire, it was as wet as if it had been soaked in water, so that he was only slightly scorched, and the verdicts were divided. But seeing that this Andrés pleaded with the Count to be put to death because he was tainted with impurity, they spared him and let him live so that he could be kept under further observation.

There were also three Celts, who were half brothers. They were the sons of one woman by three different fathers. These three displayed an unwholesome disposition to burst into horrifying laughter at things that were no laughing matter, such as a dead fox, the stump of an oak struck by lightning, or a sobbing woman. They were also in the habit of lighting a small fire of their own at night and huddling around it secretively, talking all the time in an unknown language, full of harsh consonants.

Every Sunday the three half brothers would celebrate an esoteric rite. Piling up heaps of stones, they would wring the neck of a bird and pour out its blood into a fire that they had lit in the hollow of the stones. Perhaps they used to conjure up by this means the soul of their mother.

The Celtic brothers were also gifted with extraordinary powers of marksmanship, which did more than anything else to attract to them the icy glances of the Count. Expertly they would amuse themselves by fixing an arrow into the air and piercing it with another in mid-flight. Several times they hurled a stone in the dark and brought down a night bird, guided by the sound of its wingbeats alone.

One evening Claude Crookback was sent to tell them to moderate their laughter, as befits men on a holy mission, to stop talking among themselves in their pagan tongue, and to allow him to inspect their baggage. In addition, Claude resolved inwardly to find a suitable opportunity to examine each of them while they were passing water so as to make certain that none of them was circumcised.

Claude himself, it must be admitted, loved these errands, because he felt himself humiliated by them. For the humble shall be exalted and the lowly of spirit shall be raised up.

From Grenoble the expedition continued to move slowly eastward.

The Count chose to keep away from the main roads. He was attracted to forgotten regions. Sometimes he even decided to abandon the lanes and to cut across the heathland and forest. It was not the shortest route that he preferred, but the most forsaken. In practice, Guillaume de Touron set his course afresh every morning: he simply rode in the direction of the sunrise and continued riding until the rays of the setting sun struck his helmet from behind. He put a simple explanation on the laws of the universe: whoever moves toward the light moves toward the Holy City. Insofar as it was granted to this weary soul to feel love, he loved Jerusalem. He firmly believed that in Jerusalem it is possible to die and be born again pure.

And so, while the autumn beat on their backs with fists soft as a caress, the travelers crossed the foothills of the mountains, felt their way through misty glens, and gradually advanced down the slopes toward the valley of the river Po. There was not a man among them who had ever seen the sea. Perhaps they imagined that it would appear to them as an exceedingly broad river, that if they strained their eyes they would see the opposite shore and discern the suggested outline of towers, walls, lofty steeples, a high halo of light, a holy brightness hovering over the City of God on the other side.

Meanwhile, all along the way, they sustained themselves on what the villagers offered them at the sight of the sword. They made detours around the towns and the estates of noblemen, as if they were constantly avoiding an outstretched net.

Several times on the road they met other companies of knights also making their way to the Holy Land. The Count was not willing to join those who were greater than himself and would not condescend to annex to his band those who were smaller. As they had set out from their own land, so he wanted them to arrive at the Holy City: few but pure.

. . .

One day they were almost compelled to hew their way by force of arms. Near a small village by the name of Argentera, beside the well on the way into the village, Guillaume de Touron was surprised to come across a heavy force of crusaders, at least three times as large as his own band. These were Teutonic knights with a large crowd of followers, and at their head was a young knight, fair of face and haughty of mien, Albrecht of Brunswick by name.

This was a magnificent expedition: respectable matrons borne in litters curtained with silk, a company of elderly lords in costumes of scarlet, gold-buttoned, a company of young lords wearing long, pointed helmets tipped with a silver cross, attendants decked out in velvet liveries, banners and standards carried by scar-faced standard-bearers. There were also crowds of priests, jesters, and easy women, beasts and animals. All this great abundance was carried in broad wagons the likes of which have not been seen in our country. The sides of the wagons were painted with detailed scenes from the lives of Our Lord and His Apostles, all of whom the artist had chosen to portray with stern expressions.

Albrecht of Brunswick deigned to dismount first and present himself to the lesser lord. He delivered himself of a long succession of greetings in florid Latin. He also uttered words of enticement. It was clear that he proposed to take this smaller party that had crossed his path under his wing. But when, after the formulas of greeting were finished, Guillaume de Touron maintained a frigid reserve and refrained from fulfilling the obligations of Christian fellowship, even responding to his greetings as though they were also farewells, the German smiled a faint smile and gave orders to unseat the stranger from his horse and to annex his band by force.

Before he had finished issuing the order there was a clatter as every sword was drawn. Horses began to rear and neigh, and their skins rippled like pools of water in a breeze. A great movement took hold of the men and glittered on spears and helmets. Instantly the band raised their instruments and started to play with fierce joy. Wild yet spectacular was the sudden melee of horses, banners, and accoutrements, dust, shouts, and war cries, as if a colorful dance had suddenly broken loose on those gloomy plains. Even the cries of the first casualties of battle resembled from a distance the clamor of reveling merrymakers. Everyone, even the dying men, faithfully maintained a certain style, from which they would not depart by a hair's breadth.

And so, quite soon, the knight from Brunswick said, "Stay," and the herald called, "Stay."

At once Guillaume de Touron, too, raised his visor. The music stopped and the fighting died down. The men stood where they were, breathing heavily, trying to calm their quaking mounts. Soon they began to drink, and to offer one another German ale and Avignon wine from hairy flasks. The musicians, of their own accord, immediately began to play a different tune. While the officers were still busy separating the last hot-blooded skirmishers, laughter had spread all around; the warriors blasphemed and laughed.

Among the Germans there was a holy physician. He and his assistants went through the battlefield and picked out the wounded from the dead. He tended the wounded on both sides and the dead were cast all together into the well, after sufficient water had been drawn for everyone's needs. The casualties totaled fewer than a dozen dead, all from the lower elements on both sides, and their deaths did not mar the feelings of brotherhood that quickly sprang up of their own accord around common campfires. Those who forgive shall be themselves forgiven. As evening fell the priests celebrated a great Mass, and in the night both sides together slaughtered cattle, said grace, and ate and drank. Toward dawn they exchanged maidservants.

And so Claude Crookback, drunk and foam-flecked, was sent to appease the knight from Brunswick with fifty pieces of silver as a toll and the price of peace, since Guillaume de Touron and his men were the smaller party.

Later, as the sun rose, Christian knight saluted Christian knight and both groups went their separate ways, holding high their banners and waving adieu. If sins had been committed, surely blood, prayer, and silver had made atonement. And the rain that came late in the morning, a very light and gentle rain, wiped everything away with its transparent fingers.

7

Next day they came upon a Jewish peddler by the wayside. He had a pair of goats with him, and on his back was a knapsack. As the horsemen came downhill toward him he made no attempt to hide. He doffed his cap, smiled with all his might, and bowed three times, each time lower than the last. The procession drew to a halt. The Jew, too, stopped, and laid his sack on the ground. The Christians were silent. The wayfarer, too, kept silent and did not dare to utter a word. So he stood, by the side of the road, prepared to buy or to sell, to be slain or to deliver a polite reply to any remark which might be addressed to him. And he smiled with extreme concentration.

Claude Crookback said, "Jew."

The Jew said, "Greetings, travelers. May your journey be blessed with success." And immediately he tried again in another dialect and in another language, for he did not know which was their tongue.

Claude Crookback said, "Jew, where are you going?" And without waiting for a reply he added in a honeyed whisper, "The sack. Open that sack."

Before he had stopped speaking the three Celtic half brothers suddenly burst into shrill, loud laughter, very wild but entirely free of malice, as if they were being tickled under the armpits. The peddler opened his sack, bent down, and drew out an armful of knickknacks and gewgaws of the kind that are made to amuse small children, and said very happily, "Everything cheap. Everything for coppers. Or we can arrange an exchange, for things no one wants anymore."

Claude asked, "Why are you traveling, Jew? What makes you go from place to place?"

The Jew said, "Are we alone in the world, gracious knight? Can a man choose for himself to go or not to go?"

Whereupon there was a silence. Even the Celtic brothers fell quiet. As if of her own accord, the mare Mistral moved forward and carried the Count into the center of the ring of horsemen. The smell of the horses' sweat spread around, pungent and menacing. The silence became more and more intense. A secret terror suddenly seized hold of the two goats, which were held by the Jew on a rope in his hand. Perhaps the stench of the horses brought them a premonition of evil, and the goats were alarmed. A twin bleating broke out, piercing and shrill as the ripping of cloth, as if a baby were being scorched by flames.

At this, all restraint was shattered. The Jew kicked one of the goats sharply, and Claude kicked the Jew. The peddler suddenly began giggling with all his might, his mouth gaping open from cheek to cheek. Then, radiating a politeness which was not of this world, he wiped his eyes dry with his sleeve and entreated the knights to accept everything, the goats and the merchandise, as a free gift in perpetuity, because men of every faith are ordered to love their fellow men, and there is one God over all of us. So he spoke, and his smile beneath his beard showed red as a wound. Count Guillaume de Touron made a sign with his finger that the gift should be accepted. The goats were taken, the sack was taken, and silence fell once more. Claude slowly raised his eyes toward the Count. The Count was gazing at the treetops, or through them to the patches of sky beyond. A whisper passed through the trees, thought better of it, and instantly fell quiet. Suddenly the Jew thrust his hand into the folds of his clothing and brought out a small packet.

"Take the money, too," said the Jew, and held the packet out toward the Count. The knight took the packet with a weary gesture, closed his hand round it, and concentrated his gaze as if trying hard to discover what hint the shabby cloth held for him. There was a remote sadness at that moment in Guillaume de Touron's gaze. It was as if he were searching for something in the depths of his soul while being gradually shrouded in darkness. Perhaps he was filled with sorrow for himself. Finally he spoke, and he said with suppressed pain verging on warmth, "Claude."

Claude said, "This is a Jew."

The peddler said, "I have given you everything and now I shall go happily on my way and bless you."

Claude said, "Now you shall not go and you shall not bless us."

The peddler said, "You are going to kill me."

He said this without fear and without surprise, but rather like a man who has been searching in vain for a complicated solution to a complicated problem and suddenly discovers a simple solution. And Claude Crookback replied softly, "Thou sayest."

Once again silence filled the air. In the silence birds sang. Infected with the autumn, the land stretched to the farthest distance, quiet and broad, quiet and cold. The Jew moved his head up and down a few times, concentrating, contemplating, looking as if he wanted to ask a question. And finally he asked, "How?"

"Go," said Guillaume de Touron.

A moment later, as if mistrusting his voice, he wearily repeated, "Go."

The Jewish peddler stood as if he had not heard. He began to speak, and thought better of it. He raised his arms wide, and let them drop. He turned. He walked slowly downhill as though he still carried the heavy sack on his back. He did not look around. Cautiously he quickened his pace. Then, as he neared a bend in the road, he began to run, slowly, cunningly, bent forward, dragging his feet like a sick man about to stumble and fall.

But when he reached the bend he gave a sudden bound and redoubled his pace, disappearing now with amazing speed, tracing with great care a zigzag course, and did not stop running even after the arrow hit him and lodged in his back between his shoulders. Then he stopped, twisted his arm round behind him, drew the arrow out of his flesh, and stood rocking backward and forward, holding the arrow before his eyes with both hands, as if a careful inspection were demanded of him. He stood staring at it until a second arrow dislodged the first from his grasp and pierced his forehead. Even now he stood where he was, and the arrow in his head stuck out in front, so that he looked like a stubborn ram, lowering his head to butt, his feet set firmly in the dust. Then the Jew uttered a single cry, not long and not very loud, and, as though he had finally decided to give in, he collapsed and fell on his back. He lay there without a tremor or a shudder.

The procession began to move on. Andrés Alvárez, the piper, traced a large cross with his finger over the fields and the forest and the expanse of sky. The women who followed the expedition stood for a moment beside the body, now growing cold, and one of them bent down and covered his face with the hem of his robe. Blood clung to the palms of her hands and the woman began to sob. Claude Crookback, who had moved for once to the rear of the procession, was overcome with a terrible compassion and walked behind the woman, comforting her in a soft voice with pious phrases, and so the two of them found some peace. In addition, that night they opened the peddler's sack and among a mass of old rags they discovered bracelets and earrings and women's sandals the likes of which had never been seen in the region of Avignon, extraordinarily beautiful, which could be fastened and unfastened by means of a perfectly charming and fascinating yet simple little catch.

8

Autumn, a gray and patient monk, sent out silent, icy fingers and smoothed the face of the land. Cold winds began to blow down from the mountains to the north. They penetrated every covering, and the flesh stiffened at their touch. In several places, toward dawn a fine, clear crust of ice had already begun to coat the surface of the water. The men's breath froze, caught in the hairs of their beards; their lips turned blue and cracked.

But the heavy rains of winter still held back, and the Count still hoped to reach the coast before all the roads became waterlogged. The sea held out the promise of a change, of some kind of a break. He looked forward to beholding in the sea the reflection of the Holy City, bristling with tall, insubstantial towers, glowing white as warm ice, ringed around with rocky crags and deserts, bathed in bright sunlight—and behind this light another light.

And yet sometimes the heart is smitten by a strange hesitation: Does Jerusalem really exist on the face of the earth, or is she perhaps nothing but a pure idea, which anyone who sets out to find in the substance will lose altogether?

They were passing through a monotonous gray landscape, like a long, low corridor. The melancholy of the frozen orchards around the villages was silent and terrible. To the outward eye all these plains stood open on every side as far as the horizon. And yet it was all blindly shuttered, and the travelers traveled on and on, and there was no way out.

Everything was overpowered by the fall. Sometimes the expedition marched for hours and hours on a moldering carpet of dead leaves. A venomous gloom took hold of men and beasts alike, a hidden, desperate gloom from which death itself would have come as a blessed relief. This soft, foul carpet, made up of rotting apple leaves and decomposing fodder, rustled crisply underfoot, producing a dull, monotonous melody that after a few hours imposed on knight and peasant alike a mood of silent madness.

So, like an inexorable nightmare, the silent procession advanced day after day over vast tracts of imaginary desert, which at every gust of wind and every footstep sighed and murmured. The soul's lifeblood was on the point of shriveling and disintegrating.

No one now doubted the hidden presence of a Jew in the company. In camp at night servants and knights alike kept watch on one another, feigning sleep, starting at each footfall, craning to catch every sigh or whisper, crying out in their sleep, striving to decipher the cries of other sleepers. There were occasional brawls, and some took the precaution of sleeping with a knife clutched in their hand. Secret conspiracies were formed, allegations were made, and everyone girded himself with silence. A few vanished in the night and never reappeared. A servant slit the throat of another servant, was betrayed and beaten to death. Andrés Alvárez played on his pipe, but even his cheerful tunes tore at the heart and heightened the mood of despair.

All along the way there rose the stench of squalid villages. The cloying scent of a horse's rotting carcass or the putrid odor of a man's corpse decomposing in a field. Overhead stretched low, thick skies whose grayish hues strained toward a deeper shade of black.

In this envenomed world even the echo of distant bells was turned to keening. Such solitary birds as still remained stood motionless on the tips of wet branches, as if being gradually absorbed into the realm of the inanimate.

They crossed overgrown graveyards, trampling over gravestones coated with moss and lichen, sunk into the embrace of the heavy earth. At the head of these stones stood rough, crooked crosses, two sticks of wood held together by a wooden rivet. Those moldy crosses would crumble at a slight touch.

When the expedition halted at water holes to draw water, those who peered into the depths of the water might have caught sight of an element that was not water.

Far, far away on the steep mountain slopes, one could see, for an instant, between patches of streaming mist, the vague outlines of stone-built fortifications — lingering monasteries, perhaps, or the remains of ancient castles ruined even before the coming of the Faith. Below them the river and its tributaries rushed furiously in their tangled courses, as if they, too, were desperately trying to escape.

Over everything there came at dusk a desolate, sinister power of incredible malignity, the screeching of birds of prey or wildcats. These regions were gradually being coated in rust, rotting with it to the point of death. And so Jerusalem ceased to be regarded as a destination, as the arena of glorious deeds. A change took place. Men would break the long silence to say "in Jerusalem."

And one man among them began to realize, with the gradual dawning of an inner illumination, that the Jerusalem they were seeking was not a city but the last hope of a guttering vitality.

9

This chapter of Claude's chronicle bears unambiguous witness to the force of the destructive powers which continuously emanated from the hidden presence of a malicious element that had insinuated itself

among the crusaders. No longer content with an external watch, they now appointed an internal watch as well. A few knights were detailed to eavesdrop unobtrusively. Others were instructed to keep watch on these. Claude Crookback was in a position to keep those whom he mistrusted away from the Count's presence and to surround him with those who met with his favor. Conspiracies, false accusations, and secret intrigues were rampant. In this thick, dank atmosphere of suspicion and malignant terror Claude blossomed and flourished like some swamp plant. And yet he, too, was infected by the thickening fear.

Claude wrote:

"There is a stranger in our midst. Every night as we all call on the name of Jesus Christ one of us calls with a false voice, and that man is Christ's enemy. One night, in the third watch, a hidden hand extinguished all the fires, and in the darkness there came a shout in a language that was not the language of Christian men. An enemy of Christ is concealed among us, a wolf among God's flock. That same hand that put out the fires in the night is also killing our horses, which are dying in agony one after another from an ailment that is completely unknown in our land. As we approach the villages, the villagers are warned in advance to conceal their provisions, their women, and their horses in the forest. The Jews everywhere sense our approach, and the countryside, which is hostile to us, shelters them. There is an evil in our midst. Someone among us is not one of us. He has been sent to deliver us up to the forces of defilement. O God, have mercy upon us, grant us a sign before we all perish, body and soul. Is it not for Thy sake that we walk this path of hardship and suffering? Is it not to Thy City that we are journeying—and if we do not end there, where shall we end?

"The spirit of our men is already weakened by fear of the intrigue that is being fomented in our midst, and there are some on the fringes of our contingent who are planning to turn back the remaining horses and return home empty-handed. Our lord Guillaume de Touron now rides all alone some way ahead of the party and no longer looks around, as if it is all one to him whether the others are still following him or not, as if he is traveling on alone to Jerusalem.

"Three mornings ago the Count drew up all the travelers in a row, beginning with the knights and concluding with the servants, the hangers-on, and the women, and subjected everyone to a penetrating scrutiny. He ended by suddenly calling on the Jew to fall to his knees at that instant, in that very spot, whoever he might be. Then, in total silence, he turned his back on the men and mounted his mare, slowly, as if he were ill. At first light the next day one of the women was found with her throat cut and with the point of the cross she wore around her neck buried in her breast. It was I myself who closed her eyes and drew the pointed cross out of her flesh, without wiping the blood off it. O God, whither art Thou leading Thy flock, and what will become of us tomorrow and the day after?"

And again Claude writes in his chronicle, in a spirit of humility and submission to divine judgment:

"In the course of this morning my lord the Count summoned me to follow him to the other side of a hillock. When we were out of sight of eavesdroppers my lord said to me, 'Claude, you know: why do you keep silent?' And I swore in the name of Christ, and in the name of my lord's late sister, who was my father's wife before he married my mother, I swore that I did not know, and that I was very much afraid. Then my lord the Count continued in a voice at whose memory my heart is rent with love and terror, 'Claude — are you really Claude?'

"I record here the words with which I have cried out to God all day: O God, behold us. We are being consumed by evil. Deliver us, O Lord; Thou hearest and Thou canst prevail. Sinners though we be, have compassion upon us. Is it not toward Thee that we are journeying day and night?"

Happy is the man who pours his heart out in his prayer: even if he cry out of the depths his prayer is answered.

A few days later, when the expedition had made a detour round the walls of Tortona and was pressing on eastward, the plague left the horses and the weather grew slightly warmer. The farmers surrendered large numbers of horses that sufficed for riding until better ones could be found. In one of the villages the three Celts succeeded in sniffing out great hoards of good provisions, cheeses and rye and fodder, all in one cellar, with hardly any bloodshed. Along the way we came upon two mule drivers carrying casks of wine, and we enjoyed the wine for several days. We also met a mendicant monk who sprinkled us with holy water and renewed the blessings of the Church.

And so it seemed as if our fortunes had taken a turn for the better. We did not stint our prayers and thanksgivings. Even the winter rains not only continued to hold off but even receded into the distance; for four days a benevolent sun shone down upon us. The Count distributed silver coins. The sound of singing was heard again as we set out in the morning, and Andrés Alvárez, the piper, played us merry tunes on his pipe. And at the same time we began to draw nearer to communities of Jews.

10

We began to draw nearer to communities of Jews, and our days grew brighter. Activity brought with it a new spirit: discipline improved, and industry and inventiveness reappeared among us. Some of the blazes we lit fired our hearts with joy, and the thrill of the hunt roused our slumbering senses.

We were not too ambitious. We left the Jews of the towns to stronger contingents. Count Guillaume de Touron merely passed through the remoter districts, clearing, as it were, the outer extremities of the ground — the Jews of a forgotten village or a wayside inn, or a mill hidden in a valley. Thus there fell into his hands small bands of Jews of the runaway or wandering variety. Even so, the expedition did not interrupt its eastward progress, and did not turn aside to track down fugitives or to scent out booty. They plowed a single, straight furrow, not too broad. They did not even pause to look back and see what had been accomplished and what remained to be done. The Count imposed a strict discipline on his men and refrained from lusting after bloodshed. That is not to say that they

avoided plunder, only that the Count forbade his men to take pleasure in it—and the suppressed pleasure whispered seductively.

Claude mentions in his narrative one Jewish woman, resembling a she-wolf, who, with her baby, was rooted out of her lair in the depths of a haystack. She snarled, and her fangs were whiter and sharper than human teeth. She hissed violently, as if she meant to bite or spit venom. Her breast heaved under her brown dress with a turbulence such as Claude had witnessed before only in the throes of physical ecstasy or in women who had seen a vision of a saint demanding that they throw themselves on the fire.

This Jewess even managed to keep at bay the ring of Christians who had closed around her. Not a man dared to approach within reach of claw or tooth. She stood alone in the center, and her face wore an expression which resembled a yawn. A second glance showed that this was no yawn.

She began to wheel around slowly, bent over, the baby clutched in the claws of one hand, the other hand held out in front, the fingers hooked like the talons of a bird of prey. Her movement suggested that of a scorpion or a crab. Even if Claude imagined that this Jewess was about to pounce and tear out their eyes with her nails, she did not do so. Instead, she suddenly hurled her screaming child into the arms of the youngest of the three Celts and threw herself down, rolling in the dust as if she had already been slaughtered. She did all this in complete silence, without pleading or crying, but in a fierce convulsion. Claude Crookback struggled with all his might to suppress the sobs rising in his throat. A blind, feverish urge almost forced him to fall to the ground and roll in the dust like her and kiss the soles of her feet and be trampled on by the soles of her feet. This urge burned in his veins like a flaming fury, and yet it was not fury. Hot tears ran down his beard as he put this she-wolf out of her misery with a short, sharp blow, thus sparing her the agonies of a long-drawn-out death and relieving her of the ugly sight of the crushing of the child's head, a sight both sordid and distasteful to a sensitive soul.

. . .

The region was dotted with Jewish communities. There were some towns here that had opened their doors wide to them, in defiance of the ancient curse. These Jews had put down deep roots to drink the innermost sap, and were flourishing vigorously. They were endowed with prodigious powers of suckling and growing. In these villages numerous families of Jews had spread, buying and selling, hiring and letting. They had a total monopoly on the oil and flax. Slowly, calculating and relentless, they were expanding into wool and wax, putting out feelers toward perfumes and ales, timber and spices.

Outwardly they were calm, but a closer inspection would have betrayed a nervous muscular spasm in their faces, like the ripples on the skin of a deer standing in feigned repose, poised for flight. Our language flowed from the mouths of these Jews as smooth as oil. Our silver seemed to pass into their hands of its own accord, following the natural tendency of things to roll downhill.

Thus the Jews were past masters at gathering and hoarding, exchanging one thing for another at a favorable moment and concealing one thing inside another in times of apprehension. They seemed devilishly dexterous, evasive by the very nature of their breed. The ground seemed to become pliant under their feet, and they exuded over everything around them a kind of sticky, transparent resin. They could arouse in the Christians sympathy or confidence, terror or amusement at their will. They were the pipers and we were the pipe in their hands, we were the dancing bear.

Many peasants in these regions put their faith in the Jews. Knights enticed followers to accompany them to Jerusalem with silver borrowed from the Jews. The wounds of our Lord and Savior opened anew at the sight, and His blood was spilled afresh. Even great lords, even priests and bishops were accustomed in these parts to invite Jews into their very hearths, and unawares they slowly sold their souls. Some even trusted the Jews with power. So it happened that hereabouts certain Jews had risen to such heights as to be able to exercise power behind the scenes, and to pass on moral contagion to the Christians. Twice Guillaume de Touron's band was met on the way by armed guards or even tainted priests, their swords raised as a barrier between him and the Jews, setting at nought God's curse.

In short, these Jews had raised up a shadow Judaea at the foot of the Cross, spreading all around, extending the reign of hostile forces into Christian lands. To borrow a simile that recurs several times in Claude Crookback's chronicle, the Jews were like a band of strange minstrels wandering noisily through a primeval forest. Undoubtedly there was some sweet and desolate enchantment in their music, but the forest had a music of its own, deep and dim, and it would not tolerate for long another tune.

One day Guillaume de Touron rode at the head of his men into a group of hovels that were inhabited by Jews, on the edge of a small village called Ariogolo.

As often happened, the Jews had scented what was coming and had escaped into the forest. A single spokesman came to meet the knights, to negotiate a ransom and to obtain sympathy. He also wanted to rescue from the fire a house full of old books, some of which, he claimed, were a thousand years old. Jewish books, written backward.

This man was lean and lanky; his beard was fair and his shoulders strong. Even in his manner there was nothing to suggest his base origin. His movements were few and economical, he seemed calm, and he spoke in the measured tones of one who loves words and is their master. He came out of the house toward the leading horsemen and inquired who was in command. Before they had time to speak or move, his glance rested on the Count and he said, "He is the one." Then he strode boldly between the horses, almost brushing them with his shoulders, took up his stand in front of our lord Guillaume de Touron, and said, "I was looking for you, my lord. This is your expedition."

The knight squinted, weighing with his glance the figure before him, and immediately perceived the strength of his determination. He twisted his lips and said, "You were looking for me."

"I was looking for you, my lord."

"What are you offering, Jew, and what do you want to take?"

"A house full of holy books. And if you are in great need of money, then all the rest of our houses. Payment in cash."

A faint smile, grim and rare, passed over Guillaume de Touron's face and vanished. For an instant a peasantlike expression, full of greed and loathing, played around his lips. Then his glance froze. Coldly he said, "Gold. Copper coin has no currency in the places to which I am going."

The man said, "Great quantities of gold."

Guillaume de Touron said, "You, Jew, stand on the house that you want to save from the fire, and the fire, by God's grace, will choose what to consume and what to leave untouched."

The Jew said, "Very well. You set fire to the southern side. The wind is blowing from the north. By God's grace there is a broad stream in between. The fire, as you say, will choose, by God's grace, what to consume and what to leave untouched."

The Count paused. Once again a dry smile flitted across his face. Then, twice as stern, he said, "My dear Jew, you are not afraid. Why are you not afraid of me?"

As if with a sudden sympathy the Jew uttered a short, bright laugh, carefully modulated by deep insight, and answered, "I am giving, my lord, and you want to take."

"And if I take and then kill and burn?"

"But you will swear, my lord, in the name of your Savior. Before you swear you shall not see the gold."

"And if I take by force, Jew?"

"You and I, my lord, are in the hands of a power which is greater than you or me."

"Well then," said Guillaume de Touron, in a dark tone of voice. "Well then, give me the gold. Right away. You have spoken long enough. Give it to me now."

As the Count uttered these words the nearest horsemen began to touch the Jew lightly with the tips of their lances, as if testing the thickness of the bark on a tree trunk.

The man said, "The gold is buried in the field and the spot is buried in my heart."

Guillaume de Touron said, "Then get up and go to the place. Now."

The Jew shook his head in resignation, as if disappointed at the clumsy narrow-mindedness displayed by his interlocutor. He said with exaggerated deliberateness, in the tone one would use with a stubborn peasant, "But my lord, I have not yet had your lordship's oath. Your time is short and your way is long."

"Go," said the Count. "Go and lead me to the house you spoke of."

The handsome Jew motioned with his chin. "That is the one. The books are there."

The knight raised his voice slightly, and, calling to Claude Crookback, he said, "Claude, have that house and all the houses burnt, and see that the Jew is not killed quickly, but slowly and patiently, and meanwhile tell them to turn the horses out into the field to graze and to send the servants down to the river to wash themselves before Mass—yesterday they stank to high heaven."

They began to beat the Jew at noon. Toward evening they branded him with red-hot irons. Then they soused him in salt water and asked him about Judas and Pontius Pilate and Caiaphas. They took him out of the salt water and crushed his testicles, as Claude had read in one of the books when he was a boy, and as it was written in the same book they made him drink the salty water in which he had been immersed. Later, when they were dealing with his fingers, they questioned him on the subject of the types and allegories of Jesus Christ of which the Old Testament is full. As the twilight came on they put out both his eyes, and then, finally, he opened his mouth and asked them whether, if he showed them the place where the treasure was buried, they would promise to kill him instantly, and Claude Crookback gave his word.

In the dark the treasure was dug up, and it turned out that the Jew had not lied and the treasure was very rich indeed. Then the Count told Claude to carry out his promise. The hour, he said, was advanced, and it was not fitting to delay vespers any longer, because the fire, which had burned right through the village, was dying down and the smoke was interfering with their breathing and making their eyes smart. And so they thrust a lance through the tortured body from back to chest. But the Jew went on crawling blindly hither and thither, and his blood spurted out, and he continued murmuring. So they beat him over the head with an ax haft and called him dead. The Jew, however, was not dead. He sighed deeply through the hole in his lungs, and large pink bubbles came out of him and burst. Then they stabbed him again in the chest, but apparently they missed his heart. The broken relic of a man raised a leg in the air and kicked about furiously. The people who were crowded around him wiped the sweat from their brows and consulted with one another, then ordered the servants to throw the tortured body onto the smoldering fire.

But the ignorant serfs were already seized with superstitious panic, suspecting witchcraft or portents, and stubbornly refused to touch it with their hands. Finally Andrés Alvárez, the piper, drew near, he who carried always a heavy stone tied around his neck to mortify his flesh. Alvárez fetched a long pole and pushed and rolled the remains of the palpitating body into a shallow pool. The spokesman of the Jews lay bubbling in the water. Even after vespers he had not given up the ghost.

The Count gave orders to put off halting for the night and to ride on by the light of the moon, for the moon had come out, yellow and round and of enormous size. I gave my word, thought Claude, and I did not keep it, because the task did not lie within human power, and if it was the hand of the Almighty, then who am I? Not a leaf falls to the ground without being touched by a purpose, and it is not for us to know what that purpose is. So it was by God's purpose that our Savior died on the Cross, for it was God's will that the traitor should betray Christ so that the Savior should bear our sins and carry our afflictions.

For four days more Guillaume de Touron and his men continued to plow the wild earth with their faith and to root out the hostile forces from the world. And at the end of four days, with fists of icy fury, the great rains of winter began to beat down.

Life Nowadays Is Like
a Stupid Party

from *The Hill of Evil Counsel* (1976)

1

It was dark. In the dark a woman said, I'm not afraid. A man replied, Oh, yes, you are. Another man said, Quiet.

Then dim lights came on at either side of the stage, the curtains parted, and all was quiet.

In May 1946, one year after the Allied victory, the Jewish Agency mounted a great celebration in the Edison Cinema. The walls were draped with the flags of Great Britain and the Zionist Movement. Vases of gladioli stood on the front of the stage. And a banner carried a quotation from the Bible: PEACE BE WITHIN THY WALLS AND PROSPERITY WITHIN THY PALACES.

The British governor of Jerusalem strode up to the stage with a military gait and delivered a short address, in the course of which he cracked a subtle joke and read some lines of Byron. He was followed by the Zionist leader Moshe Shertok, who expressed in English and Hebrew the feelings of the Jewish community. In the corners of the auditorium, on either side of the stage, and by all the doors stood British soldiers wearing red berets and carrying submachine guns, to guard against the Underground. In the dress circle could be discerned the stiffly seated figure of the high commissioner, Sir Alan Cunningham, with a small party of ladies and army officers. The ladies were holding opera glasses. A choir of pioneers in blue shirts sang some work songs. The songs were Russian, and, like the audience, they were wistful, rather than happy.

After the singing there was a film of Montgomery's tanks advancing across the Western Desert. The tanks raised columns of dust, crushed trenches and barbed-wire fences under their tracks, and stabbed the gray desert sky with their antennas. The auditorium was filled with the thunder of guns and the noise of marching songs.

In the middle of the film, there was a slight disturbance in the dress circle.

The film stopped suddenly. The lights came on. A voice was raised in a reproach or a curt command: Is there a doctor in the house?

In row 29, Father immediately got to his feet. He fastened the top button of his white shirt, whispered to Hillel to take care of Mother and keep her calm until things were sorted out, and, like a man plunging into a burning building at the risk of his life, turned and pushed his way to the staircase.

It transpired that Lady Bromley, the high commissioner's sister-in-law, had been taken suddenly faint.

She was wearing a long white dress, and her face, too, was white. Father hurriedly introduced himself to the heads of the administration and proceeded to lay her limp arm across his shoulders. Like a gentle knight carrying a sleeping beauty, he helped Lady Bromley to the ladies' powder room. He seated her on an upholstered stool and handed her a glass of cold water. Three high-ranking British officials in evening dress hurried after him, stood in a semicircle around the patient, and supported her head as she took a single, painful sip. An elderly wing commander in uniform extracted her fan from her white evening bag, opened it carefully, and fanned her face.

Her ladyship opened her eyes wearily. She stared almost ironically for a moment at all the men who were bustling around her. She was angular and wizened, and with her pursed lips, her pointed nose, and her permanent sardonic scowl, she looked like some thirsty bird.

"Well, doctor," the wing commander addressed Father in acid tones, "what do you think?"

Father hesitated, apologized twice, and suddenly made up his mind. He leaned over, and with his fine, sensitive fingers he undid the laces of the tight corset. Lady Bromley felt immediately better. Her shriveled hand, which resembled a chicken leg, straightened the hem of the dress. A crease appeared in the tightly closed mouth, a kind of cracked smile. She crossed her old legs, and her voice when she spoke was tinny and piercing.

"It's just the climate."

"Ma'am—," one of the officials began politely.

But Lady Bromley was no longer with him. She turned impatiently to Father.

"Young man, would you be kind enough to open the windows. Yes, that one too. I need air. What a charming boy."

She addressed him in this way because, in his white sports shirt worn outside his khaki trousers, and with his biblical sandals, he looked to her more like a young servant than like a doctor. She had passed her youth among gardens, apes, and fountains in Bombay.

Father silently obeyed and opened all the windows.

The evening air of Jerusalem came in, and with it smells of cabbage, pine trees, and garbage.

He produced from his pocket a Health Service pillbox, carefully opened it, and handed Lady Bromley an aspirin. He did not know the English for "migraine," and so he said it in German. Doubtless his eyes at that moment shone with a sympathetic optimism behind his round spectacles.

After a few minutes, Lady Bromley asked to be taken back to her seat. One of the high-ranking officials took down Father's name and address and dryly thanked him. They smiled. There was a moment's hesitation. Suddenly the official held out his hand. They shook hands.

Father went back to his seat in row 29, between his wife and his son. He said, "It was nothing. It was just the climate."

The lights went out again. Once more General Montgomery pursued General Rommel mercilessly across the desert. Fire and dust clouds filled the screen. Rommel appeared in close-up, biting his lip, while in the background bagpipes skirled ecstatically.

Finally, the two anthems, British and Zionist, were played. The celebration was over. The people left the Edison Cinema and made for their homes. The evening twilight suddenly fell upon Jerusalem. In the distance, bald hills could be seen, with here and there a solitary tower. There was a sprinkling of stone huts on the faraway slopes. Shadows rustled in the side streets. The whole city was under the sway of a painful longing. Electric lights began to come on in the windows. There was a tense expectancy, as if at any moment a new sound might break out. But there were only the old sounds all around, a woman grumbling, a shutter squeaking, a lovesick cat screeching among the garbage cans in a backyard. And a very distant bell.

A handsome Bokharan barber in a white coat stood alone in the window of his empty shop and sang as he shaved himself. At that moment, a patrolling British jeep crossed the street, armed with a machine gun, brass bullets gleaming in its ammunition belt.

An old woman sat alone on a wooden stool beside the entrance of her basement shop. Her hands, wrinkled like a plasterer's, rested heavily on her knees. The last evening light caught her head, and her lips moved silently. From inside the basement, another woman spoke, in Yiddish:

"It's perfectly simple: it'll end badly."

The old woman made no reply. She did not move.

Outside Ernpreis the pants presser's, Father was accosted by a pious beggar, who demanded and received a two-mil piece, furiously thanked God, cursed the Jewish Agency twice, and swept an alley cat out of the way with the tip of his stick.

From the east, the bells rang out continuously, high bells and deep bells, Russian bells, Anglican bells, Greek bells, Abyssinian, Latin, Armenian bells, as if a plague or a fire were devastating the city. But all the bells were doing was calling the darkness dark. And a light breeze blew from the northwest, perhaps from the sea; it stirred the tops of the pale trees that the city council had planted up Malachi Street and ruffled the boy's curly hair. It was evening. An unseen bird gave a strange, persistent cry. Moss sprouted in the cracks of the stone walls. Rust spread over the old iron shutters and veranda railings. Jerusalem stood very quiet in the last of the light.

During the night, the boy woke up again with an attack of asthma. Father came in barefoot and sang him a soothing song:

Night is reigning in the skies,
Time for you to close your eyes.
Lambs and kids have ceased from leaping,
All the animals are sleeping.
Every bird is in its nest,
All Jerusalem's at rest.

Toward dawn, the jackals howled in the wadi below Tel Arza. Mitya the lodger began to cry out in his sleep on the other side of the wall: "Leave him alone! He's still alive! *Y-a ny-e zna-yu.*" And he fell silent. Then cocks crew far away in the quarter of Sanhedriya and the Arab village of Shu'afat. At the first light, Father put on his khaki trousers, sandals, and a neatly pressed blue shirt with wide pockets, and set off for work. Mother went on sleeping until the women in the neighboring houses started beating their pillows and mattresses with all their might. Then she got up and in her silk dressing gown gave the boy a breakfast of a soft-boiled egg, Quaker Oats, and cocoa with the skin taken off, and she combed his curly hair.

Hillel said, "I can do it by myself. Stop it."

An old glazier passed down the street, shouting, "Perfessional glazing! American! Anything repaired!" And the children called after him, "Loony!"

A few days later, Father was surprised to receive a gold-embossed invitation for two to the May Ball at the high commissioner's palace on the Hill of Evil Counsel. On the back of the invitation, the secretary had written in English that Lady Bromley wished to convey to Dr. Kipnis her gratitude and profound apology, and that Sir Alan himself had expressed his appreciation.

Father was not a real doctor. He was actually a vet.

2

He had been born and brought up in Silesia. Hans Walter Landauer, the famous geographer, was his mother's uncle. Father had studied at the Veterinary Institute in Leipzig, specializing in tropical and subtropical cattle diseases.

In 1932, he had emigrated to Palestine with the intention of establishing a cattle farm in the mountains. He was a polite young man, quiet, principled, and full of hopes. In his dreams he saw himself wandering with a stick and a haversack among the hills of Galilee, clearing a patch of forest, and building with his own hands a wooden house beside a stream, with a sloping roof, an attic, and a cellar. He meant to get together some herdsmen and a herd of cattle, roaming by day to new pastures and by night sitting surrounded by books in a room full of hunting trophies, composing a monograph or a great poem.

For three months he stayed in a guesthouse in the small town of Yesud-Hama'alah, and he spent whole days wandering alone from morning to night in eastern Galilee looking for water buffalo in the Huleh Swamps. His body grew lean and bronzed, and his blue eyes, behind his round spectacles, looked like lakes in a snowy northern land. He learned to love the desolation of the distant mountains and the smell of summer: scorched thistles, goat dung, wood ash, the dusty east wind.

In the Arab village of Halsa, he met a wandering Bavarian ornithologist, a lonely and fervently evangelical man who believed that the return of the Jews to their land heralded the salvation of the world and who was collecting material for a great work on the birds of the Holy Land. Together they roamed to the Marj-'Ayun Valley, into the Mountains of Naphtali and the Huleh Swamps. Occasionally, in their wanderings, they reached the remote sources of the Jordan. Here they would sit all day in the shade of the lush vegetation, reciting together from memory their favorite Schiller poems and calling every bird and beast by its proper name.

When Father began to worry what would happen when he came to the end of the money that his mother's uncle, the famous geographer, had given him, he decided to go to Jerusalem to look into certain practical possibilities. Accordingly, he took his leave of the wandering Bavarian ornithologist, gathered his few possessions, and appeared one fine autumn morning in the office of Dr. Arthur Ruppin at the Jewish Agency in Jerusalem.

Dr. Ruppin took at once to the quiet, bronzed boy who had come to him from Galilee. He also recalled that in his youth he had studied the tropical countries in Landauer's great *Atlas*. When Father began to describe the project of a cattle farm in the hills of Galilee, he took down some hasty notes. Father concluded with these words:

"It is a difficult plan to put into practice, but I believe it is not impossible."

Dr. Ruppin smiled sadly.

"Not impossible, but difficult to put into practice. Very difficult!"

And he proceeded to point out one or two awkward facts.

He persuaded Father to postpone the realization of his plan for the time being, and meanwhile to invest his money in the acquisition of a young orange grove near the settlement of Nes Tsiyona, and also to buy without delay a small house in the new suburb of Tel Arza, which was being built to the north of Jerusalem.

Father did not argue.

Within a few days, Dr. Ruppin had had Father appointed as a traveling government veterinary officer and had even invited him for coffee to his house in Rehavia.

For several years, Father would get up before sunrise and travel on sooty buses up to Bethlehem and Ramallah, down to Jericho, out to Lydda, to supervise the villagers' cattle on behalf of the government.

The orange grove near the settlement of Nes Tsiyona began to yield a modest income, which he deposited, along with part of his government salary, in the Anglo-Palestine Bank. He furnished his small house in Tel Arza with a bed, a desk, a wardrobe, and bookshelves. Above his desk he hung a large picture of his mother's uncle, the famous geographer. Hans Walter Landauer looked down on Father with an expression of skepticism and mild surprise, particularly in the evenings.

As he traveled around the villages, Father collected rare thistles. He also gathered some fossils and pieces of ancient pottery. He arranged them all with great care. And he waited.

Meanwhile, silence cut him off from his mother and sisters in Silesia.

As the years went by, Father learned to speak a little Arabic. He also learned loneliness. He put off composing his great poem. Every day he learned something new about the land and its inhabitants, and occasionally even about himself. He still saw in his dreams the cattle farm in Galilee, although the cellar and attic now seemed to him unnecessary, perhaps even childish. One evening, he even said aloud to his granduncle's picture, "We'll see. All in good time. I'm just as determined as you are. You may laugh, but I don't care. Laugh as much as you like."

At night, by the light of his desk lamp, Father kept a journal in which he recorded his fears for his mother and sisters, the oppressiveness of the dry desert wind, certain peculiarities of some of his acquaintances, and the flavor of his travels among godforsaken villages. He set down in carefully chosen words various professional lessons he had learned in the course of his work. He committed to writing some optimistic reflections about the progress of the Jewish community in various spheres. He even formulated, after several revisions, a few arguments for and against loneliness, and an embarrassed hope for a love that might come to him, too, one day. Then he carefully tore out the page and ripped it into tiny pieces. He also published, in the weekly *The Young Worker,* an article in favor of drinking goats' milk.

Sometimes, in the evening, he would go to Dr. Ruppin's home in Rehavia, where he was received with coffee and cream cakes. Or else he would visit his fellow townsman the elderly Professor Julius Wertheimer, who also lived in Rehavia, not far from Dr. Ruppin.

Occasionally there was a distant sound of faint, persistent piano music, like the supplications of a desperate pride. Every summer the rocks on the hillside roasted, and every winter Jerusalem was ringed with fog. Refugees and pioneers continued to arrive from various foreign parts, filling the city with sadness and bewilderment. Father bought books from the refugees, some of them musty books with leather bindings and gold tooling, and from time to time he exchanged books with Dr. Ruppin or with the elderly Professor Julius Wertheimer, who was in the habit of greeting him with a hurried, embarrassed hug.

The Arabs in the villages sometimes gave him cold pomegranate juice to drink. Occasionally they would kiss his hand. He learned to drink water from an upraised pitcher without letting the pitcher touch his lips. Once a woman directed a dark, smoldering glance at him from some way off, and he trembled all over and hurriedly looked away.

He wrote in his journal:

"I have been living in Jerusalem for three years, and I continue to yearn for it as though I were still a student in Leipzig. Surely there is paradox here. And in general," Father continued thoughtfully and rather vaguely, "in general there are all sorts of contradictions. Yesterday morning, in Lifta, I was obliged to put down a fine, healthy horse because some youngsters had blinded it in the night with a nail. Cruelty for its own sake seems to me to be something sordid and thoroughly unnecessary. The same evening, in Kibbutz Kiryat 'Anavim, the pioneers played a Bach suite on the phonograph, which aroused in me profound feelings of pity for the pioneers, for the horse, for Bach, for myself. I almost cried. Tomorrow is the king's birthday, and all the workers in the department are to receive a special bonus. There are all sorts of contradictions. And the climate is not kind, either."

3

Mother said, "I shall wear my blue dress with the V-shaped neckline, and I shall be the belle of the ball. We'll order a taxi, too."

Father said, "Yes, and don't forget to lose a glass slipper."

Hillel said, "Me, too."

But children are not taken to May Balls at the high commissioner's palace. Even good children, even children who are cleverer than is usual for their age. And the ball would certainly not end before midnight. So Hillel would spend the evening next door with Madame Yabrova, the pianist, and her niece, Lyubov, who called herself Binyamina Even-Hen. They would play the phonograph for him, give him his supper, let him play a little with their collection of dolls of all nations, and put him to bed.

Hillel tried to protest. "But I still have to tell the high commissioner who's right and who's wrong."

Father replied patiently, "We are right, and I'm sure the high commissioner knows it in his heart of hearts, but he has to carry out the wishes of the king."

"I don't envy that king because God is going to punish him and Uncle Mitya calls him King Chedorlaomer of Albion and he says the Underground will capture him and execute him because of what he's done to the Remnant of Israel," the boy said excitedly and all in one breath.

Father replied mildly, choosing his words with care, "Uncle Mitya sometimes exaggerates a little. The king of England is not Chedorlaomer, but George the Sixth. He will probably be succeeded on the throne by one of his daughters, because he has no son. To kill a man except in self-defense is murder. And now, Your Majesty King Hillel the First, finish up your cocoa. And then go and brush your teeth."

Mother, with a hairpin between her teeth and holding a pair of amber earrings, remarked, "King George is very thin and pale. And he always looks so sad."

When he reached the end of the third form, Hillel wrote a letter and typed it in triplicate on his father's typewriter. He sent two of the copies to the king in London and the high commissioner, "Our land belongs to us, both according to the Bible and according to justice. Please get out of the Land of Israel at once and go back to England before it is too late."

The third copy passed from hand to hand among the excited neighbors. Madame Yabrova, the pianist, said, "A child poet!" Her niece, Lyubov-Binyamina, added, "And look at his curly hair! We ought to send a copy to Dr. Weizmann, to give him a little joy." Brzezinski the engineer said that it was no good exaggerating, you couldn't build a wall out of fine words. And from Gerald Lindley, secretary, there came a brief reply on official government notepaper: "Thank you for your letter, the contents of which have been duly noted. We are always receptive to the opinions of the public. Yours faithfully."

And how the geraniums blazed in the garden in the blue summer light. How the pure light was caught by the fingers of the fig tree in the yard and shattered into nervous fragments. How the sun burst up early in the morning behind Mount Scopus to torment the whole city and suddenly turn the gold and silver domes to dazzling flames. How joyfully or desperately the throngs of birds shrilled.

The metal drainpipe absorbed the heat and was sweet to the touch in the morning. The clean gravel that Father had spread along the path that wound down from the veranda steps to the fence and from the fig tree to the bottom of the garden was white and pleasant under bare feet.

The garden was small, logically planned, uncompromisingly well kept: Father's dreams had laid out square and rectangular flower beds among the rocky gulleys, a lonely island of clear, sober sanity in the midst of a savage, rugged wasteland, of winding valleys, of desert winds.

And surrounding us was the estate of Tel Arza, a handful of new houses scattered haphazardly on a hilltop. The mountains might move in one night and silently enfold everything, the houses, the hesitant saplings, the hopes, the unpaved road. A herd of Arab goats would arrive to munch and trample chrysanthemums, narcissuses, snapdragons, sparse beginnings of lawn here and there. And the shepherd would stand silent and motionless, watching the ravaging goats and looking perhaps like a scorched cypress tree.

All day Hillel could see the ranges of bare mountains all around. At times he could sense in the bright blue flood the autumn piling up in unseen valleys.

Autumn would come. The light would fade to gray. Low clouds would seize the mountains. He would climb to the top of the fig tree, and from there in the autumn light he might be able to see the sea and the desert, the islands in the tattered clouds, the mysterious continents that Father had told him about dryly and Mother with tears of longing.

Father used to say that the beautiful lands had vomited us up here in blind hatred, and that therefore we would build ourselves a land a thousand times as beautiful here. But Mother would call the land a backyard, and say that there would never be a river, a cathedral, or a forest here. Uncle Mitya, the lodger, used to chuckle through his rotten teeth and utter broken phrases about birth pangs, death throes, Jerusalem killing its prophets, God's curse on ruined Babylon. He was also a vegetarian.

Hillel could not make out from these words whether Mitya agreed with Father or with Mother. What Mother said seemed to him incongruous, and he would go down to the bottom of the garden to hide among the branches of the fig tree and sniff for the autumn. Autumn would come. Autumn sadness would accompany him to school, to his music lessons with Madame Yabrova, to the "Zion's Ransom" lending library, to his bed at night, into his dreams. While a rainstorm raged outside, he would compose an article for the class newspaper. The word *forest,* which Mother had used when she wanted to denigrate the land, cast a strange, melancholy spell over him.

4

Hillel was a pudgy, awkward little boy. He had a hiding place at the end of the garden, behind the fig tree or up among its branches, which he called his hideaway. He would hide himself away there and secretly eat sticky sweets that the women gave him and dream of Africa, the sources of the Nile, the lions in the jungle.

At night he would wake up with attacks of asthma. Especially in the early summer. Feverish, suffocated, he would see the horrific smile of the terrifying white thing through the slats of the shutters and burst into tears. Until Father appeared holding a small flashlight, to sit on his bed and sing him a soothing song. Aunts, neighbors, and nursery school teachers adored Hillel, with Russian kisses and Polish displays of affection. They called him "Little Cherry." Sometimes they would leave heavy lip marks on his cheeks or his mouth. These women were plump and excitable. Their faces wore an expression of bitter complaint: Life has not been as kind to me as I deserve.

Madame Yabrova, the pianist, and her niece, Lyubov, who called herself Binyamina Even-Hen, in the determined way they played the piano seemed to be nobly refraining from repaying life for what it had done to them. Mrs. Vishniak the pharmacist would grumble to Hillel and say that little children were the only hope of the Jewish people, and particularly of herself. At times Hillel wrapped himself in introspection or sadness, and then he would delight them with a sweet phrase, such as "Life is a circle. Everyone goes around and around."

And stir ripples of emotion.

But the children of Tel Arza called him by the unpleasant nickname "Jelly." Unkind, skinny girls, vicious Oriental girls, enjoyed knocking him down on a heap of gravel and pulling his blond hair. Keys and amulets hung around their necks. They emitted a pungent smell of peanuts, sweat, soap, and halvah.

Hillel would always wait until they had had enough of him and his curls. Then he would get up and shake the dust off his gym shorts and his cotton undershirt; gasping for breath, his eyes full of tears, he would bite his lip and begin to forgive. How nobly forgiveness shone in his eyes: those girls did not know what they were doing; they probably had unhappy fathers and brothers who were high up in the underworld or in football; their mothers and sisters probably went out with British soldiers. It was a terrible thing to be born an Oriental girl. And one of them had even started to grow breasts under her sweaty vest. Hillel reflected, forgave, and was filled with love of himself for his ability to understand and to forgive.

Then he would run to Mrs. Vishniak's pharmacy to cry a little, not because of the scratches but because of the cruel lot of the girls and his own magnanimity. Mrs. Vishniak would kiss him, console him with sticky candy, tell him about the mill on the banks of the blue river, which no longer existed. He would tell her, in carefully chosen words, about a dream he had had the previous night, interpret the dream himself, and leave behind a delicate mood of poetry as he went off to practice the piano in the dark, airless house of Madame Yabrova and Binyamina. He returned the caresses he had received from Mrs. Vishniak to the haughty bronze Beethoven on top of the sideboard. After all, Herzl, in his youth, was called a madman in the street. And Bialik was always being beaten.

In the evening, before he went to bed, Hillel would be summoned to his father's room in his pajamas. This room was called the study. It contained bookshelves, a desk, and a glass-fronted showcase of fossils and ancient pots; the whole was skeptically surveyed from a sepia photograph by the famous geographer Hans Walter Landauer.

He had to utter an intelligent sentence or two for the benefit of the guests. Then he was kissed and sent off to bed. From across the corridor came the sounds of the grown-ups talking passionately, and Hillel in his bed caught their passion and began to pamper his tiny organ with his fingers through the opening of his pajama trousers.

Later, the forlorn sound of Lyubov-Binyamina's cello came to him through the darkness, and he suddenly despised himself. He called himself "Jelly." He was filled with sorrow for all men and women. And fell asleep compassionately.

"He's a real *mensch*," Mrs. Vishniak would say in Yiddish. "Clever. Witty. A little devil. Just like the whole family."

Beyond the low fence, which Father had made from iron posts and old netting and had painted in bright colors, began the wasteland. Plots of scrap iron, dust, smelling of thistles, of goat dung; and farther on, the wadi and the lairs of foxes and jackals; and still far-ther down, the empty wood where the children once discovered the remains of a half-eaten Turkish soldier in the stinking tatters of a janissary's uniform. There were desolate slopes teeming with dart-ing lizards and snakes and perhaps hyenas at night, and beyond this wadi, empty, stony hills and more wadis, in which Arabs in desert robes roamed with their flocks all day long. In the distance were more and more strange mountains and strange villages stretching to the end of the world, minarets of mosques, Shu'afat, Nabi Samwil, the outskirts of Ramallah, the wail of a muezzin borne on the wind in the evening twilight, dark women, deadly sly, guttural youths. And a slight hint of brooding evil: distant, infinitely patient, forever observing you unobserved.

Mother said, "While you, Hans, are dancing like a teddy bear with that old lady you treated, I shall sit all alone in my blue dress on a wickerwork chair at the end of the veranda, sipping a martini and smiling to myself. But later on I, too, shall suddenly get up and dance, with the governor of Jerusalem, or even with Sir Alan him-self. Then it will be your turn to sit it out by yourself, and you won't feel at all like smiling."

Father said, "The boy can hear you. He understands exactly what you're saying."

And Hillel said, "So what?"

For the occasion, Father borrowed from his neighbor, Engineer Brzezinski, an English evening suit made by the Szczupak textile factory in Lodz. Mother sat on the shady balcony all morning alter-ing it to fit him.

At lunchtime, Father tried the suit on at the mirror, shrugged his shoulders, and remarked, "It's ridiculous."

Mother, laughing, said, "The boy can hear you. He understands everything."

Hillel said, "So what? 'Ridiculous' isn't a dirty word."

Father said, "No word is dirty in itself. In general, dirt lies either behind words or between them."

And Mother, "There's dirt everywhere here. Even in the grand ideas you're always putting into Hillel's head. Even in your stray remarks. And that's also ridiculous."

Father said nothing.

That morning the newspaper *Davar* said that the politics of the White Paper were leading up a blind alley. Hillel, with an effort of the imagination, could almost visualize the "blind alley."

Mitya the vegetarian lodger padded barefoot from his room to the kitchen to make himself a glass of tea. He was a tall, etiolated young man with thinning hair. His shoulders always drooped, and he walked with short, nervous steps. He had an odd habit of suddenly chewing the tip of his shirt collar, and also of angrily stroking every object he came across, table, banister, bookshelf, Mother's apron hanging on a hook in the kitchen. And he would whisper to himself. Engineer Brzezinski declared hotly that one day it would emerge that this Mitya was really a dangerous Communist in disguise. But Mother good-naturedly offered to launder his few clothes with the family wash.

As Mitya shuffled to the kitchen, he waved his hand in every direction in greeting, as though confronting a large crowd. Suddenly his glance fell on the words "blind alley" in the headline on the center page of *Davar,* lying open on the oilcloth-covered kitchen table. He bared his bad teeth and snarled furiously, "What rubbish."

Then, clasping the hot glass in his large white hands, he strode stormily back to his room, locking his door behind him.

Mother said softly, "He's just like a stray dog." After a short pause, she added, "He washes five times a day, and after each time he puts on scent, and even so he always smells. We ought to find him a girlfriend. Perhaps a new immigrant from the Women's Labor Bureau, poor but charming. Now, Hans, you go and shave. And Hillel—go on with your homework. What am I doing in this madhouse?"

5

She had come from Warsaw as a young woman to study ancient history at the university on Mount Scopus. Before a year was up, she was in despair at the country and the language. Nyuta, her elder sister in New York, had sent her a ticket to go from Haifa to America aboard the *Aurora*. A few days before the date of her departure, Dr. Ruppin had introduced her to Father, shown him her beautiful watercolors, and expressed in German his sadness that the young lady was also leaving us, that she, too, found the country unbearable and was sailing to America in disappointment.

Hans Kipnis looked at the watercolors for a while and suddenly thought of the wandering German ornithologist with whom he had traveled to the remote sources of the Jordan. He traced the lines of one of the pictures delicately with his finger, hurriedly withdrew his hand, and uttered some remarks about loneliness and dreams in general and in Jerusalem in particular.

Mother smiled at him, as though he had accidentally broken a precious vase.

Father apologized and lapsed into an embarrassed silence.

Dr. Ruppin had a pair of tickets for a concert that night by a recently formed refugee chamber orchestra. He was glad to present the tickets to the young couple: he could not go anyway, because Menahem Ussishkin, the Zionist leader, had unexpectedly arrived from abroad a day or two earlier, and as usual had convened a frantic meeting for that evening.

After the concert, they strolled together along Princess Mary's Way. The shopwindows were brightly lit and decorated, and in one of them a small mechanical doll bobbed up and down. For a moment, Jerusalem looked like a real city. Ladies and gentlemen walked arm in arm, and some of the gentlemen were smoking cigarettes in short cigarette holders.

A bus stopped beside them, and the driver, who was wearing shorts, smiled at them invitingly, but they did not get on. An army jeep with a machine gun mounted on it rolled down the street. And in the distance a bell rang. They both agreed that Jerusalem was under some cruel spell. Then they agreed to meet again the next day to eat a strawberry ice cream together at Zichel's Café.

At a nearby table sat the philosopher Martin Buber and the writer S. Y. Agnon. In the course of a disagreement, Agnon jokingly suggested that they consult the younger generation. Father made some remark; it must have been perceptive and acute, because Buber and Agnon both smiled; they also addressed his companion gallantly. At that moment Father's blue eyes may perhaps have lit up behind his round spectacles, and his sadness may have shown around his mouth.

Nineteen days later, the Nazis publicly declared their intention of building up their armed forces. There was tension in Europe. The *Aurora* never reached Haifa; she changed her course and sailed instead to the West Indies.

Father arranged to see his fellow townsman Professor Julius Wertheimer, who had been his patron ever since he had arrived in Palestine. He said he wanted to consult him on a personal matter. He was confused, furtive, obstinate, and tongue-tied. Professor Wertheimer listened in an anxious silence. Then he drove his cats out of the room and closed the door behind them. When they were alone, he warned Father obliquely not to complicate his private life unnecessarily. And it was precisely these words that brought Father to the certainty that he was finally in love.

Ruth and Hans were married in Jerusalem on the day Hitler declared in Nuremberg that he was bent on peace and understanding and that he detested war. The guests consisted of the officials of the veterinary department, including two Christian Arabs from Bethlehem; the Ruppin family; some refugees and pioneers; a few neighbors from Tel Arza; and an emaciated revolutionary student from the university who could not take his blazing eyes off the beautiful bride. He it was who toasted the happy couple on behalf of all their friends and vowed that right would triumph and that we would see as much with our own eyes. But he spoiled the effect of his words by getting thoroughly drunk on one bottle of Nesher beer and calling the bridegroom and bride respectively *burzhui* and *artistka*. The guests departed, and Father hired a taxi to convey Mother's few belongings from her simple room in Neve Sha'anan to the house he had been making ready for several years in the suburb of Tel Arza.

There, in Tel Arza, in the little stone-built house facing the rocky wadis, there was born to them a year later a fair-haired son.

When Mother and the baby came home from the hospital, Father indicated his diminutive estate with a sweep of his hand, gazed raptly at it, and pronounced these words:

"For the moment, this is a remote suburb. There are only young saplings growing in our garden. The sun beats down all day on the shutters. But as the years pass, the trees will grow, and we shall have plenty of shade. Their boughs will shelter the house. Creepers will climb over the roof and all over the fence. And the flowers will bloom. This will be our pleasure garden when Hillel grows up and we grow old together. We shall make an arbor of vines where you can sit all day through the summer, painting beautiful watercolors. We can even have a piano. They'll build a civic center, they'll pave the road, our suburb will be joined to a Jerusalem ruled by a Hebrew government with a Hebrew army. Dr. Ruppin will be a minister and Professor Buber will be president or perhaps even king. When the time comes, I may become director of the veterinary service. And immigrants will arrive from every country under the sun."

Suddenly he felt ashamed of his speech, and particularly regretted his choice of some of the words. A momentary sadness trembled around his mouth, and he added hastily, in a matter-of-fact tone, "Poetry. Philosophizing. A pleasure garden with overhanging vines, all of a sudden. Now I'll go and fetch a block of ice, and you must lie down and rest, so that you won't have a migraine again tonight. It's so hot."

Mother turned to go indoors. By the veranda steps she stopped and looked at the miserable, rusty pots of geraniums. She said, "There won't be any flowers. There'll be a flood. Or a war. They'll all die."

Father did not answer, because he sensed that these words were not directed at him and that they should never have been spoken.

His khaki shorts came down almost to his knees. Between his

knees and his sandals his legs showed brown, thin, and smooth. Behind his round spectacles his face bore an expression of permanent gratitude, or of slight, pleased surprise. And in moments of embarrassment he was in the habit of saying, "I don't know. It's just as well not to know everything. There are all sorts of things in the world that are better left alone."

6

Here is how Mother appeared as a girl in her old photograph album: a blond schoolgirl with a kind of inner, autumnal beauty. Her fingers clasping a broad-brimmed white hat. Three doves on a fence behind her, and a mustached Polish student sitting on the same fence, smiling broadly.

She had been considered the best reader in her class at the high school. At the age of twelve, she had already attracted the enthusiastic attention of the elderly Polish literature teacher. The aging humanist, Mother would recall, was deeply moved by her charming recitations of gems of Polish poetry. "Ruth's voice," the pedagogue would exclaim with hoarse enthusiasm, "echoes the spirit of poetry, eternally playing among streams in a meadow." And because he secretly considered himself a poet, he would add, overcome by the force of his emotions, "If gazelles could sing, they would surely sing like little Ruth."

When Mother repeated this sentence she would laugh, because the comparison seemed to her absurd. Not because of the idea of gazelles singing, but because she simply couldn't sing. Her affections at that time were directed toward small pets, celebrated philosophers and artists, dancing, dresses trimmed with lace, and silk scarves, and also her poor friends who had neither lace-trimmed dresses nor silk scarves. She was fond of the unfortunates she came across, the milkman, the beggar, Grandma Gittel, the maids, and her nanny, even the local idiot. Provided that suffering had not disfigured their outward appearance, and provided that they carried themselves woefully, as if acknowledging their guilt and attempting to atone for it.

She translated from Polish a story she had written on her fifteenth birthday. She copied it out neatly and told Hillel to read it aloud:

"The blue sea allows the sun's rays to draw up its water, to make clouds that look like dirty cotton wool, to pour down rain on mountains, plains, and meadows—but not on the ugly desert—and eventually all the water collects and has to flow back once more into the sea. To return to it with a caress."

Suddenly she fell into a rage, snatched the paper out of the boy's hands, and tore it into shreds.

"All gone!" she cried with desperate pathos. "Dead and done for! Lost!"

Outside, a wintry Jerusalem Sabbath, windswept, lashed by dead leaves. Inside the little house in Tel Arza, the kerosene heater burned with a blue flame. On the table there were tea and oranges, and a vase of chrysanthemums. Two of the walls were lined with Father's books. Shadows fell on them. The wind howled from the wadi. Mists touched the outside of the window, and the panes rattled. With a kind of bitter mockery, Mother spoke of her childhood in Warsaw, rowing on the Wisla, playing tennis in white clothes, the Seventh Cavalry Regiment parading down the Avenue of the Republic every Sunday. Occasionally she turned abruptly to Father and called him Dr. Zichel instead of Dr. Kipnis, Hans, Hanan. Father would rest his fingers on his high brow, unperturbed, unsurprised, silently smiling at the recollection of the acute remark he had made in Zichel's Café to the writer Agnon and the philosopher Buber. They had both been delighted; they had consulted him about the strawberry ice cream, and even complimented his companion.

When Mother was sixteen, she allowed the handsome Tadeusz to kiss her at the bridge: first on the forehead, later on the lips, but she let him go no further. He was a year and a half younger than she, an elegant, handsome youth, without a trace of acne, who excelled at tennis and sprinting. Once he had promised her that he would love her forever. But forever at that time seemed to her like a small circle bathed in pleasant light, and love like a game of tennis on a clear blue Sunday morning.

Handsome Tadeusz's father had been killed in the Polish war of independence. Tadeusz also had a cute dimple when he smiled, and wore sports shirts all through the summer. Mother loved to kiss Hillel suddenly on his own dimple and say, "Just like this one."

Every year, on the national holiday, Ruth and Tadeusz would both stand on a decorated stage in the school playground. Old chestnut trees spread their branches overhead like a rustling bridal canopy. Tadeusz's task was to light the Torch of Liberty—the same liberty for which his father had given his life. Pupils and teachers stood in serried ranks, frozen in a strained silence, while the wind toyed with the flags of the Republic—no, don't touch the photograph—and Ruth recited the immortal lines by the national poet. Bells rang out joyously from atop every church in Warsaw. And in the evening, at the ball at the home of the director of the opera house, her parents permitted her to dance one waltz with General Godzinski himself.

Then Zionism broke out. The handsome Tadeusz joined the National Youth Corps, and because she refused to spend a weekend with him at his aunt's in the country, he sent her a disgusting note: "*Zidowka.* Dirty Jewess." The old teacher who was fond of the phrase "singing gazelles" died suddenly of a liver disease. And both her parents, too, in a single month. The only memento she had left was the sepia photographs, printed on thick card stock with ornamental borders.

Nyuta, her elder sister, quickly found herself a widowed gynecologist named Adrian Staub. She married him and went with him to New York. Meanwhile, Mother came to Palestine to study ancient history on Mount Scopus. She took a small room at the end of the world, in the suburb of Neve Sha'anan. Nyuta Staub sent her a modest allowance every month. In that room she was loved by several wonderful men, including, one Hanukkah festival, the furious poet Alexander Pan.

After a year, she felt defeated by the country and the language, and decided to join her sister and brother-in-law in New York. Then Dr. Ruppin introduced her to Father, and he told her shyly about his dream of setting up a cattle farm in the hills of Galilee with his own hands. He had a fine Galilean smell. She was desperately tired. And the *Aurora* changed course, sailed to the West Indies, and never reached Haifa.

To the northeast, in the white summer light, one could see Mount Scopus from the window of the house in Tel Arza, crowned by a marble dome, a wood, and two towers. These lonely towers seemed from a distance to be shrouded in a kind of veil of solitude. At the end of the Sabbath the light faded slowly, hesitantly, poignantly.

As though forever. And as though there were no going back.

Father and Mother used to sit facing each other in the room that Father called his study. The celebrated geographer Hans Walter Landauer gazed down skeptically on them from his large portrait. And their pudgy son built complicated brick castles on the mat, demolishing each suddenly with a wave of his hand because he always wanted to build a new one. At times he would ask an intelligent question of his father, and he always received a considered reply. At other times he buried his face in his mother's dress, demanded to be cuddled, and then, embarrassed at seeing her eyes fill with tears, returned silently to his game.

Sometimes Mother asked, "What's going to happen, Hans?"

And Father would answer, "I confidently hope that things will take a turn for the better."

As Father uttered these words, Hillel recalled how last Pentecost he had gone out with his friends to hunt lions or discover the source of the Nile in the woods of Tel Arza. He recalled how a faded golden button had suddenly flashed at him, and blue cloth, how he had knelt down and dug with both hands, tearing away the pine needles, to uncover the treasure, and found a rotting military tunic, a terrible, sweet smell coming from the tarnished gold, and how as he went on digging he had discovered white ivory among disintegrating buckles, large and small white tusks, and all of a sudden the ivory was attached to an empty skull that smiled at him with a kind of chilling affection, and then the dead teeth and the eye sockets. Never, never again would he search for the source of the Nile anywhere. Never.

On weekdays Father traveled around the villages wearing khaki trousers, sandals, a neatly pressed blue shirt with wide pockets stuffed full of notebooks and writing pads. In winter he wore brown corduroy trousers, a jacket, a cap, and over his shoes he wore galoshes that looked like twin black warships.

But on Sabbath Eve, after his bath, he would appear in a white shirt and gray trousers, his damp hair combed and neatly parted, smelling of shaving lotion and almond-scented soap. Then Mother would kiss him on the nose and call him her great big child. And Hillel would laugh.

Every morning, a bib with a picture of a smiling rabbit was tied around Hillel's neck. He ate Quaker Oats, a soft-boiled egg, and yogurt. On the Quaker Oats package was a wonderful picture of an admiral with a bold and resolute look on his face, a three-cornered Napoleon hat on his head, and a telescope in his only hand.

In Europe at that time, there was a world war going on. But in the streets of Jerusalem, there were only singing bands of friendly soldiers, Australians, New Zealanders, Senegalese looking like chocolate-cream soldiers, lean Scots wallowing in beer and homesickness. The newspapers carried maps with arrows. Sometimes, at night, a long military convoy crossed Jerusalem from north to south with dimmed headlights, and a smothered roar seemed to sound in the darkness. The city was very still. The hills were hushed. The towers and domes looked thoughtful. The inhabitants followed the distant war with anxiety but without passion. They exchanged conjectures and interpretations. They expected a change for the better that would surely come about soon and might even perhaps make itself felt in Jerusalem.

A City Where All Men Are Half Prophet, Half Prime Minister

from *Fima* (1991)

PROMISE AND GRACE

Five nights before the sad event, Fima had a dream which he recorded at half past five in the morning in his dream book, a brown notebook that always lay beneath an untidy heap of old newspapers and magazines on the floor at the foot of his bed. In this book Fima had made it his habit to write down, in bed, as the first pale lines of dawn began to appear between the slats of his blinds, whatever he had seen in the night. Even if he had seen nothing, or if he had forgotten what he had seen, he still switched on the light, squinted, sat up in bed, and, propping a thick magazine on his knees to serve as a writing desk, wrote something like this:

"Twentieth of December—blank night."

Or:

"Fourth of January—something about a fox and a ladder, but the details have gone."

He always wrote the date out in words. Then he would get up to relieve himself and lie down in bed again until the cooing of the doves came into the room, with a dog barking and a bird nearby that sounded surprised, as though it could not believe its eyes. Fima promised himself he would get up at once, in a few minutes, a quarter of an hour at most, but sometimes he dropped off again and did not wake till eight or nine, because his shift at the clinic only started at one o'clock. He found less falsehood in sleeping than in waking.

Even though he had long ago come to understand that truth was beyond his reach, he wanted to distance himself as much as possible from the petty lies that filled his everyday life like a fine dust that penetrated even to the most intimate crannies.

On Monday morning early, as a murky orange glimmer began to filter through the blind, he sat up in bed and entered the following in his book:

"A woman, attractive rather than beautiful, came up to me; she didn't approach the reception desk but appeared from behind me, despite the notice saying STAFF ONLY. I said, 'Sorry, all inquiries must be made from the front of the desk.' She laughed and said, 'All right, Efraim, we heard you the first time.' I said, 'If you don't get out of here, ma'am, I'll have to ring my bell' (although I haven't got a bell). At these words the woman laughed again, a pleasant, graceful laugh, like a limpid brook. She was slim-shouldered and had a slightly wrinkled neck, but her bosom and stomach were well rounded and her calves covered by silk stockings with curving seams. The combination of curvaceousness and vulnerability was both sexy and touching. Or maybe it was the contrast between the shapely body and the face of an overworked teacher that was touching. I had a little girl by you, she said, and now it's time for our daughter to meet her father. Although I knew I wasn't supposed to leave the clinic, that it would be dangerous to follow her, especially barefoot, which I suddenly was, a sort of inner signal formed itself: If she draws her hair over her left shoulder with her left hand, then I'll have to go. She knew; with a light movement she brought her hair forward until it spread over her dress and covered her left breast, and she said, 'Come.' I followed her through several streets and alleys, several flights of steps and gates, and more stone-paved courtyards in Valladolid in Spain, though it was really more or less the Bukharian Quarter here in Jerusalem. Even though this woman in the girlish cotton dress and sexy stockings was a stranger and I had never set eyes on her before, I still wanted to see the little girl. So we walked through entrances to buildings that led to backyards full of loaded clotheslines, which led us to new alleyways and an ancient square lit by a streetlamp in the rain. Because it had started to rain, not hard, not pouring, very few drops in fact, just a thick mist in the darkening air. We didn't meet a living soul on the way. Not even a cat. Suddenly the woman stopped in a passageway that had vestiges of decaying grandeur, like an entrance to an Oriental palace, but probably it was just a tunnel joining two sodden court-yards, with battered mailboxes and flaking ceramic tiles, and, re-moving my wristwatch, she pointed to a tattered army blanket in an alcove under the steps, as though removing my watch was the prelude to some kind of nakedness, and now I had to give her a baby daughter and I asked where we were and where the children were, because somehow along the way the daughter had turned into children. The woman said, *Chili.* I couldn't tell whether this was the little girl's name or the name of the woman herself, who was clasping my hand to her breast, or if she was cold because of the nakedness of the skinny daughters, or if it was an invitation to hug her and warm her up. When I hugged her, her whole body shook, not with desire but with despair, and she whispered, Don't be afraid, Efraim, I know a way and I'll get you across safely to the Aryan side. In the dream this whispered phrase was full of promise and grace, and I continued to trust her and follow her ecstatically, and was not at all surprised when in the dream she turned into my mother, nor did I ask where the Aryan side was. Until we reached the water. At the water's edge, with a blond military mustache and legs spread wide, stood a man in a dark uniform who said, Have to separate.

"So it became clear that she was chilly because of the water, and that I would not see her again. I woke with sadness and even now as I conclude these notes the sadness has not left me."

2

FIMA GETS UP FOR WORK
Efraim got out of bed in his sweaty underwear, opened his shutters a crack, and looked out at the beginning of a winter day in Jerusa-

lem. The nearby buildings did not look near; they seemed far from him and from each other, with wisps of low cloud drifting among them. There was no sign of life outside. As though the dream were continuing. Except that there was no stone-paved alley now, but a shabby road at the southwest edge of Kiryat Yovel, a row of squat blocks of flats jerry-built in the late 1950s. The balconies had been mostly closed in with breeze-block, plasterboard, aluminum, and glass. Here and there an empty window box or a neglected flower-pot stood on a rusting balustrade. Away to the south the Bethlehem hills merged with the gray clouds, looking unattractive and grubby this morning, more like slag heaps than hills. A neighbor was having difficulty starting his car because of the cold and the damp. The starter wheezed repeatedly, like a terminally ill lung case who still insisted on chain-smoking. Again Fima was overcome by the feeling that he was here by mistake, that he ought to be somewhere completely different.

But what the mistake was, or where he ought to be, he did not know this morning. In fact he never did.

The car's wheezing brought on his own morning cough, and he moved away from the window. He did not want to start his day in such a pointless and pathetic way. He said to himself, Lazy bastard! and began to do some simple exercises, bends and stretches, in front of the mirror, which was dappled with dark islands and continents. The mirror was fixed to the front of the old brown wardrobe his father had bought for him thirty years ago. He should have asked the woman what it was he was supposed to separate. But he had missed his chance.

As a general rule Fima loathed people standing at windows. He especially loathed the sight of a woman looking out of a window with her back to the room. Before his divorce he had often irritated Yael by grumbling when she stood like that, looking out at the street or the hills.

"What's wrong? Am I breaking the rules again?"

"You know it annoys me."

"That's your problem, Effy."

This morning, even his exercises in front of the mirror annoyed and tired him. After a minute or two he stopped. Called himself lazy bastard again. He panted and added mockingly, "That's your problem, pal."

He was fifty-four, and during his years of living alone he had fallen into the habit of talking to himself. He reckoned this among his old bachelor's foibles, along with losing the lid of the jam, trimming the hair in one of his nostrils and forgetting to do the other, unzipping his fly on the way to the bathroom to save time but missing the bowl when he started to piss, or flushing in the middle in the hope that the sound of rushing water would help him overcome his stuttering bladder. He would try to finish while the water was still running, so there was always a race between his own water and that from the cistern. It was a race he always lost, and he would be faced with the infuriating alternative of standing there, tool in hand, until the cistern refilled and he could have another go, or admitting defeat and leaving his urine in the bowl till next time. He did not like to admit defeat or to waste his time waiting, so he would impatiently pull the handle before the cistern was full again. This would provoke a premature eruption that was insufficient to flush the bowl but was enough to confront him yet again with the abhorrent choice between waiting longer or giving up and going away.

In the course of his life he had had several love affairs, several ideas, a book of poems that aroused some expectations, thoughts about the purpose of the universe and clear insights into where the country had lost its way, a detailed fantasy about founding a new political movement, longings of one sort or another, and the constant desire to open a new chapter. And here he was now in this shabby flat on a gloomy wet morning, engaged in a humiliating struggle to release the corner of his shirt from the zip of his fly. While outside some soggy bird kept repeating the same three-note phrase over and over again, as though it had come to the conclusion that he was so dimwitted he would never understand.

In this way, by painstakingly identifying and classifying his middle-aged bachelor habits, Fima hoped to distance himself from himself, to open up a space for mockery and defend his longings and his self-respect. But there were times when this obsessive quest for the ridiculous in compulsive habits appeared to him in a revelation not as a line of defense between himself and the middle-aged bachelor but in fact as a stratagem employed by that bachelor to get rid of him and usurp his place.

He decided to return to the wardrobe and take a look at himself in the mirror. And to view his body not with disgust, despair, or self-pity, but with resignation. In the mirror he beheld a pale, rather overweight clerk with folds of flesh at the waist, whose underwear was none too fresh, who had sparse black hair on white legs that were too skinny in relation to the belly, and graying hair, weak shoulders, and flabby male breasts growing on the untanned plot of his chest, dotted with pimples, one of which was surrounded by a livid redness. He squeezed the pimples between his forefinger and thumb, watching in the mirror. The bursting of the pimples and the squirting of the yellowish pus afforded a vague, irritable pleasure. For fifty years, like the gestation of an elephant, this faceless clerk had been swelling inside the womb of child and youth and grown man, and now the fifty years were up, the gestation was complete, the womb had burst open, the butterfly had begotten a chrysalis. In this chrysalis Fima recognized himself.

He also saw that now the roles were reversed, that from here on, in the depth of the cocoonlike womb, the wide-eyed child with the gawky limbs would be forever hiding.

Resignation accompanied by faint mockery sometimes contains its opposite: an inner craving for the child, the youth, the grown man out of whose womb the chrysalis emerged. And so sometimes he experienced, for an instant, the restoration of that which could never be restored, in a pure refined state, immune to decay, proof against longing and sorrow. As though trapped inside a glass bubble, for an instant Yael's love was restored to him, with the touch of her lips and tongue behind his ear and her whispered, "Here, touch me here."

In the bathroom Fima was put in a quandary when he discovered that his shaving foam had run out, but he had the bright idea of trying to shave with a thick layer of ordinary toilet soap. Except that the soap turned out to have a rancid smell, like armpits in a heat wave. He scraped his jaws till they were raw but forgot to shave the bristles under his chin. Then he took a hot shower and found the courage to end with thirty seconds of cold water, and for a moment he felt fresh and vigorous and ready to open a new chapter in his life, until the towel, which was damp from the day before and the day before that and more, wrapped him again in his own stale night smell, as though he had been forced to put on a dirty shirt.

From the shower he made for the kitchen and put on the water for coffee; he washed a dirty cup from the sink, put two saccharin tablets and two spoonfuls of instant coffee in it, and went to make his bed. His struggle with the bedspread lasted several minutes. When he returned to the kitchen, he saw that he had left the refrigerator door open overnight. He took out the margarine and the jam and a yogurt he had started the day before, but it turned out that some feeble-minded insect had for some reason selected the yogurt to commit suicide in. He attempted to fish the cadaver out with a teaspoon, but succeeded only in drowning it. He dropped the yogurt pot in the bin and made do with black coffee, having decided without checking that the milk must have turned sour because the fridge door had been left open. He intended to turn on the radio and listen to the news. The cabinet had been sitting late into the night. Had the special airborne commando been parachuted into Damascus and captured President Assad? Or did Yasser Arafat want to come to Jerusalem and address the Knesset? Fima preferred to suppose that at most the news would be a devaluation of the shekel or some case of corruption. He visualized himself convening his cabinet for a midnight sitting. An old revolutionary sentiment from his days in the youth movement made him hold this meeting in a classroom in a run-down school in Katamon, with peeling benches and sums chalked on the blackboard. He himself, wearing a workman's jacket and threadbare trousers, would sit not at the teacher's desk but on the windowsill. He would paint a pitiless picture of the realities, startling the ministers with his portrayal of the impending disaster. Toward dawn he would secure a majority for a decision to withdraw all our armed forces, as a first step, from the Gaza Strip, even without an agreement. "If they fire on our settlements, I'll bomb them from the air. But if they keep quiet, if they demonstrate that they are serious about peace, then we'll wait a year or two and open negotiations with them about the future of the West Bank."

After his coffee he put on a worn brown sweater, the chunky one Yael had left behind for him, looked at his watch, and saw he had missed the seven o'clock news. So he went downstairs to collect the morning paper from the mailbox. But he had forgotten the key and had to tug the paper through the slit, tearing the front page in the process. On his way upstairs, reading the headlines as he climbed, he concluded that the country had fallen into the hands of a bunch of lunatics, who went on and on about Hitler and the Holocaust and always rushed to stamp out any glimmer of peace, seeing it as a Nazi ploy aimed at their destruction. By the time he reached his front door, he realized that he had contradicted himself again, and he warned himself against the hysteria and whining that were so typical of the Israeli intelligentsia: We must beware of the foolish temptation to assume that history will eventually punish the guilty. As he made himself a second cup of coffee, he mentally deployed, against his previous thoughts, the argument he tended to use in his political discussions with Uri Gefen and Tsvika and the rest of the gang: We've got to learn at long last how to exist and operate in interim situations that can drag on for years, instead of reacting to reality by sulking. Our lack of mental readiness to live in an open-ended situation, our desire to reach the bottom line immediately and decide at once what the ending will be, surely these are the real causes of our political impotence.

By the time he had finished reading what the television critic had to say about a program he had forgotten he meant to watch the previous evening, it was past eight o'clock and he had missed the news again. Angrily he decided that he ought to sit down to work right away. He repeated to himself the words from the dream, Have to separate. Separate what from what? A warm, tender voice that was neither male nor female but held a deep compassion said to him, And where are you, Efraim? A very good question, Fima replied.

He sat at his desk and saw the unanswered letters and the shopping list he had written out on Saturday evening, and remembered he was supposed to phone someone this morning about something that could not wait, but he could not for the life of him recall who it was. So he dialed Tsvika Kropotkin's number, woke him up, and stammered a long embarrassed apology, but still kept Tsvi on the line for a good twenty minutes about the tactics of the left and the changes that were appearing in the U.S. position and the time bomb of Islamic fundamentalism that was ticking away all around us, until Tsvi interrupted, "Fima, I'm sorry, don't be mad, but I simply have to get dressed. I'm late for a class." Fima concluded the conversation as he had begun it, with an excessively long apology, and he still could not remember whether he was supposed to call somebody this morning or instead wait for an urgent phone call, which he might have missed now because of his chat with Tsvi. Which on second thought had been less a chat than a monologue. So he dropped his idea of calling Uri Gefen as well and checked over his computerized bank statement, but he couldn't work out if six hundred and fifty shekels had been credited to his account and four hundred and fifty debited, or the other way around. His head sank on his chest, and inside his closed eyes passed crowds of Muslim fanatics excitedly chanting suras and shouting slogans, smashing and burning everything that stood in their way. Then the square was empty, with only tatters of yellowed paper fluttering in the breeze and blending with the pattering rain that fell all the way from here to the Bethlehem hills swathed in gray mist. Where are you, Efraim? Where is the Aryan side? And if she is chilly, why is she?

Fima woke to the touch of a heavy warm hand. He opened his eyes and saw his father's brown hand resting like a tortoise on his thigh. It was an old, thick hand with yellowing nails, pitted with hills and valleys, crisscrossed with dark blue blood vessels, dotted with patches of pigment and sparse tufts of hair. For a moment he panicked. Then he realized that the hand was his own. He woke and read over, three times, the headings he had written down on Saturday for an article he had promised to deliver by today's deadline. But what he had intended to write, what had excited him yesterday to polemical impishness, today seemed totally flat. The very urge to write had been dulled.

A little reflection revealed that all was not lost: it was nothing more than a technical difficulty. Because of the overcast sky and the damp mist there was not enough light in the room. He needed light. That was all. He switched on his desk lamp, hoping by so doing to make a fresh start on his article, his morning, his life. But the lamp was broken. Or perhaps it needed a new lightbulb. Angry, he hurried to the cupboard in the hall, where, contrary to his expectation, he actually did find a bulb, and he managed to replace the old one without any setback. But the new bulb must have been a dud, or perhaps it had fallen under its predecessor's influence. He went back to look for a third one, and on the way it occurred to him to try the light in the hall, and then he had to exonerate both bulbs, because it turned out there was a power cut. To save himself from idleness he decided to call Yael. If her husband answered, he would hang up. If she was there, no doubt the inspiration of the moment would tell him what to say. Like that time, after a flaming row, when he had mollified her with the words, If only we weren't married, I'd ask you to be my wife. And she, smiling, had answered through her tears, If you weren't already my husband, I think I might say yes. After ten or twenty hollow rings Fima understood that Yael did not want to speak to him, unless Ted was leaning on the phone to prevent her from picking up the receiver.

In any case he felt weary. His long nocturnal prowl through the alleys of Valladolid had ruined his whole morning. At one o'clock he had to be at his post behind the reception desk of the private clinic where he worked in Kiryat Shmuel, and already it was twenty past nine. Fima crumpled up the headings for his article and his electricity bill and his shopping list and his computerized bank statement and tossed them all in the bin, leaving his desk cleared for action at last. He went to the kitchen to make himself a fresh cup of coffee, and while he was waiting for the water to boil he stood in the half darkness remembering the evening light in Jerusalem some thirty years before, in Agrippa Street outside the Eden Cinema, a few weeks after his trip to Greece. Yael had said then, Yes, Effy, I do quite love you and I like loving you and I like it when you talk, but what makes you think that if you stop talking for a few minutes you'll stop existing? And he had shut up like a child scolded by its mother. When after a quarter of an hour the kettle was still not boiling, even though he had remembered twice to plug it in, he finally realized that without electricity he would never have his coffee. So he lay down again fully dressed under the heavy winter blanket, set the alarm for quarter to twelve, hid his dream book under the pile of newspapers and magazines at the foot of his bed, covered himself up to his chin, and concentrated his thoughts on women until he managed to arouse himself. He clasped his erection with all ten fingers, like a burglar climbing a drainpipe or, rather—he chuckled—like a drowning man clutching at a straw. But fatigue was much stronger than desire, and he let go and dropped off. Outside, the rain grew heavier.

3

A CAN OF WORMS

On the midday news he heard that an Arab youth had been hit and killed that morning by a plastic bullet fired presumably from a soldier's rifle in the Jebeliyeh refugee camp in the course of a stone-throwing incident, and that the corpse had been snatched from the hospital in Gaza by masked youths. The circumstances were being investigated. Fima pondered the wording of the announcement. He particularly disliked the expression "killed by a plastic bullet." And the word "presumably" made him seethe. He was angry, too, in a more general way, about the passive verbs that were beginning to take over official statements and seemed to be infecting the language as a whole.

Although in fact it might be a healthy and wholly laudable sense of shame that prevented us from announcing simply: A Jewish soldier has shot and killed an Arab teenager. On the other hand, this polluted language was constantly teaching us that the fault lay with the rifle, with the circumstances that were being investigated, with the plastic bullet, as if all evil were the fault of Heaven and everything was predestined.

And in fact, he said to himself, who knows?

After all, there is a sort of secret charm in the words "the fault of Heaven."

But then he was angry with himself. There was no charm and it was not secret. Leave Heaven out of it.

Fima aimed a fork at his forehead, at his temple, at the back of his head, and tried to guess or sense what it must feel like the instant the bullet pierces the skull and explodes: no pain, no noise, perhaps, so he imagined, perhaps just a searing flash of incredulity, like a child preparing himself for a slap on the face from his father and receiving instead a white-hot poker in his eyeball. Is there a fraction, an atom of time in which, who knows, illumination arrives? The light of the seven heavens? When what has been dim and vague all your life is momentarily opened up before darkness falls? As though all those years you have been looking for a complicated solution to a complicated problem, and in the final moment a simple solution flashes out?

At this point Fima croaked angrily to himself, Just stop fucking up your mind. The words "dim and vague" filled him with disgust. He got up and went out, locking the door of his flat behind him and taking particular note of which pocket he put the key in. In the entrance hall of the block of flats he spotted the white of a letter through the slit of his mailbox. But the only key in his pocket was his front-door key. The key to the mailbox was presumably still lying on his desk. Unless it was in the pocket of another pair of trousers. Or on the corner of the kitchen counter. After a moment's hesitation he shrugged; the letter was probably nothing but the water bill or the phone bill, or else just a handbill. While he lunched on a salami omelette, a salad, and a fruit compote in the café across the road, he was startled to see, through the window, that the light was on in his flat. He thought about this for a while, weighing up the faint possibility that he was in both places at once, but preferred to assume that the fault had been repaired and the current had been restored. Glancing at his watch, he decided that if he went up to the flat, switched off the light, found the key to the letter box, and retrieved the letter, he would be late for work, so he paid for his meal, saying, "Thank you, Mrs. Schoenberg." As usual, she corrected him:

"It's Scheinmann, Dr. Nisan."

"Of course," Fima replied. "I'm sorry. How much do I owe you? I've already paid? Well, all I can say is it can't have been an accident. I must have wanted to pay twice, because your schnitzel — it was schnitzel, wasn't it? — was especially tasty. I'm sorry. Thank you. Good-bye. I must run now. Just look at this rain. Aren't you looking a little tired? Or unhappy? It's probably just the weather. It'll brighten up soon. See you tomorrow."

Twenty minutes later, when the bus stopped at the National Auditorium, it occurred to Fima how ridiculous it had been to come out on a day like this without an umbrella. Or to promise the proprietress of the café that the weather would brighten up. On what grounds? Suddenly a fine, burnished sliver of reddish light piercing through the clouds dazzled him by setting fire to a window high up in the Hilton Tower. Though dazzled, he could see a towel waving on the railing of a balcony on the tenth or twentieth floor, and he sensed in his nostrils the precise scent of the woman who had just dried herself on it. Look, he said to himself, nothing is ever really wasted, nothing gets written off, and there is scarcely a moment without some minor miracle. Maybe everything is for the best after all.

The two-room flat on the edge of Kiryat Yovel had been bought for Fima when he remarried in 1961, less than a year after receiving his BA in history with distinction at the university in Jerusalem. In those days his father pinned high hopes on him. Others, too, believed in Fima's future. He was awarded a scholarship, and almost went on to do a master's degree; there were even thoughts of a doctorate and an academic career. But in the summer of 1960 Fima's life underwent a series of mishaps or complications. To this day his friends chuckled with amused affection whenever, in his absence, the conversation turned to "Fima's billy-goat year." The story ran that in the middle of July, straight after the end of his finals, in the garden of the Ratisbone Convent he fell in love with the French guide of a party of Catholic tourists. He was sitting on a bench waiting for a girlfriend, a student at the nursing college named Shula, who married his friend Tsvi Kropotkin a couple of years later. A sprig of oleander was flowering between his fingers and the birds were arguing overhead. Nicole addressed him from the next bench: Was there any water here? Did he speak French? Fima replied in the affirmative to both questions, even though he did not have the faintest idea where there was any water and he knew only a smattering of French. From that moment on he dogged her footsteps wherever she went in Jerusalem; he would not leave her alone despite her polite requests; he did not even give her up when her group leader warned him that he would be obliged to lodge a complaint about him. When she went to Mass at the Dormition Abbey, he waited for her outside like a dog for an hour and a half. Every time she came out of the Kings' Hotel, opposite the Terra Sancta Building, she encountered Fima standing in front of the revolving door, his eyes blazing. When she went to the museum, he was lurking in every room. When she flew back to France, he followed her to Paris and even to her home in Lyon. Late one moonlit night, so the story goes in Jerusalem, her father came out of the house and fired a double-barreled shotgun at him, grazing his leg. During the three days he spent in a Franciscan hospital he made inquiries about what one had to do to become a Christian. Nicole's father, visiting him in the hospital to ask his forgiveness, offered to help him convert. Meanwhile Nicole had had enough of her father too and ran away from both of them, first to her sister in Madrid and then to her sister-in-law in Málaga. Dirty, desperate, and unkempt, he pursued her on dusty buses and trains until his money ran out in Gibraltar and, with the help of the Red Cross, he was returned almost forcibly to Israel on board a Panamanian cargo vessel. On arrival at Haifa he was arrested, and he spent six weeks in a military prison because he had tampered with the date on the form authorizing a soldier on the reserve list to leave the country. They say that at the beginning of this passion Fima weighed seventy-two kilograms and that in September, in the prison hospital, he weighed less than sixty. He was released from prison after his father interceded for him with a senior official, whose wife, a well-known woman-about-town with a famous collection of etchings, subsequently fell outrageously in love with him; she was ten years younger than her husband and at least eight years older than Fima. In the autumn she became pregnant by him and moved into his lodgings in Mousrara. They were the talk of the whole city. In December Fima boarded another cargo boat, a Yugoslav one this time, and turned up in Malta, where he spent three months working on a tropical-fish farm and writing his cycle of poems, *The Death of Augustine and His Resurrection in the Arms of Dulcinea*. In January the woman who owned the cheap hotel where he was staying in Valletta fell for him and moved his luggage into her own apartment. Afraid she might get pregnant too, he decided to marry her in a civil ceremony. This marriage lasted less than two months, because meanwhile his father, with the help of friends in Rome, had managed to discover his whereabouts; he informed Fima that his Jerusalem lover had lost the baby, succumbed to depression, and returned to her husband and her etchings. Fima decided that there was no forgiveness for him and made up his mind to leave his landlady at once and give women a wide berth forever. He decided that love leads inexorably to disaster, whereas relations without love cause only humiliation and hurt. He left Malta without a penny, on the deck of a Turkish fishing boat. His plan was to hole up for at least a year in a certain monastery on the island of Samos. On the way he was smitten with panic at the thought that his ex-wife might also be pregnant and wondered if he ought to go back to her, but at the same time he felt he had acted wisely in leaving her his money but no address that she could trace him by. He disembarked at Thessaloniki and spent a night in a youth hostel, where with sweetness and pain he dreamed of his first love, Nicole, whom he had lost track of in Gibraltar. In the dream her name had changed to Thérèse, and Fima saw his father with a loaded shotgun holding her and the baby prisoner in the cellar of the YMCA in Jerusalem, except that by the end of the dream he himself had become the captive child. The next morning he set off to look for a synagogue, even though he had never been a practicing Jew and was certain that God was not in the least religious and had no use for religion. But, having no other address, Fima decided to try and see. Outside the synagogue he came across three Israeli girls who were backpacking around Greece and were about to head north, into the mountains, because by now spring had arrived. Fima joined them, and on the way, so they say, fell head over heels for one of them, Ilia Abravanel, from Haifa, who to him was the image of Mary Magdalene in a painting he had seen somewhere — he could not remember where or who the artist was. And as Ilia did not yield to his advances, he slept a few times with her friend Liat Sirkin, who invited him to share her sleeping bag as they spent the night in some highland valley or sacred grove. Liat Sirkin taught Fima one or two unusual, exquisite pleasures, but he felt, beyond the carnal thrills, faint hints of spiritual elation: almost day by day he fell under the spell of a secret mountain joy mingled with a sense of exaltation that endowed him with heightened powers of vision such as he had never experienced before or since. During these days in the mountains of northern Greece he was able, looking at the sunrise over a clump of olive trees, to see the creation of the world. And to know with absolute certainty, as he passed a flock of sheep in the midday heat, that this was not the first time he had lived. And actually to hear, sitting on the vine-shaded terrace of a village tavern, over wine and cheese and salad, the roar of a snowstorm in the polar wastes. He played tunes to the girls on a pipe he had fashioned from a reed, and was not ashamed to leap and whirl in front of them like a crazy child until he brought them to peals of laughter and simple happiness. All that time he could see no contradiction between pining for Ilia and sleeping with Liat, but he barely noticed the third girl, who mostly chose to stay silent. Though she was the one who dressed his foot when he cut it on a piece of broken glass. These three girls, with the previous women in his life, including his mother, who had died when he was ten, almost merged into a single woman in his mind. Not because he thought that a woman is only a woman, but because with his inner illumination he sometimes felt that the differences between people, any people — men, women, or children — were of no consequence except perhaps for the outermost layer, the ephemeral surface. Just as water took the form of snow or mist or steam or a lump of ice or clouds or hailstones. Or just as the bells of the monasteries and village churches differed only in their pitch and rhythm, all having the same meaning. He shared these thoughts with the girls, two of whom believed, whereas the third called him a simpleton and contented herself with patching his shirt; in this, too, Fima saw only different expressions of a single statement. This third girl, Yael Levin from Yavne'el, did not refrain from joining in their nude swimming on warm moonlit nights if they found a spring or stream. Once, they watched stealthily, from a distance, a fifteen-year-old shepherd boy satisfying his urges on a nanny goat. And once, they saw a pair of pious old women in widow's weeds with large wooden crosses on their chests sitting silently on a rock in the middle of a field in the noonday heat, motionless, their fingers interlaced. One night they heard sounds of music coming from an empty ruin. And one day a wizened old man walked past them, going the other way, playing on a broken accordion that made no sound. The next morning there was a brief cloudburst, and the air became so clear that they could see the shadows of trees shifting on the red-tiled roofs of little villages in distant valleys, and could almost make out the individual needles of the cypress and pine trees on the flanks of the mountains. One of the peaks still wore a cap of snow, which looked silver rather than white against the deep blue of the sky. Flocks of birds were performing a sort of scarf dance overhead. Fima, for no particular reason, suddenly said something that made all the girls laugh:

"This," he said, "is where the dog is buried."

Ilia said, "I feel dreamier than in a dream and more awake than waking. I can't explain it."

Liat said, "It's the light. That's all."

And Yael: "Who's thirsty? Let's go down to the water."

Less than a month after the conclusion of this trip Fima went to Yavne'el to look for the third girl. He discovered that Yael Levin was a graduate of the aeronautical engineering department of the Haifa Technion and worked in a top-secret air force installation in the hills west of Jerusalem. After a few meetings he found that her presence made him feel restful, while his presence amused her in her placid way. When he asked her, hesitantly, whether she thought they were suited to each other, she replied, "I quite like the way you talk." He thought this indicated a hint of affection. Which he treasured. Next he sought out Liat Sirkin and sat with her for half an hour in a little seaside café, simply to make certain he had not made her pregnant. But afterward he allowed himself to sleep with her again in a cheap hotel in Bat Yam, so he wasn't certain anymore. In May he invited all three girls to Jerusalem to meet his father. The old man charmed Ilia with his old-style courtesy, entertained Liat with anecdotes and fables with morals, but he preferred Yael, who showed, he thought, "signs of depth." Fima agreed with him, although he was not entirely sure he understood what the signs were. He continued to go out with her, until one day she said to him, "Look at your shirt, half inside your trousers and half outside. Wait. I'll sort it out for you."

And in August 1961 Yael and Efraim Nisan were married in the small flat his father had bought him on the edge of Kiryat Yovel, on the edge of Jerusalem, after Fima had given in and signed, in the presence of a notary, an agreement drawn up by his father, containing a solemn undertaking to refrain henceforth from any act that his father might define as an "adventure." He also undertook to begin, at the end of the wasted year, studying for a master's degree. The father, for his part, agreed to finance his son's studies as well as the final stage of Yael's training, and even granted them a modest monthly allowance for the first five years of their marriage. From then on Fima's name was no longer mentioned in Jerusalem gossip. The adventures had come to an end. The billy-goat year was finished, and the tortoise years began. But he did not go back to the university, except perhaps with one or two ideas that he gave to his friend Tsvi Kropotkin, who had meanwhile proceeded without a pause from MA to doctorate and was already laying the foundation for a great tower of historical articles and books.

In 1962, at the urging of his friends and thanks to special efforts on the part of Tsvika, Fima published the cycle of poems he had written during his short-lived marriage in Malta: *The Death of Augustine and His Resurrection in the Arms of Dulcinea*. For a year or two there were some critics and readers who saw in Efraim Nisan a promise waiting to be fulfilled. But after a time even the promise faded, because Fima's muse fell silent. He wrote no more poems. Every morning Yael was picked up by a military vehicle and taken to work at a base whose location Fima did not know, where she was engaged in some technological development that he neither understood nor wanted to. He would spend the entire morning prowling around the flat, listening to every news broadcast, raiding the fridge and eating standing up, arguing aloud with himself and with the news readers, furiously making the bed that Yael had not managed to make before she went out, in fact couldn't, because he was still asleep in it. Then he would finish reading the morning paper, go out to buy one or two things at the grocer's, come back with two afternoon papers, immerse himself in them until the evening and leave their pages scattered all over the flat. Between reading the papers and listening to the news, he made himself sit down at his desk. For a while he was occupied by a Christian book, the *Pugio Fidei* of Father Raymond Martini, published in Paris in 1651 to refute once and for all the faith of the "Moors and the Jews." Fima was contemplating a fresh study of the Christian origins of anti-Semitism. But his work was interrupted by a vague interest in the idea of the Hidden God. He plunged himself into the biography of the hermit Eusebius Sophronius Hieronymus, who learned Hebrew from a Jewish teacher, settled in Bethlehem in 386, translated both

Testaments into Latin, and may have deliberately deepened the rift between Jews and Christians. But this study did not quench Fima's thirst. Lassitude got the better of him, and he sank into idleness. He would leaf through the encyclopedia, forget what he was looking for, and waste a couple of hours reading through the entries in alphabetical order. Almost every evening he would pull on his battered cap and go out to visit his friends, chatting till the early hours about the Lavon affair, the Eichmann trial, the Cuban missile crisis, the German scientists in Egypt, the significance of the pope's visit to the Holy Land. When Yael got home from work in the evening and asked if he had eaten, Fima would reply irritably, Why? Where does it say I've got to eat? And then, while she was in the shower, he would explain to her through the closed door who was really behind the assassination of President Kennedy. Later, when she asked if he was going out to have another row with Uri or Tsvika, he would answer, No, I'm going to an orgy. And he would ask himself how he had allowed his father to attach him to this woman. But there were other times when he suddenly fell in love all over again with her strong fingers as they rubbed her little ankles at the end of the day, or with her habit of stroking her eyelashes, lost in thought, and he would court her like a shy, passionate youth until she allowed him to give pleasure to her body, and then he would thrill her eagerly and precisely, with a sort of profound attentiveness. Sometimes he would say to her, as some petty quarrel brewed, Just wait, Yael, it'll pass. It won't be long before our proper life starts. Sometimes they would go for a walk together in the deserted lanes of north Jerusalem on a Friday evening, and he would talk to her with barely suppressed excitement about the union of body and light according to the ancient mystics. This made her feel so joyful and tender that she snuggled against him and forgave him for putting on weight, for forgetting to change his shirt again for the weekend, for his habit of correcting her Hebrew. Then they would go home and make love as if they were beyond despair.

In 1965 Yael went to work, on special contract, at the Boeing research center in Seattle. Fima declined to join her, arguing that a period of separation might do them both good. He stayed behind in the two-room flat in Kiryat Yovel. He had a modest post as receptionist in a private gynecological clinic in Kiryat Shmuel. He kept his distance from academic life, unless Tsvi Kropotkin dragged him to a one-day conference on the importance of personality in history, or on the notion of the historian as eyewitness. At weekends he would turn up at Nina and Uri Gefen's or at other friends', and was easily caught up in their political discussions; he would occasionally astound all those present with some mordant summing-up or paradoxical prediction, but he never knew how to stop when he was winning, he would persist like a compulsive gambler, arguing volubly on subjects he knew nothing about, even over trivial details, until he wore out even his most loyal friends. Sometimes he would arrive with a few books and keep an eye on his friends' children while they went out for the evening. Or cheerfully offer to help them with an article, by proofreading, copyediting, or preparing an abstract. Sometimes he would undertake shuttle diplomacy on a mission of mediation for a feuding couple. Every now and again he would publish a short trenchant article in *Ha'aretz* on some aspect of the current political scene. Once in a while he would take a few days' holiday alone in a private guesthouse in one of the older settlements in northern Sharon. Every summer he attempted with renewed enthusiasm to learn to drive, and every autumn he failed the driving test. Now and again a woman he had met at the clinic or through friends found her way to his untidy bachelor flat and into his bed, whose sheets needed changing. She would soon discover that Fima was more interested in her pleasure than his own. Some women found this wonderful and moving; others found it unsettling and hastened to disengage themselves. He could spend an hour or two inflicting endless varied exquisite sensations full of playful inventiveness and physical humor, before casually snatching his own satisfaction, and then, almost before his partner noticed that he had exacted his modest commission, he would be devoting himself to her again. Any woman who tried to obtain a measure of continuity or permanence in her relationship with Fima, who succeeded in extracting a key from him, caused him to take refuge after a week or two in a run-down guesthouse in Pardés Hanna or Magdiel and not come home until she had given him up. But even these episodes had become rare in the past five or six years.

When Yael wrote to him from Seattle early in 1966 to say there was another man in her life, Fima laughed at the trite expression. The love affairs of his billy-goat year, his marriage to Yael, Yael herself, now seemed as trite, as overacted, as childish as the underground revolutionary cell he had tried to set up when he was in high school. He decided to write her a line or two simply to send his best wishes to her and the other man in her life. He sat down at his desk that afternoon, and did not stop writing until midday the following day: in a feverish missive of thirty-four pages he confessed the depth of his love for her. After reading it through, he rejected it, tore it up, and flushed it down the lavatory. You cannot describe love in words, and if you can, that's a sign the love no longer exists. Or is on the way out. Finally he tore a page of graph paper from a notebook and scrawled on it: "I can't stop loving you because it's not up to me, but of course you're a free agent. How blind I've been. If there's anything you need from the flat, let me know and I'll send it. Meanwhile I'm sending you a parcel with three of your nighties and your furry slippers and the photos. But if you don't mind, I'd like to keep the picture of the two of us at Bethlehem in Galilee." Yael took this letter to mean that Fima would not place any obstacles in the way of a divorce. But when she came back to Jerusalem and introduced a colorless, inexpressive man with a jaw that was too broad and thick eyebrows like a pair of bushy mustaches, saying, Efraim Nisan, Ted Tobias, let's all be friends, Fima changed his mind and adamantly refused to grant a divorce. So Ted and Yael flew back to Seattle. They lost contact, apart from a few aerograms and postcards about practical matters.

Several years later, early in 1982, Ted and Yael turned up at Fima's flat one winter afternoon with their three-year-old son, a slightly cross-eyed albino child-philosopher with thick glasses, dressed in an American astronaut's space suit bearing a shiny metal badge inscribed with the word CHALLENGER. The little fellow soon revealed an ability to compose complicated conditional sentences and to duck awkward questions. Fima instantly fell for little Dimi Tobias. Regretting his earlier opposition, he offered Yael and Ted a divorce, his assistance, and his friendship. Yael, however, no longer attached any importance to the religious divorce and saw no point in friendship. In the intervening years she had managed to leave Ted twice and have affairs with other men before making up her mind to go back to him and to have Dimi at what was almost the last moment as far as she was concerned. Fima won the heart of the thoughtful little Challenger with a story about a wild wolf who decided to give up being wild and tried to join a colony of rabbits. When the story was over, Dimi offered his own ending, which Fima found logical, sensitive, and not unfunny.

Thanks to the intervention of Fima's father, the divorce was arranged discreetly. Ted and Yael settled in the suburb of Beit Hakerem, found jobs together in a research institute, and divided their year into three: the summer in Seattle, the fall in Pasadena, the winter and spring in Jerusalem. Sometimes they invited Fima round on Friday evening, when the Kropotkins and the Gefens and the rest of the group were there. Sometimes they left Dimi with Fima in Kiryat Yovel and went off to Elat or Upper Galilee for a couple of days. Fima became their unpaid babysitter, because he was available and because a friendship had grown up between him and Dimi. By some odd logic Dimi called him Grandpa. He called Fima's father Grandpa too. Fima taught himself to make houses, palaces, and castles with openings out of matchsticks, matchboxes, and glue. This was totally at odds with the image of Fima shared by his friends, by Yael, and by Fima himself, namely, a clumsy oaf who was born with two left hands and could never get the hang of replacing the washer on a tap or sewing on a button.

Apart from Dimi and his parents, there was the gang: pleasant, respectable people, some of whom had known Fima from their student days and had been indirectly involved in the ordeals of the billy-goat year, and some of whom still hoped that one day the lad would wake up, get his act together, and one way or another take Jerusalem by the ears. True, they said, he sometimes gets on your nerves, he overdoes it, he has no sense of proportion, but on the other hand when he's brilliant he's really brilliant. One day he's really going to get somewhere. He's worth investing in. Last Friday, for example, early in the evening, before he started making a fool of himself with his imitations of politicians, the way he snatched the word *ritual* out of Tsvi's mouth and held us all spellbound like little kids when he suddenly said, "Everything is ritual" and fired his theory at us straight from the hip. We haven't stopped talking about it all week. Or that amazing comparison he threw out, of Kafka and Gogol, and of the two of them with Hasidic folktales.

Over the years some of them grew fond of Fima's unique combination of wit and absentmindedness, of melancholy and enthusiasm, of sensitivity and helplessness, of profundity and buffoonery. Moreover, he was always available to be roped in to do some proofreading or to discuss a draft of an article. Behind his back they said, not unkindly, True, he's a—how to put it?—he's an original, and he's good-hearted. The trouble is, he's bone idle. He has no ambition. He simply doesn't think about tomorrow. And he's not getting any younger.

Despite which, there was something in his podgy form, his shuffling, abstracted way of walking, his fine, high brow, his weary shoulders, his thinning fair hair, and in his kindly eyes that always seemed lost and looking either inward or out beyond the mountains and the desert, something in his appearance that filled them with affection and joy and made them smile broadly even when they caught sight of him from a distance, on the other side of the street, wandering around the city center as though he did not know who had brought him there or how he was going to get out again. And they said, Look, there's Fima over there, waving his arms. He must be having an argument with himself, and presumably he's winning it.

In the course of time a certain uneasy friendliness, filled with anger and contradictions, developed between Fima and his father, the well-known cosmetics manufacturer Baruch Nomberg, who was a veteran member of the right-wing Herut Party. Even now, when Fima was fifty-four and his father eighty-two, the father would slip a couple of ten-shekel notes, or a single twenty-shekel note, into his son's pocket at the end of every visit. Meanwhile Fima's little secret was that he deposited eighty shekels each month in a savings account in the name of Ted and Yael's son, who was ten now but still looked like a seven-year-old, dreamy and trustful. Strangers on buses sometimes noticed a vague resemblance between Fima and the child, in the shape of the chin or the forehead, or in the walk. The previous spring Dimi had asked to keep a pair of tortoises and some silkworms in a little storage space that Fima and Ted cleared for him on the balcony of the messy kitchen of the flat in Kiryat Yovel. And even though Fima was considered by others and even by himself to be incorrigibly idle and absentminded, all through the summer there was not a single day when he forgot to attend to what he took to calling "our can of worms." Now, in the winter, the silkworms were dead, and the tortoises had been set free in the wadi, at the point where Jerusalem abruptly ends and a rocky wilderness begins.

4

Hopes of Opening a New Chapter

The private clinic in Kiryat Shmuel was approached through the garden behind the building, along a pathway paved with Jerusalem stone. Now that it was winter, the path was covered with slippery rain-soaked pine needles. Fima was totally absorbed in considering whether a frozen bird he had just spotted on a low branch could hear the thunder that was rolling from west to east; the bird's head and beak were buried deep in the plumage of its wing. Struck by a sudden doubt, he turned back to see if it really was a bird or if it was just a wet pinecone. That was how he came to slip and fall to his knees. He stayed crouching, not because he was in pain, but because of self-mocking pleasure at his own predicament. Softly he said, Well done, pal.

For some reason he felt he had deserved this fall as a sort of logical sequel to the minor miracle he had experienced outside the Hilton Hotel on his way here.

When he eventually managed to get to his feet, he stood absent-mindedly in the rain, looking like someone who does not know where he has come from or where he must go. Raising his head toward the upper floors, he saw nothing but closed shutters or blank curtained windows. Here and there on a balcony was a geranium in a pot. The rain had given them a sensual sparkle that brought to his mind the painted lips of a vulgar woman.

Beside the entrance to the clinic there was an elegantly restrained plate of black glass inscribed in silver lettering: DR WAHRHAFTIG DR EITAN CONSULTANT GYNECOLOGISTS. For the thousandth time Fima asked himself why there were not specialists for male disorders too. He also objected to the Hebrew phrase in question, which contained a construction that the language does not tolerate. Then he found himself ridiculous for using such an absurd expression. And felt shame and confusion as he recalled how indignantly he had reacted to the news, not because of the death of an Arab boy in the Jebeliyeh refugee camp but because of the phrase "killed by a plastic bullet."

As if it's the bullets that do the killing.

And was he getting soft in the head himself?

He summoned his cabinet for another meeting in the dilapidated classroom. At the door he posted a burly sentry in khaki shorts, Arab headdress, and knitted cap. Some of his ministers sat on the bare floor at his feet, others leaned against the wall, which was covered with educational diagrams. In a few well-chosen words Fima presented them with the need to choose between the territories conquered in '67 and our very identity. Then, while they were still buzzing excitedly, he called for a vote, which he won, and immediately gave them his detailed instructions.

Before we won the Six-Day War, he mused, the state of the nation was less dangerous and destructive than it is now. Or perhaps it wasn't really less dangerous, just less demoralizing and less depressing. Was it really easier for us to face up to the danger of an-

nihilation than to sit in the dock facing the accusations of international public opinion? The danger of annihilation gave us pride
and a sense of unity, whereas sitting in the dock now is gradually
breaking our spirit. But that's not the right way to state the alternatives. In fact, sitting in the dock may be breaking the spirit only of
the secular intelligentsia of Russian or Western origin, whereas the
ordinary masses are not in the least nostalgic for the pride of David
standing up to Goliath. Anyway, the expression "ordinary masses"
is a hollow cliché. Meanwhile, because you fell, your trousers are
covered with mud and the hands that are wiping them clean are
also muddy and the rain is pouring down on your head. It is already five past one. However hard you try, you'll never get to work
on time.

The clinic was two ground-floor flats joined together. The windows, guarded by arabesque grilles, looked out on a typical back
garden, damp and deserted, shaded by dense pine trees around
whose bases a few gray boulders sprouted. A rustle of treetops
started at the slightest breeze. Now, with a strong wind blowing,
Fima had a fleeting image of a remote village in Poland or one of
the Baltic States, with storms shrieking through the surrounding
forest, whipping across snowbound fields, assailing thatched cot-
tage roofs, and making the church bells ring out. And wolves howling not far away. In his head Fima already had a little story about
this village, about Nazis, Jews, and partisans, which he might tell
to Dimi this evening, in exchange for a ladybug in a jam jar or a
spaceship cut out of orange peel.

From the first floor came the sounds of piano, violin, and cello
being played by the three elderly women who lived there and gave
private music lessons. They also probably gave recitals and played
at memorial meetings, at the presentation of a prize for Yiddish literature, at the inauguration of a community center or a day center for the elderly. Although Fima had worked at the clinic for several years now, their playing still wrung his heart, as though a cello
deep inside him responded with its own mute sounds of longing to
the one upstairs. As though with the passing years, a mystic bond

was growing stronger between what was being done down here to women's bodies with stainless-steel forceps and the melancholy of the cello upstairs.

The sight of Fima, podgy and disheveled, smiling sheepishly, with his hands and knees covered with mud, filled Dr. Wahrhaftig as usual with good humor mingled with affection and a strong urge to reprimand him. Wahrhaftig was a gentle, rather shy man, so emotional that he had difficulty holding back his tears at times, especially when anybody apologized to him and asked to be forgiven. Maybe that was why he cultivated a severe manner, and always tried to terrorize those around him by shouting rebukes at them. Rebukes that turned out to be mild and inoffensive.

"Hah! Your Excellency! Herr Major General von Nisan! Straight from the trenches, I see! We should pin a medal on you!"

"I'm a little late," Fima replied bashfully. "I'm sorry. I slipped on the path. It's so wet outside."

"Ach so!" roared Wahrhaftig. "Once more this fatal lateness! Once again force majeure!" And he recounted for the nth time the joke about the dead man who was late for his own funeral.

He was a stocky man with the build of a basso profundo, and his face had the florid, flabby look of an alcoholic's, crisscrossed with an unhealthy network of blood vessels that were so near the surface, you could almost take his pulse by their throbbing. He had a joke for every occasion, invariably introduced with the phrase "There is a well-known story about . . ." And he always burst out laughing when he got close to the punch line. Fima, who had already heard ad nauseam why the dead man was late for his own funeral, nevertheless let out a faint laugh, because he was fond of this tender-hearted tyrant. Wahrhaftig was constantly delivering long lectures in his stentorian voice about such subjects as the connection between your eating habits and your worldview, or about the "socialistic" economy and how it encouraged idleness and fraud and was therefore unsuited to a civilized country. Wahrhaftig would utter these last words in a tone of mystical pathos, like a true believer praising the works of the Almighty.

"It's quiet here today," Fima remarked.

Wahrhaftig replied that they were expecting a famous artist any minute now with a minor obstruction of the tubes. The word "tubes," in its medical usage, reminded him of a well-known story, which he did not spare Fima.

Meanwhile, stealthily as a cat, Dr. Gad Eitan emerged from his office. He was followed by the nurse, Tamar Greenwich, who looked like an early pioneer, a woman of forty-five or so in a light-blue cotton dress with her hair pinned neatly back into what looked like a small ball of wool at the base of her skull. As a result of a pigment peculiarity one of her eyes was green and the other brown. She crossed the reception hall supporting a pale patient, whom she escorted to the recovery room.

Dr. Eitan, lithe and muscular, leaned on the desk, chewing gum with a leisurely motion of his jaws. He replied with a movement of the chin to Fima's greeting or to a question from Wahrhaftig, or perhaps to both at once. His watery blue eyes were fixed on a spot high above the reproduction Modigliani on the wall. With his self-satisfied expression and his thin blond mustache, he looked to Fima like an arrogant Prussian diplomat who has been posted against his will to Outer Mongolia. He allowed Wahrhaftig to finish another well-known story. Then there was a silence, after which, like a lethargic leopard, almost without moving his lips, he said quietly, "Let's cut the chatter and get on with it."

Wahrhaftig obeyed at once and followed him to the treatment room. The door closed behind them. A sharp, antiseptic whiff escaped between its opening and closing.

Fima washed his hands and made a cup of coffee for the patient in the recovery room. Then he made another cup for Tamar and one for himself, donned a short white coat, sat down behind his desk, and began to look through the ledger in which he kept track of patients' visits. Here too he wrote the numbers out in words, not figures. He noted down accounts that were settled or deferred, dates for laboratory tests and their results, and any alterations to appointments. He also managed the filing cabinet that contained patients' medical records and details of prescriptions, ultrasound tests, and X-rays. This, with answering the telephone, was the sum total of his job. Apart from making coffee every couple of hours for the two doctors and the nurse, and occasionally also for a patient if her treatment had been painful.

Across the hall from his desk there was a small coffee table, two armchairs, a rug, the reproduction Modigliani and Degas on the walls: the waiting area. Sometimes Fima would help a patient through the difficult period of waiting by engaging her in light conversation about some neutral subject such as the rising cost of living or a TV program that had been shown the previous evening. Most of the visitors, however, preferred to wait in silence, leafing through magazines, in which case Fima would bury his eyes in his papers and minimize his presence so as not to cause embarrassment. What went on behind the closed doors of the treatment rooms? What caused the groans that Fima sometimes heard or thought he heard? What did the various women's faces express when they arrived and when they left? What was the story that ended in this clinic? And the new story that was just beginning here? What was the male shadow behind this or that woman? And the child that would not be born, what was it? What would it have turned out to be? These things Fima tried at times to decipher, or to invent, with guesswork linked to a struggle between revulsion and the feeling that he ought to participate, at least in his imagination, in every form of suffering. Sometimes womanhood itself struck him as being a crying injustice, almost a cruel illness that afflicted half the human race and exposed it to degradations and humiliations that the other half was spared. But sometimes a vague jealousy stirred inside him, a sense of deprivation or loss, as though he had been cheated of some secret gift that enabled *them* to relate to the world in a way that was barred to him forever. The more he thought about it, the less he was able to distinguish between his pity and his envy. The womb, conception, pregnancy, childbirth, motherhood, breastfeeding, even menstruation, even miscarriage and abortion — he tried to imagine them all, struggling over and over again to feel what he was not meant to feel. Sometimes, while he was thinking, he absently fingered his own nipples. They seemed a hollow joke, a sad relic. Then he was swept by a wave of profound pity for all men and women, as though the separation of the sexes were nothing but a cruel prank. He felt that the time had come to rise up and with sympathy and reason do something to put an end to it. Or at least minimize the suffering that resulted from it. Without being asked, he would get up, fetch a glass of cold water from the refrigerator, and with a faint smile hand it to a woman waiting her turn, and murmur, It'll be all right. Or, Have a drink, you'll feel better. Usually this only provoked mild surprise, but occasionally he generated a grateful smile, to which he replied with a nod, as if to say, It's the least I can do.

When he had free time between answering the telephone and keeping his records up to date, Fima would read a novel in English or a biography of a statesman. Generally, though, he did not read books, but devoured the two evening papers he had bought on the way, taking care not to miss even the short news items, the commentary, the gossip: embezzlement in the co-op in Safed, a case of bigamy in Ashkelon, a story of unrequited love in Kfar Saba. Everything concerned him. After scouring the papers, he would sit back and remember. Or convene cabinet meetings, dressing his ministers up as revolutionary guerrillas, lecturing them, prophesying rage and consolation, saving the children of Israel whether they wanted it or not, and bringing peace to the land.

Between treatments, when the doctors and the nurse emerged for their coffee break, Fima would sometimes suddenly lose his ability to listen. He would wonder what he was doing here, what he had in common with these strangers. And where he ought to be if not here. But he could find no answer to that question. Even though he felt, painfully, that somewhere someone was waiting for him, surprised he was so late. Then, after scrabbling for a long time in his pockets, he would find a heartburn tablet, swallow it, and continue scanning the newspapers in case he had missed what really mattered.

Gad Eitan was Alfred Wahrhaftig's ex–son-in-law: he had been married to Wahrhaftig's only daughter, who ran away to Mexico with a visiting poet she had fallen for while working at the Jerusalem Book Fair. Wahrhaftig, the founder of the clinic and the senior partner, held Gad Eitan in strange awe: he would lavish on him little gestures of submission and deference, which he camouflaged with explosions of polite rage. Dr. Eitan, who although his particular specialty was infertility also served whenever necessary as the anesthetist, was an icy, taciturn man. He had a habit of staring long and hard at his fingers. As if he were afraid of losing them, or as if their very existence never ceased to amaze him. The fingers in question were well shaped and long, and wonderfully musical. He also moved like a drowsy wild beast, or one that was just waking up. At times a thin, chilly smile spread over his face; his watery eyes took no part in it. Evidently his coolness aroused in women a certain confidence and excitement, and an urge to shake him out of his indifference or to melt his cruelty. Eitan would ignore any hint of an overture, and respond to confessions on the part of a patient with a dry phrase such as "Well, yes, but there's no alternative" or "What can one do: these things happen."

In the middle of Wahrhaftig's stories Eitan would sometimes turn quickly 180 degrees, like the turret of a tank, and vanish on cat's paws through the door of his consulting room. It seemed as though all people, men and women alike, caused a faint revulsion in him. And because he had known for several years that Tamar was in love with him, he enjoyed occasionally firing an acerbic remark at her:

"What do you smell of today?"

Or:

"Straighten your skirt, will you, and stop wasting your knees on us. We have to watch that kind of view at least twenty times a day."

This time he said, "Would you kindly put that artist's vagina and cervix on my desk. Yes, the famous lady. Yes, the results of her tests. What did you think I meant? Yes, hers, I've no use for yours."

Tamar's eyes, the green left one and the brown right one, filled with tears. And Fima, with an air of someone rescuing a princess from the dragon's jaws, got up and placed the file in question on the doctor's desk. Eitan shot a vacant glance at him and then turned his icy eyes to his own fingers. Under the powerful theater lights his womanly fingers took on an unnatural pink glow: they looked almost transparent. He saw fit to aim a lethal salvo at Fima too:

"Do you happen to know what *menstruation* means? Then please tell Mrs. Licht, today—yes, on the phone—that I need to have her here exactly two days after she next menstruates. And if that doesn't sound nice on the phone, you can say two days after her next period. I don't care what you say. You can say after her festival, for all I care. The main thing is to fix an appointment for her accordingly. Thank you."

Wahrhaftig, like a man catching sight of a fire and hurrying over to throw the contents of the nearest bucket on it without stopping to check whether the bucket contained water or gasoline, intervened at this point:

"Festivals—that reminds me of a well-known story about Begin and Yasser Arafat."

And he embarked for the nth time on the story of how Begin's shrewdness once got the better of Arafat's villainy.

Eitan replied, "I'd hang the pair of them."

"Gad's had a hard day," said Tamar.

And Fima added his own contribution: "These are hard times all round. We spend all our time trying to repress what we're doing in the Territories, and the consequence is that the air's full of anger and aggression, and everybody's at everybody else's throat."

At this point Wahrhaftig asked what the difference was between Ramallah and Monte Carlo, and then launched into another anecdote. He started laughing heartily halfway between Monte Carlo and Ramallah. Then, remembering his position, he suddenly puffed himself up, flushed deep red with the network of veins throbbing in his cheeks, and thundered carefully, "Please! The break is finished. Sorry. Fima! Tamar! Please close this beer garden right away! This whole country of ours is more Asian than Asia! Not even Asia! Africa! But at least in my clinic we are still working as in a civilized country." A superfluous exhortation, since by then Eitan had shrunk back to his room, Tamar had gone to wash her face, and Fima had in any case not left his desk.

At half past five a tall, golden-haired woman in a beautiful black dress came out. She stopped at Fima's desk and asked, almost in a whisper, whether it showed. Whether she looked a fright. Fima, who had not heard the question, replied mistakenly to another one, "Naturally, Mrs. Tadmor. Of course nobody will find out. You can rest assured. We are totally discreet here." Although he tactfully refrained from looking at her, he sensed her tears and added, "There are some tissues in the box."

"Are you a doctor too?"

"No, ma'am. I'm only the receptionist."

"Have you been here long?"

"Right from the start. Ever since the clinic opened."

"You must have witnessed all sorts of scenes."

"We do have our awkward moments."

"And you're not a doctor?"

"No, ma'am."

"How many abortions do you do a day?"

"I'm afraid I can't answer that question."

"I'm sorry for asking. Life has suddenly dealt me a cruel blow."

"I understand. I'm sorry."

"No, you don't understand. I didn't have an abortion. Just a little treatment. But it was humiliating."

"I'm very sorry. Let's hope you'll feel better now."

"You've probably got it on record, exactly what they did to me."

"I never look into the medical notes, if that's what you mean."

"You're lucky you weren't born a woman. You can't even begin to guess what you were spared."

"I'm sorry. Can I get you some coffee, or tea?"

"You're always sorry. Why are you so sorry? You haven't even looked at me. You keep looking away."

"Sorry. I didn't notice. Instant or Turkish?"

"Strange, isn't it? I could have sworn you were a doctor, too. It's not the white coat. Are you a student? Doing your practical stint?"

"No, ma'am. I'm just a clerk. Would you rather have a glass of water? There's some mineral water in the fridge."

"What's it like, working in a place like this for such a long time? What sort of a job is it for a man? Don't you develop an aversion to women? A physical aversion even?"

"I don't think so. Anyway, I can only speak for myself."

"So what about you? You don't have an aversion to women?"

"No, Mrs. Tadmor. If anything, the opposite."

"Oh! What's the opposite of an aversion?"

"Sympathy, perhaps? Curiosity? It's hard to explain."

"Why aren't you looking at me?"

"I don't like to cause embarrassment. There, the water's boiling. What's it to be, then? Coffee?"

"Embarrassment to yourself or to me?"

"Hard to say exactly. Maybe both. I'm not sure."

"Do you happen to have a name?"

"My name is Fima. Efraim."

"I'm Annette. Are you married?"

"I have been married, ma'am. Twice. Nearly three times."

"And I'm just getting divorced. To be more accurate, I am being divorced. Are you too shy to look at me? Afraid of being disappointed? Or maybe you just want to make sure you never have to hesitate whether to say hello to me if we meet in the street?"

"Sugar and milk, Mrs. Tadmor? Annette?"

"It would actually suit you, to be a gynecologist. Better than it suits that ridiculous old man who can't stick a rubber-gloved finger into me without trying to distract my attention with some joke about the Emperor Franz Josef deciding to punish God. May I use the phone?"

"Of course. I'll be back there, in the records room. When you've finished, just call me so we can make you another appointment. Do you need one?"

"Fima Efraim. Please. Look at me. Don't be afraid. I'm not going to cast a spell on you. Once, when I was beautiful, men used to fall for me like flies; now, even the assistant in the clinic won't look at me."

Fima looked up. And at once recoiled, because the combination of anguish and sarcasm he saw on her face made him throb with desire. He lowered his eyes to his papers and said carefully, "But you are still a very beautiful woman. At least, to me you are. You don't want to make a phone call?"

"Not anymore. I've changed my mind. I'm changing my mind about lots of things at the moment. So I'm not ugly?"

"On the contrary."

"You're not too good-looking yourself. Pity you've made the coffee. I didn't ask for anything. Never mind. You can drink it. And thank you." She stopped at the door and added, "You have my phone number. It's in your files."

Fima pondered this. The words "a new chapter" seemed rather cheap, yet he knew that in other times he might well have fallen for this Annette. But why only in other times? Finally, in Yael's old words, he said to himself, "Your problem, pal."

And, after filing the papers away, he locked the records room and washed the cups, ready to shut up shop.

In the
Promised Land

The Meaning of Homeland

from *Under This Blazing Light*
(First published in 1967)

Let me begin with a few things that seem to me to be self-evident. I shall have to reformulate some accepted phrases about identity and identification, because there has been a massive upheaval recently, an erosion of words and their meanings: "Jewishness," "Zionism," "homeland," "national right," "peace"—these words are being dragged into new spaces, and laden with interpretations that we could not have imagined previously. And anyone who stands up and speaks out these days risks being stoned in the marketplace and suspected of Jewish self-hatred or betraying the nation or desecrating the memory of the fallen, whose very rest is being disturbed so that they may be used as ammunition in our domestic quarrels.

TO BE A JEW

I am a Jew and a Zionist. In saying this, I am not basing myself on religion. I have never learned to resort to verbal compromises like "the spirit of our Jewish past" or "the values of Jewish tradition," because values and tradition alike derive directly from religious tenets in which I cannot believe. It is impossible to sever Jewish values and Jewish tradition from their source, which is revelation, faith, and commandments. Consequently nouns like "mission," "destiny," and "election," when used with the adjective "Jewish," only cause me embarrassment or worse.

A Jew, in my vocabulary, is someone who regards himself as a Jew, or someone who is forced to be a Jew. A Jew is someone who acknowledges his Jewishness. If he acknowledges it publicly, he is a Jew by choice. If he acknowledges it only to his inner self, he is a Jew by the force of his destiny. If he does not acknowledge any connection with the Jewish people either in public or in his tormented inner being, he is not a Jew, even if religious law defines him as such because his mother is Jewish. A Jew, in my unhalachic opinion, is someone who *chooses* to share the fate of other Jews, or who is *condemned* to do so.

Moreover: to be a Jew almost always means to relate mentally to the Jewish past, whether the relation is one of pride or gloom or both together, whether it consists of shame or rebellion or pride or nostalgia.

Moreover: to be a Jew almost always means to relate to the Jewish present, whether the relation is one of fear or confidence, pride in the achievement of Jews or shame for their actions, an urge to deflect them from their path or a compulsion to join them.

And finally: to be a Jew means to feel that wherever a Jew is persecuted for being a Jew—that means you.

To Be a Zionist

Anyone who believes in the power of words must be careful how he uses them. I never use the word *shoah* ("catastrophe") when I want to refer to the murder of the Jews of Europe. The word *shoah* falsifies the true nature of what happened. A shoah is a natural event, an outbreak of forces beyond human control. An earthquake, a flood, a typhoon, an epidemic is a shoah. The murder of the European Jews was no shoah. It was the ultimate logical outcome of the ancient status of the Jew in Western civilization. The Jew in Europe, in Christendom, in the paganism within Christendom is not a "national minority," "a religious minority," or "a problem of status." For thousands of years the Jew has been perceived as the symbol of something inhuman. Like the steeple and the cross, like the devil, like the Messiah, so the Jew is part of the infrastructure of the Western mind. Even if all the Jews had been assimilated among the peoples of Europe the *Jew* would have continued to be present. Someone had to fill his role to exist as an archetype in the dungeons of the Christian soul. To shine and repel, to suffer and swindle, to be fated to be a genius and an abomination. Therefore, being a Jew in the diaspora means that Auschwitz is meant for you. It is meant for you because you are a symbol, not an individual. The symbol of the justly persecuted vampire, or the symbol of the unjustly persecuted innocent victim — but always and everywhere, you are not an individual, not yourself, but a fragment of a symbol.

I am a Zionist because I do not want to exist as a fragment of a symbol in the consciousness of others. Neither the symbol of the shrewd, gifted, repulsive vampire, nor the symbol of the sympathetic victim who deserves compensation and atonement. That is why my place is in the land of the Jews. This does not make me circumvent my responsibilities as a Jew, but it saves me from the nightmare of being a symbol in the minds of strangers day and night.

The land of the Jews, I said. The land of the Jews could not have come into being and could not have existed anywhere but here. Not in Uganda, not in Ararat, and not in Birobidjan. Because this is the place the Jews have always looked to throughout their history. Because there is no other territory to which the Jews would have come in their masses to establish a Jewish homeland. On this point I commit myself to a severe, remorseless distinction between the *inner motives* of the return to Zion and *its justification to others*. The age-old longings are a motive, but not a justification. Political Zionism has made political, national use of religious, messianic yearnings. And rightly so. But our justification vis-à-vis the Arab inhabitants of the country cannot be based on our age-old longings. What are our longings to them? The Zionist enterprise has no other objective justification than the right of a drowning man to grasp the only plank that can save him. And that is justification enough. (Here I must anticipate something I shall return to later: there is a vast moral difference between the drowning man who grasps a plank and makes room for himself by pushing the others who are sitting on it to one side, even by force, and the drowning man who grabs the whole plank for himself and pushes the others into the sea. This is the moral argument that lies behind our repeated agreement in principle to the partition of the Land. This is the difference between making Jaffa and Nazareth Jewish, and making Ramallah and Nablus Jewish.) I cannot use such words as "the promised land" or "the promised borders." Happy are those who believe, for theirs is the Land. Why should they trouble themselves with questions of morality or the rights of others? (Although perhaps those who believe in the promise ought to wait humbly for the Author of the promise to decide when the right moment has come for Him to keep it.) Happy are those who believe. Their Zionism is simple and carefree. Mine is hard and complicated. I also have no use for the hypocrites who suddenly remember the divine promise whenever their Zionism runs into an obstacle or an inner contradiction (and go charging off in their cars with their wives and children every Sabbath to cherish the dust of the holy places). In a nutshell, I am a Zionist in all that concerns the redemption of the Jews, but not when it comes to the "redemption of the Holy Land." We have come here to live as a free nation, not "to liberate the land that groans under the desecration of a foreign yoke"—Samaria, Gilead, Aram, and Hauran, up to the great Euphrates River. The word "liberation" applies to people, not to dust and stone. I was not born to blow rams' horns or "purge a heritage that has been defiled by strangers."

Why here of all places? Because here and only here is where the Jews were capable of coming and establishing their independence. Because the establishment of the political independence of the Jews could not have come about in any other territory. Because here was the focus of their prayers and their longings.

To tell the truth, those longings were organically linked with the belief in the promise and the Promiser, the Redeemer, and the Messiah. Is there a contradiction here? As I have already said, religious feelings helped a secular, political movement to achieve an aim that was historical, not miraculous or messianic. The ancient yearning for the Land of Israel was part of a total faith in the coming of the Redeemer. Faith, side by side with a common destiny, maintained the continuing unity of the Jewish people. But let us not forget, or allow others to forget, that it was not God or the Messiah or a miracle or an angel that achieved the independence of the Jews in their own land, but a secular, political movement with a modern ideology and modern tactics. Therefore the Zionism of a secularist may contain a structural fault. I do not intend to gloss over this fault with phrases and slogans. I accept this contradiction, if such it be, and I say: Here I stand. In our social life, in love, in our attitude to others and to death, we the nonreligious are condemned to live with inconsistencies and faults. And that goes for Zionism too.

Consequently, my Zionism may not be "whole." For instance, I see nothing wrong with mixed marriage or with conversion, if it is successful. Only those Jews who *choose* to be Jews or who are *compelled* to be Jews belong, in my view, to this tribe. For them, and only for them, the State of Israel is a present possibility. I would like to make it an attractive and fascinating possibility.

I do not regard myself as a Jew by virtue of "race," or as a "Hebrew" because I was born in the Land of Canaan. I *choose* to be a Jew, that is, to participate in the collective experience of my ancestors and fellow Jews down the ages. Albeit a selective participation: I do not approve of everything they approved of, nor am I prepared to continue obediently living the kind of life that they lived. As a Jew, I do not want to live among strangers who see in me some kind of symbol or stereotype, but in a State of Jews. Such a state could only have come into being in the Land of Israel. That is as far as my Zionism goes.

Confronting the Jewish Past

I do not live here in order to renew the days of old or to restore the glory of the past. I live here because it is my wish to live as a free Jew.

Admittedly, it would be foolish to deny the religious experience that lies at the root of Jewish independence. Even the first founders of the New Land of Israel, who broke out of the straitjacket of religion and revolted against it, brought to their Tolstoyan or Marxist or nationalist enthusiasm a religious temperament, whether Hasidic or messianic or reverential. "Restoring the glory of the past," "renewing the days of old," "bringing redemption to the Land"—such common expressions testify to a powerful religious current flowing beneath the crust of the various secular Zionist ideologies. Actually, there is often an unpleasant deception at work in this masked ball of phrases arbitrarily plucked from their religious context to serve as faded garlands for an essentially national ideology. The false note becomes particularly disturbing when the State of Israel is adorned with messianic attributes and we are told that the coming of the Messiah is evident in every Jewish goat, every Jewish acre, every Jewish gun, and every act of Jewish villainy. You can read some powerful words on this subject in the writings of Brenner.

But the experience that has taken shape and grown in the Land of Israel in the last two or three generations has already begun to develop a new appearance of its own: the main thing is neither the liberation of the ancestral heritage nor the restoration of old-time Judaism, but the liberation of the Jews.

The new Israel is not a reconstruction of the kingdom of David and Solomon or of the Second Jewish Commonwealth, or the shtetl borne to the hills of Canaan on the wings of Chagall. On the other hand, one cannot regard it as merely a synthetic Australian-type land of immigration on biblical soil. Neither chained nor unchained, neither continuation nor revolution, neither resurrection nor reincarnation, this State is in the curious and fascinating situation of being "over against." The Law and the Prophets, the Talmud and the Midrash, the prayers and the hymns are all present and visible here, but we are neither entirely within them nor entirely outside them.

Over against: neither uninterrupted continuity, nor a new start, but a continual reference to the Jewish heritage and traditions. The Hebrew language, law and justice, table manners, old wives' tales, lullabies, superstitions, literature—all refer continually to the Jewish past. We relate nostalgically, defiantly, sardonically, calculatingly, resentfully, penitently, desperately, savagely, in a thousand and one ways—but we relate. It is not merely a new interpretation of an ancient culture, as the disciples of Ahad Ha'am would have it, but neither is it a leap across the past to link up with ancient pre-Judaic Hebrew strata, as the school of Berdyczewski claims. It is a powerful yet complex love-hate relationship, burdened with conflicts and tensions, oscillating between revolt and nostalgia, between anger and shame. Perhaps this is what Brenner meant when he spoke of "a thorny existence."

I, for one, am among those who believe that the conflicts and contradictions — the love-hate relationships with the Jewish heritage — are not a curse but contain a blessing: a prospect of profound fruitfulness, of that creative suffering and cultural flowering which is always and everywhere the outcome of souls divided against themselves. A great richness lies hidden in this experience of existing neither within Judaism nor outside it but incessantly and insolubly over against it.

FACING THE ARAB POPULATION

"A people without land for a land without people" — this formula offered those who propounded it a simple, smooth, and comfortable Zionism. Their way is not my way.

It seems that the enchantment of "renewing the days of old" is what gave Zionism its deep-seated hope of discovering a country without inhabitants. Any movement that has a melody of return, revival, reconstruction tends to long for a symmetrical coordination between the past and the present. How pleasant and fitting it would have been for the Return to Zion to have taken our land from the Roman legions who subjugated it and drove us into exile. How pleasant and fitting it would have been to come back to an empty land, with only the ruins of our towns and villages waiting for us to bring them back to life. From here it is only a short step to the kind of self-induced blindness that consists of disregarding the existence of the country's Arab population or discounting their importance (on the dubious grounds that "they have created no cultural assets here and have not developed the Land"). Many of those who returned to Zion wanted to see the Arab inhabitants as a kind of mirage that would dissolve of its own accord, or as a colorful component of the biblical setting, or at best as natives who would drool with gratitude if we treated them kindly. (In time, Naomi Shemer was to express this state of mind with terrifying, transparent simplicity by describing East Jerusalem in these terms: ". . . the market place is empty / And no one goes down to the Dead Sea / By way of Jericho . . ." Meaning, of course: the market place is empty *of Jews,* and *no Jew* goes down to the Dead Sea by way of Jericho. A revelation of a common and characteristic way of thinking.)

This is also what some of my teachers taught me when I was a child: After our Temple was destroyed and we were banished from our Land, the gentiles came into our heritage and defiled it. Wild desert Arabs laid the land waste, destroyed the terraces on the hillside that our ancestors had constructed, and let their flocks ravage the vegetation. When our first pioneers came to the land to rebuild it and be rebuilt by it and to redeem it from its desolation, they found an abandoned wasteland. True, there were a few uncouth nomads roaming around in it, and here and there a filthy cluster of primitive hovels.

Some of our first arrivals thought the Ishmaelites ought to return to the desert from which they had crept into the Land, and if they refused—"Arise and claim your inheritance," like those who "conquered Canaan in storm" in the prophecy of Saul Tschernichowsky: "A melody of blood and fire . . . / Climb the mountain, crush the plain, All you see—inherit" (Tschernichowsky, "I Have a Tune").

Most of the first settlers, though, loathed blood and fire and kept faith with the Jewish heritage and the principles of Tolstoy, and therefore they sought ways of love and pleasantness, for "the Bedouin are people like us" (!) So we brought light into the darkness of the tents of Kedar, we healed ringworm and trachoma, we paved roads, we built and improved and let the Arabs share in the benefits of prosperity and civilization. But they, being by nature bloodthirsty and ungrateful, listened willingly to the incitements of strangers, and they also envied us our possessions and our industry, and lusted after our houses and womenfolk, which is why they fell upon us and we were compelled to repel them with the revolt of the few against the many; again we held out our hand in peace, and again it was refused; they fell upon us again, and thus the war between the Sons of Light and the Sons of Darkness goes on unto this day. (It should be stressed that this primitive, simplistic depiction was not universal, though it was popular and current among the Zionist settlers. Many of the best minds inside and outside the Labor movement, from A. D. Gordon to Ben-Gurion and from Brenner and Martin Buber to Moshe Shertok, had a far more complex understanding of the situation.)

Moreover, the question of our attitude to the Arab population provided from the very beginning the meeting point for two extreme and opposed trends of thought: Revisionist nationalism and "Canaanism" (which, incidentally, had grown up on the soil of Revisionism). Many years before the surprising and ironical meeting of Uri Zvi Greenberg and Aharon Amir in the "Committee for the Greater Land of Israel," the "Canaanites" and the nationalists had met in their common view of the Arabs as the reincarnation of the ancient Canaanites, Amorites, Ammonites, Amalekites, Jebusites, and Girgashites. Both the romantics and the counter-romantics wanted to paint the present in the colors of the biblical period. Admittedly, their conclusions were opposed: the Revisionists dreamed of a holy war against the tribes of Canaan, the direct continuation of the wars of Joshua, David, and Alexander Jannaeus, "revenging the spilt blood of Thy servants"; the "Canaanites," on the other hand, dreamed of returning in order to be restored to the bosom of the Semitic ethnos and the magical oriental paganism from which we had been uprooted thousands of years ago by namby-pamby "phylactery Judaism," fatally tainted by Yiddishkeit.

However, for all the romantic picture that the Jewish faithful and the Jewish apostates, each in his way, so fondly treasure, the people that returned to contemporary Zion found no Canaanite tribes, so they would neither return to the bosom of those tribes nor "settle the ancestral blood feud" with them. The people that returned to

Zion found itself facing an Arab population that could not be fitted conveniently into any biblical picture or any plan to "restore the days of old," because it was not these Arabs who had expelled our ancestors from their country and robbed us of our heritage. For a thousand and one irrelevant reasons, but also because of the first beginnings of normal and natural national consciousness, this Arab population was not impressed by the spectacle of the Jews coming from the ends of the earth and settling all over this land. They began to suspect that if this became a Jewish land it would not be an Arab land. As simple as that. Hence they did not show us the traditional cordial oriental hospitality and did not spread out their arms in love to embrace the returning prodigal sons. Hence much violence and anger.

So the returning Jews confronted the Arab population in panic or resentment, fawning or closing their eyes, behaving arrogantly or unctuously, galloping around in desert robes or indignantly plucking the sleeve of the British, consoling themselves with memories of Joshua, Ezra, and Nehemiah, amusing themselves with exotic oriental gestures, occasionally sensing vaguely the existence of a tragic undertone, trumpeting a civilizing missionary destiny, but generally alien, muddled, and remote.

RIGHT AGAINST RIGHT

I have tried to describe, perhaps a little too starkly, both the view that regards the dispute as a kind of western with the civilized good guys fighting the bloodthirsty natives, and also the romantic conceptions that endow it with the attributes of an ancient epic. As I see it, the confrontation between the Jews returning to Zion and the Arab inhabitants of the country is not like a western or an epic, but more like a Greek tragedy. It is a clash between right and right (although one must not seek a simplistic symmetry in it). And, as in all tragedies, there is no hope of a happy reconciliation based on a clever magical formula. The choice is between a bloodbath and a disappointing compromise, more like enforced acceptance than a sudden breakthrough of mutual understanding.

True, the dispute is not "symmetrical." There is no symmetry between the constant, eager attempts of Zionism to establish a dialogue with the local Arabs and those of the neighboring states, and the bitter and consistent hostility the Arabs, with all their different political regimes, have for decades shown us in return.

But it is a gross mistake, a common oversimplification, to believe that the dispute is based on a misunderstanding. It is based on full and complete understanding: we have repeatedly offered the Arabs goodwill, good neighborliness, and cooperation, but that was not what they wanted from us. They wanted us, according to the most moderate Arab formulation, to abandon the idea of establishing a free Jewish State in the Land of Israel, and that is a concession we can never make.

It is the height of naivety to believe that but for the intrigues of outsiders and the backwardness of fanatical regimes, the Arabs would realize the positive side of the Zionist enterprise and straightaway fall on our necks in brotherly love.

The Arabs did not oppose Zionism because they failed to understand it but because they understood it only too well. And that is the tragedy: the mutual understanding *does* exist. We want to exist as a nation, as a State of Jews. They do not want that state. This cannot be glossed over with high-sounding phrases, neither the noble aspirations to brotherliness of well-meaning Jews, nor the clever Arab tactics of "We will be content, at this stage, with the return of all refugees to their previous place of residence." Any search for a way out must start from a fundamental change of position preceded by the open-eyed realization of the full extent of the struggle: a tragic conflict, tragic anguish.

We are here because this is the only place where we can exist as a free nation. The Arabs are here because Palestine is the homeland of the Palestinians, just as Iraq is the homeland of the Iraqis and Holland the homeland of the Dutch. The question of what cultural assets the Palestinians have created here or what care they have taken of the landscape or the agriculture is of no relevance to the need to discuss their right to their homeland. Needless to say, the Palestinian owes no deference to God's promises to Abraham, to the longings of Yehuda Hallevi and Bialik, or the achievements of the early Zionist pioneers.

Current talk about pushing the Palestinian masses back to oil-rich Kuwait or fertile Iraq makes no more sense than would talking about our own mass emigration to "Jewish" Brooklyn. Knaves and fools in both camps might add, "After all, they'll be among their brothers there." But just as I am entitled to see myself as an Israeli Jew, not a Brooklynite or a Golders Greener, so a Palestinian Arab is entitled to regard himself as a Palestinian, not an Iraqi or Kuwaiti. The fact that only an enlightened minority of Palestinians seem to see it that way at the moment cannot prejudice the national right to self-determination when the time comes. Let us remember, with all the reservations the comparison requires, that it was only a Zionist-minded minority of Jews who—justly!—claimed the right to establish a Hebrew State here in the name of the entire Jewish people for the benefit of the Jews who would one day come to a national consciousness.

This land is our land. It is also their land. Right conflicts with right. "To be a free people in our own land" is a right that is valid either universally or not at all.

As for the war between Israel and the neighboring Arab States, it is an indirect outcome of the confrontation between us and the Palestinians. Of course I am not going to explain everything away in terms of "devotion" or "brotherliness" on the part of the neighboring states. I only want to emphasize that the strife that has developed in the Land of Israel must be resolved here, between us and the Palestinian people. There is nothing tragic in our relations with Cairo, Baghdad, or Damascus. The war they are waging against us is basically a war of aggressors against victims of aggression, even though our neighbors are armed, as usual, with self-righteous rhetoric. The Arab-Jewish tragedy does not extend, therefore, to the whole Middle East, as the Arab States claim, but is confined to this land, between the sea and the desert.

AGAINST CONSISTENCY AND AGAINST JUSTICE

From its inception, Zionism has contained currents of thought that played overambitious fantasy games over the whole map of the Middle East and entertained colossal geopolitical speculations. This motif is apparent from the start, in the thought and actions of Herzl, and the Revisionist movement in its different guises has still not been weaned off it. Its global strategists have more than once tried to square the circle, to stand Columbus's eggs on their end, and to cut Gordian knots with one stroke of a geopolitical formula. The Labor movement, on the other hand, has generally treated all these geo-political manifestations with ironical reserve and wry suspicion.

It is easy enough to represent this contrast as one between gi-ants with wide vision on the one hand and narrow-minded dwarfs on the other. Actually, it was a conflict of temperaments and men-talities, a contrast between childishly simplistic romanticism and restrained romanticism.

The Six-Day War and its aftermath have revitalized, right across the political spectrum, a craving for "mighty" geopolitical formu-las: you read in the press elated calls for a Palestinian protector-ate under the Israeli aegis, an Ottoman-style Hebrew empire with a Kurdistan and Druzistan created by the might of the Israeli Defense Forces, and similar far-fetched speculations on the theme of a "pax Israeliana." What all these formulas have in common is the desire to raise our sights beyond the fact of the existence, under our mili-tary rule, of a one-million-strong Arab population with a burgeon-ing national consciousness.

All the thinkers who have sprung up on every side since the Six-Day War, spouting brilliant geopolitical ideas, all, even those who promise to do wonderful favors for the Palestinian Arabs and give them all sorts of benefits, try to bypass the need sooner or later to "consult the bride."

I do not undertake to determine whether the Arabs in this country regard themselves as Palestinians, Hashemite Jordanians, part of greater Syria, or descendants of the ancient Hebrews whose ancestors were forcibly Islamized and who have been redeemed at last. I do not know. But I am almost certain that they are not over-joyed to entrust their future to even the most enlightened and be-nevolent Jews. They doubtless regard themselves as the despoiled owners of the whole country, some of whom reluctantly accept the loss of part of it while others do not accept it at all. In any case, this population has never been given an opportunity to define itself and express its wishes democratically, whether as a Palestinian people or as a branch of the greater Arab nation. Its demand for self-determination is legitimate. One can postpone its realization, for no less a reason than Israel's existence, but the day that our existence is recognized this demand will have to be met.

Where right clashes with right, either the issue can be decided by force, or some unsatisfactory, inconsistent compromise develops that does not seem right to either of the sides.

If might prevails, I am not sure whose might it will be. We know that conflicts that last for generations are fought out not between armies but between systems of national potential. They may eventually manage to drive us out of the Land. We may manage to push them into the desert. We may both succeed: then the land will be a desolate ruin without Jews or Arabs, with only justice hovering over the debris.

If a compromise is reached, it will be between an inconsistent Zionist and an inconsistent Palestinian. Justice, total, brutal justice, is of course on the side of those who argue that in principle there is no difference between Ramallah and Ramleh, between Gaza and Beersheba, between Jerusalem and Jerusalem. This, of course, is precisely what the Palestinian and Zionist fanatics claim with a single voice: "It's all mine!"

In the life of nations, as in the life of individuals, existence, albeit a complicated and painful existence, can sometimes only be made possible by inconsistency. Tragic heroes, consumed by the desire for justice and purity, destroy and annihilate each other because of the consistency that burns like a fire in their bones. Whoever sets his sights on total justice is seeking not life but death.

CONFRONTING THE ARAB STATES

It would be well to clear the path of this discussion of certain stumbling blocks. One of them is the inane phrase "return of territories."

The areas occupied by the Israeli forces during the Six-Day War may be divided into two categories: those populated by Palestinian Arabs and those that were unpopulated and served as a springboard for a war of attrition and annihilation. East Jerusalem, Judaea and Samaria and the Gaza Plain are one thing, the Sinai Peninsula and the Golan Heights another. In the case of the Sinai Peninsula and the Golan Heights, the question is comparatively simple. Egypt and Syria have not been deprived of their independence by the Israeli conquest of those territories. We crushed their armies and deprived them of a springboard for renewed aggression. When those countries deign to enter into peace negotiations with us, one of the subjects we will discuss with them is the drawing of permanent borders, and we shall not commit ourselves in advance to the straight line between Rafah and Eilat, and certainly not to the stupid line in the north drawn by the clumsy hands of Messrs. Sykes and Picot. For the present, as long as Syria and Egypt refuse to sign proper peace treaties with us there is nothing hard or objectionable in keeping these territories under military occupation. Meanwhile, they may as well serve to warn and deter Cairo and Damascus, instead of being a violent threat to the heart of the State of Israel.

Where Judaea and Samaria and the Gaza Plain are concerned, the expression "return of territories" is meaningless. The future of those districts is a matter between us and the Palestinian Arabs who inhabit them. As I have said, this is a problem quite unlike the Gordian knot or Columbus's egg, one that cannot be settled with a single clever formula, such as the simplistic formula of those who see peace as a matter of generosity and goodwill, or the foolish formula of those who calculate that military strength times determination equals peace plus territories.

From the viewpoint of the Arab States, one of the roots of the conflict is their mortal fear of the momentum of the Zionist effort and the legendary potential they attribute to the Jewish people. For all that moderate Israeli leaders declare that all we want is "a piece of land for refuge and shelter," the Arabs have seen Zionism in its eighty years of development going from strength to strength, from a ragged, starving handful of nondescript settlers encamped among the marshes to a minor world power.

From the viewpoint of anxious or frightened Arabs, the inner rhythm of the achievement of Zionism seems to consist in a recurrent cycle of consolidation and expansion. Hence the widespread feeling in the neighboring countries that there are many more areas in the Middle East that could become the object of Zionist "redemption" and "liberation." In this respect the Arabs' belief in the secret power of Zionism is, paradoxically, even greater than that of our own most fanatical extremists. And while there is no denying the helpful and perhaps decisive contribution the stupidity of the Arab leaders has made to the increasing strength of Zionism, that does not diminish the widespread fear of the Satanic power of Zionism, and fear, as usual, increases stupidity.

For the national movements in the Arab countries, with the demonic superhuman powers they ascribe to the "Zionist monster" (verging on classical anti-Semitism and the mythology of the secret power of "international Jewry"), the fate of Arab Palestine is a fearsome vision of their own future. It is their view of us as a "bridgehead" that threatens to overwhelm the entire Middle East if it is not smothered in its infancy that drives them to launch against us one desperate war of destruction after another.

And so we return to our starting point. If in Israel after the Six-Day War those trends in Zionism for which the "redemption of the Land" is the most important thing, if the nationalistic and Canaanite ambitions to become a Jewish power as great as the kingdom of David and Jeroboam prevail, then the darkest fears of the Arabs about the "true meaning" of Zionism will be confirmed and reinforced, as will their sense that their war against us is a life-and-death struggle.

On the other hand, if a victorious Israel, from a position of strength, allows Palestine to develop gradually in the direction of the realization of its national right to part of the land, the Arab world will be exposed to a mental shock that may perhaps, in the course of time, force it to reassess the nature of Zionism. Such a re-interpretation, accompanied by a shrewd awareness of Israel's determination and ability to defend itself, may bring the Arab States to a gradual if grudging acceptance of the fact that we exist. Not, of course, to an enthusiastic brotherly reconciliation.

BETWEEN TWO POSSIBILITIES OF ZIONISM

I am not one of those who hold the fatalistic view that there is no other way out of the Jewish-Arab war than the ultimate defeat of one side in blood and fire. On the other hand, I do not share the melodramatic vision of the two reconciled sides embracing each other as soon as the magic geopolitical formula is found. The best we can expect, in the usual way of tragic conflicts between individuals or between peoples, is a process of adaptation and psychological acceptance accompanied by a slow, painful awakening to reality, burdened with bitterness and deprivation, with shattered dreams and endless suspicions and reservations that, in the way of human wounds, heal slowly and leave permanent scars.

Some people say that "reality dictates" this and "the situation demands" that, or that "there is no choice at this moment because there is no one to talk to." There is truth and its opposite in such talk. The fact is that the immediate conclusion of my reasoning puts me in a position that is not far from the declared policy of the government of Israel.* Yet one would have to be blind to fail to realize that the results of the recent war have placed before Zionist ideology an urgent and fateful choice: if from now on the current that has flowed within Zionism almost from the beginning, the current of nationalistic romanticism and mythological delusions of greatness and renewal, the current of longing for a kingdom and blowing rams' horns and conquering Canaan by storm, the national superiority complex based on military enthusiasm in the guise of

---

*The position of the Eshkol government (late 1967): no withdrawal without peace agreements; everything is open to negotiation.

crude biblical nostalgia, the conception of the entire State of Israel as one giant act of retaliation for the "historical humiliation" of the diaspora — if that trend prevails among us, then the Middle East is fated to be the battleground of two peoples, both fighting a fundamentally just war, both fighting essentially for their life and liberty, and both fighting to the death.

I believe in a Zionism that faces facts, that exercises power with restraint, that sees the Jewish past as a lesson, not as a mystical imperative or as an insidious nightmare; that sees the Palestinian Arabs as Palestinian Arabs, not as the camouflaged reincarnation of the ancient tribes of Canaan or as a shapeless mass of humanity waiting for us to form it as we see fit: a Zionism *also* capable of seeing itself as others may see it; and finally, a Zionism that recognizes both the spiritual implications and the political consequences of the fact that this small tract of land is the homeland of two peoples fated to live facing each other, willy-nilly, because no God and no angel will come to judge between right and right. The lives of both, the lives of all of us, depend on the hard, tortuous, and essential process of learning to know each other in the curious landscape of the beloved country.

Thank God for His Daily Blessings

from *In the Land of Israel* (1983)

And how are things going in the port city of Ashdod?

A bright sea-blue washes over the broad avenues and apartment buildings this morning. Vines have climbed up the rows of identical buildings, forming their lacy patterns over the cinder blocks. Shade trees grace the yards. On almost every corner is a kindergarten, and from almost every kindergarten drift the voices of children's songs. A bell from a nearby school rings, and a river of blue uniforms sweeps into the asphalt school yard. I linger at the fence for a moment to overhear a snatch of conversation. One of the pupils says, "He brings politics into everything. Even into Bible class. Does he think the Bible's a newspaper? A book about politics? It's a spiritual book! It's symbolic."

Another pupil cuts him off, grabs his wrist, and says, "Listen, now listen—you're too extreme; of course there are political implications to everything, even in the Bible, just like you could say that politics has biblical implications. It all ties in to the same subject."

"Do you have any idea of what you're saying? Abraham and Isaac—and politics? The Prophets—and politics? What do you think—Moses was a member of the Likud? Or Labor? It's an inter-Jewish book. Well, I'd say it's even an interhuman book!"

Later, at the street corner, an elderly man, his sad face tight in concentration, carefully parks his car, locks it, and has started to walk away when he suddenly slaps his forehead and returns to the car to remove a package wrapped in brown paper. At 9:30, an attractive woman unlocks her perfume shop. She goes out, a straw broom in hand, and sweeps the sidewalk in front of her shop.

Not far away, on a park bench, sits a bespectacled old man in a faded black suit, reading a Romanian-language newspaper. I sit down beside him, trying to imprint the morning voices of urban Ashdod on my memory; somewhere close behind me, pigeons coo. Noisy birds chatter from the branches of the trees on the avenue. At a distance a large truck passes, its brakes panting, its gears grinding. A woman beats a rug or a mattress. A disco song drifts from the radio, then an Israeli folk song, and after that a soft instrumental piece. Ashdod in the morning. A ship bellows from the direction of the port and the birds answer. The elderly Romanian suddenly turns to me and speaks in a broken Hebrew jargon mingled with Yiddish and a touch of French: "Now is not winter, not summer. Now is something very good. Can breathe a little."

I concur.

"Too bad is not this way all the time," he says. "In summer is hot and in winter is strong wind and is rain. But rain — very important, yes! For our agriculture!"

I concur once more, and ask the man where he is from.

"From Dalet quarter. But now I am pensioner. There is time."

And from where did he come to Ashdod?

"Ploiesti. Is the oil city. *Rumanish*. Here, in Ashdod, we also have oil. They say — is right underneath Dalet quarter. Nobody dig it now, but when they dig it — will be very good here. Will come prosperity to the city and to Israel — will be peace."

And now? Things are not good?

"Oh, very good. Is prosperity now, too. The Arabs should only let live without the wars, we have here a paradise. Paradise with all kinds tsuris, is true, but what is life without the troubles? Me, I have the kidney troubles. Live from the dialysis. But you know, mister, a man what has been where I was, don't complain no more. We shouldn't complain. I seen Hitler; I seen Stalin — maybe you're too young — I seen the bestiality from the goyim. Then, after, I was living in Paris a couple years — is no paradise there, for sure: the people there is alonely. They make maybe a living, but is no life for them. I mean the Jews there, along with the goyim. Here is a so-so living, medium, but the people is always together. I don't mean about the politics, about the arguing. I mean about the life. The life here is all the time together—the troubles together, the happiness together. You remember when was the Europe song contest, mister? Everybody cried with happiness how the Jews beat the goyim: the Sephardim, the Ashkenazim, the religious, the Likud, the kibbutzim, everybody felt together. Or like now from the dead what we lost in the Galilee war: so everybody cried together. I don't say . . . of course there is no-goodniks, even cheaters, there is uneducated, but is a minority. The majority—is very good. Better than the goyish man. Mister don't think so? For instance, I had yesterday an incident. I brung the plumber, a Moroccan, name of Abram, a good friend from my boy. I had a whole wall was broken in my house, from the leaks. He fixes it all up, worked maybe three hours, and finally he takes the mop and the pail and cleans the whole mess what he made from the work and fixes up the tiles. With the zinc glue. So how much I owe you, I ask him. So he says to me, Aren't you ashamed, Gramps? Didn't your boy help me out of my troubles in the army? And this is true: my son was giving him all sorts help. So I say to him: What, a beggar I am? Thanks God, I can pay. You tell me what I owe you and you don't shame me! So he laughs and says to me, Okay, Gramps, never mind, give me five bucks and I'll take a cup of coffee. Five dollars—for three hours working! And the materials—his! It was only so not to shame me. I tell you, that's the way it is in Eretz Yisrael when a Jew has a Jewish heart. With the goyim, the Jew becomes like a goy.

"I'll tell you what I believe, mister. Listen, everyone is good. Begin is good. Peres is good. Rabin is good. Of course, His Honor the president is good. And David Levy, too. Yossi Sarid was a pilot from the army before. Everybody's a hero. From all the communities. Everybody wants it should be good. Everybody gives from his life to the country. They should get respect for that! This argument what we got—is nothing; they have such in the best families. They argue? So they make up. Me—I'm for everybody. I already seen with my own eyes what the goyim got and what we got. The

State of Israel—a very nice thing! There's even a lot of goyim what tell us bravo! You know what my dream is? I'll tell you. Mister is still young, maybe, but I'll tell you anyways. My dream is—before my time comes, they should give me two minutes on the television Friday night, when everybody is listening, and I will tell the young people what everybody should be saying here every morning and every night, should say thanks God for everything what we got here in this country: the army, the ministers by the Knesset, the El Al, the income tax even, the streets, the kibbutzim, the factories—the everything! What is this?! They forgot how we had it in this country in the beginning? There wasn't nothing! Sand and enemies! Now, thanks God, we got the State and everybody has what to eat and clothes and education—not enough yet, the education—and we even got a lot of luxury! What did we have in the Diaspora? We had bubkes, that's what! This is a great honor to the Jewish people, what they done in this country so quick! Against all the tsuris! Only, all the Jews what lives in America, in France, in Russia, by Khomeini even, should all come here quick, we should have all the Jewish people at home.

"That's what I want to say on the television. From a simple man in the street. In Romania I was a woodworker. In Ashdod I worked in wood, too. Now—a pensioner. Once I saw Mrs. Golda Meir, she should rest in peace, by the city Afula. This was before she died. They gave me a great honor, to talk to Mrs. Golda Meir, she should rest in peace. So I said to her, I said, Mrs. Prime Minister, in Romania I had much criticism, but there wasn't no freedom to talk. There was fear. In Eretz Yisrael, there is freedom to say anything, no fear, but you know what? I got no criticism. Nothing. Only compliments . . . only thanks God. That's what I said to her. I didn't want to tell her about the tsuris: doesn't she have enough troubles already? I got to add her another kvetch? But the young people we got today, they see the holes—they don't see the cheese. That's a saying in French. It is ten o'clock already? Excuse me, mister, I got to go by the bank here. You're still young. Don't worry!"

· · ·

In the center of town, near a movie theater, is an enclosed, paved square surrounded by shops and shaded by one giant, heavy-topped tree. Tables snake their way into the square from several cafés. And there is a boutique, a perfumery, bank branches, a bookstore, a hardware store, and a restaurant. Mothers sit near their babies' carriages and pass the morning in the sea breeze. Two beauties, well aware of their attractions, enter the perfumery, seemingly ignoring my glances and the glances of three suntanned wolves—dandies—their shirts carelessly open to reveal the gold chains at their necks as they sit at the adjacent table, exchanging experienced glances and loud, clever expert opinions. The afternoon newspapers arrive at 10:30, and soon everyone, including me, the wolves, and even several of the mothers, is absorbed in the headlines.

At a side table sits a man of about forty, modishly dressed, an attaché case open before him. He is industriously writing something without lifting his head; he might be filling out income-tax forms or the football lottery, or preparing a legal brief. Perhaps he, like me, joins word to word.

A small Mediterranean city is Ashdod, a pleasant city, unpretentious, with a port and a lighthouse, and a power station and factories and many landscaped avenues. Not pretending to be Paris or Zurich or aspiring to be Jerusalem. A city planned by social democrats: without imperial boulevards, without monuments, without grandiose merchants' homes. A city living entirely in the present tense, a clean city, almost serene. The horns of passing cars do not squeal, the pedestrians do not run. It seems that almost everybody here knows almost everybody. If there is poverty here it is not glaring. Even the wealth of the suburb of villas near the beach is not ostentatious. A city of workers and businessmen and artisans and housewives. Of the sixty or seventy thousand souls here, about half are immigrants from North Africa, approximately one-third come from Western Europe and the Americas, and the remainder are native-born. At this morning hour, a weekday serenity rests on Ashdod: the men at work, some of the women at work, some at home. The children have gone off to day-care centers or to school.

You will find no Light unto the Nations here, but also no ghetto or slum—only a small, bright port city rapidly growing and expanding to the south and east.

Back in '48, the Egyptian army columns reached Ashdod on their way to Tel Aviv, only twenty miles to the north. Here they were stopped by two daring pilots, one of whom was shot down, and here they were repelled in a desperate night attack by the fighters of the fledgling Israeli army. After the Egyptians were repelled, only the barren sand dunes remained. Later a transit camp of tin shacks was put up between the dunes, under blazing sun, amid the garbage dumps, the flies, and the treacherous sandy roads. Taking hasty leave of their homes, Jewish refugees were brought here, people persecuted and bitter. And there was a cry of injustice, of injury, but worse than the cry was their humbled submission.

In '57 the beginnings of a city were built here. In '66 the port was dedicated. Afterward the large power station was built. In the early '70s the country was in an uproar over the violent strikes and the bitter labor disputes that broke out here. But nowadays Ashdod is not in the headlines.

From a wooden tray slung from his neck, a wrinkled peddler offers me a comb or a pair of scissors or a bar of soap. I tell him that I don't need anything. And he, for no reason, wishes me well. At the corner of the square a youth in his high school uniform sets up an easel and begins to sketch something. About half an hour later I peek at his work: it is a sketch of this very square as captured through his own strange, private vision. A thread of sadness is woven through the drawing. He has added long shadows to each of the objects. And the figures he has scattered across the square are thin, long, faceless, all of them for some reason wrapped in black monks' cowls. What does this young artist see here? What has he brought to this scene? And from where? My two neighbors sitting on the bench and chatting in soft voices are joined by a woman, full-bodied, with large earrings and a dress that generously reveals the slopes of her attractive breasts. I eavesdrop and jot down crumbs of conversation.

"So, how's life, Jeanette?"

"Slipping through my fingers—like my salary. How're things by you, Yosef? How's the new house coming along?"

"Terrific! I finished the roof—you wouldn't believe it—all by myself—no contractor, no laborers, with these two hands. Only, with the concrete Asulin came to help me out. It's coming along great. Maybe it'll be finished by Passover and we'll be able to move in. Only thing is, the money has to hold out. How those greenbacks go! Incredible!"

"And how are the kids?"

"Rami got out of the army the day before yesterday. Yael probably told you: he did two months in Damour, and after that he was in Beirut—got as far as Yuniye, he did. He came back a bit depressed, like all of them. There are arguments in the house—it's awful. Only thing is, next week he starts in Beersheba. At the university. He's taking literature and Judaica, he is."

"What kind of living is he going to make out of literature and Judaica?"

"I ask myself the same question, believe me. He don't know the first thing about anything, this kid. Maybe he'll be a teacher. A welfare case. Maybe he'll get a job with some newspaper. Or he'll go into politics. Always had a brain, he did. And what a gift of gab—a silver tongue! Like Begin. Actually, he's not for Begin, but he talks every bit as pretty as Begin. His opinions he gets from his mother, not from me. I'm no match for him in an argument. Takes me out on points, this kid. Even when I'm all riled up, I get a kick out of listening to how he builds an argument. Like pouring concrete, I swear!"

"Why don't you come over on Friday? And you'll bring him along? David'll work on him a little. Besides, David brought us a video. We'll watch movies from the cassette. Later on you can talk politics, have a drink. Why don't you come?"

"This Friday—it's out. We're in Tiberias, only Yael doesn't know about it yet: I'm going to surprise her. A treat. Five-star hotel. But why don't you come to us next Friday? And maybe we won't talk politics, after all. I've got a headache and a butt-ache from this stuff already. We'll talk something else. This country can really get right into your bones. There're other things in life, no?"

Three months have passed since that morning in Ashdod. The country really gets right into your bones. On Tuesday, the conclusions of the Kahan Commission of Inquiry concerning the massacre in Lebanon were published and the country was in an uproar. On Thursday, Defense Minister Sharon presented/didn't present his resignation/nonresignation. That same evening Emil Grunzweig was murdered and some of his friends who had participated in a Peace Now demonstration in Jerusalem were injured, after they marched through a jeering crowd that did not cease to shower them with spit and threats and stones.

Nineteen eighty-two is over and eighty-three has begun. A hard winter in the Land of Israel. Rain and mist and great waters. Snow in the mountains. An icy wind blows in Jerusalem. The water and the frost polish the stones. The strong wind sweeps the hillsides. At night the floodwaters flow down to the sea. Last autumn seems far away, and what was written then seems part of another era. Snow on the graves of the soldiers who died in the war in Lebanon. Snow on the soldiers still fighting in Lebanon to separate the Druzes from the Christians in the Shouf Mountains, the Christians from the Palestinians in Tyre and Sidon, to separate curse from curse.

Several hours after the grenade was thrown at the Peace Now demonstrators, close to midnight, friends of Emil, who has been killed, still sit in a small circle on the rocky hill facing the halls of power. Menachem Begin and his ministers went home long ago. The demonstrators huddle in their jackets against the cold as they sing softly into the winter darkness, "Bring near the day which is neither day nor night." A Hasidic song with a Hasidic melody. Their hands cup small candles. It is a hard winter in Jerusalem.

The next day people from Gush Emunim ask to attend Emil's funeral. The leaders of Peace Now tell them not to come. Emil's friends interrupt the high-flown eulogy delivered by Chief Rabbi Goren at the funeral.

. . .

On the day the Kahan Commission's report was released — Tuesday, February 8, 1983 — the chief of staff testified at the court-martial of soldiers and officers charged with harassing Arab inhabitants in the West Bank. Did you give orders or were you aware, General Eitan was asked, that Arab parents are severely punished when their children are caught throwing stones at Israeli vehicles?

"Affirmative," answered the chief of staff. "That's the way it is. And, on the Arabs, it works very well!"

The Kahan Commission report said, among other things, "We have no doubt that no conspiracy or plot was entered into between anyone from the Israeli political echelon or from the military echelon in the Israeli Defense Forces and the Phalangists, with the aim of perpetrating atrocities in the camps. . . . No intention existed on the part of any Israeli element to harm the noncombatant population in the camps. . . . We assert that . . . no intention existed on the part of anyone who acted on behalf of Israel to harm the noncombatant population. . . . [Nonetheless] we perceive it to be necessary to deal with objections that have been voiced on various occasions, according to which if Israel's direct responsibility for the atrocities is negated — i.e., if it is determined that the blood of those killed was not shed by IDF soldiers . . . or others operating at the behest of the State . . . then there is no place for further discussion of the question of indirect responsibility. . . . A certain echo of this approach may be found in statements made in the cabinet meeting of September 19, 1982. . . . We cannot accept this position."

And, further on: ". . . those who made the decisions and those who implemented them are indirectly responsible for what ultimately occurred, even if they did not intend this to happen and merely disregarded the anticipated danger. . . . It is not possible to absolve of such indirect responsibility those persons who, when they received the first reports of what was happening in the camps, did not rush to prevent the continuation of the Phalangists' actions and did not do everything within their power to stop them. . . . As far as the obligations applying to every civilized nation and the ethical rules accepted by civilized peoples go, the question of indirect responsibility cannot be avoided. A basis for such responsibility may be found in the outlook of our ancestors, which was expressed in things that were said about the moral significance of the biblical reference to the beheaded heifer (in the Book of Deuteronomy, chapter 21)."

A civilized nation. Civilized peoples. I have already said, on several occasions, that the question that cleaves us "to the bone" is not the famous question "Who is a Jew in the eyes of the law?" but precisely the opposite question: "What is the law in the eyes of the Jew?" What is the rule we determine for ourselves? Who are we?

Many would be delighted to forgo the "family of civilized nations" and send it down the drain along with the Kahan report, claiming that "what is permissible for all the stinkers in the world is permissible for us too," and that "after what the gentiles did to us, no one has the right to preach morality to us." Certain religious circles reacted thus to the report's reference to the portion in Deuteronomy about the beheaded heifer: "How is it that these ignorant judges don't know that the rule of the beheaded heifer applies only in the case of Israelites?"

Again in today's mail I received, among other things, a fascinating little threat. It said, "You PLO agent destroyer of the nation filthy traitor Nazi heir you better stop you satanic antiks before we finish you off the Likud government will last forever with Begin on top because the Labor Party is all Arabs and kibutzniks one after the other We know your communistic PLO views—you and Yosi Sarrid and Wilner and Peres and Mota Gur and Shulamit Aloni and Peace Now are all on our hit list the hell with you defeetist leftists beware what you say—you'll get what you've got coming to you all you lousy bastards. Whear were you when the Arabs butchered us? Why didn't you make your big demonstarations then? Braggart supporter of assassins your end is near!"

Who is the writer? I don't know, but it is not difficult for me to assemble a profile of him. More exactly, I can figure out his sources of inspiration from his linguistic repertoire: "Nazi heirs," "antics," "satanic," "defeatist," "assassins."

"Assassins," not "murderers." In my laboratory of stylistic identification these words—and particularly that last one—are something like a fingerprint. Can one look here, too, for the "question of indirect responsibility"?

A veteran member here in Kibbutz Hulda says to me, "You should tell them—the youth, the Oriental communities, all those who were not here—what we went through when we came to this country. They just don't know anything; that's the whole problem. They don't know in Bet Shemesh, and the youth don't know, and in the bright lights of Tel Aviv they don't know, all those bohemians. Gush Emunim doesn't know, either. How should they know? Who talks today about what went on in those days? Begin, with his distortions? The television with all that *Dallas* stuff? Who? You know a little. You have a sort of feeling for it. And to you they'll listen. You should write, make speeches, even appear on television, and tell the whole truth about us. To tell them that we suffered poverty and want worse than what they are suffering today, and even worse than their parents suffered in the transit camps. Much worse! And to tell them that even though we didn't go to synagogue and observe the customs, we were religious people, in the internal sense of the word—much more than the Orthodox, who walk around in skullcaps. We would work hard all day, from morning to night, and every evening we talked about ideology and all kinds of 'isms' until late at night. But later at night, when each of us was alone on his mattress—that's when each of us talked to God! Tearfully! In his heart, not out loud! And you know something—listen—sometimes God would talk to us, too. Even though we were great skeptics then. And we were paupers. Paupers—that's not the word for it! Penniless! There was one pair of shoes for the whole community, and whoever had to go into town to take care of something received these shoes, no matter whether they were too big or too small for him. Besides, he carried the shoes over his shoulder and didn't wear them, so as not to wear out the soles! Only when he went into some office, to stand before the clerks or the authorities, would he put on our pair of shoes. And today? Is it a crime that we have a room or two with a kitchenette, fifty or sixty square meters, and a television and a fan and a heater? You tell them, tell all those angry folks you allowed to cry on your shoulder. And tell it to the Arabs, and to Bet Shemesh, too, to everyone. Tell them that we still work, every one of us, as much as his health permits, doing physical labor. And that our sons serve in the frontline combat units. Tell them not to believe the agitators: we don't have any castles of gold here, we haven't cheated anyone. They ought to know that, in general, under Begin's government we feel angrier and more insulted even than they say they felt under our government. Why do they make us out to be monsters? Exploiters? Patronizing? Corrupt? Traitors? Do they even hear what they're saying? Aren't they ashamed? Do you really think they believe what Begin puts into their heads—that we're Nazis? And how can he, that refugee from the Holocaust, who never stops talking about the Holocaust all the time, how can he bear to hear them call us Nazis and remain silent? Maybe he encourages it? No, I can't believe that.

"And also tell them, those angry people of yours in Bet Shemesh, that a man like me wouldn't throw stones or go disrupt their meetings with shouts of 'Peres! Peres!' and throw tomatoes, but tell them that my heart bleeds. Write just that. And ask them, please, after all their complaints against me—let's assume that the way they paint history is all true and just—then what do they want now? Revenge? To humiliate me? To make me crawl in the dirt? To expel me? To shut our mouths? Ask them—'hand on your heart,' as they said to you in Bet Shemesh—whether now, when the power is in Begin's hands, and in theirs, they really think it pays to settle accounts with us like this, the night of the long knives. And ask them another thing as well, 'hand on your heart': Was everything we did in this country in fifty years, or eighty years, so bad? Was it all malicious? Everything we built here at such great sacrifice, everything we created here out of nothing, including the mistakes we surely made? What would the Land of Israel look like without the Labor movement? So where does this blind hatred come from? Where?

"And I have a serious complaint against you as well: why did

you present all those terrible things from every side in the newspaper, without any reply? Don't you have any answer to the Arabs
who want to annihilate us? Have you nothing to say to those ultra-
Orthodox who also await the destruction of the state? Have you
lost your tongue? Why did you keep silent in Bet Shemesh while
they insulted and sullied everything that is dear and sacred to us?
But beyond that—why did you suddenly decide to present our case
with the rumblings of some fanatic here or some psychopath there?
Aren't there any normal people left in this country, people who
don't want to annihilate the Jews or exterminate the Arabs, and
don't want to humiliate the Ashkenazim or drag in the Messiah by
his beard? Didn't you find anyone like that? What's the matter with
you? You're not a reporter! You're not a tape recorder! You're supposed to speak for us! They'll listen to your voice. They'll pay attention! Forgive me for bursting out like this—it's not like me—but
when you go wrong, at least someone should tell you you've gone
wrong. And you have gone wrong! Tell me, what is it that attracts
you to all these extremist types? To people eaten up by hatred? To
religious zealots? You're supposed to be our spokesman, not theirs!
Let Begin be their spokesman! So far he's managing very nicely
even without your help! Don't be angry with me for speaking so
openly to you like this, but in my opinion you have to publish a
response! Something in the style of Berl [Katznelson] or Pinchas
[Lavon]! An answer to the slanderers! A reply to your own articles!
And very cuttingly! No, no—don't under any circumstances quote
me. I'm not willing to be publicized; I'm only a simple worker who
has some thoughts of his own, not a speaker and not a wheeler-
dealer, and I trust you not to let it go like this but to leave no stone
unturned in answering it all. Forgive me, I hope you aren't hurt.
Are you hurt? No? Thank heaven. So sit down! Write! Write *our*
truth!"

N.S., from Haifa, also has thoughts on the question of what I should
and should not write. And this, in excerpt, is what she wrote in
her letter to me: "Forgive me for interfering. I know this is perhaps

presumptuous, but I feel the need to tell you something. I have read almost everything you have written in the newspapers lately (including the pieces against the war in Lebanon) and I asked myself if one of our writers hasn't burned himself out. We have a number of those who can write in newspapers, I think. Perhaps I have no right to interfere, but in my estimation you should stay away from current-affairs writing and the cheap publicity that accompanies it, and instead isolate yourself and in that way make your contribution to Israeli literature. That is more your field. Please do not interpret this to mean that I was not impressed by your reporting (although I don't particularly agree with some of your opinions). I only think that literature suffers because of it, and that is a pity. I imagine that many people write to you suggesting what to write, something I am opposed to (if the writer is not completely unencumbered, then he is not a writer!). I simply felt a need to write you what I, as one of your steady readers, feel. You are not obliged to pay any attention or send me a reply."

Not obliged, but I will try.

Look. For us, history is interwoven with biography. And not just from this morning. One can almost say that history *is* biography. Private life is virtually not private here. A woman might say, for example, "Our oldest son was born while Joel was in the bunkers, during the War of Attrition." Or, "We moved into this apartment exactly one week before the Six-Day War." Or, "He came back from the States during Sadat's visit."

How can one fix boundaries between areas here?

Our dear teachers once used to divide Bialik's poems between "poems of private agony" and "poems of public agony." But Bialik wrote "public" poems in the first person singular. "On the Slaughter," for instance, is a poem that was apparently written in an outburst of fury, masochism, and despair, and in it the poet turns to the murderer with the "ax in hand" shouting, "O hangman—take my neck, up and slay, / scalp me like a dog, my blood is forfeit." And in the same breath he continues and threatens the murderer, "And on your blouse / shall spring the blood of the suckling babe / and of the sage, / never to be erased, for eternity." In other words, chop my own neck and you shall be defiled by the blood of all Jews, "suckling babe and sage." I-us. Us-I. And so in Brenner and so in Alterman. The habit of the poet-emperor. ("I," once said the Russian czar to the German kaiser, "suffer from the highest infant-mortality rate in Europe. But, on the other hand, I multiply at the fastest rate in Europe!")

The hardest question is how to distance oneself a bit, how to preserve a measure of internal detachment.

No. The genuine question is, What is the meaning of distancing oneself? Is it possible? And if it is possible — is it right?

The man from Ashdod said, We'll talk something else. "This country can really get right into your bones. There are other things in life, no?"

Of course there are. If there aren't, the state turns into a monster and history becomes a merciless tyrant.

Perhaps we must compromise a little?

The insult and the fury of Bet Shemesh are a result of the magnitude of the promise this land proffered to all who sought it, a promise that was not fulfilled, and could not be fulfilled: not merely a land of refuge for emigrants, not just a house and yard and a living and entertainment, but the realization of all hope. A community of brothers. "A life of purity. A life of liberty," as the popular Zionist song goes.

Perhaps it was a lunatic promise: to turn, in the space of two or three generations, masses of Jews, persecuted, frightened, full of love-hate toward their countries of origin, into a nation that would be an example for the Arab community, a model of salvation for the entire world. Perhaps we bit off too much. Perhaps there was, on all sides, a latent messianism. A messiah complex. Perhaps we should have aimed for less. Perhaps there was a wild pretension here, beyond our capabilities — beyond human capabilities. Perhaps we must limit ourselves and forgo the rainbow of messianic dreams, whether they be called "the resurrection of the kingdom of David and Solomon" or "the building of a model society, a Light unto the

Nations," "fulfillment of the vision of the Prophets," or "to become the heart of the world." Perhaps we should take smaller bites, relinquish the totality of the Land for the sake of internal and external peace. Concede heavenly Jerusalem for the sake of the Jerusalem of the slums, waive messianic salvation for the sake of small, gradual reforms, forgo messianic fervor for the sake of prosaic sobriety. And perhaps the entirety of our story is not a story of blood and fire or of salvations and consolations but, rather, a story of a halting attempt to recover from a severe illness.

Perhaps there is no shortcut.

What, then, does one find in the autumn of 1982 and in the hard winter of 1983? Not "the land of our forefathers' glory" and not "days of yore" but simply the State of Israel. With the territories it occupies, which are — ironically enough — biblical regions arousing longings and aspirations. And with almost half of the territory of Lebanon, where crime and punishment have become one.

Not "the land of the heart" and not "the divine city reunited," as the clichés would have it, but simply the State of Israel. Not the "Maccabeans reborn" that Herzl talked of, but a warm-hearted, hot-tempered Mediterranean people that is gradually learning, through great suffering and in a tumult of sound and fury, to find release both from the bloodcurdling nightmares of the past and from delusions of grandeur, both ancient and modern; gradually learning to cling to what it has managed to build here over the course of one hundred difficult years, despite the "sand and enemies," as the man from Ashdod put it. Gradually learning to hold on by its fingernails to what there is.

Are we gradually learning, or perhaps not? But we should learn.

And what is, at best, is the city of Ashdod.

A pretty city and to my mind a good one, this Ashdod. And she is all we have that is our own. Even in culture and in literature: Ashdod. All those who secretly long for the charms of Paris or Vienna, for the Jewish shtetl, or for heavenly Jerusalem: do not cut loose from those longings — for what are we without our longings? — but let's remember that Ashdod is what there is. And she is not quite the grandiose fulfillment of the vision of the Prophets and of the dream of generations; not quite a world premiere, but simply a city on a human scale. If only we try to look at her with a calm eye, we will surely not be shamed or disappointed.

Ashdod is a city on a human scale on the Mediterranean coast. And from her we shall see what will flower when peace and a little repose finally come.

Patience, I say. There is no shortcut.

Yours with Great Respect and in Jewish Solidarity

from *Black Box* (1987)

6.7.1976

Mr. M. H. Sommo
7 Tarnaz St.
Jerusalem

BY REGISTERED POST

Dear Mr. Sommo,

You are hereby warned not to address any further requests/ demands for financial favors, whether directly or through your wife or through your wife's son, to my client Dr. A. A. Gideon, additional to the *ex gratia* payments you have already received from him.

Permit me hereby to draw your attention to the fact that my client has authorized me by cable to veto absolutely any transfer of funds extracted from him by means of emotional or other pressure. In plain words, you had better get it into your head that if there is anything else you want, there is no point in pestering Dr. Gideon, personally or via your relations. Try addressing yourself to me, and if you behave properly you will find me responsive. For your own good, sir, I suggest you bear in mind that we possess all the information we require to deal with any difficulties that may arise on your part in the future.

Your obedient servant,
M. Zakheim
Lawyer and Business Manager

*

By the Grace of G-d
Jerusalem
13th of Sivan 5736 (6.10.76)

Mr. M. Zakheim, Lawyer
Mr. Zakheim & Mr. di Modena
36 King George St.

LOCAL

Esteemed Mr. Zakheim,

First of all my respectful greetings to you on the occasion of the Festival of Shavuot!

Heaven forbid that you should think that I have any complaint or grievance against you. As it is written, "May He Who protects the simple protect me from suspecting the righteous or from casting aspersions." On the contrary, I think that you do your job of acting for Professor Gideon as well as possible. Likewise I appreciate the efforts you made on our behalf to renew contact with Boaz, apologize for any distress that has been caused you, thank you for your trouble, and express my confidence that your virtuous actions will stand you in good stead.

Nevertheless, and with all due respect, you will forgive me for finding myself under the necessity to observe, in response to your letter, that you are disqualified from acting as an intermediary between me and my family and Professor Gideon. This is for the simple reason that you are completely identified with the other party, and quite rightly so as long as he is paying you for your pains. So, as it is written, "no to your sting and no to your honey," Mr. Zakheim. If Professor Gideon should come to be persuaded out of the goodness of his heart to make a donation toward the rebuilding of the Land, with all due respect you have no right of veto or *locus standi,* you do not belong in the picture, and I'll thank you to step out of it.

On the other hand, if you decide that you would also like

to contribute something toward our holy sacred cause, your contribution will be most welcome and will be accepted with appreciation and without too close a scrutiny.

Moreover I have made a note of your explicit hint about the material that you claim to have assembled against us. I was not unduly impressed, however, for the simple reason that we have nothing to hide. As it is written, "Who shall ascend unto the hill of the Lord? or who shall stand in his holy place? He that hath clean hands, and a pure heart; who hath not lifted up his soul unto vanity," etc. Your explicit hint can only embarrass you, Mr. Zakheim. And I for my part, obedient to the command "You shall take no vengeance nor bear any grudge," have decided to overlook it and consider it as though it never existed.

My dear Mr. Zakheim, I should have thought that you, as someone who came here perhaps from the Holocaust, would be the first to wish to strengthen the state and consolidate its borders. Without, save the mark!, assailing the honor or property of the Arab inhabitants. I should like to propose you for membership in our organization, the Jewish Fellowship Movement (I enclose a prospectus with full details). What is more, Mr. Zakheim, by virtue of the legal prowess you have displayed in the service of Professor Gideon, I have the honor to offer you hereby the position of legal representative of the Movement, either on a voluntary basis or in return for full and proper fees.

Moreover I hereby request you to accept the position of private property manager for me and my family, in light of the fact that with God's help, and with your own deeply welcome help, part of the plundered property has been restored to us, and I am confident that the rest will come as well.

I am prepared to pay you for your trouble at the usual commission and a little over. We could even operate on a partnership basis, Mr. Zakheim, since I am intending to invest a good deal of money through our organization in certain business enterprises connected with the redemption of the liberated territories. A partnership between us should bring ample rewards to both parties, besides rewards for the State of Israel and the Jewish people. As it is written, "Will two walk together if they have not agreed?" My proposal, therefore, is that you should come over to our side, without of course abandoning your client Professor Gideon. Please think about this seriously. There is no urgency about replying. We are accustomed to waiting and do not believe in haste.

Professor Gideon may represent the achievements of the past, but it is my conviction that the future belongs to us. Take thought for the future, Mr. Zakheim!

Yours with great respect and in Jewish solidarity,
Michael (Michel-Henri) Sommo

*

6.11.76

Rahel Morag
Kibbutz Beit Avraham
Mobile Post, Lower Galilee

Dear normal Rahel,

And yet I still owe you a line or two. I didn't answer you before because I was up to here in Boaz's problems. No doubt you've put on your understanding-forgiving-Rahel look, and in your elder-sister tone you're remarking to yourself that I haven't been concerned about Boaz but, as usual, about myself. After all, ever since we were children you were always the one to save me from my crazes. "My dramas," to use your term. And you'll start feeding me a stew of that applied psychology you picked up from your child-care course. Until I go out of my mind and scream: Leave me alone! And then you'll smile at me sadly, refrain as usual from taking offense, keep quiet, and let me reach by myself the realization that my outbursts only exemplify what you have been wise enough to diagnose already. That tolerant, pedantic wisdom of yours — which has infuriated me all these years, until I almost choke with rage and explode and insult you, thus giving you a perfect opportunity to forgive and also reinforcing your constant anxiety about my condition. Aren't we a perfect team, the two of us? You see, I only meant to write you a couple of lines to thank you—you and Yoash—for being willing to drop everything and come to Jerusalem to help. And look what came out. Forgive me. Even though if it weren't for my dramas, what connection would there be between the two of us? And where would you send your salvos of crushing kindness?

As you know, Boaz is okay. And I am trying hard to calm down. Alec's lawyer hired some investigators, who discovered that he was working on some sort of tourist boat on the Sinai coast and didn't need any of us. I managed to persuade Michel not to go to him in the meantime. You see, I accepted your advice to leave him alone. As for your other advice, to forget Alec for good and to refuse his money, don't be angry if I tell you you don't understand a thing. Give my regards and thanks to Yoash and kisses to the children.

> *Your intolerable*
> *Ilana*

Best wishes to all of you from Michel. He is starting to extend the flat with the money we got from Alec. He's already got permission to add two rooms on the back, into the yard. Next summer you'll be able to come and stay with us for a break, and I'll be on my best behavior.

*

From worldwide press reviews of *The Desperate Violence: A Study in Comparative Fanaticism* by Alexander A. Gideon (1976).

"This monumental work by an Israeli scholar sheds new light—or, rather, deep shade—on the psychopathology of various faiths and ideologies from the Middle Ages to the present day. . . ."   *Times Literary Supplement*

"A must . . . an ice-cold analysis of the phenomenon of messianic fervor in both its religious and its secular guise . . ."

New York Times

"Fascinating reading . . . vital for an understanding of the movements that have shaken and still shake our century . . . Professor Gideon describes the phenomenon of faith . . . any faith . . . not as a source of morality but as its precise opposite . . ."   *Frankfurter Allgemeine Zeitung*

"The Israeli scholar maintains that all world-reformers since the dawn of history have actually sold their souls to the devil of fanaticism. . . . The fanatic's latent desire to die a martyr's death on the altar of his idea is, in the author's view, what enables him to sacrifice the lives of others, sometimes of millions, without batting an eyelid. . . . In the fanatic's soul, violence, salvation, and death are fused into a single mass. . . . Professor Gideon bases this conclusion not on psychological speculations but on a precise linguistic analysis of the vocabulary that is characteristic of all fanatics of all ages and of all positions in the religious and ideological spectrum. . . . This is one of those rare books that force the reader to reexamine himself and all his views fundamentally and to seek within himself and his surroundings manifestations of latent sickness. . . ."   *New Statesman*

"Ruthlessly lays bare the true face of feudalism and capitalism. . . . With great skill he exposes the Church, Fascism, nationalism, Zionism, racism, militarism, and the extreme right. . . ."   *Literaturnaya Pravda*

"You sometimes have the feeling as you read that you are looking at a painting by Hieronymus Bosch. . . ."   *Die Zeit*

*

To Dr. A. Gideon
Via Mr. M. Zakheim

Dear Monk,

If only you had given me a hint seven years ago, at the trial,
that you were not plotting to take advantage of my admitting
adultery to take Boaz away from me I should have had no reason
to object to the paternity test, which in any case would have been
unnecessary. How much suffering could have been spared if you
had only said two words then. But what's the point of asking a
vampire how he can drink fresh blood?

I am doing you an injustice. You forfeited your son because
you wanted to spare him. You were even intending to donate
a kidney to him. Even now you could photocopy these letters
of mine and send them to Michel. But something interferes
with your hatred. Something whispers to you like wind in dry
grass, interrupting the arctic silence. I can remember you with
your friends having the usual ritual Friday-night argument:
your long legs stretched out under the coffee table, your eyes
only half opened, the rough suntanned skin of your arms, your
pensive fingers slowly kneading some absent object. For the rest,
a motionless fossil. Like a lizard watching an insect. Your glass
precariously balanced on the arm of your chair. The din of voices
in the room, the arguments, the counterarguments, the cigarette
smoke — they all seem to be happening a long way below you.
Your best white shirt, starched and neatly pressed. And your
face sealed in contemplation. And all of a sudden, like a viper,
you dart your head forward and spit into the conversation: "Just
a minute. I'm sorry. I must have missed something." The din
of the argument fades instantly. And you scythe through the
discussion with a sentence or two, cut across the positions from
a sharp, unexpected angle, demolish the point of departure,
and conclude with, "Sorry. Carry on." Then you settle back into

your disconnected position. Indifferent to the silence that you
have generated. Letting someone else formulate in your name
the conclusion that might possibly be implied by the question
you have put. Slowly, sheepishly, the argument warms up again.
Without you. By then you are completely engrossed in a solemn
study of the ice cubes in your glass. Until the next interjection.
Who was it who warped your mind and made you see compassion
as weakness, gentleness and sensitivity as shameful, love as a sign
of effeminacy in a man? Who was it who banished you to the
snowy steppes? Who was it who corrupted a man like you into
obliterating the stain of his compassion for his son, the shame
of his longing for his wife? What a grim horror, Alec. And the
crime is its own punishment. Your monstrous suffering is like a
thunderstorm behind the mountains at dawn. I hug you.

Meanwhile the Hebrew edition of your book is all the rage
here now. Your picture stares out at me from every newspaper.
Except that the picture is ten years old at least. It shows your face
as lean and concentrated, with your military sternness stretched
the width of your lips, as if you are about to give the order to fire.
Was it taken when you left the regular army and went back to
the university to finish your doctorate? As I look at it the arctic
brilliance flashes opposite me out of the gray cloud. Like a spark
trapped in an iceberg.

Ten years ago. Even before you finished building the
house that looks like a castle in Yefe Nof, from the money that
Zakheim managed to extract for you from your father, who was
already disappearing into the distance toward the steppes of his
melancholy, like an old Indian heading for the happy hunting
ground.

We were still living in our old flat in Abu Tor, with that rocky
yard and its pine trees. And I remember particularly the rainy
winter weekends. We would stay in bed till ten o'clock, battered
and exhausted from the cruelty of our night, almost tolerating
each other, like a pair of boxers between rounds. Almost leaning
on each other. Punch-drunk. When we emerged from the

bedroom we would find Boaz already awake. He had dressed himself two hours earlier (with his shirt buttoned up wrongly and with odd socks) and would be sitting in academic earnestness at your desk, with your lamp lit in front of him, your pipe in his mouth, drawing instrument panels of spaceships on one sheet of paper after another. Or an airplane crashing in flames. Sometimes cutting out for you a pile of wonderfully neat rectangular little cards, his contribution to your doctorate. Or for the Armored Corps. It was before the period of the balsa airplanes.

Outside it was raining gloomily, persistently. The wind dashed the rain against the tops of the pine trees and the rusty iron shutters. Through the streaming window the yard seemed to have been drawn with a Japanese brush: pine needles trembling in the mist with droplets of water trapped at their tips. In the distance, between blocks of cloud, domes and minarets floated as though also joining the caravan that was rolling with the thunder eastward toward the desert.

When I went to the kitchen to get breakfast ready I discovered that Boaz had already laid the table for three. Red-eyed, you and I would avoid looking at each other. Sometimes I would fix you with my eyes as though I were hypnotizing you, only so you would not be able to look at me. And the child, like a social worker, would act as intermediary for us, asking me to pour you more coffee, you to pass me the cream cheese.

After breakfast I would put on that blue woolen dress, comb my hair and make my face up, and sit down with a book in the armchair. Except that the book would almost always stay open upside down on my lap: I could not take my eyes off you and your son. You would sit together at the desk, cutting out, sorting, and pasting pictures from your *Geographical Magazine*. You worked in almost total silence, the child skillfully guessing your wishes, passing you just at the right moment scissors, paste, penknife, even before you could ask for them. As though you were practicing some ritual together. And all in deep seriousness. Apart from the hum of the kerosene heater, there was no sound to be heard in the flat. And occasionally you would unconsciously lay your strong hand on his fair hair, and dirty it with glue. How different was that purposeful masculine silence from the desperate silence that came down on you and me the moment the last spasm of desire left us. How I trembled to see the touch of your fingers on his head, and compared it with the nocturnal rage they had bestowed on me a few hours earlier. When did we see Death winning at chess in *The Seventh Seal*? Where were the frozen tundras that gave you the vicious strength to disown that child? Where do you draw the frozen power from to compel your fingers to write the words *your son*?

And at the end of those Saturdays, at the close of the Sabbath in the twilight between rain showers, even before we had put Boaz to bed, you would suddenly stand up, angrily pour yourself a quick brandy, down it in one gulp without screwing up your face, deliver a couple of violent pats on your son's back, as if he were a horse, roughly shrug on your coat, and hurl at me from the doorway, "I'll be back on Tuesday evening. Try to evacuate the zone before then if you can." Then you would go out, closing the door with a sort of desperate self-control beyond all slamming. Through the window I would see your back disappearing into the gathering darkness. You have not forgotten that winter. In you it goes on and on, but growing ever grayer, moss-covered, sinking into the ground, like an old tombstone.

If you can, try to believe me when I say that Michel does not read your letters. Even though I have mentioned to him that we are corresponding through Zakheim. Don't worry. Or perhaps I should write: Don't hope?

Despite your denial, I still see you sitting at your window with a vista of snowfields, brilliant plains without tree, hill, or bird, stretching away until they merge with masses of gray fog, all as in a woodcut. All in the heart of the winter.

Whereas here, meanwhile, the summer has arrived. The nights are short and cool. The days are blazing, dazzling like molten steel. Through the window of my room I can see the three Arab laborers that Michel has hired digging trenches for the foundations of the extension that Michel is building with your money. Michel himself works with these laborers every day when he gets home from school. He doesn't need a contractor, since he was once a builder himself, the first year after he came to Israel. Every couple of hours he takes some coffee out to them and exchanges jokes and sayings with them. His brother-in-law's nephew, who is an official in the city council, got us our building permit early. A cousin of his friend Janine has promised to do the electrical wiring for us, and to charge us only for the materials.

On the other side of the fence are two fig trees and an olive. Beyond them begin the steep slopes of the wadi. And you can see on the other side of the wadi the Arab quarter, half suburb and half village, a flock of little stone houses clustering around a minaret. Before dawn the cocks call to me from there insistently, as though trying to seduce me. At sunrise goats bleat, and sometimes I manage to hear the bells of the herd going off to nibble on the edge of the desert. A whole battalion of dogs bursts at times into a barking that is dulled by the distance. Like the ashes of old passions. At night their barking descends to a strangled howling. The muezzin responds with his own wailing, guttural, unbridled, consumed with veiled longings. It is summer in Jerusalem, Alec. Summer has come and you have not.

But Boaz has turned up—the day before yesterday. As if nothing had happened. And his manner was almost joking: "Hi, Michel. Ilana. I've come to eat up your Yifat. But first of all, here, little one, eat these sweets so that you'll be sweeter for me to eat." A Bedouin Viking, sun-scorched, smelling of sea and dust, his shoulder-length hair white-hot, like burnished gold. He already has to stoop when he comes through the doorway. He turns and addresses Michel with a deep bow, as though of reverence, as though performing deliberately and consciously a ritual gesture of respect. Whereas for Yifat he went down on all fours, and she, a dark-skinned monkey, climbed up and clung to his limbs until she could touch the ceiling. And dribbled a sticky mess from the candy he had given her into his hair.

Boaz brought with him a skinny, silent girl, who was neither pretty nor ugly. A math student from France, a good four years older than he is. Michel, after investigating her background and discovering that she came from a Jewish family, calmed down and suggested that they stay the night on the carpet in front of the television. For greater security he left the light on in the shower and the door between us and them wide open, so as to insure "that Boaz doesn't get up to any nonsense in my house."

What brings Boaz here? It appears that he turned to Zakheim and asked for a sum of money for purposes you know. For some reason Zakheim decided to tell him about the hundred thousand you gave Michel, but refused to give Boaz so much as pocket money. Some sort of sly scheme that I can't decipher is apparently brewing inside his devilish shaven skull, and that's why he suggested to Boaz that he come and see Michel "and claim what is rightfully yours."

Perhaps you are also a party to this plot? Perhaps it's your very own? Is it just obtuseness that always prevents me from anticipating your next blow, even when it is just about to hit me? Surely Zakheim is merely a kind of exuberant operetta puppet in which you sometimes choose to conceal your grim fist.

Boaz came to suggest nothing less than to take Michel into partnership in some business to do with tourist boats in the Red Sea. That was why he came up to Jerusalem. He needs, as he puts it, a preliminary investment, which, he is sure, he will recover in a few months. While he was talking, he dismantled a matchbox and made Yifat a sort of camel on chicken's legs. This child is you: enthralled, I watched his fingers recklessly squandering rivers of strength just to refrain from breaking a matchstick. Such a dazzling waste, at the sight of which I was instantly nearly filled with an overwhelming physical envy of his French dropout.

On hearing the offer of a partnership, Michel stood up and, as usual, did the right and fitting thing at the most appropriate moment. That is to say, he suddenly climbed onto the windowsill and opened up the box of the roller blind to dismantle and reassemble the screw and so release the blind, which was stuck. Then he remained standing on the windowsill, and thus was able to talk to your son *de haut en bas*, as though from the bridge of a ship. Michel explained to Boaz dispassionately, without either losing his temper or in any way softening the blow, that there was nothing to talk about, neither loans nor investments, and that even if Boaz was "the epitome of wisdom, like King Solomon in his day, still the Sommo family will not finance either the harem or the ships of Tarshish." And he also nailed Boaz with the verse "in the sweat of your brow you shall eat your bread."

But immediately afterward he got down from his launching pad and went to the kitchen and made Boaz and his friend regal hamburgers, fried potatoes, and a virtuoso salad. And in the evening he asked the neighbors' boy to babysit Yifat again and took the two of them and me out to the cinema and afterward for ice cream. It was only when we returned home, close to midnight, that Boaz summoned up enough courage to ask Michel whose "that money from America" was. Michel, who symbolically had not got down for an instant from his pedestal, replied calmly, "The money is your mother's, your sister's, and yours in three equal parts. But for the time being you and Yifat are still minors as far as the law is concerned, and naturally as far as I am, too. Meanwhile your mother is responsible for the two of you and I am responsible for her, so go and tell that to Mr. Zakheim, and tell him to stop boring us all. As for you, Boaz, even if you grow to be taller than the Eiffel Tower, for me you will still have the status of a minor Eiffel Tower. If you want to study, that's another matter altogether: just say so, and the money's yours. But to waste money that you didn't earn on fishes and tourists and girls? That I won't finance, even if it is happening in the liberated Sinai. That money is intended to make you into a human being. Now if by any chance you have an urge to hit me over the head with a vegetable crate, go ahead, Boaz; there's one under Yifat's bed."

Boaz listened and said nothing, merely spread that thoughtful smile of his on his mouth, and his regal, tragic beauty filled the room like an aroma. He did not stop smiling even when Michel changed over to French and plunged into a lengthy conversation with the girl student. I am fascinated by the way my husband and your son, out of the depths of contempt and humiliation,

are silently fond of each other. Be careful, sir: your victims are
only too likely to make common cause against you. And I get
a thrill out of your jealousy, which no doubt has just made you
purse your lips like wire. And close by an inch or two the space
between your spectacles and your pen on your desk. But don't
touch the whiskey again: your illness is outside the rules of the
game.

This morning some friends of Michel's, skullcapped Russians
and Americans, came in a van and took Michel and Boaz and
his friend for a trip around Bethlehem. So I am here by myself,
writing to you on pages torn out of an exercise book. Yifat is
at the nursery. She looks like Michel but with a sort of comical
exaggeration, as though she had been specially made to be a
parody of him: she is thin, curly-haired, has a slight squint, and
is obedient, even though she is given to occasional tantrums. But
most of the time she radiates shy friendliness, which she lavishes
indiscriminately on objects, animals, and people, as though the
world were waiting to receive grace and favor from her tiny self.
Almost since the day she was born Michel has addressed her as
"Mademoiselle Sommo." He pronounces it "Mamzelle," and she
responds by innocently calling him *mamzer,* "bastard."

Did you know, Alec, that Michel has decided to leave his job
as a French teacher at the end of the year? To leave the school
and also give up his private lessons? He has dreams of dealing in
real estate in the territories, of a political career, following in the
footsteps of a brother he hero-worships. Not that he tells me much
about it. Your money has changed his life. It may not be what
you had in mind, but it happens sometimes that even a dragon
produces some noble result, fertilizes a plot of land that will one
day yield crops.

At eleven o'clock I have to go to the Café Savyon, to give this
letter to Zakheim at a secret rendezvous. As you have instructed.
Even though Michel knows. And Zakheim? He is thrilled. He
comes to these meetings arrogant, stylish, and deadly. Wearing a
sporty jacket with a bohemian silk scarf around his neck, his Tatar
shaven head gleaming and perfumed, his fingernails carefully

manicured, the effect spoiled only by the clumps of black hairs
sprouting from his nostrils and ears. Time after time he manages
to break down my resistance and force a coffee and cake on me.
And then he starts to ooze extravagant compliments, double
entendres; sometimes he even touches me accidentally, and
hastens to apologize with veiled eyes. By our last meeting he had
advanced as far as the flower stage. Not a whole bunch, of course,
just a single carnation. I forced myself to smile and to sniff the
bloom, which smelled of Zakheim's scent rather than its own. As if
it had been soaked in it.

You ask what I saw in Michel. And I have to admit it: I
was lying again. And I am taking back that tale about Michel
the virtuoso lover. So meanwhile you can relax. Michel is all
right in bed, and he's trying hard to go on improving. I even
found a handbook in French that he had hidden from me in his
toolbox. I'm sorry if I've taken away one of your instruments of
mortification. I'll let you have others, even sharper ones. Michel
and I met a year or so after the divorce. He used to come to the
bookshop where I was working, and he used to wait for me,
browsing among the magazines until the shop closed. Then he
used to take me to a cheap restaurant, to the cinema, to public
discussion groups. After the film we sometimes walked mile after
mile through the empty night streets of south Jerusalem — he did
not dare to invite me up to his room. Perhaps he was ashamed of
his lodgings in the laundry room on the roof of a house belonging
to one of his relatives. And he would shyly describe his views and
plans to me. Can you imagine a bashful ego trip? Even to put his
arm through mine was beyond his courage.

I waited patiently for nearly three months, until I had had
enough of the sidelong hungry-but-well-trained-dog looks he kept
giving me. Finally one night I grabbed his head and kissed him
in a back street. So we began to kiss occasionally. But he was still
apprehensive about my meeting his family and about my reaction
to his partial piety. I liked his timidity. I tried not to put pressure
on him. When several more months had passed, and the winter
chill had turned our strolls to martyrdom, I took him to my room,

undressed him like a child, and folded his limbs around me. Nearly an hour passed before he managed to relax a little. And after that I still had quite a struggle before he showed signs of life. It transpired that the little he knew he had learned as a youth in Paris from girls who were apparently as frightened as he was. And perhaps, despite his denials, in some paupers' brothel. When I let out a little sigh, he was terrified and began to murmur *Pardon*. And then he got dressed, went down solemnly on his knees, and desperately asked for my hand in marriage.

I became pregnant after our wedding. Another year passed after the baby was born before I managed to teach him how to wait for me. How to wean himself from behaving like a bicycle thief whenever he made love. When he finally succeeded in wringing from me for the first time the sound that you can draw out of me even by mail, Michel resembled the first astronaut to land on the moon: his modest, ecstatic pride made my heart tremble with love. The next day, in a transport of enthusiasm, he did not go to school but borrowed some money from his brother to buy me a summer dress. He even bought me a little electric mixer. And in the evening he cooked me a regal four-course meal, complete with a bottle of wine. He did not stop plying me with little treats and favors. Since then he has slowly improved and sometimes manages to get a clear sound.

Have you relaxed, Alec? Did the vampire's smile appear like a crack between your lips? Are your fangs shining white by the light of the flickering fire? Is the gray malice capering behind the cold stare? Wait. We haven't finished yet. You have never reached and never will as far as Michel's feet. The silent respect, Alec, the shy flicker of gratitude with which he defers to my body before love and after it, the dreamy glow that spreads over his face at night: like a humble restaurant violinist who has been permitted to touch a Stradivarius. Every night, as though this were the first time in his life, his fingers explore my body, surprised by a blow that never falls. And afterward, by the light of the bedside lamp when he gets up to fetch me my nightie, his myopic eyes tell me in fervent silence that the regal favors that I have undeservedly bestowed upon him exceed his humble deserts. A wavering, spiritual glow, like a prayer, lights up his brow from within.

But what can a scaly, bone-plated dragon like you understand of grace and kinship and tenderness? You have never had anything, and you never will have, besides your torture dungeons. Which my flesh longs for. Your tropical hell. The steamy jungles bubbling with warm decomposition, and glowing dimly in the half-light filtering through the foliage where the oily rain rises from the earth that simmers with fat wanton marrow, catches in the dense treetops, and spills back again, melting, from the treetops to the mud and to the rotting roots. After all, I was not the one who got up and ran away. It was you who smashed it all up. I was prepared to carry on, and I still am. Why did you divorce me? Why did you bring me to the heart of darkness and leave me and run away? And you are still hiding from me in your black-and-white room. You will not return. You are paralyzed by fear. You exhausted, feeble male, hiding, trembling, in your hole. Is the dragon really so shabby? Such a floppy, sloppy dragon? A vampire stuffed with rags? Write and tell me where you are. Tell me of your doings. And the truth about your health.

Weeping Willow

*

Tel Aviv
6.18.1976

To Mr. M. Zakheim, Attorney
Zakheim & di Modena
36 King George St.
Jerusalem

PERSONAL — ATTENTION OF ADDRESSEE ONLY

Dear Mr. Zakheim,

Following your telephone request earlier this week I flew to Sharm al-Sheikh for a few hours and checked out the story. My assistant, Albert Maimon, also succeeded in tracking the youth and discovering his whereabouts up to two days ago. The report is as follows:

During the night of June 10–11, the tour boat on which BB has been working lately was stolen from the civilian anchorage at Ophira. The same night, at two o'clock in the morning, the boat was discovered abandoned not far from Ras Muhammad, after apparently being used by Bedouin smugglers to transport drugs (hashish) from the Egyptian coast. The patrol that discovered the boat set off in pursuit of the smugglers. At five o'clock (dawn on June 11) a young Bedouin by the name of Hamed Mutani was arrested. He was living with BB at a gas station, together with three young women from abroad. The Bedouin resisted arrest (he denies this) and I have reason to believe that he was beaten up on the spot by the police and the military (they deny this). BB got involved in the incident, and with the help of a tire attached to a rope he went berserk and injured nine soldiers and five members of the Ophira police force before he was eventually overpowered. He was arrested and charged with obstructing a lawful arrest. BB's version, as it was taken down at the police station, is that it was those conducting the arrest who employed violence against his friend the Bedouin, who was acting, as was BB, in "self-defense." The Bedouin was released after a few hours, once his interrogators were convinced that he had had nothing whatever to do with either the theft of the boat or the smuggling.

After less than twenty-four hours, during the night of June 11–12, BB succeeded in breaking down the wall of the prefabricated structure housing the police station and escaped. The officer on duty at the time believes that the youth is still wandering around in the desert, and may have taken shelter with the Bedouin. It was in this direction that the Ophira police continued to search for him. As mentioned above, investigator Albert Maimon of our staff (who submitted a brief report on BB to you on a previous occasion) turned in a completely different direction (MHS) and indeed quickly obtained positive results. The youth BB stayed until two days ago in a rented apartment in Kiryat Arba, near

Hebron, inhabited by a group of five unmarried religious men of American and Russian origins. These young men are attached to a small right-wing organization calling itself the Jewish Fellowship. As you are aware, MHS is also associated with this cause.

In accordance with our legal responsibility, we communicated this discovery to the police. But meanwhile the youth has disappeared again. That is the extent of the information in our possession. (Invoice enclosed.) Please inform us promptly if you wish us to continue working on this case.

[*Signed*] *Shlomo Zand*
S. Zand Private Investigations Ltd., Tel Aviv

*

A GIDEON HILTON AMSTERDAM

ARE YOU STILL INTERESTED IN MY SELLING PROPERTY
ZIKHRON I HAVE PURCHASER ON EXCELLENT TERMS ADVISE
PROMPT ACTION AWAITING INSTRUCTIONS MANFRED

*

PERSONAL ZAKHEIM JERUSALEM ISRAEL

NEGATIVE ALEX

*

GIDEON GRANDHOTEL STOCKHOLM

TRIED TO REACH YOU BY TELEPHONE THIS IS
UNREPEATABLE OFFER CALL IMMEDIATELY FOR DETAILS
NOT LONG AGO YOU WERE PRESSING ME TO SELL WHATS
THE MATTER WITH YOU MANFRED

*

PERSONAL ZAKHEIM JERUSALEM ISRAEL

I SAID NEGATIVE ALEX

*

GIDEON NICFOR LONDON

BOAZ IN TROUBLE AGAIN POLICE LOOKING FOR HIM YOU
MAY REQUIRE FUNDS URGENTLY PURCHASER IS WILLING TO
PAY NINE HUNDRED IMMEDIATELY IN WILLIAM TELL SALVO
TO YOUR ACCOUNT IN MAGIC MOUNTAIN THINK CAREFULLY
MANFRED

*

PERSONAL ZAKHEIM JERUSALEM ISRAEL

GIVE BOAZ MY ADDRESS SO HE CAN CONTACT ME DIRECT
AND STOP NAGGING ALEX

*

GIDEON NICFOR LONDON

THE DEVIL KNOWS WHERE BOAZ IS WHAT ABOUT ZIKHRON
PROPERTY STOP CHANGING YOUR MIND EVERY FIVE
MINUTES OR YOULL END UP LIKE YOUR FATHER MANFRED

*

PERSONAL ZAKHEIM JERUSALEM ISRAEL

GIVE ME A BREAK ALEX

*

SOMMO 7 TARNAZ JERUSALEM ISRAEL

INFORM ME IMMEDIATELY WHATS UP WITH BOAZ DO YOU
NEED MY HELP WIRE ME AT NICFOR LONDON ALEXANDER
GIDEON

*

DOCTOR GIDEON C/O NICFOR LONDON

EVERYTHING IS ALL RIGHT NOW WE GOT THE NEW POLICE
RECORD CLOSED TOO ONCE HE UNDERTOOK TO STUDY AND
WORK IN KIRYAT ARBA DONT NEED ANY FAVORS WHAT
ABOUT YOUR DONATION MICHAEL SOMMO

*

Chicago
6.28.76

To Ilana, PRIVATE
By hand of Mr. M. Zakheim, Attorney

Dear Weeping Willow,

I got back here this morning after my term in London and a
few lectures in Holland and Sweden. Just before I left London I
got your long letter, which dear old Zakheim forwarded to me.
The letter with the juices and the jungles. I read it in the plane
somewhere over Newfoundland. Why did I divorce you? That's
your question this time. We'll deal with that in a minute.

But meanwhile I hear that Boaz has struck again. And that
Sommo has come to the rescue again. I'm beginning to like this
fixed pattern. My only reservations are about the bill that he'll be
sending me soon no doubt, together with interest.

Has Boaz started to grow side locks yet? Is he going to live
with the religion freaks on the West Bank? Has Sommo given him

a choice between a pioneering settlement and a reform school? That's just fine. If I know Boaz, it won't be long before the settlers start cursing Sommo and the day they agreed to take on our skull-smasher.

My answer to your question is: No, I shall not come to see you, except perhaps in dreams. If you had pleaded with me to stay far away from you, to have pity on you and not sully with my presence your pure new life with your humble restaurant violinist, who is playing on your Stradivarius, I might just have come running. But you are imploring me, Ilana. The thick smell of your desire, the smell of figs that were picked too long ago, reaches all the way here. Although I won't deny that I am astonished at your efforts to avoid your fixed habit and write a letter without any lies in it. It's nice that you're working on yourself. We can carry on for a while.

I owe you an answer to your simple, cunning question: Why did I divorce you seven and a half years ago?

Well done, Ilana. Ten points for putting the question. I'd like to put it in the newspapers, on television even: "Rahab rides again — sleeps with three divisions then wonders why she's been divorced. Says: All I really wanted was to come out all right in the end."

I'm evading the issue. I'll try to find an answer for you. The sad thing is, my hatred is starting to go. It's getting thin and gray, just like my hair. And apart from my hatred, what have I got left? Only money. Which is also being gradually drained out of my veins into Sommo's tanker. Don't interfere with my death, Ilana. For seven years I was slowly sinking into the fog, and all of a sudden you swooped down on me to wreck my death as well. You attacked without warning with your fresh troops while my tired old tanks are silent, without fuel or ammunition. Perhaps even starting to rust.

And in the middle of this assault you have the nerve to write to me that grace and tenderness and compassion exist. The murderess starts chanting psalms to elevate her victim's soul?

Did you happen to notice the motto from the New Testament that I chose as the epigraph for my book? I borrowed it straight from Jesus, who remarked at one moment in one of his inspired moods, "Those who live by the sword shall die by the sword." Which did not prevent that delicate zealot from raising his voice on another occasion and roaring, "Do not think I came to bring peace to the world; I did not come to bring peace but a sword." And the sword ended up by eating him as well.

What will you do with your sword once you have felled the dragon? Will you present it to Gush Emunim,* the scabbard to Mazkeret Gideon and the blade to Tel Alexander, those two great West Bank settlements that will be built with my money?

But surely the sword you wrenched from my grasp will wilt and fade and melt between your fingers. The blade will turn into a jellyfish. And in the strategic reserve, fresh and ready for the fray, fueled with deadly hatred and armed to the teeth with my arctic malice, Boaz Gideon is waiting for you. Your pincer movement, your plot to team Boaz up with Sommo so as to outflank me, will end badly for you. Boaz will gobble up Sommo and you will be left with nowhere to flee to, face to face with my killer child, who can slay a thousand men with the jawbone of an ass.

I ask myself why I did not follow your good advice, why I didn't throw your first letter, like a live scorpion, straight into the fire, as soon as I read the opening sentence. Now I don't even have the right to resent you; after all, you generously offered me in advance the way to avoid the trap you were laying for me. You did not fear for a moment that I would get out of the net. You recognized an insect that was out of its mind at the smell of a female in heat. I didn't have a chance. You are stronger than I am, in the same ratio as the sun is stronger than snow. Have you ever heard of carnivorous plants? They are female plants that can exude a scent of sexual juices over a great distance, and the poor

---

*Gush Emunim is a spiritual-political movement that seeks to build Jewish settlements throughout the Israeli-occupied territories, in order to retain "greater Israel," including the West Bank and Gaza. It consists mostly of religious Jews.

insect is drawn from miles away into the jaws that are going to
close around it. It's all over, Ilana. Checkmate. As after a plane
crash, we have sat down and analyzed, by correspondence, the
contents of the black box. And from now on, in the words of our
decree, we have no further demands on each other.

But what will your victory give you?

Thousands of years ago a certain man of Ephesus looked at
the fire burning in front of his eyes and proclaimed, "Its victory
will be its destruction." What will you do with the sword when
you have wiped me out? What will you do with yourself? You will
be extinguished pretty damn quick, Madame Sommo. You will
age. You will put on a lot of weight. Your golden hair will grow
dull. You will have to bleach it a ghastly peroxide blond. As long
as you don't take to wearing a head scarf. You will have to drown
the smells of your degenerating body in deodorants. Your breasts
will fill with fat, and your dazzling bosom, as usually happens to
Polish matrons, will rise up to meet your chin. Which for its part
will lengthen and go halfway to meet the bosom. The nipples will
become pale and bloated, like drowned corpses. Your legs will
swell. A network of varicose veins will spread from hip to foot.
The corsets in which you will be obliged to contain your cascades
of flesh will groan fit to burst as you fasten them. Your posterior
will become beastlike. Your vulva will flap and stink. Even a
virgin soldier or a retarded youngster will flee from your charms
as from the wild advances of a female hippopotamus in heat.
Your tame party hack, little Monsieur Pardon, will trail around
after you in a dazed state, like a puppy dog after a cow, until he
stumbles on some lively girl student who will effortlessly pull him
out and extricate him, thankful and out of breath, from under the
mountain lying on top of him. And so the episode of your Saharan
carnival will finally come to an end. A lover who knows neither
laughter nor levity is getting closer and closer to you. Perhaps for
you he will put on his black robe and cowl as you asked.

I stopped writing to you and stood at my high window (on
the twenty-seventh floor of an office building by the lakeside
in Chicago, built of glass and steel and somewhat resembling a

ballistic missile). I stood there for about half an hour looking
for a truthful and lethal answer to your question: mate in three
moves.

Try to picture this man, if you can, thinner than you
remember and with much less hair, in dark blue corduroy trousers
and a red cashmere sweater. Even though in principle, as you say,
he is in black and white. Standing at the window with his brow
pressed against the glass. The eyes in which you detect an "arctic
malice" search the outside world where the light is fading. And his
hands are in his pockets. Clenched. Every few minutes he shrugs
his shoulders for some reason and hums in a British sort of way.
A coldness passes through his bones. He shudders, removes his
hands from his pockets, and clasps his shoulders with his arms
crossed. This is the embrace of those who have nobody. And yet,
for all that, a tight-coiled animal element still endows his silent
standing by the window with some characteristic of inner tension:
as though flexed to leap back like lightning and anticipate his
assailants.

But there is no reason for tension. The world is red and
strange. A strong wind blows off the lake and dashes clumps of
fog against the silhouettes of the tall buildings. The dusk light
pours over the clouds, the water, the nearby towers, an alchemical
quality. A transparent orange hue. Opaque and yet transparent.
Not a single sign of life can he spy from his window. Apart from
millions of salvos of foam capering on the surface of the lake,
as though the water had rebelled and tried to convert itself into
another substance altogether: slate, for example. Or granite. Every
now and again the wind erupts and the windowpanes chatter
like teeth. Death appears to him now not like a hovering threat,
but like an event that has been going on for some time already.
And here is a strange bird being swept toward his window with
spasmodic flapping, describing circles and loops as though
trying to sketch an inscription in space: perhaps the wording of
the answer to you that he is looking for? Until all of a sudden
it comes rushing toward the glass and almost bursts in his face

as he realizes at last that it is not a bird at all but just a sheet of newspaper trapped in the claws of the wind. Why did we part, Ilana? What took hold of me and made me suddenly extinguish the furnaces of our hell? Why did I betray us? An empty evening is falling violently on Chicago. Lightning flashes of white-hot iron bluster from horizon to horizon like flares, and now convoys of thunder are starting to roll in the distance, as though my tank battles are pursuing me here all the way from the Sinai. Has it ever occurred to you to ask yourself how a monster mourns? The shoulders heave in a rapid, compulsive rhythm, and the head extends forcefully forward and downward. Like a dog coughing. The belly is seized by frequent cramps, and the breathing becomes a hoarse gurgling. The monster chokes with rage at the fact of being a monster and writhes in monstrous spasms. I have no answer, Ilana. My hatred is dying and my wisdom is expiring with it.

As soon as I came back to my desk to continue writing to you, there was a power cut. Just imagine: America — and power cuts! After a moment of blackness, the emergency lighting came on: pale, skeletal neon, looking like moonlight on chalk hills in the desert. The most electric moments in my life were spent in the desert, charging and trampling under my tracks all that lay in my path, smashing with my gunfire whatever displayed signs of life, raising columns of fire and smoke, causing clouds of dust to billow up, shaking the whole world with the roar of thirty engines, inhaling like an intoxicating drug the smell of scorched rubber, the stench of charred flesh and burning metal, leaving behind me a trail of destruction and empty shell cases, and at night, hunched over a map, devising clever stratagems by the light of the dead moon, shedding its silver over the dead chalk hills. To be sure, I could have answered you with a burst of machine-gun fire: I could have said, for example, that I threw you out because you had started to rot. Because your carryings-on, even with apes and he-goats, had begun to get boring. Because I had had enough. Lost interest.

But we had agreed to dispense with lies. After all, all these years I could sleep only with you. All my life, in fact, because I was a virgin when I met you. When I take into my bed some little admirer, pupil, secretary, interviewer, you appear and intrude yourself between us. If ever you forget to turn up, my sleeping partner has to help herself out. Or make do with an evening of philosophy. If I am a demon, Ilana, then I am a genie, and you are my bottle. I've never managed to escape.

Nor have you, for that matter, Lady Sommo. If you are a demon, I am *your* bottle.

I read in Bernanos that unhappiness is a source of blessing. To this Catholic honeydew I replied in my book that all happiness is basically a trite Christian invention. Happiness, I wrote, is kitsch. It has nothing in common with the *eudaimonia* of the Greeks. Whereas in Judaism the whole idea of happiness does not exist; there isn't even a word corresponding to it in the Bible. Apart, perhaps, from the satisfaction of approval, a positive feedback from God or your neighbor: "Blessed are the undefiled in the way," for instance. Judaism recognizes only joy. As in the verse "Rejoice, O young man, in thy youth." Ephemeral joy, like the fire of the cryptic Heraclitus, whose victory is its destruction, joy whose converse is wrapped up in it and in fact actually makes it possible.

What is there left of all our joy, yours and mine, Ilana? Only perhaps joy at the other's misfortunes. Embers of a dead fire. And here we are, puffing on those embers from halfway around the globe in the hope of fanning a momentary flicker of malice. What a foolish waste, Ilana. I give in. I'm ready to sign a document of capitulation here and now.

And what will you do with me? Of course. There is no other way. Nature herself decrees that the routed male be enslaved. He is castrated and made to serve. He shrinks to the size of a Sommo. So you will have two of us: one to worship you and sweeten your nights with his religious passion, the other to finance these spiritual nuptials. What should I write on the next check?

I'll buy you both whatever you want. Ramallah? Bab Allah? Baghdad? My hatred is dying and in its place I am falling under the spell of my father's impetuous generosity. He intended to leave his fortune, at the end of his days, to build homes for consumptive poets on top of Mount Tabor and Mount Gilboa. I shall use my money to arm both sides in the battle that will erupt one day between Boaz and Sommo.

And now I shall tell you a story. A sketch for a romantic novel. An opening for a *tragedia dell'arte*. The year is 1959. A young major in the regular army brings his intended to meet his almighty father. The girl has a Slavic face, sexy in a dreamy way, but not particularly beautiful in the accepted sense. There is something beguiling in her expression of childlike surprise. Her parents brought her here from Lodz when she was four. They have both died on her. Apart from a sister in a kibbutz, she has no family left in the world. Since leaving the army she has earned her living as a copy editor for a popular weekly. She is hoping to publish some poetry.

And this morning she is visibly worried: what she has heard about the father does not bode well. Her personality and background are certain not to be to his liking, and she has heard alarming stories about his fits of rage. She sees the meeting with the father therefore as a sort of fateful interview. After some hesitation, she decides to wear a shiny white blouse and a flowery spring skirt, perhaps to emphasize the surprised-little-girl effect. Even her hussar, magnificent in his starched uniform, appears a little tense.

And at the gateway to the estate between Binyamina and Zikhron Yaakov, pacing up and down on his gravel path and fingering a fat cigar as though it were a gun, Volodya Gudonski, the great dealer in land and importer of iron, awaits them. Tsar Vladimir the Terrible. Among the many stories circulating about him they tell how, when he was still a pioneer in charge of stone quarries, in 1929, he killed three Arab brigands by himself, with a sledgehammer. And they tell how he was the lover of two Egyptian princesses. And they also tell how, after he had embarked on his import business and made a small fortune out of his dealings with the British army, it once happened that the high commissioner at a reception affectionately called him a "clever Jew," and the Tsar, on the spot, roared at the high commissioner and challenged him to a fistfight in the middle of the party, and when the man declined called him a "British chicken."

The hussar and his intended were greeted on their arrival with iced pomegranate juice and then taken on a long tour of inspection of the length and breadth of the estate, whose fields were worked by Circassian laborers from Galilee. And there was an ornamental pool with a fountain and goldfish, and a rose garden with a collection of rare varieties imported from Japan and Burma. Zeev-Benjamin Gudonski talked without stopping, lecturing with picturesque enthusiasm, wooing, as though overflowing with whimsical exaggeration, his son's fiancée. Cutting and handing her whatever flower her eyes lighted upon. Clasping her shoulders in an expansive gesture. Jokingly kneading her fine shoulder blades. Bestowing upon her the honorary rank of thoroughbred filly. His deep Russian voice waxed enthusiastic over the elegance of her ankles. And suddenly he demanded with a roar to be shown her knees at once.

Meanwhile the crown prince was firmly and absolutely deprived of the right of speech for the whole duration of the visit. He was not permitted to utter a single cheep. What alternative did he have, therefore, but to grin like an idiot and occasionally relight the cigar that had gone out in his father's mouth. Even now, in Chicago, as he writes down for you his memories of that day, seventeen years later, he suddenly has the feeling that that idiotic grin is spreading over his face again. And a ghostly breeze blows on the embers of his hatred for you, because you were so thrilled to join in the tyrant's game. You even, with peals of schoolgirlish laughter, repeatedly exposed your knees to his gaze. An enchanting blush colored your cheeks as you did so. Whereas I must have been as pale as a corpse.

Next the young couple was invited to a meal in the dining room, where French windows afforded a view of the Mediterranean from the top of the escarpment of Zikhron. Christian Arab servants in tailcoats served pickled fish with vodka, consommé, meat, fish, fruit, cheese, and ice cream. And a regular caravan of glasses of steaming tea straight from the samovar. Every refusal or apology provoked bellows of titanic rage.

As evening came on, the Tsar, in the library, still determinedly strangled at birth any sentence that the cowed prince tried to speak: the father was busy up to his ears with the *krassavitsa* and must not be disturbed. She was asked to play the piano. Requested to recite a poem. Examined in literature, politics, and art history. A record was placed on the phonograph and she was obliged to dance a waltz with the tipsy giant, who trod on her toes. To all these challenges she responded readily, good-humoredly, like someone trying to please a child. Then the old man began to tell rude jokes of the spiciest variety. Her face reddened, but she did not deny him her rippling laughter. At one o'clock in the morning the dictator finally fell silent, grasped the tip of his bushy mustache between brown finger and thumb, closed his eyes, and fell fast asleep in his armchair.

The couple exchanged glances and gestured to each other to leave him a note and depart: they had not planned to spend the night there. But as they were leaving on tiptoe, the Tsar leapt from his place and kissed the beauty on both cheeks, and then, lengthily, on her mouth. And delivered a stunning clap on the back of the neck to his son and heir. At half past two he called Jerusalem, woke a dazed Zakheim from a sweet conspiratorial dream, and bombarded him with instructions to purchase an apartment in Jerusalem for the young couple first thing in the morning and to invite "the world and his wife" to the wedding, to take place "ninety days from yesterday."

And we had only gone to see him so that he could meet you. We had not yet discussed the question of marriage. Or if we had, you had spoken and I had hesitated.

To our wedding, which did indeed take place three months later, he actually forgot to come: he had found himself a new mistress in the meantime and had taken her to the Norwegian fjords for a honeymoon. As he regularly did with his new mistresses, at least twice a year.

One bright morning, a short time after our wedding, when I was away on brigade maneuvers in the Negev, he turned up in Jerusalem and started to explain to you delicately, almost sheepishly, that his son—to his great sorrow—was merely a "bureaucratic spirit," whereas the two of you were "like a pair of trapped eagles." And therefore on his bended knee he implored you to consent to spend with him "just one magical night." And he immediately swore to you by all that was precious and holy to him that he would not touch you with so much as his little finger—he was no villain—but would merely listen to your playing and your reading of poems and go for a walk with you in the mountains around the city, concluding with the view of the "metaphysical sunrise" from the top of the YMCA tower. When you refused him, he called you a "little Polish shopkeeper" who had lured his son into your "clutches" with your "tricks," and he took his presence elsewhere. (During those nights you and I had already started to excite ourselves by playing at threesomes. Even if at that time we had not yet advanced beyond the realm of the imagination. Was the Tsar the first third man in your fantasies? The first lie you told me?)

When Boaz was born, for some reason Volodya Gudonski was staying in northern Portugal. But he managed to send a check from there to some dubious Italian firm, which dispatched to us an official certificate testifying that somewhere in the Himalayas there was a godforsaken peak that would henceforth and forevermore be named on all maps "Boaz Gideon Peak." You must check to see if the piece of paper still exists. Perhaps your messiah will found a settlement there. And in 1963, when Boaz was two or three years old, Volodya Gudonski decided to become a recluse. He sent his army of mistresses scattering to the four corners of the globe, Zakheim he tortured like a Scythian, and us he adamantly refused to see even for a brief audience—he considered us to be degenerates. (Had he noticed something from his exalted throne? Did he nurse some suspicion?) He shut himself away within the four walls of his estate, hired a couple of armed guards, and devoted his days and nights to learning Persian. And then astrology and the Doctor Feldenkreis Method. Doctors hired by Zakheim he sent packing like dogs. One day he up and dismissed all his workmen with a wave of the hand. Since then the orchard has gradually been turning into a jungle. One day he up and sacked the domestic servants and guards as well, leaving himself only one old Armenian to play billiards with him in the cellar of the dilapidated house. Father and the Armenian slept on camp beds in the kitchen and lived on canned food and beer. The door from the kitchen to the rest of the house was secured with a crossbeam and nails. Branches of the trees in the garden began to grow through the broken upstairs windows into the bedrooms. Plants and bushes grew in the ground-floor rooms. Rats and snakes and night birds nested in the corridors. Creepers climbed up the two staircases, reached the first floor, ramified from room to room, penetrated the ceiling, pushed up a few roof tiles, and so found their way out to the sunshine again. Eager roots sprouted between the decorated floor tiles. Tens or hundreds of pigeons requisitioned the house for their own use. But Volodya Gudonski chatted in fluent Persian to his Armenian. He also discovered the weak point in the Feldenkreis Method and burned the book.

One day we risked our lives, defied his Biblical curse, and went to see him, the three of us. To our great surprise he received us gladly and even tenderly. Large tears rolled down his new beard, a Tolstoyan beard that covered his Brezhnevian features. He addressed me in Russian, using an expression that can best be translated as "foundling." He used the same expression in speaking to Boaz. Every ten minutes he would drag Boaz down to the cellar, and after each of these excursions the boy would return clutching a present of a coin from the time of Turkish rule. You he called "Nusya," "Nusya maya," after my mother, who died when I was five. He bewailed your pneumonia and blamed the doctors and himself. Finally he roared at you with his last strength that you did away with yourself deliberately, just to torment him, and therefore he would leave his "fortune" to build a home for starving poets.

And indeed he began to scatter his wealth in all directions: rogues and charlatans swarmed around him, demanding donations to funds to make Galilee Jewish or the Red Sea blue. Not unlike what has been happening to me recently. Zakheim worked away patiently, discreetly, at transferring the property to my name. But the old man summoned up the strength to fight back. Twice he sacked Zakheim (and I hired him). He set up a panel of lawyers. He paid for three dubious professors to come from Italy and sign an attestation of sanity for him. For nearly two years the property went on leaking. Until Zakheim managed to get him taken in for observation and eventually committed. And then he changed his tune again and wrote and signed a detailed will in our favor, together with a short, melancholy letter in which he forgave us and asked our forgiveness and warned us against each other and implored us to have pity on the child, and signed it with the words "I bow down in awe before the depth of your afflictions."

Since 1966 he has been living in a private room in a sanatorium on Mount Carmel. Silently staring at the sea. Twice I went to see him, but he did not recognize me. Is it true, as Zakheim tells me, that you still visit him occasionally? What for?

It was with his money that we built the villa in Yefe Nof. Even though the abandoned castle between Binyamina and Zikhron is still registered in my name. Zakheim maintains that its value has reached a peak, and begs me to sell quickly, before the fashion changes. Perhaps I should leave it all for some scheme? To drain the Huleh Marshes? Or to paint the Black Sea white? Or to rescue stray dogs? In fact, why not to Boaz? To Sommo? To both of them? I shall compensate your Sommo for everything: his color, his height, his humiliation. I shall give him a belated dowry. I have nothing to do with my property. Or with the time I have left.

Or perhaps I won't leave it to anybody just yet. On the contrary, I'll come back. I shall move into the crumbling kitchen, remove the beam from the door leading to the rest of the house, and slowly restore it. I shall mend the broken fountain. Restock the pool with goldfish. I shall establish my own settlement. Perhaps we shall run away there, the two of us? And live like a couple of pioneers in the crumbling building? In your honor I shall dress in black robes and put a cowl over my head.

Only write and let me know what you want.

I am left owing you an answer: Why did I divorce you? Among the papers on my desk is a note in which I wrote that the word *ritual* comes from the Latin *ritus*, which means something like "right condition." Or perhaps "fixed habit." As for *fanaticism*, it may possibly come from *fanum*, meaning "temple" or "place of worship." And what of *humility*? *Humility* comes from *humilis*, which comes, it seems, from *humus*, "earth." And is there humility in the earth? Apparently anyone can come and do whatever he feels like doing to it. Dig and plow and sow. But eventually it swallows all its masters. Standing there, eternally silent.

You have the womb — you have the advantage. That is the answer to your question. I never had a chance and that was why I ran away from you. Until your long arm reached me in my hideaway. Your victory was child's play. From a range of twelve thousand miles you managed to score a bull's-eye on an empty abandoned tank.

Ten to midnight. The storm has died down a little but there is still no regular power. Perhaps I'll call Annabel, my secretary, and wake her up. I'll tell her to get the Scotch out and make me a light supper. I'll tell her I'm on my way. She is a divorcée, about thirty, embittered, diminutive, bespectacled, ruthlessly efficient, always dressed in jeans and chunky sweaters. Chain-smokes. I'll

call a taxi and in half an hour I'll be ringing her bell. The moment
she opens the door I'll shock her with a hug and proceed to crush
her lips with mine. Before she can collect herself I'll ask her to
marry me and demand an instant reply. My famous name, plus
my aura of grim manliness, plus the smell of battlefields that
clings to me, plus my property, minus love, plus the growth that
has been removed from my kidney, in return for her stunned
consent to bear my surname and look after me if my illness gets
worse. I'll buy her a sweet house in one of the delightful suburbs,
on condition that we share it with a mentally disturbed giant of
sixteen, who will have permission to invite girls home without
any obligation to leave a light on in the shower or inspection
doors open. The ticket will be sent to him in Hebron tomorrow
morning. Zakheim can worry about the rest.

It's no good, Ilana. My hatred is peeling away from me like
old plaster. By the neon light in the room, with the lightning
falling into the lake in the darkness, I do not have it in my power
to thaw the cold in my bones. In fact, it's extremely simple: when
the electricity was cut, the heating also stopped working. And so
I got up and put on a jacket. But no improvement was apparent.
My hatred is being dashed from my grasp like the sword from
the hands of Goliath after the pebble sank into him. This is the
sword you will lift and kill me with. But you have nothing to boast
about: you slew a dying dragon. Perhaps you will get the credit for
putting me out of my misery?

Just now there was a hoot outside in the darkness. Because the
darkness outside is complete, apart from a thin line of radioactive
purple on the horizon. A hoot from the outer darkness where
according to Jesus there is "howling and gnashing of teeth." Was
it a boat? Or a train arriving from the prairies? It is hard to know,
because the wind is frenziedly whistling a single sharp, high
note. And the power is still off. My eyes ache from writing in this
mortuary light. I have here in my office a bed, a closet, and a small
bathroom. But the narrow bed, between two metal file cabinets,
suddenly frightens me. As though there were a corpse laid out on

it. Surely it is only the clothes I unpacked in a hurry when I got back from London this morning.

There is that hooting again. This time nearby. So it wasn't a boat or a train, but the plaintive siren of an emergency vehicle. An ambulance? A police car? There's been a crime in one of the neighboring streets. Somebody is in big trouble. Or is there a fire—a building on fire and threatening to take its neighbors and all the neighborhood with it? Has a man decided he's had enough and jumped from the top of a skyscraper? Someone who lived by the sword dying by the sword?

The emergency lighting sheds its pallor on me. It is a ghostly mercury light, the kind used in operating theaters. I loved you once and there was a picture in my brain: You and me on a summer's evening sitting on the veranda of our home facing the Jerusalem hills and the child playing with bricks. Sundae glasses on the table. And a newspaper that we are not reading. You are embroidering a tablecloth and I am making a stork from a pinecone and slivers of wood. That was the picture. We weren't able. And now it's late.

Your Vampire

*

(Note delivered by hand)

Dear Mr. Zakheim, I shall hand you this note at the end of our meeting today at the Café Savyon. I'm not going to go on meeting you. My ex-husband will have to find another way of getting his letters to me. I can't see why he doesn't send them by mail, as I shall do from now on. I am writing this note only because it would be difficult for me to tell you to your face that you disgust me. Every time I have had to shake hands with you I have felt as if I were holding a frog. The shady "deal" that you hinted at, in connection with Alex's inheritance, was the last straw. Perhaps the fact that in the past you were a witness to my misfortune has unsettled you completely. You did not understand my misfortune and even today you understand nothing. My ex-husband, my present husband, and perhaps my son, too, know and understand what happened then, but you do not, Mr. Zakheim. You are on the outside.

Ilana Sommo

Despite everything, I would do what you want if only you could find a way of bringing him back to me. And because of his illness it is urgent.

And So Yoel Ravid Began to Give In

from *To Know a Woman* (1989)

FORTY-ONE

The next day, the seventeenth of February, was a gray day, and the air seemed to be congealed. But it was not raining and there was no wind. After taking Netta to school and his mother to the foreign-language lending library he drove on to the filling station; he filled the tank right up and went on pressing until the pump cut out automatically; then he checked the oil and water and the battery and the tire pressures. When he got home he went into the garden and pruned the rosebushes, as he had planned. He spread manure over the lawns, which were yellowing because of the winter rain and the cold. He also mulched the fruit trees in readiness for the approaching spring, mixing the manure in with rotting leaves that were moldering under the trees and spreading the mixture with a fork and rake. He repaired the irrigation basins and weeded the flower beds a little, with his fingers, bending over as though prostrating himself, and removing the first shoots of couch grass, wood sorrel, and bindweed. It was from this deep crouching position that he saw her blue flannel dressing gown coming out of the kitchen door, he could not see her face, and he shrank back as though he had received a well-aimed punch in the solar plexus or as though some kind of inner collapse had occurred in his stomach. Instantly his fingers stiffened. Then he gained control of himself, stifled his anger, and said, "What's happened, Avigail?" She burst out laughing and replied: "What's the matter, did I startle you? Just look at your face. You look as though you're about to kill somebody.

Nothing's happened, I just came out to ask you if you'd like your coffee out here or if you're coming in soon." He said, "No, I'm just coming," and then he changed his mind and said, "Or rather, bring it out here, so it doesn't get cold." Then he changed his mind again and said in a different voice, "Never, do you hear me, don't you ever put her clothes on again." What Avigail heard in his voice made her broad, bright, placid Slavic peasant's face turn a deep red. "It's not her clothes. This is a dressing gown she gave me five years ago when you bought her a new one in London."

Yoel knew he ought to apologize. Only a couple of days earlier he had pleaded with Netta to wear the nice raincoat that he had bought Ivria in Stockholm. But his rage, or perhaps his anger at the appearance of this rage, made him not apologize but hiss grimly, almost menacingly, "It makes no difference. This is my house and I won't put up with it."

"Your house?" Avigail inquired in her pedagogic tone of voice, like a tolerant headmistress of a liberal school.

"My house," Yoel repeated quietly, wiping the damp soil off his fingers on the seat of his jeans. "And here in my house you're not to wear her things."

"Yoel," she said after a moment in a tone of sadness tinged with affection, "would you mind me saying something to you? I'm beginning to think that your condition may be as bad as your mother's. Or Netta's. Except that of course you're better at concealing your problems, and that makes your condition even worse. In my opinion, what you really need is—"

"OK," Yoel cut in, "that'll do for today. Is there some coffee or isn't there? I ought to have gone inside and made it myself instead of relying on favors. It won't be long before they have to send in the antiterrorist troops."

"And talking of your mother," Avigail said, "you know very well that we have a very meaningful relationship, the two of us, but when I see—"

"Avigail," he said, "the coffee."

"I understand," she said, going indoors and returning with

a mug of coffee and a grapefruit on a plate, carefully peeled and opened out like a chrysanthemum. "I see. Talking hurts you, Yoel. I should have sensed it myself. Seemingly everybody has to bear his affliction in his own way. I want to say I'm sorry if I hurt you."

"All right, let's drop it," said Yoel, suddenly filled with loathing because of the way she said "see-eemingly." He wanted to think about something different, but suddenly there floated into his mind the image of Shealtiel Lublin, the policeman, with his walrus mustache, his rough kindness, his clumsy generosity, his jokes about sex and other bodily functions, and his habitual smoke-scorched sermons on the subject of the tyranny of the gonads or the community of secrets. He found that the loathing welling up inside him was directed neither against Lublin nor against Avigail, but against the memory of his wife, against her icy silence and her white clothes. With difficulty he forced himself to take a couple of sips of coffee, like someone bending over sewage, and immediately handed the mug and the grapefruit-flower back to Avigail. Without another word he prostrated himself once more over the cleared flower bed, and resumed his hawk-eyed search for signs of sprouting weeds. He even decided to put on his black-framed glasses to help him in his search. After twenty minutes, however, he went into the kitchen and saw her frozen in a stiff sitting position, with her widow's mantilla draped around her shoulders, looking the very picture of the unknown bereaved mother, staring unmovingly through the window at the precise spot in the garden where he had been working a moment before. Unthinkingly, he followed her gaze with his eyes. But the spot was empty. He said, "All right. I've come to apologize. I didn't mean to upset you."

Then he started the car and went back to Bardugo's Nurseries.

And where else could he go during these days at the end of February, when Netta had already been twice to the recruiting center, at a week's interval, and now they were waiting for the results of her medical. He took her to school every morning, always at the last minute. Or later. But on her visits to the recruiting center it was Duby, one of Arik Krantz's two sons, who accompanied her, a skinny, tousled lad who for some reason made Yoel think of a Yemeni newsboy from the early years of the state. It turned out that his father had sent him and apparently also instructed him to wait outside on both occasions until she had finished and then drive her home in the little Fiat.

"Tell me something, do you happen to collect thistles and sheet music too, by any chance?" Yoel asked this Duby Krantz. And the young man, totally ignoring the irony or incapable of detecting it, replied softly, "Not yet."

Besides driving Netta to school, Yoel also drove his mother for regular checkups at Litwin's private clinic, not far from Ramat Lotan. On one of these trips she suddenly asked him, without any warning or connection, if the business with the neighbor's sister was serious. And without thinking he answered her with the same words that Krantz's son had used to answer him. He often spent an hour or more at Bardugo's Nurseries in the middle of the morning. He bought various window boxes, large and small flowerpots of earthenware or synthetic materials, two different types of enriched potting compost, a tool for loosening the soil, and two sprays, one for watering and another for pesticides. The whole house was filling up with plants. Especially ferns, which hung from the ceilings and door frames. To put them up, he had to bring his electric drill with its extension cord back into service. Once, when he was on his way home from the nursery at half past eleven in the morning, with his car looking like a tropical jungle on wheels, he noticed the Filipino maid from the house down the road pushing her laden shopping cart up the steep slope a quarter of an hour's walk from their street. Yoel stopped and made her accept a lift. Even though he was unable to engage her in conversation beyond the necessary expressions of politeness. After that he lay in wait for her on several occasions at the corner of the car park by the supermarket, alert behind the wheel and hidden behind his new sunglasses, and when she emerged with her cart he drove up sharply and managed to waylay her. It turned out that she knew a little Hebrew and a little English and made do for the most part with three- or four-word answers.

Without being asked, Yoel volunteered to improve the shopping cart: he promised to fit it with rubber-rimmed wheels instead of the noisy metal ones. And he did indeed go into the hardware store in the shopping center and among other things bought some wheels with rubber rims. But he never managed to bring himself to the front door of the strangers the woman worked for, and on the occasions when he succeeded in waylaying her with her cart on the way out of the supermarket and taking her home in his car, he could hardly stop suddenly in the middle of the road in the middle of the neighborhood in full view and start emptying the shopping out of the heavily laden cart, turning it upside down, and changing its wheels. And so it was that Yoel did not keep his promise and even pretended that he had never made it. He hid the new wheels from himself in a dark corner of the garden shed. Even though in all his years in the service he had always been particular about keeping his word. Apart, perhaps, from his last day at work, when he had been summoned back in a hurry from Helsinki and had not managed to keep his promise to get in touch with the Tunisian engineer. When this comparison occurred to him, he discovered to his amazement that even though the month of February had just ended and so it was a year or more since the day he had seen the cripple in Helsinki, the telephone number that the engineer had given him was still engraved on his memory. He had memorized it at the time, and never forgotten it.

That evening, when the women had left him alone in the living room to watch the midnight news and the snowflakes that filled the screen afterward, he had to fight against the sudden temptation to call the number. But how could someone with no limbs pick up the receiver? And what could he say? Or ask? As he got up to switch off the uselessly flickering television, it dawned on him that the month of February had indeed just ended the day before, and that consequently today was actually his wedding anniversary. So he picked up the big flashlight and went outside into the dark garden to check the state of each and every sapling and seedling.

One night after checking, over a glass of steaming punch, Ralph asked if he could offer him a loan. For some reason Yoel got the impression that Ralph was asking him for a loan and he had asked him how much, and Ralph had said, "Up to twenty or thirty thousand" before Yoel caught on that he was being offered the money, not asked for it. He was surprised. Ralph said, "Whenever you like. Be my guest. We won't rush you." Suddenly Annemarie, clutching the red kimono to her slight body, intervened, saying, "I object to this. There'll be no business before we find ourselves."

"Find ourselves?"

"I mean, all of us tidy up our lives a bit."

Yoel looked at her and waited. Ralph did not speak, either. Some dormant sense of survival stirred suddenly deep inside Yoel and warned him that it would be best to interrupt her at once. Change the subject. Look at his watch and say good night. Or at least team up with Ralph and make fun of what she had said and what she was about to say.

"Musical chairs, for instance," she continued, bursting out laughing. "Who remembers how to play?"

"That will do," Ralph urged, as though he sensed Yoel's anxiety and saw reasons to share it.

"For instance," she said, "there's an old man living across the street. From Romania. He talks to your mother in Romanian for half an hour at a stretch over the fence. And he also lives on his own. Why shouldn't she move in with him?"

"But why?"

"Why, then Ralphie can move into your house with the other mom and live with her. At least for a trial period. And you could move in here. Huh?"

Ralph said, "Like Noah's Ark. She pairs everyone off. What's the matter? Is there a flood coming?"

And Yoel, taking care not to sound angry, but rather amused and good-natured, said, "You've forgotten about the child. Where do we put her in your Noah's Ark? Can I have some more punch?"

"Netta," said Annemarie so softly that her voice was almost inaudible and Yoel almost missed the words and the tears that filled her eyes at that moment. "Netta is a young woman. Not a child. How long will you go on calling her a child? I think, Yoel, you've never known what a woman is. You don't even understand the word. Ralph, don't interrupt. You've never known it, either. How do you say 'role' in Hebrew? I wanted to say that you always either make us play the role of a baby or you act it out yourselves. Sometimes I think, What a sweet little, nice little baby, but we have to kill the baby. I'd like some more punch, too."

FORTY-TWO

During the days that followed, Yoel thought over Ralph's offer. Particularly once it became clear to him that the new lines of battle set him and his mother, the objectors, against his mother-in-law and Netta, who both supported the idea of renting the penthouse flat in Karl Netter Street. Even before the approaching examinations. On the tenth of March, Netta received a notification from the army computer to say that her call-up would be in seven months' time, on the twentieth of October. From this Yoel deduced that she had not informed the doctors at the recruiting center about her problem, or perhaps she had but the tests had revealed nothing. At times he asked himself whether his silence was irresponsible. Was it not his clear duty, as a single parent, to contact them on his own initiative and bring the facts to their notice? The findings of the doctors in Jerusalem? On the other hand, he thought, which of the divided opinions was it his duty to present to them? And would it not be wrong and irresponsible to initiate such a step behind her back? To stamp her for the rest of her life with the stigma of an illness that was the butt of all sorts of superstitions? And was it not a fact that Netta's problem had never manifested itself outside the home? Not once. Since Ivria's death there had only been one solitary occurrence even within the home, and even that had been some time earlier, at the end of August, and since then there had been no further sign. In fact even what had happened in August had involved at the least a certain slight ambivalence. So why should he not go to Karl Netter Street in Tel Aviv, check out the room that allegedly had a view of the sea, investigate the neighbors, find out discreetly about the roommate, this classmate called Adva, and if it turned out that everything was aboveboard she would receive a hundred and twenty dollars a month, or more, and in the evenings he could look in for a coffee and so make sure day by day that everything was OK. And what if it really turned out that the Patron was seriously intending to offer her a minor clerical job in the office? Some sort of junior secretarial work? He could always decide to exercise his veto and frustrate Teacher's schemes. On second thought, why should he forbid her to work a little in the office? It would spare him the need to pull strings, to reactivate old contacts, to release her from her call-up without making use of the pretext of defective health and without branding her with the stigma of having been exempted on medical grounds. The Patron could easily arrange to have her work in the office recognized as a substitute for military service. Moreover, it would be splendid if he, Yoel, with a few well-thought-out moves, could rescue Netta both from the army and from the stigma that Ivria had sometimes insanely accused him of trying to brand his daughter with. Moreover, shifting his ground on the question of the apartment in Karl Netter Street might bring about a change in the balance of power in the house. Even though, on the other hand, it was clear to him that the moment his daughter was on his side once more, the alliance between the two old women would be renewed. And vice versa: if he managed to recruit Avigail to his camp, his mother and his daughter would join ranks across the barricade. So what was the point of bothering? And so he left the matter for the time being, without doing anything either about the call-up or about the apartment. Once more he decided that there was no rush, tomorrow was another day, and the sea would not run away. And in the meantime he repaired the landlord, Mr. Kramer's, broken vacuum cleaner, and spent a day and a half helping the cleaner to clean every last speck of dust from the house, just as he had done every spring in their apartment in Jerusalem. So immersed was he in the operation that when the phone rang and Duby Krantz asked when Netta would be home, Yoel announced curtly that they were in the middle of spring-cleaning and could he please call back another time. As for Ralph's suggestion that he should invest money in a discreet fund linked to a consortium in Canada that would double his investment in eighteen months, Yoel examined the proposition again in relation to all those other ideas that had been put to him. For instance, there was the hint his mother had dropped several times concerning the large sum of money that she was keeping to start him off in the business world. Or the fabulous rewards that his ex-colleague from the service promised him if he would only agree to set up with him in a private investigation agency. Or Arik Krantz, who never stopped begging him to share his adventure: twice a week putting on a white robe and spending four hours on a night shift as a volunteer auxiliary in the hospital where he had earned the devotion of Greta the volunteer, and where Krantz had earmarked two other volunteers, Christina and Iris, for Yoel, and he could choose between them or indeed choose them both. But the fabulous rewards said nothing to him. Nor did the tempting investments or Krantz's volunteers. Nothing stirred in him, beyond a vague but constant feeling that he was not really awake: that he was walking about, brooding, looking after the house and the garden and the car, making love to Annemarie, driving backward and forward between the nurseries, the house, and the shopping center, cleaning the windows for Passover, that he had nearly finished reading the biography of Chief of Staff Eleazar, all in his sleep. If he still retained a hope of deciphering something, of understanding, or at least of formulating the question clearly, he must get out of this thick fog. He must wake up at all costs from this slumber. Even if it needed a disaster. If only something would come and slice away the soft fatty jelly that was closing in around him from every direction and stifling him like a womb.

Sometimes he would recall the sharp, vigilant moments of his career, when he would steal down the streets of a foreign city as though slipping through a narrow crack between two razors, physically and mentally acute as while hunting or making love, when even simple, trivial, everyday things yielded hints to him of the secrets they enfolded: The evening lights reflected in a puddle. The folds of a passer-by's sleeve. A glimpse of the daring cut of a woman's underwear under a summer dress. Sometimes he even managed to guess something several seconds before it actually happened. Like a breeze getting up, or which way a cat crouching on a wall would leap, or the certainty that a man coming toward him would stop, tap his forehead, turn around, and retrace his steps. His perceptional life had been so sharp in those years, and now everything was blunt. Slowed down. As though the glass were clouding over and you had no way of discovering whether the mist were on the outside or the inside, or whether, worse than that, it was neither of these, but the glass itself that was suddenly discharging the opaque, milky element into itself. And if he did not wake up and smash it now, it would go on clouding over, the somnolence would deepen, the memory of the moments of alertness would gradually fade, and he would die unawares, like a wayfarer falling asleep in the snow.

At the optician's in the shopping center he purchased a powerful magnifying glass. And when he was alone in the house one morning he finally inspected the strange spot by the entrance to one of the Romanesque abbeys in the photographs that had belonged to Ivria. He scrutinized it intensely for a long time, with the help of a focused beam of light and his glasses and Ivria's country doctor's glasses and the magnifying glass that he had just bought, now from one angle and now from another. Until he began to feel inclined to accept the hypothesis that it was neither an abandoned object nor a stray bird but some sort of flaw in the photographic plate. Perhaps a tiny scratch that had occurred during development. The words of Jimmy Gal, the earless regimental commander, about the two points and the line connecting them, struck Yoel as correct beyond any doubt but also trite, and evincing, ultimately, a measure of intellectual dullness that he deemed himself not free from, though he still hoped he might manage to rid himself of it.

FORTY-THREE

Suddenly the spring exploded in the humming of swarms of wasps and flies and eddies of scents and colors that struck Yoel as almost overdone. All of a sudden the garden seemed to be overflowing and discharging a mass of blossom and seething vegetation. The fruit trees came into flower and three days later they were aflame. Even the cactuses in their flowerpots on the porch erupted in scarlet and flaming orange-yellow, as though trying to talk to the sun in its own tongue. There was a kind of swell that Yoel almost imagined he could hear foaming if only he listened hard enough. As though the roots of the plants had turned into sharpened claws that were ripping at the earth in the blackness and drawing from it dark juices that were shooting upward in the tunnels of the trunks and stems and being proffered in the unfolding of the blossoms and foliage to the blinding light. Which tired his eyes again, despite the sunglasses that he had bought himself at the beginning of the winter.

Standing beside the hedge, Yoel reached the conclusion that the apple and pear trees were not enough. But ligustrum and oleander and bougainvillea, and even hibiscus bushes, suddenly struck him as boring and vulgar. He therefore decided to do away with the stretch of lawn at the side of the house, under the windows of the two children's rooms where the old women slept, and plant figs and olives and perhaps even pomegranates. In due course the vines that he had planted round the new pergola would also spread to this part, so that in ten or twenty years there would be a perfect miniature replica of a thick dark biblical orchard such as he had always envied around the homes of Arab villagers. Yoel planned it all down to the last detail: he shut himself away in his room and studied the relevant chapters of the agricultural handbook, drew up a table of the advantages and drawbacks of different varieties, and then went outside and measured the space there would be between the saplings, marked the positions with small pegs, telephoned Bardugo every day to see if his order had arrived. And waited.

On the morning of Passover Eve, when the three women had gone off to Metullah, leaving him on his own, he went into the garden and dug five nice square holes where the pegs were. He lined the bottom of each hole with a layer of fine sand mixed with chicken dung. Then he drove to Bardugo's Nurseries to collect his saplings, which had just arrived: a fig, a date palm, a pomegranate, and two olives. He drove back in second gear all the way so as not to upset the plants, and found Duby Krantz sitting on the front doorstep, looking thin, curly, and dreamy. Yoel knew that both the Krantz boys had finished their military service, yet this young lad looked as if he were no older than sixteen.

"Did your father send you over to bring me the spray?"

"Well, it's like this," said Duby, drawing out the syllables as though he had difficulty parting with them, "if you need the spray I can pop back and get it. No problem. I've got my parents' car here. They're away. Mom's abroad and Dad's gone to Eilat for the festival and my brother's gone to stay with his girlfriend in Haifa."

"What about you? Have you locked yourself out?"

"No, it's something else."

"Like what?"

"The fact is, I came to see Netta. I was thinking, maybe to-night—"

"It's a pity you were thinking, chum," Yoel burst out laughing, surprising himself and the boy. "While you were busy thinking, she went off to the other end of the country with her grandmas. Can you spare five minutes? Come and help me unload these trees."

For three quarters of an hour they worked without talking, apart from essential words like "Hold this" or "Straighter" or "Firm it down well, but take care." They cut away the metal containers and managed to release the saplings without disturbing the ball of earth around the roots. Then silently and meticulously they performed the burial ceremony, including filling in the holes and firming down the soil, building up a ring of earth around each tree for irrigation purposes. Yoel was pleased with the young man's finger-work, and he almost began to appreciate his shyness or reticence. Once, one evening, at the end of an autumn day in Jerusalem, it was a Friday evening and the sadness of the hills was filling the air, he had taken a walk with Ivria and they had gone into the Rose Garden to watch the sunset. Ivria said, "You remember when you raped me under the trees in Metullah? I thought you were dumb." And

Yoel, who knew that his wife rarely joked, at once corrected her and said, "That's not right, Ivria. It wasn't rape; if anything, it was the opposite—seduction. That's point number one." But then he forgot to say what point number two was. Ivria said, "You always file every detail away in that awesome memory of yours, you never lose the slightest crumb. But you always process the data first. After all, that's your profession. But on my side it was love."

When they had finished, Yoel said, "Well, what does it feel like planting trees at Passover as if it were Tu Bishvat?" And he invited the boy into the kitchen for a cold orangeade because they were both pouring with sweat. Then he made some coffee too. And interrogated him a bit about his army service in Lebanon, about his political views, which according to his father were extremely left-wing, and about his current activities. It turned out that the boy had served in field engineering, that he thought Shimon Peres was doing quite a good job, and that right now he was studying precision mechanics. It happened to be his hobby, and now he'd decided to make it his career, too. He believed, even though he had not had a lot of experience, that the best thing that could happen to a man was when his hobby filled his life.

Yoel intervened here, jokingly, "Some people say that the best thing in life is love. Don't you agree?"

And Duby, intensely serious, with an emotion that he managed to overcome so successfully that all that remained was a glint in his eye, said, "I don't pretend to understand all that yet. Love and so on. When you look at my parents—you know them, after all—you might think the best thing is to keep feelings and so forth on a back burner. No, the healthy thing is to do something that you do well. Something that somebody needs. That's the two most satisfying things. Anyway, the two most satisfying things for me: to be needed, and to do a good job."

And since Yoel was in no hurry to reply, the boy made a further effort and added, "Excuse me asking. Is it true you're an international arms dealer or something like that?"

Yoel shrugged his shoulders, smiled, and said, "Why not?" Suddenly he stopped smiling and said, "That was a joke. The fact is, I'm nothing more than a government employee. On a kind of extended leave at the moment. Tell me something, what exactly are you looking for in Netta? An introduction to modern poetry? A crash course on the thistles of Israel?"

And so he managed to embarrass and even frighten the boy. He hurriedly put the coffee cup he was holding down on the table, then picked it up again and put it carefully onto the saucer, chewed his thumbnail for a moment, instantly thought better of it and stopped, and said, "Nothing special. We just chat."

"Nothing special," Yoel said, spreading on his jaws for a moment the stony, frozen-eyed feline cruelty that he had employed at will to frighten runts, small-time villains, crooks, creatures crawling out of the dirt. "If it's nothing special you've called at the wrong address, chum. You'd better try somewhere else."

"All I meant was—"

"Anyway, you'd best keep away from her. Haven't you heard? She's not a hundred percent. She's got a minor health problem. But don't you dare breathe a word about it."

"I did hear something like that," said Duby.

"What?!"

"I heard something. So what?"

"Just a minute. I want you to repeat it. Word for word. What did you hear about Netta?"

"Forget it," Duby spun the words out. "All sorts of rumors. Rubbish. Don't get worked up over it. I had the same thing myself once, rumors buzzing about, an item about nerves and so forth. Let them buzz, that's what I say."

"You have a problem with your nerves?"

"Hell, no."

"Listen carefully. I can easily check, you know. Do you or don't you?"

"I did once. I'm OK now."

"That's what you say."

"Mr. Ravid?"

"Yes."

"Can I ask you what you want with me?"

"Nothing. Only don't start filling Netta's head with all sorts of nonsense. She's got enough of that already. So have you, by the sound of it. Have you finished your coffee? So there's nobody at home? Do you want me to make you a snack?"

The boy said good-bye and drove off in his parents' blue Audi. Yoel got under a very hot shower, soaped himself twice, rinsed in cold water and got out muttering, *Please yourself.*

At four-thirty Ralph arrived to say that he and his sister realized that Yoel wouldn't be celebrating the festival, but seeing that he was all on his own, would he like to join them for supper and watch a comedy film on the video? Annemarie was making a Waldorf salad, and he was trying an experiment with veal stewed in wine. Yoel promised to come, but when Ralph came in to fetch him at seven o'clock he found him sleeping fully dressed on the living-room sofa surrounded by pages from the special supplement of the newspaper. He decided to let him sleep. Yoel slept long and deeply in the empty, dark house. Only once, after midnight, did he get up and grope his way to the lavatory without opening his eyes and without switching the light on. The sounds of the television or the video from next door were mingled in his sleep with the balalaika of the truck driver who might have been a sort of lover of his wife's. Instead of the lavatory door he found the door of the kitchen and he groped his way out into the garden and pissed with his eyes closed; returning to the sofa in the living room, with his eyes still closed, he wrapped himself in the checked bedspread and sank back into his sleep, as an ancient stone sinks into the dust, until nine o'clock the following morning. And so that night he missed a mysterious sight taking place right overhead, vast flights of storks, in a broad stream, one after another without a break, sailing northward under a full spring moon, in a cloudless sky, thousands, perhaps tens of thousands of lithe silhouettes floating over the earth with a silent swishing of wings. It was a long, relentless, irrevocable yet delicate movement, like masses of tiny white silk handkerchiefs streaming across a vast black silk screen, all bathed in a luminous silvery lunar-astral glow.

FORTY-FOUR

When he got up at nine o'clock on Passover morning he padded to the bathroom in his crumpled clothes, shaved, took another long, thorough shower, put on clean white sports clothes, and went outside to see how his new plants, the fig, the pomegranate, the two olive trees, and the date palm, were feeling. He gave them a light watering. He plucked out here and there tiny tips of new weeds that had apparently sprouted during the night, since his careful search of the previous day. While the coffee was percolating he rang the Krantzes' number to apologize to Duby for possibly treating him rather rudely. At once he realized that he would have to apologize twice, the second time for waking him up from his holiday lie-in. But Duby said, It's nothing, it's only natural you should worry about her, it doesn't matter, though you ought to know that actually she's quite good at worrying about herself. By the way, if you need me again for the garden or anything, I've got nothing special to do today. It was nice of you to ring, Mr. Ravid. Of course I'm not angry.

Yoel asked when Duby's parents were due back, and when he learned that Odelia was expected back from Europe the following day and that Krantz was returning from his sortie to Eilat that same evening, so as to be home in time to turn over a new leaf again, Yoel said to himself that the expression *a new leaf* was unsatisfactory because it sounded flimsy, like paper. And he asked Duby to tell his father to give him a call when he got back, there might be a little something for him.

Then he went into the garden and looked at the bed of carnations and snapdragons for a while, but he could not see what else he could do there, and he said to himself, Enough. On the other side of the fence the dog, Ironside, sitting on the pavement in a formal pose with his legs together, was trying to follow with a speculative gaze the flight of a bird whose name Yoel did not know but which thrilled him with its brilliant blue color. The truth is that there can be no new leaf. Only perhaps a prolonged birth. And birth is a form of parting and to part is hard, and anyway who can part all the way? On the one hand you carry on being born to your parents for years upon years, and on the other hand you start giving birth even before you have finished being born, and so you get caught up in battles for disengagement to the front and the rear. It suddenly occurred to him that there was reason to envy his father, his melancholy Romanian father in the brown striped suit, or his unshaven father in the filthy ship, both of whom had vanished without trace. And what was it that stopped you vanishing without a trace, too, during all those years, assuming the identity of a driving instructor in Brisbane or living as a trapper and fisherman in a forest north of Vancouver, in a log cabin you built for yourself and the Eskimo mistress who so aroused Ivria? And what is it that prevents you from vanishing now? "What a fool," he said affectionately to the dog, who had suddenly decided to cease looking like a china ornament and become a hunter, standing on his hind legs and resting his front paws on the fence, presumably in the hope of catching the bird. Until the middle-aged neighbor opposite whistled to him and took the opportunity to offer Yoel the season's greetings.

All of a sudden Yoel felt sharp pangs of hunger. He remembered that he had eaten nothing since lunch the previous day, because he had fallen asleep fully dressed. And he had had nothing but coffee this morning. So he went next door and asked Ralph if there was any of last night's veal left and if he could have the leftovers for breakfast. "There's some Waldorf salad left, too," Annemarie said cheerfully, "and some soup. But it's very highly seasoned, and it might not be a good idea to have it first thing in the morning." Yoel chuckled because he suddenly remembered one of Nakdimon Lublin's rhymes, "Muhammad said, Make no mistake, when my belly's empty I could swallow a snake." Without troubling to reply he simply gestured, Bring out whatever you've got.

It seemed as though there was no limit to his eating capacity on that festival morning. Having demolished the soup and the leftover veal and salad, he did not hesitate to ask for breakfast as well: toast and cheeses and yogurt. And when Ralph opened the door of the refrigerator for a moment to get out the milk, Yoel's well-trained eyes spotted a jug of tomato juice and he shamelessly asked if he could demolish that too.

"Tell me something," Ralph Vermont began. "Heaven forbid that I should try to rush you, I just wanted to ask."

"Go ahead," said Yoel, with his mouth full of cheese on toast.

"I wanted to ask you, if you don't mind, something like this: Are you in love with my sister?"

"Right now?" Yoel muttered, startled by the question.

"Now, too," Ralph specified, calmly but with a kind of clarity, like a man who knows where his duty lies.

"Why are you asking?" Yoel hesitated, as though playing for time. "I mean to say, why are you asking instead of Annemarie? Why isn't she asking? Why does she need a go-between?"

"Look who's talking," said Ralph, not sarcastically but blithely, as though amused at the sight of the other's blindness. And Annemarie, almost devoutly, with her eyes nearly closed, as though in prayer, whispered, "Yes. I am asking."

Yoel ran his finger slowly between his neck and his shirt collar. He filled his lungs with air and let it out slowly. Shame, he thought, shame on me, for not gathering any information, not even the most basic details, about these two. I haven't got a notion who they are, where they sprang from or why, what they're after here. Still, he refrained from speaking a lie. The true answer to their question he did not know yet.

"I need a bit more time," he said. "I can't give you an answer right away. It needs some more time."

"Who's rushing you?" Ralph asked, and for a moment Yoel thought he saw a swift flash of paternal irony cross his middle-aged schoolboy's face, which life's sorrows had left no trace on. As if the placid face of an aging child were only a mask, and for an instant a bitter or sly line had been revealed underneath it.

Still smiling affectionately, almost stupidly, the overgrown farmer took Yoel's broad, ugly hands, which were brown like bread, with garden soil under the fingernails, between his own pink, abundantly freckled hands, and placed each of them slowly and gently on one of his sister's breasts, so accurately that Yoel could feel the stiffened nipple in the exact center of each hand. Annemarie laughed softly. Ralph sat down clumsily, with a chastened air, on a stool in a corner of the kitchen, and asked sheepishly, "If you do decide to take her, do you think I . . . that there'll be some room for me? Around the place?"

Then Annemarie released herself and got up to make the coffee, because the water was boiling. While they were drinking it the brother and sister suggested that Yoel watch the comedy that they had seen the previous evening on the video, the one he had missed because he had fallen asleep. Yoel stood up and said, "Perhaps in a few hours' time. I've got to go and take care of some business right now." He thanked them and left without explaining, started the car, and drove out of the neighborhood and the city. He felt good and well within himself, within his body, within the sequence of his thoughts, as he had not done for a long time. It might have been because he had satisfied his huge appetite by eating a lot of delicious things, or else because he knew exactly what he had to do.

FORTY-FIVE

Along the coast road he recalled the various details he had heard here and there over the years about the man's private life. He was so deep in thought that the Netanya interchange caught him by surprise, heaving suddenly into view barely past the northern exit from Tel Aviv. He knew that his three daughters had been married for some time; one was in Orlando, Florida, one was in Zurich, and the last was, or at least had been a few months previously, on the staff of the embassy in Cairo. It followed that his grandchildren were scattered over three continents. His sister lived in London. As for his ex-wife, his daughters' mother, she had been married for upward of twenty years to a world-famous musician; she, too, lived in Switzerland, not far from the middle daughter and her family, perhaps in Lausanne.

The only member of the Ostashinsky family left in Pardés Hanna, if his information was correct, was the old father, who must now, Yoel calculated, be at least eighty. Perhaps closer to ninety. Once when the two of them had waited all night in the Operations Room for a message that was supposed to be coming in from Cyprus, the Acrobat had said that his father was a fanatical, mad chicken breeder. More than that he had not said, and Yoel had not asked. Everyone has his own shame in the attic. Although now, as he drove along the coast road north of Netanya, he was surprised to see how many new houses were being built with pitched roofs and storage space in the loft. Whereas until a little while before, cellars and attics had hardly existed in Israel. Yoel reached Pardés Hanna soon after hearing the one o'clock news on the car radio. He decided not to visit the cemetery, because the village was already subsiding into the calm of a festival day's siesta, and he did not want to cause a disturbance. He asked twice before he discovered where the house was. It was set apart somewhat, near the edge of an orange grove, at the end of a muddy track overgrown with thistles that reached up to the car's windows. After parking, he had to force his way through a thick hedge that had run wild and almost grown together from either side of a path of broken and uneven paving stones. He therefore prepared himself to encounter a neglected old man in a neglected house. He even entertained the possibility that his information was out-of-date and that the old man had passed away or been moved into an institution. To his surprise, when he emerged from the overgrowth he found himself standing before a door painted a psychedelic blue surrounded by standing, hanging, and hovering pots of petunias and white cyclamens blending into the bougainvillea that trailed over the front of the house. Among the flowerpots masses of little china bells hung from intertwined strings, making Yoel think he detected the hand of a woman, and a young woman at that. He knocked five or six times, pausing between knocks and knocking harder each time, because it occurred to him that the old man might be hard of hearing. And all the time he felt embarrassed to be disturbing the still, small silence of the vegetation that filled the place by making such an impertinent noise. He even felt, with a pang of longing, that he had been in a place like this once before, and that it had been good and pleasant. The memory was heart-warming and dear to him, even though in fact there was no memory, since he was unable to focus his feeling and locate the place.

As there was no answer, he started off round the bungalow and tapped at a window that was framed by white curtains draped in a pair of rounded wings, like the curtains painted at the windows of the symmetrical houses in children's books. Between the two wings he could see a tiny but pleasant and extremely clean and tidy living room, a Bukhara rug, a coffee table made from the stump of an olive tree, a single deep armchair and also a rocking chair in front of a television set on which stood a glass jar, of the sort that yogurt used to be sold in thirty or forty years ago, containing a bunch of chrysanthemums. On the wall he saw a painting of a snowcapped Mount Hermon with the Sea of Galilee below, all wreathed in bluish early morning mist. Out of professional habit Yoel identified the painter's vantage point, apparently on the slope of Mount Arbel. But what was the explanation for the increasingly painful feeling that he had been in this room once before, and not only been there but lived there, a life full of powerful, forgotten joy?

He went round to the back of the house and knocked on the kitchen door, which was painted the same dazzling pale blue and was also surrounded by masses of petunias in flowerpots amidst china bells. But there was no answer here either. Pressing down the handle, he discovered that the door was not locked. Behind it he found a tiny, splendidly clean and tidy kitchen, all painted pale blue, though its furnishings and equipment were ancient. Here, too, Yoel saw the same old yogurt jar, on the kitchen table, except that here it was sprouting marigolds instead of chrysanthemums. From another jar, which stood on the old refrigerator, a sturdy, attractive sweet-potato plant trailed along the wall. It was only with difficulty that Yoel resisted the sudden desire to sit down on the rush stool and settle here in this kitchen.

Eventually he left and after a slight hesitation decided to inspect the outbuildings before coming back and penetrating deeper into the house itself. There were three matching henhouses, well kept, enclosed by tall cypress trees and small squares of lawn finished off in the corners with cactuses growing in rockeries. Yoel observed that the henhouses were air-conditioned. And in the doorway of one of them he saw a skinny, small-framed, compressed-looking man standing, squinting at a test tube that was half full of a cloudy liquid. Yoel apologized for his unannounced visit. He introduced himself as an old friend and colleague of the man's late son. Of Yokneam, that was.

The old man stared at him in amazement, as though he had never heard the name Yokneam in his life. For a moment Yoel's confidence was shaken. Had he come to the wrong old man, after all? He asked the man if he was Mr. Ostashinsky, and whether he was disturbing him. The old man wore neatly pressed khaki clothes with wide military pockets, which might have been an improvised uniform from the time of the War of Independence; the skin of his face looked as rough as raw flesh, and his back was slightly hunched and bent, vaguely suggesting a nocturnal predator, a badger or pine marten, but his little eyes flashed sharp blue sparks that matched the doors of his house. Without responding to Yoel's outstretched hand, he said in a clear tenor voice with the accent of the early settlers, "Yeis. You are disturbing me. And yes again, I am Zerach Ostashinsky." After a moment, slyly, with a shrewd wink, he added, "Ve didn' see you et de fuineral." Once more Yoel had to apologize. He almost uttered the excuse that he had been abroad at the time. But as ever he avoided telling an untruth. He said, "You are right. I didn't come." He added a compliment to the old man on his excellent memory, which the man ignored.

"And for vy hef you come here today?" he asked. As he did so he looked not at Yoel but, squinting sideways against the daylight, at the spermlike liquid in the glass test tube.

"I've come to tell you something. And also to see if there's some way I can be of help here. But, if it's possible, perhaps we could talk sitting down?"

The old man thrust the stoppered test tube with the opaque liquid in it like a fountain pen into the pocket of his khaki shirt.

He said, "I'm sorry. I'm not free." And also, "Are you also a secret agent? A spy? A licensed killer?"

"Not anymore," said Yoel. "Couldn't you spare me just ten minutes of your time?"

"Vell, five then," the old man compromised. "Please. Begin. I em all ears." But with these words he spun round and quickly entered the dark battery house, obliging Yoel to follow on his heels, almost running after him as he darted from battery to battery adjusting the water taps attached to the metal troughs that ran along the cages. A constant quiet cackle, like busy gossip, filled the air, which was heavy with the smell of dung and feathers and chicken feed.

"Speak," said the old man. "But keep it short."

"It's like this, sir. I came to tell you that your son actually went to Bangkok instead of me. I was the one who was told to go first. And I refused. And your son went instead of me."

"Nu? So what?" the old man said without surprise. And without interrupting his brisk, efficient progress from battery to battery.

"You might say that I have some responsibility for the disaster. Responsibility, though naturally not guilt."

"Nu, so it's nice of you you should say det," declared the old man, still darting along the alleys in the henhouse. Occasionally he would disappear for an instant and reappear on the other side of a battery, leading Yoel almost to suspect that he had a network of secret passages.

"It's true that I refused to go," Yoel said as though arguing, "but if it had been up to me your son would also have stayed at home. I would never have sent him. I wouldn't have sent anyone. There was something there that I didn't like right from the start. It doesn't matter. The truth is that to this day it isn't clear to me what really happened."

"Vot heppened. Vot heppened. Dey kilt him. Det's vot heppened. Vid a revolver dey kilt him. Vid five billets. Vould you hold dis please?"

Yoel held the rubber hosepipe with both hands at the two points indicated by the old man, who suddenly, as quick as lightning, drew a flick-knife from his belt, made a small hole in the pipe, and at once fitted a sparkling metal tap in it, tightened it, and pressed on, with Yoel at his heels.

"Do you know," Yoel asked, "who killed him?"

"Who kilt him. Who kilt him. De Jew-haters kilt him. Vy, who did you tink, de stuidents of Greek philosophy?"

"Look here," Yoel said, but at that instant the old man vanished. As though he had never existed. Or as though he had been swallowed up by the ground, which was covered here with a layer of pungent-smelling chicken droppings. Yoel began hunting for the old man between the rows of batteries, peering underneath the cages, walking faster and faster, breaking into a run, peering down the alleys to left and right, mixing them up as though lost in a maze, retracing his steps, going up to the entrance and returning by a parallel alley, until he finally gave up in despair and shouted at the top of his voice, "Mr. Ostashinsky!"

"It seems, your five minutes are over," replied the old man, suddenly springing up behind a small stainless-steel counter immediately to Yoel's right, this time holding a reel of fine wire.

"I only wanted you to know that they ordered me to go, and your son was only sent because I refused."

"Det I heard you say already."

"And I would never have sent your son. I wouldn't have sent anyone."

"Det also I heard you say. Vos dere something else?"

"Did you know, sir, that your son once saved the lives of the Philharmonic Orchestra, when they were about to be massacred by terrorists? May I tell you that your son was a good man? An honest man? A brave man?"

"*Nu?* So, for vot do ye need an orchestra? Vot good can orchestras do for us?"

A lunatic, Yoel decided, peaceable, but definitely certifiable. And I was mad, too, to come here.

"Well, anyway, I share your grief."

"After all, in his own way he vos a terrorist himself. And if any man seeks his own private death, de death det suits him, den in de fullness of time he vill surely find it. And vot is so special about det?"

"He was a friend of mine. Quite a close friend. And I would like to say, seeing that, if I have understood correctly, you are on your own here . . . maybe you'd like to come and be with us? To stay? To live? Even maybe for quite a long time? We are, I should say, an extended family . . . a sort of urban kibbutz. Almost. And we could easily, how should I put it, absorb you. Or maybe there's something else I can do for you? Something you need?"

"Need? Vot do I need? *And purify our hearts to serve Thee in truth*—det's vot ve all need. But in dis you don' help and you don' get help. It's every man for himself."

"Still I wish you wouldn't turn it down just like that. Just think if there isn't something I can do for you, Mr. Ostashinsky."

Again the slyness of a badger or a pine marten flashed across the old man's rough face, and he almost winked at Yoel as he had winked at the cloudy liquid in the test tube when he had held it up to the sunlight.

"Did you have a hend in my son's death? Have you come here to buy yourself forgiveness?"

And as he made his way to the electrical control panel by the entrance to the henhouse, walking fast and weaving slightly, like a lizard crossing an exposed patch of ground between two shadows, he suddenly turned his shriveled face and transfixed Yoel, who was running behind him, with his glance:

"*Nu?* So who did?"

Yoel did not understand.

"You told me it vosn' you det sent him. And you asked me vot I need. So, vot I need is I should know who did send him."

"Of course," Yoel said keenly, as though he were trampling the divine name underfoot, with vindictive glee or righteous zeal. "Of course. For your information. It was Yirmiyahou Cordovero who sent him. Our Patron. The head of our office. Our Teacher. The famous mystery man. The father of us all. My brother. He sent him."

The old man surfaced slowly from under his counter, like a drowned corpse rising from the deep. Instead of the gratitude Yoel was expecting, instead of the absolution he imagined he had rightfully earned by his candor, instead of an invitation to tea in the house that glowed with the magic of a childhood he had never known, in the little kitchen that had won his heart like a promised land, instead of the open arms, came a blow. Which somehow, secretly he had been expecting. And even waiting for. The father suddenly erupted, puffed himself up, bristled like an attacking pine marten. And Yoel recoiled from the spit. That never came. The old man merely hissed at him: "Traitor!"

As Yoel turned to effect his retreat, with measured steps yet inwardly in headlong flight, the old man shouted after him again as though stoning him: "Cain!"

It was important to him to avoid the house with its charms and to cut straight through to his car. So he plunged among the overgrown bushes that had once been a hedge. Very soon a bristly darkness, a thick, humid coat of ferns, closed round him. Gripped by claustrophobia, he began to trample on the branches, to flail, to kick out at the dense foliage, which simply absorbed his kicks, bending stems and twigs; scratched all over, panting hard, his clothes covered in burrs and thorns and dry leaves, he seemed to be sinking in the folds of thick, soft, twisted, dark green cotton wool, struggling with strange pangs of panic and seduction.

He cleaned himself up to the best of his ability, started the car, and reversed rapidly down the dirt track. He only came to when he heard the sound of the taillight being crushed as the car hit the trunk of a eucalyptus that was leaning across the path. Yoel could have sworn it was not there when he arrived. But the accident restored his self-control, and he drove carefully all the way home. When he reached the Netanya interchange he even turned on the radio and managed to hear the end of an old piece for harpsichord, although he did not catch the name of the piece or of the composer.

Then there was an interview with a Bible-loving woman who described her feelings about King David, a man who often in his long life received news of a death, and each time tore his clothes and uttered heartrending lamentations, even though in fact each news of a death was good news to him, because it brought him relief and sometimes even rescue. So it was in the case of the deaths of Saul and Jonathan at Gilboa, of Abner son of Ner, of Uriah the Hittite, and even of his son Absalom. Yoel turned off the radio and parked the car expertly, in reverse gear, with the bonnet toward the road, dead in the center of the new pergola he had constructed. Then he went indoors to take a shower and change.

As he was getting out of the shower the telephone rang; he picked it up and asked Krantz what he wanted.

"Nothing," said the agent. "I thought you left a message for me with Duby, to ring you the moment I got in from Eilat. So now here I am, back with that chick, and now I've got to clear away the evidence because Odelia's flying back from Rome tomorrow and I don't want to have any trouble with her first thing."

"Yes," said Yoel, "I remember now. Listen. I've got some business to talk over with you. Could you drop round tomorrow morning? What time does your wife get in? Hold on a minute. Actually tomorrow morning is no good. I've got to take the car in to be fixed. I've smashed a taillight. And the afternoon's no good either, because my women are coming back from Metullah. How about the day after tomorrow? Have you got the whole week off for Passover?"

"What the hell, Yoel," said Krantz. "What's the problem? I'll come round right away. I'll be with you in ten minutes. Put the coffee on and stand by to repel boarders!"

Yoel made coffee in the percolator. He'd have to go and see about the insurance tomorrow too, he thought. And spread some fertilizer on the lawn, because spring is here.

Hebrew Melodies

from *The Slopes of Lebanon* (1987)

It was June 1987. Exactly five years had passed since the invasion of Lebanon, and everyone was trying to forget it. Radio, television, and the press held a festival to mark the twentieth anniversary of the Six-Day War. They sponsored symposia, played Hebrew songs ("I Remember Bet H'arava," "The Western Wall," "Ammunition Hill"), held memorial services at military cemeteries, expressed their nostalgia for that smashing victory, and swooned over "Jerusalem of Gold." And they also argued at length about what we describe with the loathsome phrase "the fruits of victory."

Nobody here commemorated the war in Lebanon during that week. The fallen soldiers of the Six-Day War "belong to all of us," but those who died in Lebanon belong only to their mothers now.

Until the Lebanon War, even someone like me had an admission ticket (perhaps for a place in some rear corner of the balcony, standing room only) to the enchanted world of "the beautiful Land of Israel," to the Hebrew melodies, to the feelings of "a man [who] wakes up one morn, feels he is a people reborn, and begins to move forward," in the words of A. Gilboa. During the Lebanon War, it was possible to hope that the blindness, the hunger for power, and the self-righteousness so evident then were only side effects of the war, and that when peace came, our health would be restored. But during the Lebanon War I understood, or thought I understood, at last, that the disease was deep-seated and widespread, that it might be something more than a by-product. Even now, after Lebanon, from time to time I search for something on which to pin my hope and in which to become involved. But life is not as it was before that war. What once was will never be again.

There are people on the left who, at this point, would say to me, "Good morning! Welcome to the real world." In their eyes Israel was the bad guy long before Lebanon—ever since the rise of the Likud* to power, or since the administration of Golda Meir, or since the occupation of the West Bank and Gaza in 1967, or maybe ever since the beginning of the "Zionist penetration." I do not agree with them. That debate has been aired in other places. I wrote this essay in June 1987 only in order to present what I remembered from the summer of 1982.

In August 1981, through the mediation of the American diplomat Philip Habib, a cease-fire agreement was reached between Israel and the PLO. Both sides honored that agreement along the Lebanese border. It was, I believe, the year with the fewest casualties since the establishment of our state. The PLO was distracted by its attempt to take control of wide areas in a disintegrating Lebanon. Another year and yet another, and part of Lebanon might perhaps have turned into a Palestinian state. And, indeed, the PLO invested great effort in establishing the infrastructure for a quasi-regular army, including several dozen obsolete tanks and considerable artillery. Despite the exaggerations of Israeli propaganda, which publicized reports during the Lebanon War of "mammoth arms stockpiles," the organized strength of the PLO did not come close to the strength of even a single Syrian or Jordanian division. The PLO had the power to be a nuisance and to draw blood before the Lebanon War, and it continues to have that capacity after the war. But it did not have the power to pose a threat to the survival of Israel, nor can it ever, by virtue of the limits of its potential, pose unaided such a threat in the future. All was quiet on the northern front.

On the night between Wednesday, June 2, and Thursday, June

---

*Likud is the major right-wing party in Israel and led the country from 1977 to 1984.

3, 1987, the Israeli ambassador to Great Britain, Shlomo Argov, was shot in the head. Abu Nidal's group claimed responsibility. The PLO spokesman in Beirut was quick to disassociate his organization from the crime, because the PLO was just then concentrating on a not entirely unsuccessful attempt to achieve international recognition so that Israel might be forced to accept it as a partner in negotiations over the future of the occupied territories. The government of Israel, however, placed full responsibility on the PLO for the attempted assassination of the ambassador. On Thursday afternoon, an acquaintance telephoned me and said, "Get ready, ol' buddy! There's going to be a little war pretty soon. Something like an expanded performance of the Litani raid in 1978. Only this time we'll go as far as the Awali River or maybe even up to the Zaharani. Find it on the map. And we won't pull back unless we can hand the whole package over to the good ol' boys of Major Haddad." And then he added another, cryptic, sentence, "Unless the whole of that Lebanon falls apart completely from our kick — in which case, anything may happen."

That same night several reservists from Kibbutz Hulda were called up. Not many — maybe four or five. Early that Friday morning, convoys of military trucks, covered with tarpaulins, passed through nearby Bilu junction. At noon we could hear preparations going on at the Tel Nof air base. The regional civil-defense headquarters called our kibbutz coordinator and asked him to beef up our night watch. The army radio station began to put on special newscasts, and everything was just as it had been in the good old days, just as before the Sinai campaign of 1956, just as before the Six-Day War of 1967, just as before Yom Kippur of 1973. It was like a traveling troupe that completes its tour every few years and then returns for a repeat performance, except that in the meantime the actors have aged a bit, the old familiar stage props have become threadbare, and the whole audience recites the lines before the actors can utter the words. Only the children who have not seen the previous performances are excited.

But this time there is something missing. This time the famil-

iar show seems to have shrunk. After a while you can feel a difference between this time and previous times; this time your stomach doesn't contract in spasms of anxiety. Also missing is the fear
that the war may descend upon our own red-tiled roofs here at the
kibbutz. Unlike earlier wars, no one bothers to clean out the bomb
shelters or to reinforce the windowpanes with strips of masking
tape, to wash the heavy blackout curtains or to make up a duty ros-
ter for the infirmary. And suddenly it dawns on you: This game is
fixed. The results of this war are clear from the outset, and in any
event, not one sliver from it will reach us here. The whole war will
be taking place in another country, and may Allah have mercy on
them. This time our whole country is not the battlefield, nor the
people the army, and this time it is not a life-and-death struggle.
This time Israel will have a war deluxe, and if someone should have
doubts as to whether he'll survive—well, it's only the guy who's being sent there, to the arena. The spectators can sit in the stands
and munch popcorn. Or, instead of sitting and watching, they can
go about their business as usual—everyone, that is, who doesn't
happen to care particularly for this war. For instance, they can go
abroad for that planned vacation in Spain or Portugal, or they can
finally get around to enclosing that porch, or they can open that
restaurant, produce that first play, or trade in that old car. I mean, of
course, everyone who hasn't been called up himself, or whose loved
ones haven't been drafted. This time it's not the whole nation that
is at war; it is just the army, the government, and the newspapers.
These lines bear witness to the abomination of this war, which was
not forced upon us and was not fought to anticipate a threat to our
survival, but, rather, to "achieve a result" or to "strike while the iron
is hot." It's something like a timely investment in the stock market.
This was never the case in Israel's previous wars, not even in those
that were regarded as controversial for one reason or another. And
that is the essence of the horror that Menachem Begin was to describe a few weeks later as a "war of choice," arguing that it is conve-
nient, cheaper, and more worthwhile than "wars in which we have
no alternative." And, at the same time, his followers, in order to jus-

tify this war, will try retroactively to defile the earlier wars, claim-ing—along with Israel's enemies—that actually we always did have a choice, that we always were the aggressor, that we always were lying when we claimed that our back was to the wall, and that Is-rael always flaunted specious, self-righteous arguments in order to cover up its gluttony; and it is no big deal, so what's the *shpiel*, and would you kindly cut the crap and shut up.

All this surfaced only in the weeks ahead. On Friday, June 4, there was quite a different sort of discussion around the lunch ta-ble in Kibbutz Hulda's dining hall. M., one of the old-timers in the kibbutz, said, "Begin is just looking for some resounding military success to give his supporters new inspiration and make them for-get about having had to quit our settlements in Sinai two months ago."

Redhead said, "This time we've got to finish them once and for all, not like during the Litani operation. And if the Egyptians make a peep, that'll be our opportunity to take back Sinai."

Said A., "Forget about Sinai now. Reagan told Begin to take Lebanon and give it to the Christian Phalangists. Maybe we should keep everything up to the Litani, so we'll have enough water for our country. And if, by chance, the result is that Mr. Assad* falls, the Egyptians will be sending us flowers. You can believe me. After that, maybe we'll be able to give the Arabs a slice of the territories, or a little autonomy, and that'll be that. We might just come out from this deal with a comprehensive, total peace, on our own terms."

M. said, "Begin just wants to go down in history as more of a Ben-Gurion than Ben-Gurion. And that Raful [Rafael Eitan] and that Arik [Ariel Sharon]†—well, they've had itchy trigger fingers for a long time."

L. added, "All those bickering factions in Lebanon will come to us for help in putting their houses in order. The Christians, the

---

*Hafez al-Assad, born in 1928, was president of Syria from 1971 to 2000.

†Sharon, general, politician, and a leader of Likud, was minister of defense during the Lebanon War. Rafael Eitan, also a general, was chief of staff from 1978 to 1983.

Druze, the Whatzits, and even the Palestinians themselves, after the way the Phalangists and the Syrians slaughtered them at Tel Azaatar."

Redhead said, "It's all an American plot. Maybe they worked the whole thing out at Camp David, sort of on the quiet, on the side. And do you know what? Hussein and the Saudis are going to lick their lips when Arafat's end arrives. It's going to be a great little war! The Three-Day War—that's what they'll call it."

That afternoon, alone at home, I lay on the couch and read the weekend newspapers. I wondered whether I, too, was going to be called up for reserve duty. I hoped I wouldn't be, and I was a little ashamed of that hope. The afternoon papers struck a tone of forced gaiety, as though the old marching tune this time had a counterfeit ring. If you believed the papers, Israel was like an aging gentleman, portly and well established, who locks himself in the bathroom to get spruced up for a prurient rendezvous that has come his way without any effort on his part. Humming to himself before the mirror, he tries to get into the proper spirit with memories of his wild youth, when his back ached from all the pats of admiration.

But now, the code words from the days of 1967 sounded tired and worn out. "A preemptive strike," somebody wrote. "To take them off the playing field for the next ten years," another analyst explained. And someone else even resurrected the one about "reviving the element of deterrence." They wrote that our peace treaty with Egypt would prevent the opening of a second front on that side and allow us a lightning victory "in view of the balance of power," particularly if the Syrians had the good sense to sit this one out. They also wrote about the need to "root out international terrorism at its source, once and for all." Someone else, in fatherly, forgiving tones, appealed to the leaders of the opposition Labor Party* to remember—for their own good—that they had paid

---

*The Labor Party, the major center/left-wing party in Israel, led the country from 1948 to 1977. In 1984, it formed a "national unity" coalition with Likud and other parties.

dearly in the elections of the year just past for their opposition to the bombing of the Iraqi nuclear reactor. This time, the journalist advised the Labor leaders, they ought to go along with the people and not act against them.

That afternoon, Israeli air force planes launched a massive bombing attack on the suburbs of Beirut. They destroyed, as the newscasts reported, the municipal stadium, which had served as a huge arsenal for the terrorists. The flames, it was gleefully reported, "could be seen for dozens of kilometers." The evening news informed us, as usual, that "Arafat himself had miraculously escaped from the bombing."

Later that evening, at long last—as promised, as written in the program—the army radio station started to broadcast old-time Hebrew melodies: "There in the Hills of Galilee," "In the Eucalyptus Grove," and perhaps even "Mount Hermon's Majesty" ("We climbed with the wind / to her shining peak. . . .").

All day long, that Saturday, the Israeli government waited for the PLO's response to the bombings near Beirut the day before: flurries of Katyusha rockets on the villages of Galilee, which would provide justification for an invasion. For a full day and night, the PLO managed to restrain itself, perhaps because its leaders sensed what was about to happen and did not want to play into Israel's hands.

On Saturday morning, M. and I drove in the kibbutz Subaru to a meeting of Peace Now supporters in the kibbutz movement, which took place at a kibbutz in the north. All the northbound roads were jammed with long military convoys: tanks piggybacked on huge carriers, mobile artillery pieces, jeeps, trucks open and closed, some of them towing enormous spotlights and others dragging elongated tools of war covered by khaki tarpaulins, buses filled with soldiers (none of whom were singing), and among the vehicles, as always in the wars of David against Goliath, there were civilian trucks that had been drafted—Berman's Bakery, Tadiran Co., Amcor Enterprises, Marbek, Inc., and so forth.

At the kibbutz conference, they talked as usual about the "cor-

rupting occupation" and about the "nationalist-religious fanaticism"
that had shown up "in all its ugliness" two months earlier, during
the evacuation of the Jewish settlements in the Sinai Peninsula. They
condemned false messianism and warned about the "waning of the
spirit of Camp David." Opinions were aired for and against Yigal
Allon's plan for territorial compromise. A young woman with an
American accent compared Israel to the United States in the Viet-
nam War and expressed her understanding of the "Palestinian resistance movement." And there was a slightly built, emotional young
man—from Latin America, I think—whose name I have forgotten,
but whose words I remember well. He said that there was going
to be a blitzkrieg in Lebanon and, as a result of the quick and easy
victory, Lebanon would become West Bank Number 2. First they'd
occupy half of Lebanon to prevent Katyusha attacks. Then they'd
say there was no one to give it back to because there was no one
to talk to. Later, they would say that perhaps there was someone to
talk to, but that without a stable and durable peace we will return
nothing. Whereupon they would say: What's the noise all about?
What occupiers are you talking about? What occupation? Why, all
we did was liberate the biblical portion of the tribe of Asher. And
then a squad of rabbis would be sent to renovate the ruins of an ancient synagogue in Nabatiyah or a Jewish cemetery in Sidon. After
that, a settler's group from Gush Emunim (Bloc of the Faithful) will
set up house there in order to pray at the grave of Queen Jezebel.
And then lands will be expropriated for military maneuvers and
installations. These lands will be held by paramilitary settlement
groups with such names as Cedar Trees and Leaders, to prevent
incursions by local *fellaheen* into restricted military areas. These
settlements would support themselves by growing cherries for ex-
port, and when they were handed over to civilian authorities they
would live on tourism and skiing in the snowy Lebanese mountains. The centrist United Kibbutz Movement would refuse, at first,
to set up kibbutzim north of the generally accepted boundary, the
"Katyusha range," along the Litani River. The Hashomer Hatzair
kibbutz movement would agree to settle only within a "cosmetic

distance" of several hundred meters from the old border. In the early years, only Gush Emunim followers would settle north of the Litani. The rabbinate would decree that the Bible forbids us to turn our ancestral inheritance over to the Gentiles, and that decision will receive wide support because this ancestral inheritance also happens to be very important for defense and very strategic as well as rich in water and arable land, which will gradually be expropriated. Apart from that, they will say that no one except ourselves has a historic right to Lebanon, which was, after all, the artificial creation of French imperialism and, when you get down to it, there is no such thing as a Lebanese people anyway: Lebanon already exists in Syria. Besides, the Arabs already have enough territory, and if they don't like it, they can lump it and go back to their own countries. The upshot of all this will be that, twenty years later, the right will refuse to relinquish a single inch, while the left, taking a balanced, realistic stand, will propose a territorial compromise: annex only the territory up to the Litani and return the rest in exchange for a true, stable, and lasting peace with appropriate security arrangements. That's what will happen.

A giggle rippled through the audience at the young man's words. Many thought he was exaggerating a little.

(Four months later, a government spokesman was to make a slip of the tongue that spoke volumes: "The Israel Defense Forces will not pull out of Lebanon until the Syrian Army, too, pulls out of Syria." Under the Dostoevskian title "Crime and Punishment," Rabbi Dov Lior would soon publish an article in the *B'nai Akiva Journal* in which he would claim that the war in Lebanon was a punishment from heaven for "the sin of having handed over the Sinai Peninsula to the Egyptians," but at the same time it was the beginning of the Redemption, since we had liberated the Land of Cedars, which, according to the Bible, was part of the inheritance of the Children of Israel who had gone forth from Egypt. We had been commanded, as far back as the days of Joshua, son of Nun, he said, to conquer it, but had been a little remiss about this until now.)

Toward evening M. and I returned from the conference at Kibbutz Ma'ayan Tsvi. By twilight we had counted almost 150 tanks headed north on tank carriers. The car radio showered us with nostalgic Hebrew melodies, not the marching songs other nations play on the eve of war, but soul melodies full of charm and longing: "The Two of Us from the Same Hometown," "Oh, the Open Road," "Night of Roses," "I Bear the Pain of Silence."

To what tribal codes did those melodies address themselves? What did the tribe want to whisper to itself in the few precious hours that were left before it set out to overrun Lebanon under a pretext that was mendacious, self-righteous? What emotions were those cloying tunes meant to arouse — or to silence? Perhaps this: That we are beautiful, gentle people, righteous, pure, and sensitive, completely out of touch with our actions; that we will be forgiven because our pure and poetic hearts know nothing about the filth that is on our hands; that the evening scent of roses will come to perfume the stench of dead bodies that will pile up by the hundreds and thousands in the days to come.

The hands are the hands of Begin and the voice is the voice of the Geveatron Kibbutz folk choir.

Since the Sabbath had come and gone without a barrage of PLO rockets on the villages in Galilee, the air force was sent on another bombing raid on Lebanon on Saturday night. It was clear that Israel would not tolerate the self-restraint of the PLO and would not countenance Arafat's decision to keep quiet. And indeed, just as the architects of this war had hoped, the barrage on Galilee came on the night between Saturday and Sunday. Most of the shells fell somewhere between the villages, not on them — this time. Only one person was wounded and almost no damage was done — in the words of the official announcement, which, this time, seemed to carry a slight undertone of frustration. The PLO spokesman, on the other side, said something about a "warning response."

That same night some more reservists were drafted from Kibbutz Hulda. Over early-morning coffee in the dining hall, the local pundits were saying "They are going to grandstand it." H. stopped me near the laundry house. She was almost at the end of her pregnancy and she told me that her husband had been called up at dawn that morning. Then she burst into tears. I, in my great wisdom, told her in authoritative tones that everything would be just fine, that it would all be over in a few days.

That afternoon several Israeli military formations crossed the Lebanese border along several main axes. Afterward a task force was put ashore north of Sidon in order to block enemy routes, and perhaps to cut off lines of retreat as well. During the night between June 7 and 8, Israeli forces gained control over the 45-kilometer area between the international border and the Sidon-Jezzin line — that same area the government spokesman had initially declared to be the goal of the "operation." Fierce fighting continued in that area for another week with PLO troops that included little boys carrying RPG bazookas, who holed up mostly in the refugee camps between Tyre and Sidon. The entire population of Sidon — men, women, and children — were ordered to leave their houses and to assemble at the seashore. Air force planes were sent, wave after wave, to bomb the firing sites in the Rashidiyeh and Einal-Hilwah refugee camps and Sidon itself. The trouble was that those gun emplacements happened to be in the midst of densely populated side streets, and thousands suffered death and destruction. ("Well, who told those bastards to hide behind old women and children?")

The official spokesmen used the deceitful name "Peace for Galilee." (No war, not even a justifiable war of defense, can be called "peace.") They talked a lot about "innocent women and children" — in the villages of northern Israel. (The women and children of the other side are not "innocent," and, of course, men are never "innocent.") They talked about intolerable provocations (although the year prior to the war had been calm to an unprecedented degree). They talked about "enlightened world public opinion" (which very quickly became "the hypocritical world"). They talked about "limited objectives, which have been achieved almost entirely thus far" (while the Israeli forces had been given orders to engage the

Syrian army and drag it into the war). From newspeak to newspeak, the radio continually perfumed the airwaves with "The Scent of the Apple, the Blush of the Rose," "The Forgotten Melody Returns," "Let It Be, Let It Be, All That We May Ask, Let It Be," "Would That All Lovers," and a new song, "Do Not Uproot the Sapling." Behind the deceitful screen of folk melodies and self-righteousness, the decision was made to broaden the scope of the war. The Israeli formation, which had reached the Shouf Mountains and was met by the local population with applause and a shower of rice, was now ordered to advance to the Beirut-Damascus highway and there to link up with our Christian brethren, who, anticipating their liberation, were busy preparing royal banquets for us. The decision was apparently made on June 8, if not much earlier—if, indeed, it had not been part of the original plot of calculated disinformation. That same day, the Syrian forces were overrun at Jezzin; Syria finally got the message and entered the war.

It was a war of deceit and brainwashing, the true goals of which had been concealed from the nation, from the soldiers, from the Knesset, and from most of the Cabinet. Under the guise of peace for Galilee, Begin was going to crown the corrupt Gemayel family as rulers over all Lebanon, and turn Lebanon into a client state of Israel. ("So what? Why is it okay for Brezhnev? Why is it okay for Assad?") He was going to strike at the Syrian army although it had not provoked Israel and had not caused a single Israeli casualty during the eight years since the signing of the Syrian-Israeli agreement at the end of the Yom Kippur War. He would do the Western world ("the ingrates!") a favor by finishing off the PLO and thus, as these geniuses saw it, putting an end to the Palestinian problem. He would win, as Chief of Staff Lieutenant General Eitan put it, "the war for the Land of Israel" (in other words, for the territories that we occupied during the Six-Day War), and perhaps clean up, once and for all, the mess in the Middle East. The history writers were asked to take note that, unlike the Christian world, which had stood aside while Jews were being slaughtered, the Jews had not stood aside, but had gone to the rescue of their Christian brethren in Lebanon (to save them from the disaster they had brought down on themselves). The role of the sweet, innocent Little Red Riding Hood was thus given to the rotten Christian Phalangists, whose creation had been inspired by fascism. Begin assumed the role of the noble woodsman who rescues Little Red Riding Hood from the jaws of the Islamic wolf, if not the role of the last Crusader.

Indeed, if we are to judge by his speeches during that war, Menachem Begin went into Lebanon to fight a worldwide war against the enemies of Israel, from Amalek to Chmielnicki to Hitler: an awesome retribution for all that the Jews had suffered. Once and for all.

"We love you, precious Homeland / in joy, in song, and toil / Down from the slopes of Lebanon to the shores of the Dead Sea / We will rake your fields with plows. . . ." On June 9, the Israeli air force swept away virtually all the ground-to-air missiles the Syrians had installed in the Lebanon rift (without asking our permission!). In air battles that same day, twenty-nine Syrian planes were shot down, with all Israeli planes returning safely to their base. The following day, the Syrian forces were struck near Lake Karoun and the Syrian First Division was defeated in heavy armored fighting. During the night between June 10 and 11, an Israeli spearhead force reached the Beirut-Damascus highway. The Lebanese capital was cut off. (I am told that the code name for Beirut in Israel Defense Forces documents was "Bar-Lev," which is not only the name of Haim Bar-Lev, the Israeli army's deputy chief of staff during the Six-Day War, but the Hebrew acronym for Birat Levanon — the capital of Lebanon.) Fifteen thousand Syrian soldiers and PLO fighters were trapped in what Arafat would later glorify as the Palestinian Leningrad.

Y. came over to see me later that evening. "You see?" he said. "We screwed them quick, hard, and neat." "This won't end well," I said. I didn't know what else I could have told him. "Are you starting that all over again?" said Y. "You'd do better if you got up the courage to send an article to *Davar,* that newspaper of yours, retracting all those gloom-and-doom prophecies you've been publishing these last few days. You're making a fool of yourself."

Then came the cease-fire of June 11, which wasn't a cease-fire. And after that came the battles of Aley and Bachamdoun and Baabdeh and the Galerie Semaine Square, spiced with parties and fancy banquets given by the Christian Phalangists (as their contribution toward their own liberation) honoring officers of the Israel Defense Forces and delegations of Israeli dignitaries. Then came two months of the cruel siege of the city of Beirut, including massive shelling of residential neighborhoods, which cut off electricity and water. Meanwhile, in Israel, the rift deepened between those who supported the war and the critics who publicly demonstrated their protest. There was controversy even among the soldiers, many of whom discovered they had fallen victim to a cynical lie — that they were being used to achieve objectives of which no one could have conceived at the beginning of the "operation." High-ranking army commanders aired criticism of the plan to enter West Beirut. Colonel Eli Geva was relieved of his command and dismissed from the army because of his refusal to take part, as commander, in an operation he considered unconscionable. Public opinion in Western nations was not ecstatic about the Israeli crusade "to rescue the Christians in Lebanon." Strong criticism of the military operation quickly escalated into poisonous criticism of Israel and of Zionism itself, with more and more blatantly anti-Semitic undertones.

On August 21, in accordance with an agreement reached under American auspices, the beleaguered Syrian and PLO forces were evacuated from West Beirut. A multinational force was supposed to take their place in the city. Two days later Bashir Gemayel was elected president of Lebanon by the vote of a phony parliament ringed by Israeli tanks. Within three weeks Gemayel was murdered by Syrian agents, and the Israel Defense Forces quickly took control of West Beirut. In coordination with the Israel Defense Forces, the heroic Phalangists, who until then had not lifted a finger to help "save the Christians," took upon themselves the task of "purifying" the Palestinian refugee camps in the city. Within earshot of Israeli army positions, the illustrious Phalangist heroes of Eli Houbeike and his cohorts, their way lighted by flares of the Israeli army, slaughtered men, women, and children in the Shatilla and Sabra camps.* "The Phalangists went overboard this time," said Chief of Staff Eitan without elaborating. Speech is silver. . . .

Then from all the radio stations, simultaneously—as though by command from the top—the charming Hebrew melodies suddenly vanished. The Israeli nightingale seemed to have swallowed its tongue. Other songbirds were heard in the land, including the grenade explosion that murdered Emil Grunzweig, the Peace Now demonstrator, and wounded some of his friends in the square in front of Begin's office.

And then began the retreat from Lebanon and in its wake came amnesia. Uncle Sharon was forced to leave, Uncle Raful, the chief of staff, went away, and Grandpa Begin was gathered up into his own bosom. The entire Lebanon War was retired to the cellars of collective oblivion. Some seven hundred soldiers were gone, along with thousands of the enemy. And gone, too, it is said, were more than ten thousand civilians, "innocent" even in the vocabulary of those who had abetted the crime.

And in time we started playing those melodies again—"How Shall I Bless," "He Will Bring Us," and "Would That Buds Could Speak."

It is time to go back to the beginning—the beginning of that war. To a picture of Menachem Begin, pale, leaning on a cane, surrounded by his generals and his advisers, at the top of captured Beaufort, the old Crusader castle in southern Lebanon. The blood of the dead from the previous night's battle has not yet dried beneath his feet, but this man is standing there, "tired but happy." Happy? Gleeful and arrogant, crowing that this "great" fortress had been captured "with no losses." And with fatherly satisfaction, he questions one of

---

*In the Shatilla and Sabra refugee camps on the southern outskirts of Beirut, eight hundred Palestinian civilians were murdered by Lebanese Phalangist forces in 1982. In the worldwide uproar that followed, Israel was blamed for allowing the Phalangists to enter the camps.

the stunned soldiers: "What used to be over here? Machine guns?" Then, as though assuming the role of a biblical king in a Cecil B. DeMille spectacular, he "bestows" Beaufort upon the armies of Major Haddad.

Thus began the new era: King Solomon granted "forty cities" as a gift to Hiram, king of Tyre; Israel dispensed fiefdoms to its vassals.

This was only the prologue. Several days later, the prime minister appeared on television, bemused, sarcastic, in a verbal blast against all the Gentile hypocrites. ("Look who dares preach morality to us!") He trampled upon his domestic opponents, promoted Arafat to the rank of a new Hitler, and in the next breath demoted him to the rank of a "hairy-faced" two-legged beast, treating viewers at home to a "strategic" comparison in which he contrasted "Hannibal who had outflanked the Romans one way" with his own minions, "who had, on the contrary, outflanked both this way and that." What his words did not reveal was written on his face: he was smug. To listen to him, the war seemed like a toy that had finally been presented to him after a long, frustrating wait, which had gone on, perhaps, since his youth. Pugnacious, petty, and vengeful toward his opponents, and indifferent to the horrors of the war, he was consumed by a hatred of "the Gentile world," born of a feeling of inferiority that was cloaked in a pose of sarcastic superiority. "And now," he happily promised us, "there will be peace in the land for forty years."

As fate would have it, several months later Begin himself became a "hairy-faced" man. Photographers were requested to show tact and to refrain from photographing him with the stubble of mourning he had grown in accordance with religious custom after the death of his wife and, later, not with the beard he grew because he was stricken by a skin disease. Some say he was stricken by remorse as well.

But what do I care about Begin? May he find a little peace in his seclusion. We will cast no stone on his sufferings. The guilt for Lebanon lies not with Begin alone, and certainly not just with Eitan and

Sharon, who carried out his orders (or carried out his orders and then some). We will have to grit our teeth and admit that this war was a war of the people. The people wanted it and the people (most of them) supported it, took pleasure in it, and hated the handful who were opposed to it. At least that is how it was until the war got "bogged down"; at that point, this good people simply forgot about the war and its dead.

But who are "the people" in this case? We cannot simply place the spilled blood at the doorstep of the ecstatic masses who shouted "Begin! Begin!" Many of them celebrated the war and spat their hatred in every direction, but they weren't the ones who had started it and they weren't the ones who allowed it to go on. The Labor Party, and the centrist Shinui Party (Democratic Party for Change), and some of the members of the dovish left wing of the Knesset either voted with the government or abstained in the vote of no confidence when the war broke out. M. K. Imri Ron, of the left-wing Mapam, was photographed in his army uniform and his officer's insignia, calling upon his party to support the war and not to incense the people. Labor's Motta Gur volunteered to serve as Sharon's unofficial adviser. And Labor Party leader Yitzhak Rabin recommended "tightening the siege on Beirut." Thus spoke the representatives of enlightened Israel, the land of the pioneer folk songs. And even *Ma'ariv,* the afternoon newspaper, published a political cartoon portraying the Israeli army, tiny but unyielding, standing all alone against a ferocious, hairy terrorist giant, armed to the teeth, while a knife held by Peace Now is being plunged in the back of the brave little IDF.

In Tel Aviv and the development towns, at kibbutzim, just as in Juniyeh, the Christian suburb of Beirut, the dead died and the bathers bathed in the sea, businessmen transacted business, and vacationers took package trips to Scandinavia—returning, of course, in time for the opening of school for their children. No one heard, or could have heard, the wail of an air-raid siren. No one (except the Israeli residents along the northern border during the first two nights) hurried into bomb shelters. The newspapers were filled with Lebanese cherries, with obituaries, Beirut restaurant reviews, nightclub features in the Christian enclave, and shouts of merrymaking. There were endless television broadcasts of joyous Lebanese civilians showering the rice of welcome on Israeli military convoys and just a handful of left-wing pictures of burning cities, maimed children, and weeping women. ("They're used to that sort of thing over there," several newspapers wrote. "Why, up there in Lebanon, slaughter is a way of life.")

And the radio dipped it all in the oil of idyllic nostalgia while Begin and his friends presented the ongoing horror as a sort of neurotic mixture of a new Eichmann trial (with Arafat, if and when he was caught, in the lead role), the Sinai campaign in an expanded edition (with Israel in the role of scourge for the Western world), together with the fall of Nazi Berlin (with Arafat's bunker cast as the bunker of Adolf Hitler), and "The Six-Day War Rides Again" (down to the "poetic" touch of identical dates), topped off by "healing the trauma of the Yom Kippur War" (in the words of the Great Traumatizer).

Right up until the BBC reported the slaughter that the Phalangists had conducted by the light of our flares in Shatilla and Sabra. Until Emil Grunzweig was murdered by a hand grenade intended for all the opponents of this war. That grenade closed a circle: Jerusalem had gone off to clean up Beirut and now Beirut had reached the heart of Jerusalem to turn Jerusalem into a Beirut.

Not one popular song was born out of the Lebanon War, except "Planes come down from up anon / Taking us to Lebanon / For Sharon, O, we will fight / And come home in coffins tight," which was composed by defeatist soldiers, plunging their knives into their own backs. Perhaps it would have been proper to set to music the poems of despair, anger, and loss written during those days by Israel's poets, young and old, or the elegies written by Raya Harnik for her son Goni, the Peace Now activist, who had died at Beaufort, and then to play them on the Hebrew hit parades. But no, the metabolism of the idyllic Hebrew melodies would not have been able to absorb them. So they would have no place even among such elegies to heroes of past wars as "A Palmachnik Named Dudu," "In the Plains of the Negev a Defender Fell," "Accept, Ye Hill of Ephraim, This New Young Sacrifice."

There would be no more songs about "The Bitter and the Sweet," only about the bitter and the hasty.

Seven years have passed since then. I have tried to replace my alienation of those days with various kinds of involvement, engagements, petitions, and public stands. This collection of essays deals with these issues.

There are times when I forget a little, when I try to persuade myself that the "people" learned a lesson, that they have learned — the hard way — the limits of power, that there's a catch in a philosophy based on violence. There are times when I think that "it" can't happen again.

Perhaps.

But among the victims of the Lebanon War was "the Land of Israel, small and brave, determined and righteous." It died in Lebanon perhaps precisely because, in Lebanon, its back was not to the wall. *It* was the wall and *they,* the Palestinians in Lebanon, had their backs pressed to the wall. From underneath the "ponytail and pinafore" of the myths, the claws peeked out. Just as they continue to peek out daily, not only in the occupied territories, but also in the "good Israel of old" — in the suburbs and in the cities, on the crazy peripheries as well as in the enlightened, sane center, in the slums and on the campuses, among the hotheads and among the intelligentsia, and in the heart of the corridors of power.

After Lebanon, we can no longer ignore the monster, even when it is dormant, or half asleep, or when it peers out from behind the lunatic fringe. After Lebanon, we must not pretend that the monster dwells only in the offices of Meir Kahane, or only on General Sharon's ranch, or only in Raful's carpentry shop, or only in the Jewish settlements in the West Bank. It dwells, drowsing, virtually everywhere, even in the folksinging guts of our common myths. Even in our soul melodies. We did not leave it behind in Lebanon, with the Hezbollah. It is here, among us, a part of us, like a shadow, in Hebron, in Gaza, in the slums and in the suburbs; in the kibbutzim and in my Lake Kinneret—"O Lake Kinneret mine, were you real or only a dream? . . ."

That which you have done—whether it be only once in your life, in one moment of stupidity or in an outburst of anger—that which you were capable of doing—even if you have forgotten, or have chosen to forget, how and why you did it—that which you have done and regretted bitterly, you may never do again. But you are capable of doing it. You may do it. It is curled up inside you.

In an
Autobiographical Vein

An Autobiographical Note

from *Under This Blazing Light*
(First published in 1975)

Shortly after the October Revolution, my grandfather, Alexander Klausner, a businessman and poet, fled from Odessa in southern Russia. He had always been a "Lover of Zion," and was one of the first Zionists. He believed wholeheartedly that the time had come for the Jews to return to the Land of Israel, so that they could begin by becoming a normal nation like all the rest, and later perhaps an exceptional nation. Nevertheless, after leaving Odessa my grandfather did not head for Jerusalem—that Jerusalem that all his poems had yearned for (in Russian)—but settled with his wife and two sons in Vilna, which was then in Poland. In addition to his profound affection for the ancestral land, my grandfather was also a thoroughgoing European in his bearing, his habits, his dress, and his principles. He considered that conditions in the Land of Israel were as yet insufficiently European. That is why he settled in Vilna, where he once more divided his time between business and poetry. He raised his two sons in a spirit of European and Zionist idealism.

However, in those days no one in Europe, apart from my grandfather and some other Jews like him, was a European: they were all either pan-Slavists, or communists, or pan-Germanists, or just plain Bulgarian nationalists. In 1933, having been taunted by his anti-Semitic or order-loving neighbors to "Go to Palestine, little Yid," Grandfather reluctantly decided to go to "Asia" with his wife and his younger son.

As for the elder son, my uncle David, he resolutely refused to succumb to chauvinism and barbarism: he stood at his post and continued lecturing on European literature at Vilna University until the Nazis arrived and murdered him, together with his wife and their baby son, Daniel, to purge Europe of cosmopolitanism and Jews.

In Jerusalem Alexander Klausner continued with his business and his poetry, despite the heat, the poverty, the hostility of the Arabs, and the strange Oriental atmosphere. He went on writing poems in Russian about the beauty of the Hebrew language and the splendor of Jerusalem, not this wretched, dusty Jerusalem, but the other one, the real one.

His son, my father, obtained a post as a librarian that allowed him to eke out a living, but at night he sat up writing articles on comparative literature. He married the middle daughter of a former mill owner from Rovno in Ukraine, who for ideological reasons had become a carter in Haifa Bay. My parents made themselves a simple but book-filled home in Jerusalem with a black tea trolley, a painting of a European landscape, and a Russian-style tea set. They told each other that someday Hebrew Jerusalem would develop into a real city.

I was born in 1939, shortly before the outbreak of war, when it became clear to my parents that there was no going back. They may have dreamed in Yiddish, spoken to each other in Russian and Polish, and read mainly in German and English, but they brought me up speaking one language only: Hebrew. I was destined to be a new chapter, a plain, tough Israeli, fair-haired and free from Jewish neuroses and excessive intellectualism.

The Jerusalem of my childhood was a lunatic town, ridden with conflicting dreams, a vague federation of different ethnic, national, and religious communities, ideologies, and aspirations. There were ultrapious Jews who sat waiting prayerfully for the Messiah to come, and there were active revolutionary Jews who aimed to cast themselves in the role of Messiah; there were Oriental Jews who had lived in Jerusalem for generations in their placid Mediterranean fashion, and there were various fanatical sects of Christians who had come to Jerusalem to be "reborn"; there were also the Arabs, who sometimes called us "children of death" and threw stones at us. Besides all these there were weird and crazy people from just about everywhere in the world, each with his own private formula for saving mankind. Many of them may have been secretly longing to crucify or to be crucified. My parents chose to send me to a Hebrew school of strong National Religious leanings, where I was taught to yearn for the glory of the ancient Jewish kingdoms and to long for their resurrection in blood and fire. My Jerusalem childhood made me an expert in comparative fanaticism.

I was nine when the British left Palestine and Jewish Jerusalem underwent a long siege in the War of Independence. Everyone believed that victory would bring a free Hebrew State, where nothing would be as it was before. Three years after Hitler's downfall, these survivors believed that they were fighting the final battle in the War of the Sons of Light and the Sons of Darkness, and that Jewish independence would be a decisive sign of the salvation of the whole world.

The War of Independence culminated in a great victory. More than a million Jewish refugees arrived in Israel within a few years. But the siege and the suffering had not ended, universal salvation did not happen, and the trivial pains of a very small state made themselves felt. After the sound and the fury came the morning after. Jerusalem did not turn into a "real" European city. The Jews did not become "a merry, contented race of rugged peasants."

Some continued to wait. Even in advanced old age, and he is now over ninety, my grandfather Alexander Klausner continues to write poems of longing for Jerusalem: a different, real, pure Jerusalem redeemed by the Messiah, freed from all suffering and injustice. To the day of his death, in October 1970, my father, Yehudah Arieh Klausner, went on making literary comparisons in fifteen languages. Only my mother, Fania, could not bear her life: she took her own life in 1952, out of disappointment or nostalgia. Something had gone wrong.

Two years later, when I was fourteen, I left home, walked out on the good manners and the scholarship, changed my surname from

Klausner to Oz, and went to work and study in Kibbutz Hulda. I was hoping to start a new chapter in my life, away from Jerusalem. For several years I worked a bit on the land and took my lessons in a free socialist classroom, where we sat barefoot all day long learning about the source of human evil, the corruption of societies, the origins of the Jewish disease, and how to overcome all these by means of labor, simple living, sharing, and equality, a gradual improvement in human nature. I still hold to these views, albeit with a certain sadness and an occasional fleeting smile. In their name I still reject any radical doctrine, whether in socialism, Zionism, or Israeli politics. My wife, who was born on the kibbutz, my daughters, Fania and Gallia, and my son, Daniel, may be spared certain Jewish and Jerusalemite afflictions that tormented my parents and their parents and me myself: I see this as an achievement.

As a child I wrote biblical poems about the restoration of the Davidic kingdom through blood and fire and a terrible vengeance wrought on all the foes of the Jewish people. After serving in the regular army I returned to the kibbutz; by day I worked in the cotton fields and by night I penned ironic stories about the distance between the pioneers and their dreams. Then the kibbutz assembly sent me to study philosophy and literature at the university in Jerusalem, on the understanding that I would teach the kibbutz children on my return. At night I could hear jackals howling in the fields and occasionally shots could be heard. I heard people crying out in their sleep, refugees who had come to the kibbutz from various countries: some of them had seen the Devil himself with their own eyes. So I wrote about the haunting phantoms: nostalgia, paranoia, nightmare, messianic hopes, and the longing for the absolute. I also wrote so as to capture in words where my family had come from and why, what we had been hoping to find here and what we actually found, and why different people in different times and places have hated us and wished us dead. I wrote so as to sort out what more could be done and what could not be done.

Twice, in 1967 with the victorious armored divisions in the Sinai

Desert and in 1973 amid blazing tanks on the Golan Heights, I saw for myself that there is no hope for the weak and the slain, while the strong and triumphant have only a limited hope. After the wars I wrote again about the closeness of death, the power of the desire for salvation, the nostalgic energy motivating all around me, the depth of fear and the impetus of the resolve to start a new chapter. I write so as not to despair, nor to yield to the temptation to return hatred for hatred. I have written stories and novels set in Jerusalem and in the kibbutz, in the medieval crusades and Hitler's Europe. I have written about Jewish refugees, about Zionist pioneers, and about the new Israelis. I have also written articles and essays in which I have called for a compromise, grounded neither in principles nor even perhaps in justice between the Israeli Jews and the Palestinian Arabs, because I have seen that whoever seeks absolute and total justice is seeking death. My stories and my articles have often unleashed a storm of public fury against me in Israel. Some have asserted that I am harming Zionist ideological fervor, or providing "ammunition" for the enemy, or damaging the image of the kibbutz. Some claim that I am touching a raw nerve and inflicting unnecessary pain.

I write to exorcise evil spirits. And I write, as Natan Zach puts it in one of his poems,

> this is a song about people,
> about what they think, and what they want,
> and what they think they want.

Father and Son in a
Search for Love

from *The Same Sea* (1999)

AN UGLY BLOATED BABY

After his mother became ill, Rico stayed out quite a lot. It was use-less his father pleading with him. That winter he came home at two o'clock almost every night. Only rarely did he sit by the invalid's bedside. The selfish love of an only child. Sometimes when he was little he used to imagine that his father had gone away, that he had been sent to Brazil, or moved in with another woman, and the two of them were left on their own in a pleasantly enclosed life, consol-ing each other. At least he wanted all the traffic between his parents to flow through his own junction and not through a tunnel behind his back. Her illness seemed to him as though she had suddenly had a baby daughter, a demanding pampered creature, a little like him, it was true, but a spoiled child. He imagined that if he went away his mother would have to choose between the two of them, and he was sure that she would never give him up. How astonished he was when she eventually chose the ugly bloated baby and left him alone with his father.

. . .

DITA OFFERS

Give me five minutes to try to sort out this screwed-up business.
   People are
constantly being ditched. Here in Greater Tel Aviv for example I bet
the daily total of ditchings is not far short of the figure for burglaries.
In New York the statistics must be even higher. Your mother killed
   herself

and left you quite shattered. And haven't you yourself ditched any
    number
of women? Who in turn had ditched whoever they ditched in favor of
    you,
and those ditched guys had certainly left some wounded Ditchinka
    lying
on the battlefield. It's all a chain reaction. OK, I'm not saying, I admit
being ditched by your own parents is different, it bleeds for longer.
Specially a mother. And you an only son. But how long for? Your
    whole life?
The way I see it being in mourning for your mother for forty-five
    years is
pretty ridiculous. It's more than ridiculous: it's insulting to other
    women.
Your wife, for instance. Or your daughters. I find it a turnoff myself.
Why don't you try and see it my way for a moment: I'm twenty-six
    and you'll
soon be sixty, a middle-aged orphan who goes knocking on women's
    doors
and guess what he's come to beg for. The fact that before my parents
were even born your mother called you Amek isn't a life sentence. It's
high time you gave her the push. Just the way she chucked you. Let her
wander round her forests at night without you. Let her find herself
some other sucker. It's true it's not easy to ditch your own mother, so
    why
don't you stick her in some other scene, not in a forest, let's say in a lake:
cast her as the Loch Ness monster, which as everyone knows may be
down there or may not exist, but one thing is certain, whatever you
    see or
think you see on the surface isn't the monster, it's just a hoax or an
    illusion.

BUT HOW

Ditch her, you say, it's easy for you to say it,
bail out like a fighter pilot ditching a plane
that's in a spin or on fire. But how can you jump from a plane
that's already crashed and rusted or sunk under the waves?

My Mother Was Thirty-eight When She Died

from *A Tale of Love and Darkness* (2003)

A week or so before her death my mother suddenly got much better. A new sleeping pill prescribed by a new doctor worked miracles overnight. She took two pills in the evening, fell asleep fully dressed at half past seven on my bed, which had become her bed, and slept for almost twenty-four hours, until five o'clock the following afternoon, when she got up, took a shower, drank some tea, and must have taken another pill or two, because she fell asleep again at half past seven and slept through till the morning, and when my father got up, shaved, and squeezed two glasses of orange juice and warmed them to room temperature, Mother also got up, put on a housecoat and apron, combed her hair, and made us both a real breakfast, as she used to before she was ill, fried eggs done on both sides, salad, pots of yogurt, and slices of bread that she could cut much finer than Father's "planks of wood," as she affectionately called them.

So there we sat once more at seven o'clock in the morning on the three wicker stools at the kitchen table with its flower-patterned oilcloth, and Mother told us a story, about a rich furrier who had lived in her hometown, Rovno, an urbane Jew who was visited by buyers from as far away as Paris and Rome because of the rare silver fox furs he had that sparkled like frost on a moonlit night.

One fine day this furrier forswore meat and became a vegetarian. He put the whole business, with all its branches, into the hands of his father-in-law and partner. Some time later he built himself a little hut in the forest and went to live there, because he was sorry for all the thousands of foxes that his trappers had killed on his behalf. Eventually the man vanished and was never seen again. "And," she said, "when my sisters and I wanted to frighten each other, we used to lie on the floor in the dark and take turns telling how the formerly rich furrier now roamed naked through the forest, possibly ill with rabies, uttering bloodcurdling fox howls in the undergrowth, and if anyone was unfortunate enough to encounter the fox-man in the forest, his hair instantly turned white with terror."

My father, who intensely disliked this kind of story, made a face and said, "I'm sorry, what is that supposed to be? An allegory? A superstition? Some kind of *bubbe-meiseh*?" But he was so pleased to see Mother looking so much better that he added with a dismissive wave of his hand, "Never mind."

Mother hurried us along so my father would not be late for work and I would not be late for school. At the door, as my father was putting his galoshes on over his shoes and I was getting into my boots, I suddenly let out a long, bloodcurdling howl, which made him jump and shiver with fear, and when he recovered himself, he was just about to hit me when Mother interposed herself between us, pressed me to her breast, and calmed us both down, saying, "That was all because of me. I'm sorry." That was the last time she hugged me.

We left home at about half past seven, Father and I, not saying a word because he was still angry with me over the rabid fox howl. At the front gate he turned left toward the Terra Sancta Building and I turned right toward Tachkemoni School.

When I got home from school, I found Mother dressed up in her light skirt with two rows of buttons and her navy jumper. She looked pretty and girlish. Her face looked well, as though all the months of illness had vanished overnight. She told me to put my school satchel down and keep my coat on, she put her coat on too, she had a surprise for me:

"We're not going to have lunch at home today. I've decided to take the two men in my life out to a restaurant for lunch. But your father doesn't know anything about it yet. Shall we surprise him? Let's go for a walk in town, and then we'll go to the Terra Sancta Building and drag him out of there by force, like a blinking moth out of a heap of book dust, and then we'll all go and eat somewhere that I'm not even going to tell you, so that you'll have some suspense, too."

I didn't recognize my mother. Her voice was not her usual voice, it was solemn and loud, as though she were speaking a part in a school play; it was full of light and warmth when she said, "Let's go for a walk," but it shook a little at the words "blinking moth" and "book dust"; for an instant it made me feel a vague fear, which gave way at once to happiness at the surprise, at Mother's cheerfulness, at the joy of her return to us.

My parents hardly ever ate out, although we often met up with their friends in cafés on Jaffa Road or King George Street.

Once, in 1950 or 1951, when the three of us were staying with the aunts in Tel Aviv, on the last day, literally just before we left for Jerusalem, Father uncharacteristically declared himself to be "Baron Rothschild for the day" and invited everybody, my mother's two sisters with their respective husbands and only sons, out to lunch at Hamozeg Restaurant on Ben Yehuda Street, at the corner of Sholem Aleichem Street. A table was laid for the nine of us. Father sat at the head, between his two sisters-in-law, and seated us in such a way that neither sister sat next to her husband and none of us children sat between his parents: as though he had made up his mind to shuffle all the cards. Uncle Tzvi and Uncle Buma were slightly suspicious, as they could not understand what he was up to, and firmly refused to join him in a glass of beer, as they were not used to drinking. They chose not to speak, and left the floor to my father, who apparently felt that the most urgent and exciting topic must be the Dead Sea Scrolls that had been found in the Judaean desert. So he embarked on a detailed lecture that lasted right through the soup and the main course about the significance of the scrolls that had been found in some caves near Qumran and the possibility that more and more priceless hidden treasures were waiting to be discovered among the ravines in the desert. Eventually Mother, who was sitting between Uncle Tzvi and Uncle Buma, remarked softly, "Perhaps that's enough for now, Arieh?"

Father understood and left off, and for the rest of the meal the conversation broke up into separate conversations. My older cousin, Yigal, asked if he could take my younger cousin, Ephraim, to the nearby beach. After a few more minutes I also decided I had had enough of the company of the grown-ups and left Hamozeg Restaurant to look for the beach.

But who could have imagined that Mother would suddenly decide to take us out for lunch? We had become so accustomed to seeing her sitting day and night staring at the window and not moving. Only a few days earlier I had given up my bedroom for her and run away from her silence to sleep with Father in the double sofa bed. She looked so beautiful and elegant in her navy jersey and light skirt, in her nylon stockings with a seam at the back and her high-heeled shoes, that strange men turned around to look at her. She carried her raincoat over one arm and linked the other arm in mine as we walked along.

"You'll be my cavalier today."

And as though she had adopted Father's normal role as well, she added, "A cavalier is a knight: *cheval* is a horse in French, and *chevalier* is a horseman or knight." Then she said, "There are lots of women who are attracted to tyrannical men. Like moths to a flame. And there are some women who do not need a hero or even a stormy lover but a friend. Just remember that when you grow up. Steer clear of the tyrant lovers, and try to locate the ones who are looking for a man as a friend, not because they are feeling empty themselves but because they enjoy making you full, too. And remember that friendship between a woman and a man is something much more precious and rare than love: love is actually something quite gross and even clumsy compared to friendship. Friendship includes a measure of sensitivity, attentiveness, generosity, and a finely tuned sense of moderation."

"Good," I said, because I wanted her to stop talking about things that had nothing to do with me and talk about something else instead. We hadn't talked for weeks, and it was a pity to waste this walking time that was just hers and mine. As we approached the city center, she slipped her arm through mine again, gave a little laugh, and asked suddenly, "What would you say to a little brother? Or sister?"

And without waiting for a reply, she added with a sort of jocular sadness, or rather a sadness wrapped in a smile that I could not see but that I heard in her voice as she spoke, "One day when you get married and have a family of your own, I very much hope you won't take me and your father as an example of what married life ought to be."

I am not just re-creating these words from memory, as I did a dozen lines earlier with her words about love and friendship, because I remember this plea not to take my parents' marriage as an example exactly as it was said to me, word for word. And I remember her smiling voice precisely too. We were on King George Street, my mother and I, walking arm in arm past the building called Talitha Kumi on our way to the Terra Sancta Building to take Father away from his work. The time was 1:30 P.M. A cold wind mixed with sharp drops of rain was blowing from the west. It was strong enough to make passersby close their umbrellas so they would not blow inside out. We did not even attempt to open ours. Arm in arm, Mother and I walked in the rain, past Talitha Kumi and the Frumin Building, which was the temporary home of the Knesset, and then we passed the Hamaalot Building. It was at the beginning of the first week of January 1952. Five or four days before her death.

And as the rain grew heavier, Mother said, with an amused tone to her voice, "Shall we go to a café for a bit? Our Father won't run away."

We sat for half an hour or so in a German Jewish café at the entrance to Rehavia, in JNF Street, opposite the Jewish Agency Building, where the prime minister's office was also located at the time. Till the rain stopped. Meanwhile, Mother took a little powder compact and a comb from her handbag and repaired the damage to her hair and face. I felt a mixture of emotions: pride in her looks, joy that she was better, a responsibility to guard and protect her from some shadow whose existence I could only guess at. In fact I did not guess, I only half sensed a slight strange uneasiness in my skin. The way a child sometimes grasps without really grasping things that are beyond his understanding, senses them and is alarmed without knowing why.

"Are you all right, Mother?"

She ordered a strong black coffee for herself and for me a milky coffee, even though I was never allowed coffee-is-not-for-children, and a chocolate ice cream, even though we all knew perfectly well that ice cream gives you a sore throat, especially on a cold winter day. And before lunch to boot. My sense of responsibility forced me to eat only two or three spoonfuls and to ask my mother if she didn't feel cold sitting here. If she didn't feel tired. Or dizzy. After all she'd only just recovered from an illness. And be careful, Mummy, when you go to the toilet, it's dark and there are two steps. Pride, earnestness, and apprehension filled my heart. As though as long as the two of us were sitting here in Café Rosh-Rehavia, her role was to be a helpless girl who needed a generous friend, and I was her cavalier. Or perhaps her father.

"Are you all right, Mother?"

When we got to the Terra Sancta Building, where several departments of the Hebrew University were relocated after the road to the campus on Mount Scopus was blocked in the War of Independence, we asked for the newspaper department and went up the stairs to the second floor. (It was on a winter's day like this that Hannah in *My Michael* slipped on these very stairs, and might have twisted her ankle, and the student Michael Gonen caught her by the elbow and said he liked the word *ankle.* Mother and I may well have walked past Michael and Hannah without noticing them. Thirteen years separated the winter's day when I was in the Terra Sancta Building with my mother from the winter's day when I began to write *My Michael.*)

When we entered the newspaper department, we saw facing us the director, gentle, kindly Dr. Pfeffermann, who looked up from the pile of papers on his desk, smiled, and beckoned us with both his hands to come in. We saw Father too, from behind. For a long moment we did not recognize him, because he was wearing a gray librarian's coat to protect his clothes from the dust. He was standing on a small stepladder, with his back to us and all his attention concentrated on the big box files he was taking down from a high shelf, leafing through and returning to the shelf, before taking down another and another file, because apparently he could not find what he was looking for.

All this time, kind Dr. Pfeffermann did not make a sound, but sat comfortably in the chair behind his big desk, his smile growing broader and broader in an amused sort of way, and two or three other people who worked in the department stopped working and smirked as they looked at us and at Father's back without saying anything, as though they were sharing in Dr. Pfeffermann's little game and watching with amused curiosity to see when the man would finally notice his visitors, who were standing in the doorway patiently watching his back, the pretty woman's hand resting on the little boy's shoulder.

From where he was standing on the top step of the ladder Father turned to his head of department and said, "Excuse me, Dr. Pfeffermann, I believe there is something . . . ," and suddenly he noticed the director's broad smile — and he may have been alarmed because he could not understand what was making him smile — and Dr. Pfeffermann's eyes guided Father's bespectacled gaze from the desk to the doorway. When he caught sight of us, I believe his face went white. He returned the large box file he was holding with both hands to its place on the top shelf and carefully climbed down the ladder, looked around, and saw that all the other members of staff were smiling, and as though he had no choice, he remembered to smile too, and said to us, "What a surprise! What a great surprise!" and in a quieter voice he asked if everything was all right, if anything had happened, heaven forbid.

His face was as strained and anxious as that of a child who in the middle of a kissing game at a party with his classmates looks up and notices his parents standing sternly in the doorway — who knows how long they have been standing there quietly watching or what they have seen?

First of all, he tried to shoo us outside very gently, with both hands, into the corridor, and looking back he said to the whole department and particularly to Dr. Pfeffermann, "Excuse me for a few minutes?"

But a minute later he changed his mind, stopped edging us out, and pulled us back inside, into the director's office, and started to introduce us; then he remembered, and said, "Dr. Pfeffermann, you already know my wife and son." And then he turned us around and formally introduced us to the rest of the staff of the newspaper department with the words, "I'd like you to meet my wife, Fania, and my son, Amos. A schoolboy. Twelve and a half years old."

When we were all outside in the corridor, Father asked anxiously, and a little reproachfully, "What has happened? Are my parents all right? And your parents? Is everyone all right?"

Mother calmed him down. But the issue of the restaurant made him apprehensive: after all, it was not anyone's birthday today. He hesitated, started to say something, changed his mind, and after a moment he said, "Certainly. Certainly. Why not. We'll go and celebrate your recovery, Fania, or at any rate the distinct and sudden amelioration in your condition. Yes. We must definitely celebrate."

His face as he spoke, however, was anxious rather than festive.

But then my father suddenly cheered up, and fired with enthusiasm he put his arms around both our shoulders, got permission from Dr. Pfeffermann to leave work a little early, said good-bye to his colleagues, took off his gray dust coat, and treated us to a thorough tour of several departments of the library, the basement, and the rare manuscripts section; he even showed us the new photocopying machine and explained how it worked, and he introduced us proudly to everyone we met, as excited as a teenager introducing his famous parents to the staff of his school.

The restaurant was a pleasant, almost empty place tucked away in a narrow side street between Ben Yehuda Street and Shammai or Hillel Street. The rain started again the moment we arrived, which Father took as a good sign, as though it had been waiting for us to get to the restaurant. As though heaven were smiling on us today.

He corrected himself immediately: "I mean, that is what I would say if I believed in signs, or if I believed that heaven cares at all about us. But heaven is indifferent. Apart from Homo sapiens, the whole universe is indifferent. Most people are indifferent, too, if it comes to that. I believe indifference is the most salient feature of all reality."

He corrected himself again: "And anyway, how could I say that heaven was smiling on us when the sky is so dark and lowering and it's raining cats and dogs?"

Mother said, "Now, you two order first, because it's my treat today. And I'll be very pleased if you choose the most expensive dishes on the menu."

But the menu was a modest one, in keeping with those years of shortages and austerity. Father and I ordered vegetable soup and chicken rissoles with mashed potato. I conspiratorially refrained from telling Father that on the way to Terra Sancta I'd been allowed to taste coffee for the very first time. And to have a chocolate ice cream before my lunch, even though it was winter.

Mother stared at the menu for a long time, then placed it face down on the table, and it was only after Father reminded her again that she finally ordered a bowl of plain boiled rice. Father apologized amiably to the waitress and explained vaguely that Mother was not entirely recovered. While Father and I tucked into our food with gusto, Mother pecked at her rice as though she were forcing herself, then stopped and ordered a cup of strong black coffee.

"Are you all right, Mother?"

The waitress returned with a cup of coffee for my mother and a glass of tea for my father, and she placed in front of me a bowl of quivering yellow jelly. At once Father impatiently took his wallet out of his inside jacket pocket. But Mother insisted on her rights: Put it right back, please. Today you are both my guests. And Father obeyed, not before cracking some forced joke about her inheriting an oil well apparently, which explained her newfound wealth and her extravagance. We waited for the rain to let up. My father and I were sitting facing the kitchen, and Mother's face opposite us was looking between our shoulders at the stubborn rain through the window that gave onto the street. What we spoke about I can't remember, but presumably Father chased away any silence. He may have talked to us about the Christian Church's relations with the Jewish people, or treated us to a survey of the history of the fierce dispute that broke out in the middle of the eighteenth century between Rabbi Jacob Emden and the adherents of Shabbetai Tsevi, particularly Rabbi Jonathan Eybeschütz, who was suspected of Sabbataean leanings.

The only other customers in the restaurant that rainy lunchtime were two elderly ladies who were talking in very refined German in low, well-mannered voices. They looked alike, with steely gray hair and birdlike features accentuated by prominent Adam's apples. The elder of the two looked over eighty, and at second glance I supposed that she must be the other one's mother. And I decided that the mother and daughter were both widows, and that they lived together because they had no one else left in the whole wide world. In my mind I dubbed them Mrs. Gertrude and Mrs. Magda, and I tried to imagine their tiny, scrupulously clean apartment, perhaps somewhere in this part of town, roughly opposite the Eden Hotel.

Suddenly one of them, Mrs. Magda, the younger of the two, raised her voice and hurled a single German word at the old woman opposite. She pronounced it with venomous, piercing rage, like a vulture pouncing on its prey, and then she threw her cup against the wall.

In the deeply etched lines on the cheeks of the older woman, whom I had named Gertrude, tears began to run. She wept soundlessly and without screwing up her face. She wept with a straight face. The waitress bent down and silently picked up the pieces of the cup. When she had finished, she disappeared. Not a word was spoken after the shout. The two women went on sitting opposite each other without uttering a sound. They were both very thin, and they both had curly gray hair that started a long way up their foreheads, like a man's receding hairline. The older widow was still weeping silent tears, with no contortion of her face; they drained down to her pointed chin, where they dripped onto her breast like stalactites in a cave. She made no attempt to control her weeping or to dry her tears. Even though her daughter, with a cruel expression on her face, silently held out a neatly ironed white handkerchief. If indeed it was her daughter. She did not withdraw her hand, which lay extended on the table in front of her with the neatly ironed handkerchief on top of it. The whole image was frozen for a long time, as though mother and daughter were just an old, fading sepia photograph in some dusty album. Suddenly I asked, "Are you all right, Mother?"

That was because my mother, ignoring the rules of etiquette, had turned her chair slightly and was staring fixedly at the two women. At that moment it struck me that my mother's face had turned very pale again, the way it was all the time she was ill. After a while she said she was very sorry, she was feeling a little tired and wanted to go home and lie down. Father nodded, got up, asked the waitress where the nearest phone booth was, and went off to call a taxi. As we left the restaurant, Mother had to lean on Father's arm and shoulder; I held the door open for them, warned them about the step, and opened the door of the taxi for them. When we had got Mother into the backseat, Father went back into the restaurant to settle the bill. She sat up very straight in the taxi, and her brown eyes were wide open. Too wide.

That evening the new doctor was sent for, and when he had left, Father sent for the old one as well. There was no disagreement between them: both doctors prescribed complete rest. Consequently Father put Mother to bed in my bed, which had become her bed, took her a glass of warm milk and honey, and begged her to take a few sips with her new sleeping pills. He asked how many lights she wanted him to leave on. A quarter of an hour later I was sent to peep through the crack in the door, and I saw that she was asleep.

She slept till next morning, when she woke up early again and got up to help Father and me with the various morning chores. She made us fried eggs again while I set the table and Father chopped various vegetables very fine for a salad. When it was time for us to go, Father to the Terra Sancta Building and me to Tachkemoni School, Mother suddenly decided to go out, too, and to walk me to school, because her good friend Lilenka, Lilia Bar-Samkha, lived near Tachkemoni.

Later we discovered that Lilenka had not been at home, so she had gone to see another friend, Fania Weissmann, who had also been a fellow pupil at the Tarbuth gymnasium in Rovno. From Fania Weissmann's she had walked just before midday to the Egged Central Bus Station halfway down Jaffa Road and boarded a bus bound for Tel Aviv, to see her sisters, or perhaps she intended to change buses in Tel Aviv and go on to Haifa and Kiryat Motskin, to her parents' hut. But when my mother got to the Central Bus Station in Tel Aviv, she apparently changed her mind: she had a black coffee in a café and returned to Jerusalem late in the afternoon.

When she got home, she complained of feeling very tired. She took another two or three of the new sleeping pills. Or perhaps she tried going back to the old ones. But that night she could not get to sleep, the migraine came back, and she sat up fully dressed by the window. At two o'clock in the morning my mother decided to do some ironing. She put the light on in my room, which had become her room, set up the ironing board, filled a bottle with water to sprinkle on the clothes, and ironed for several hours, until dawn broke. When she ran out of clothes, she took the bed linen out of the cupboard and ironed it all over again. When she had finished that, she even ironed the bedspread from my bed, but she was so tired or weak that she burned it: the smell of burning woke Father, who woke me too, and the two of us were astonished to see that my mother had ironed every sock, handkerchief, napkin, and table-cloth in the place. We rushed to put out the burning bedspread in the bathroom, and then we sat Mother down in her chair and got down on our knees to remove her shoes: my father took off one, and I took off the other. Then Father asked me to leave the room for a few minutes and kindly close the door behind me. I closed the door, but this time I pressed myself against the door because I wanted to hear. They spoke to each other for half an hour in Russian. Then Father asked me to look after my mother for a few minutes, and he went to the pharmacist's and bought some medicine or syrup, and while he was there, he phoned Uncle Tsvi in his office at Tsahalon Hospital in Jaffa and he also phoned Uncle Buma at work at the Zamenhof clinic in Tel Aviv. After these calls Father and Mother agreed that she should go to Tel Aviv that very morning, Thursday, to stay with one of her sisters, to get some rest and a change of air and atmosphere. She could stay as long as she liked, till Sunday or even till Monday morning, because Lilia Bar-Samkha had managed to get her an appointment on Monday afternoon for a test at Hadassah Hospital in Heneviim Street, an appointment that without Aunt Lilenka's good connections we would have had to wait several months for.

And because Mother was feeling weak and complained of dizziness, Father insisted that this time she should not travel to Tel Aviv alone, but that he would go with her and take her all the way to Auntie Haya and Uncle Tsvi's, and he might even stay the night: if he took the first bus back to Jerusalem the next morning, Friday, he could manage to get to work for a few hours at least. He took no notice of Mother's protests—that there was no need for him to travel with her and miss a day's work, that she was perfectly capable of taking the bus to Tel Aviv on her own and finding her sister's house. She wouldn't get lost.

But Father would not hear of it. He was gray and stubborn this time, and he absolutely insisted. I promised him that after school I would go straight to Grandma Shlomit and Grandpa Alexander's in Prague Lane, explain what had happened, and stay overnight with them till Father got back. Only don't be a nuisance to Grandma and Grandpa, help them nicely, clear the table after supper, and offer to take the trash out. And do all your homework, don't leave any of it for the weekend. He called me a clever son. He may even have called me young man. And from outside we were joined at that moment by the bird, Elise, who trilled her morning snatch of Beethoven for us three or four times with clear, limpid joy: "Ti-da-di-da-di . . ." The bird sang with wonderment, awe, gratitude, exaltation, as though no night had ever ended before, as if this morning was the very first morning in the universe and its light was a wondrous light the like of which had never before burst forth and traversed the wide expanse of darkness.

Imagining the Other Is a Deep and Subtle Human Pleasure

upon acceptance of the Goethe Prize

FRANKFURT AM MAIN, AUGUST 28, 2005

Dear friends,

I would like to speak today about Goethe, and about the devil, and about Lotte, and about the tree of the knowledge of good and evil, and finally about a certain secret pleasure.

When I was a child in Jerusalem, the teacher at our school taught us the book of Job. All Israeli children, to this day, study the book of Job. Our teacher told us how Satan traveled all the way from that book to the New Testament, and from there to Goethe's *Faust* and many other works of literature. And although each writer made something new of Satan, the devil, *der Teufel,* he was always the very same Satan: cool, amused, sarcastic, and skeptical. A deconstructor of human faith, love, and hope.

Job's Satan, like Faust's Satan, makes a wager. His big prize is neither a hidden treasure, nor the heart of a beautiful woman, nor even a promotion to a higher position in the heavenly hierarchy. No: Satan takes up the gamble out of a didactic urge. He wishes to make a point. To prove something, and to refute something else. With enormous argumentative zeal, the biblical Satan and the Enlightenment Satan try to show God and his angels that man, when given the choice, will always opt for evil. He will choose bad over good, willingly and consciously.

Shakespeare's Iago may well have been motivated by a very similar didactic zeal. Indeed, such has been the motive of almost every thorough evildoer in world literature.

Perhaps this is why Satan is often so charming. So beguiling. Milton may have misunderstood the devil when he called him the infernal serpent. Heinrich Heine knew better, when he wrote:

> *I call'd the devil, and forth he came,*
> *With wonder his form did I closely scan;*
> *He is not ugly, he is not lame,*
> *But really a handsome and charming man.*
> *A man in the prime of his life, this devil,*
> *Obliging, a man of the world, and civil,*
> *A diplomatist too, well skill'd in debate,*
> *Who talks quite glibly of church and state.*

Man and the devil have understood each other so well because in some ways they are so alike. In the book of Job, Satan, the perverse educator, innately understands how human pain breeds evil: "Put forth thy hand now, and touch all that he has, and he will curse thee to thy face." Shakespeare's witches, in *Macbeth,* can sense the arrival of an evil man from afar. "By the pricking of my thumbs, something wicked this way comes." Goethe, for his part, observes that the devil, like so many human beings, is simply a selfish charmer: "*Der Teufel ist ein Egoist.*" The devil is an egotist. He helps others only to serve his own ends. Not, as God and Kant would have us do, to serve others alone.

And this is the reason that from the time of Job until not so long ago, Satan, man, and God lived in the same household: all three seemed to know the difference between good and evil. God, man, and the devil knew that evil was evil and good was good. God commanded man to make one choice. Satan seduced him to try the other. God and Satan played on the same chessboard, and man was their pawn. It was as simple as that.

Personally, I believe that every human being, in his or her heart of hearts, is capable of telling good from bad. We may pretend that we cannot, but we have all eaten of that tree of Eden whose full name is the Tree of the Knowledge of Good and Evil. *Etz ha-da'at tov va-ra.*

The same distinction may apply to truth and falsehood. It is immensely difficult to detect the truth, yet quite easy to smell a lie. Just so, it has sometimes been hard to define good, but evil has always had an unmistakable odor: every child knows what pain is. Therefore, each time we have deliberately inflicted pain on another, we have known what we were doing. We were doing evil.

But the modern age has changed all that. It has blurred the clear distinction that humanity has made since its very beginning in the Garden of Eden. Sometime in the nineteenth century, not so long after Goethe died, a new type of thinking entered Western culture, a type that brushed evil aside, indeed denied its very existence. That intellectual innovation was called social science. For some of the new, self-confident, exquisitely rational, optimistic, thoroughly scientific practitioners of psychology, sociology, anthropology, and economics, evil was not an issue. Come to think of it, neither was good. To this very day, certain social scientists simply do not talk about good and evil. To them, all human motives and actions derive from circumstances, which are often beyond personal control. "Demons," Freud said, "do not exist any more than gods do, being only the products of the psychic activity of man." We are controlled by our social background. For about one hundred years now, they have been telling us that we are motivated exclusively by economic self-interest, that we are simply products of our respective ethnic cultures, or else puppets of our subconscious.

In other words, these modern social sciences represent the first major attempt to kick both good and evil off the human stage. For the first time in their long history, good and bad were both overruled by the idea that circumstances are always responsible for human decisions, human actions, and especially human suffering. Society is to blame. A painful childhood is to blame. Politics are to blame—colonialism, imperialism, Zionism, globalization—what is not? So began the great world championship of victimhood.

For the first time since long before the book of Job, the devil found himself out of a job. He could no longer play his ancient game with human minds. This was the modern age.

Well, the times may be changing again. Satan had been sacked, but he did not remain unemployed. The world of the twentieth century saw the worst cold-blooded evil in human history. The social sciences failed to predict, confront, or even grasp this modern, highly technologized evil. Very often, this twentieth-century evil disguised itself as world reform, as idealism, as reeducation or enlightenment of the masses. Totalitarianism was presented as secular redemption for some lives, at the expense of millions of others.

Today, having emerged from the evil of totalitarian rule, we have developed an enormous respect for other cultures, for diversities, for pluralism. Some people are willing to kill anyone who is not a pluralist. Satan has once again been hired—this time by postmodernism, but by now his professional standing verges on kitsch. He has become that small, secretive bunch of shady forces that are blamed for everything from poverty and discrimination and war and global warming to September 11, to the Indian Ocean tsunami. Ordinary people are always innocent. Minorities are never to blame. Victims are, by definition, morally pure.

Have you noticed that today the devil never seems to tempt individuals? We have no Fausts anymore. Today, evil is a conglomerate. Systems are evil. Governments are bad. Faceless institutions run the world for their own sinister gain. The devil is no longer in the details. Individual men and women cannot be bad as that concept is understood in *Macbeth* or *Othello* or *Faust*.

You and I are always nice people. The devil is always the establishment.

This, in my view, is ethical kitsch.

Let us consult our own most gifted adviser, *der Geheimrat* Johann Wolfgang von Goethe. Let us look at his *West-eastern Divan,* one of the earliest great tributes of Western culture to its own curiosity and attraction toward the East. Was Goethe a condescending orientalist, as Edward Said might have called him? Or was Goethe a multiculturalist in the fashion of today's guilt-ridden Europeans when they pay lip service to everything distant, everything different, everything decisively non-European?

I think Goethe was neither an orientalist nor a multiculturalist. It was not the extreme and imagined exoticism of the East that tempted him, but the strong and fresh substance that Eastern cultures, Eastern poetry and art give to universal human truths and feelings. Good, and indeed God, are universal:

> *God is of the East possess'd,*
> *God is ruler of the west;*
> *North and South alike, each land*
> *Rests within His gentle hand.*

Even more so, love is universal, whether it is for Gretchen or for Zuleika. So a German poet may well write a love poem for an imagined Persian woman — or a real Persian woman — and speak the truth.

And yet more touchingly, pain is universal. As "Let Me Weep," one of the finest poems in *The West-eastern Divan* has it:

> *Let me weep, hemmed in by night,*
> *In the boundless desert.*
> *Camels are resting, likewise their drivers;*
> *Calculating in silence, the Armenian is awake;*
> *But I, beside him, calculate the miles*
> *That separate me from Zuleika, reiterate*
> *Those wretched turns that lengthen out the road.*
> *Let me weep. It is no shame.*
> *Weeping men are good to see.*
> *Didn't Achilles weep for his Briseis?*
> *Xerxes wept for his unslain host;*
> *Over his self-murdered darling*
> *Alexander wept.*
> *Let me weep. Tears give life to dust.*
> *Already it grows green.*

Goethe does not recruit the East to prove anything. He takes humans, all humans, seriously. East or West, good men weep.

I would like to take a moment here, with you, to weep for Johann Wolfgang von Goethe. I would like to weep for Weimar. Because Goethe's Weimar is gone forever. Thomas Mann's Weimar is gone for good. Not that Weimar today is not a beautifully restored historical town. But Weimar today lies across the forest from

Buchenwald. We may lament the passing of memories, the fading of landscapes, growth and change in long-established cities. But this is not what we are lamenting in Goethe's Weimar. Not the teeth of time, but the extreme and total evil of man has taken Goethe's Weimar away from us.

Thomas Mann, in his novel *Lotte in Weimar,* made Charlotte Kestner, who was once Lotte Buff, the real-life beloved of the young Werther, come to visit the old and famous Goethe in Weimar. *Lotte in Weimar* is an exquisite study in the slow fading of memory: even when Goethe was still alive, the spirit of his time was slipping away, becoming the stuff of legend. That is normal; that is the way human life and memory, like human houses and streets, flow and ebb as history moves on.

But Goethe and his old love Lotte could still walk together to the woodland outside the town and observe the blissful, tranquil scenery of the Thuringian countryside. And maybe they could walk up to the beautiful oak tree out there that would be known for many years to come as Goethe's oak. And years went by, and generations, but that oak tree still stood. Until it was bombed by Allied aircraft toward the end of the Second World War, when Weimar became the neighboring town, the "market town" of the death camp Buchenwald.

Thus did the Nazis not only kill their victims but also destroy the slow, aging innocence of Weimar and Goethe and Lotte. The subtitle of *Lotte in Weimar* was *The Beloved Returns.* But the beloved can no longer return. Not ever.

Which brings me to another Lotte, Lotte Wreschner, the mother of my son-in-law. She was born here in Frankfurt am Main, 174 years after Goethe and not far from his house. Not for nothing did the name Lotte run in her family. She grew up in a home full of books, shelves upon shelves of German, Jewish, and German-Jewish spiritual treasures. Schiller and the Talmud. Heine and Kant. Buber and Hölderlin—all were there. One of her uncles was a rabbi, the other a psychoanalyst. They all knew Goethe's poetry by heart. The Nazis imprisoned her, along with her mother and sister, and sent them to Ravensbrück, where her mother died of typhus and hard labor. Lotte and her sister Margrit were transferred to Theresienstadt. I wish I could tell you that they were liberated from Theresienstadt by peace demonstrators carrying placards saying MAKE LOVE, NOT WAR. In fact, they were set free by soldiers wearing helmets and carrying machine guns. We Israeli peace activists never forget this fact, even as we struggle against our country's attitude toward the Palestinians, even as we work for a livable, peaceful compromise between Israel and Palestine. Lotte and Margrit Wreschner came home to find all the books waiting, but none of their family. Not a living soul. Margrit Wreschner is sitting here with us tonight. She can bear witness to what all survivors of that mass murder can say. There are good people in the world. There are also evil people in the world, and evil cannot always be repelled by incantations, by demonstrations, by social analysis, or by psychoanalysis. Sometimes, as a last resort, it has to be confronted by force.

In my view, the ultimate evil in the world is not war itself, but aggression. Aggression is the mother of all wars. And sometimes aggression has to be repelled by the force of arms before peace can prevail.

Lotte Wreschner settled in Jerusalem. Eventually she became a leader in the Israeli civil rights movement, as well as a deputy mayor of Jerusalem under Teddy Kollek. Her son, Eli, and my daughter Fania, who are also with us in the audience, are both civil rights and peace activists, as are my other children, Gallia and Daniel.

Let me turn back to Goethe, and to my feelings about Germany. Goethe's *Faust* reminds us forever that the devil is personal, not impersonal. That the devil puts every individual to the test, which every one of us can pass or fail. That evil is tempting and seductive. That the impulse to aggression has a potential foothold inside every one of us.

Personal good and evil are not concepts exclusive to any religion. They are not necessarily religious terms. The choice to inflict pain or not, to look it in the face or to turn a blind eye to it, to get personally involved in healing pain, like a devoted country doctor, or to make do with organizing angry demonstrations and signing general petitions — this spectrum of choice confronts each one of us several times a day.

Of course, we might occasionally take a wrong turn. But even as we stray, we know what we are doing. We know the difference between good and evil, between inflicting pain and healing, between Goethe and Goebbels, Heine and Heydrich, Weimar and Buchenwald. And between individual responsibility and collective madness.

Dear friends, let me conclude with one more personal recollection: as a very nationalistic, even chauvinistic little boy in Jerusalem of the 1940s, I vowed never to set foot on German soil, never even to buy any German product. The only thing I could not boycott were German books. If you boycott the books, I told myself, you will become a little bit like them. At first I limited myself to reading prewar German literature and anti-Nazi writers. But later, in the 1960s, I began to read, in Hebrew translations, the works of the postwar generation of German writers and poets—in particular, the works of the Group 47 writers. They made me imagine myself in their place. I'll put it more strongly: they seduced me into imagining myself in their stead back in the dark years, and just before the dark years, and just after. Reading these authors, and others, I could no longer go on simply hating everything German, past, present, and future.

I believe that imagining the other is a powerful antidote to fanaticism and hatred. I believe that books that make us imagine the other may make us more immune to the ploys of the devil, including the inner devil, the Mephisto of the heart.

Thus, Günter Grass and Heinrich Böll, Ingeborg Bachmann and Uwe Johnson, and in particular my beloved friend Siegfried Lenz, opened the door to Germany for me. They, along with a number of dear personal German friends, made me break my taboos and open my mind, and eventually my heart. They reintroduced me to the healing powers of literature. It is very much thanks to them that I am standing here in front of you today.

Imagining the other is not only an aesthetic tool. It is, in my view, also a major moral imperative. And finally, imagining the other—if you promise not to quote this little professional secret—imagining the other is also a deep and very subtle human pleasure.

Thank you very much.

INDEX

CREDITS